Semantics with Assignment Variables

This pioneering study combines insights from philosophy and linguistics to develop a novel framework for theorizing about linguistic meaning and the role of context in interpretation. A key innovation is to introduce explicit representations of context — *assignment variables* — in the syntax and semantics of natural language. The proposed theory systematizes a spectrum of "shifting" phenomena in which the context relevant for interpreting certain expressions depends on features of the linguistic environment. Central applications include local and nonlocal contextual dependencies with quantifiers, attitude ascriptions, conditionals, questions, and relativization. The result is an innovative, philosophically informed compositional semantics compatible with the truth-conditional paradigm. At the forefront of contemporary interdisciplinary research into meaning and communication, *Semantics with Assignment Variables* is essential reading for researchers and students in a diverse range of fields.

ALEX SILK is a senior lecturer in philosophy at the University of Birmingham and the author of *Discourse Contextualism*. He has earned international recognition for research in philosophy of language, normative theory, and linguistic semantics. He is the recipient of the Sanders Prize in Metaethics and grants from the Arts and Humanities Research Council and Leverhulme Foundation.

T0384645

Semantics with Assignment Variables

Alex Silk
University of Birmingham

Shaftesbury Road, Cambridge CB2 8EA, United Kingdom

One Liberty Plaza, 20th Floor, New York, NY 10006, USA

477 Williamstown Road, Port Melbourne, VIC 3207, Australia

314–321, 3rd Floor, Plot 3, Splendor Forum, Jasola District Centre, New Delhi – 110025, India

103 Penang Road, #05–06/07, Visioncrest Commercial, Singapore 238467

Cambridge University Press is part of Cambridge University Press & Assessment, a department of the University of Cambridge.

We share the University's mission to contribute to society through the pursuit of education, learning and research at the highest international levels of excellence.

www.cambridge.org
Information on this title: www.cambridge.org/9781108799126

DOI: 10.1017/9781108870078

First published 2021
First paperback edition 2023

A catalogue record for this publication is available from the British Library

Library of Congress Cataloging-in-Publication data
Names: Silk, Alex, author.
Title: Semantics with assignment variables / Alex Silk.
Description: New York: Cambridge University Press, 2021. | Includes bibliographical references and indexes.
Identifiers: LCCN 2020042259 (print) | LCCN 2020042260 (ebook) | ISBN 9781108836012 (hardback) | ISBN 9781108799126 (paperback) | ISBN 9781108870078 (epub)
Subjects: LCSH: Semantics. | Grammar, Comparative and general–Quantifiers.
Classification: LCC P325 .S5443 2021 (print) | LCC P325 (ebook) | DDC 401/.43–dc23
LC record available at https://lccn.loc.gov/2020042259
LC ebook record available at https://lccn.loc.gov/2020042260

ISBN   978-1-108-83601-2   Hardback
ISBN   978-1-108-79912-6   Paperback

Contents

Preface

I began developing the ideas in this book in spring 2017. Thanks to Yogurt World UCSD for early inspiration. For helpful discussion, thanks to Billy Dunaway, Daniel Rothschild, and participants at a 2018 Pacific APA symposium. I am also grateful to two readers for Cambridge University Press for valuable feedback. Thanks to Helen Barton and Izzie Collins at Cambridge University Press for their patience and assistance throughout the process. Thanks also to Justin Clarke-Doane, Jenn McDonald, Maja Spener, and Gaines Johnsen. Thanks especially to my better counterpart, without whom this book would not exist. The book was completed under the support of an Arts & Humanities Research Council Early Career Research Grant and a Leverhulme Research Fellowship.

Some conventions and abbreviations: I use bold and single quotes for object-language expressions, e.g.: 'puppy', **puppy**. For non-English expressions I use italics, e.g.: *chiot* 'puppy'. In bracketed expressions in numbered examples, I use plain font; in trees, I use bold, e.g.:

(i)   [$_S$ puppies [are cute]]

(ii)

For readability, in bracketed expressions I sometimes use dashes to indicate constituents, e.g. [$_S$ **puppies are-cute**]. In numbered examples, '?'/'??' are used to indicate (mild) degradedness, '#' for semantic infelicity on the relevant reading, and '*' for ungrammaticality. Subscript/superscript indices may be used informally to indicate intended readings and binding/coreference relations, e.g.:

(iii)   a.   *She$_i$ likes Fluffy$_i$.
        b.   #The unicorn likes Fluffy.
        c.   ??[Which puppy]$_i$ did only its$_i$ owner like?

In semantic derivations I use '≈' to indicate equivalences with certain irrelevant assignment modifications suppressed, e.g.: $g[x/3](2) \approx g(2)$; and I often omit '= 1' in conditions, e.g. abbreviating '$f(x) = 1$' with '$f(x)$'. Depending on the purposes at hand, I often simplify glosses in non-English examples and omit explicit indications for φ-features, classifiers, case, tense, aspect. Readers interested in specific morphemic analyses are advised to consult the original sources.

1

Introduction

This book develops a syntactic and semantic framework for natural language. The principal focus is a spectrum of "shifting" phenomena in which the context relevant for interpreting certain expressions depends on features of the linguistic environment. A key innovation is to introduce explicit representations of context in linguistic structure and meaning. Positing variables for context in the syntax — formally, assignment variables — can help account for a wide range of linguistic phenomena which have resisted systematic explanation. Central applications include local and nonlocal contextual dependencies with quantifiers, attitude ascriptions, conditionals, questions, and relativization. The project integrates insights from philosophy of language, formal tools from theoretical syntax and semantics, and empirical data in linguistic typology. The proposed theory affords a standardization of quantification across domains and an improved framework for theorizing about linguistic meaning and the role of context in interpretation. The result will be a novel philosophically and empirically informed compositional semantics compatible with the truth-conditional paradigm.

1.1 Overview

A distinctive feature of human language is displacement (Hockett and Altmann 1968). We use language to communicate about things other than what is happening in the current context. An utterance of (1.1) makes a claim about a raining event in the here and now. In (1.2), the string in (1.1) is used to make a claim about a raining event in possibilities compatible with Gabe's beliefs.

(1.1) It's raining.

(1.2) Gabe thinks it's raining.

Such *linguistic shifting*, where the interpretation of an expression depends on features of the linguistic environment, is pervasive in natural language. It can be observed across semantic domains and types of expression — e.g., with worlds, as with the nominal and verbal predicates in (1.2)–(1.3); times, as with tense in (1.4); individuals, as with the personal and demonstrative pronouns in (1.5)–(1.6); norms, as with the deontic modal in (1.7). For instance, the truth of the belief ascription in (1.3) is independent of whether there are monsters in the world of the discourse context.

(1.3)   Timmy thinks Bert is a <u>monster</u>.

(1.4)   Whenever it rains, Timmy <u>cries</u>.

(1.5)   Every child who got a toy liked <u>it</u>.

(1.6)   je   mee-Ti okhane   dãRie ache <u>Se</u>   lOmba.
        which girl   there.DEICT stand be   that.ANAPH tall
        (lit. 'Which girl is standing over there, that is tall')
        'The girl who is standing over there is tall.'
                                    (Bagchi 1994: ex. 3; Bangla (Indo-Aryan))

(1.7)   I wonder whether Bert <u>should</u> give to charity.

Despite extensive cross-disciplinary interest in such phenomena, theoretical work has been largely piecemeal and insulated from developments in associated domains. This has led to hasty conclusions and a proliferation of resources for capturing the different cases. The aim in this book is a more systematic theory which integrates insights from philosophy of language, technical innovations in theoretical syntax and semantics, and crosslinguistic work in linguistic typology to deepen our understanding of linguistic shifting and the nature of linguistic meaning.

The present project pursues a fundamental reorientation in theorizing about context-sensitivity. The traditional approach takes unshifted readings for context-sensitive expressions as paradigmatic. Here is Kaplan: "What is common to [indexical words] is that the referent is dependent on the context of use and that the meaning of the word provides a rule which determines the referent in terms of certain aspects of the context" (1989: 490). Recent debates have focused on shifting contrasts between paradigm context-sensitive expressions such as indexicals, and expressions such as epistemic modals, deontic modals, predicates of personal taste (Yalcin 2007, Weatherson 2008, Lasersohn 2009, Dowell 2011, Silk 2013, 2016a, 2017). When embedded under 'think' in (1.8), the pronoun 'I' and perspectival expression 'local' can receive their interpretation from the discourse context; yet there seems to be no reading of (1.8) which ascribes to Al a belief about the information available in the discourse, s_c.

(1.8)   *Bo:* Al$_i$ thinks I$_c$ might$_{i/*c}$ be at a local$_{i/c}$ bar.
        ≉ "Al thinks it's compatible with s_c that Bo is at a bar local to Al/Bo"

Many theorists have responded by adopting revisionary theories and reconceiving the nature of truth, meaning, and communication (see also Yalcin 2011,

MacFarlane 2014). Such reactions are premature. Shifted interpretations may be optional, obligatory, or unavailable. Possibilities for shifted/unshifted interpretations may vary for different expressions in a given category and for a given expression in different linguistic contexts. In (1.3) the modal interpretation of the nominal predicate is obligatorily linked to the attitude state; the attitude ascription can only be interpreted as saying that Bert is a monster in the possibilities compatible with Timmy's beliefs. In (1.9) the nominal 'murderer' can receive shifted or non-shifted modal interpretations when used with 'every'; yet it can only receive the (sadistic) shifted interpretation in (1.10) when used with 'sm' (unstressed 'some').

(1.9)   [It would be better]$_i$ if every murderer$_{i/c}$ was a priest.

    a. ≈ "for all worlds u in which every murderer in u is a priest in u, things are better in u"

    b. ≈ "it would be better if everyone who is actually a murderer was a priest"

(1.10) [It would be better]$_i$ if sm murderers$_{i/*c}$ were priests.

    a. ≈ "for all worlds u in which some murderers in u are priests in u, things are better in u"

    b. ≉ "it would be better if some people who are actually murderers were priests"

As a counterpoint to indexical pronouns, classically understood — expressions which must receive their interpretation from the discourse context — common across language families are conventionalized anaphoric pronouns (dedicated reflexive and reciprocal forms aside). In (1.11), whereas the 3rd-person pronoun *ea* 'he' cannot receive the shifted interpretation, the reduced form *a* cannot be used referentially (see also Gair 1998, Gair et al. 1999, Bhat 2004, Dixon 2010: 251–252). Such intralinguistic and crosslinguistic variation can be observed even with paradigmatic referential expressions. Unlike in English, the proper name in (1.12) can receive a bound-variable interpretation.

(1.11) a. Gestan   hot ea$_c$/*a$_c$ gsunga.
        Yesterday has he   sung
        'Yesterday he sang.'

    b. Neta do Hons$_i$ hot a Frog   kriagt wos   a$_i$/*ea$_i$ vastondn   hot
        Only DET Hans has a question gotten which he   understood has
        'Only Hans$_i$ got a question which he$_i$ understood.'

                         (Wiltschko 2016: exs. 35, 37; Upper Austrian German)

(1.12)   Gye'eihlly-dihs$_i$ r-ralloh   r-yulàààa'z-ënn Gye'eihlly$_i$
         Mike-only   HAB-think HAB-like-1PL   Mike
         'Only Mike thinks we like him' (i.e., no other person x thinks we like x)
                                           (Lee 2003: ex. 61; Zapotec)

The project in this book is to develop a compositional semantic framework better
suited to the rich array of shifting phenomena that we find in natural language.

Following Stalnaker (1970), Kamp (1971), Lewis (1980), and Kaplan (1989),
it is standard in formal semantics to interpret expressions with respect to two
general parameters: to a first approximation, a context c which takes expressions
to intensions, and a circumstance (index) i which takes intensions to extensions.
To handle quantification and the interpretation of free pronouns, the context may
be treated as determining an assignment function g_c, which maps typed numerical
indices $\langle n, \tau \rangle$ (abbreviated: $n\tau$) to items in the model. Roughly put, (1.13) says
that S = 'It$_{7e}$ jumped' is true in c (written: $\llbracket S \rrbracket^{g_c, i} = 1$) iff such-and-such individual
relevant in c, $g_c(7e)$, jumped in the circumstance i (type e for individuals, 7 an
arbitrary syntactic index).[1]

(1.13)   a.   [$_S$ it$_{7e}$ jumped]
         b. $\llbracket S \rrbracket^{g_c, i} = 1$ iff $g_c(7e)$ jumped in i

Diverse linguistic data have led many theorists to posit reference to various
parameters of interpretation in the syntax (e.g., Partee 1973, Cresswell 1990,
Percus 2000, Schlenker 2003, 2006, Hacquard 2006, 2010). For instance, tenses
may be treated as pronouns referring to times; modals may be treated as binding
implicit world pronouns. Compositional semantic details aside, the interpretation
function, now $\llbracket \cdot \rrbracket^{g_c}$, may return a semantic value as in (1.14), where $g_c(1m)$ is a
time earlier than the time of the context (type m for times, ignoring worlds).

(1.14)   a.   [$_S$ PAST$_{1m}$ [it$_{7e}$ jump]]
         b. $\llbracket S \rrbracket^{g_c} = 1$ iff $g_c(7e)$ jumped at $g_c(1m)$

This book investigates the prospects for a linguistic framework that that goes the
further step of positing object-language pronouns for context — formally, *assignment variables*. Although there are precedents for introducing a semantic type for
assignments (Sternefeld 1998, Kobele 2010, Rabern 2012b, Kennedy 2014) and
for introducing pronouns for items determining shifted interpretations of referential expressions (Percus and Sauerland 2003, Elbourne 2005, Johnson 2012,

---

[1] Some authors distinguish the context c and assignment g_c, reserving c for specific features of
discourse contexts such as speaker, addressee, etc. For present purposes I simplify by identifying the
context coordinate with the contextually determined assignment.

Charlow and Sharvit 2014), the project of developing a syntax/semantics with assignment variables — variables for the sort of item responsible for interpreting context-sensitive language generally — hasn't been pursued. I will argue that by representing the assignment function in the syntax, we can capture a wide range of linguistic phenomena previously explained by varied syntactic and semantic mechanisms. A theory with assignment variables affords a unified analysis of the context-sensitivity of various theoretically recalcitrant expressions, and systematizes a spectrum of seemingly disparate shifting data across domains.

One way of understanding the assignment-variable-based approach is as formally implementing Stalnaker's (1988, 2014) seminal "multiple context" treatment of attitude ascriptions (cf. Swanson 2011). On Stalnaker's view, there are multiple contexts "available to be exploited" (Stalnaker 1988: 156) in describing individuals' states of mind — the "basic" ("global") discourse context, and a "derived" ("local," "subordinate") context representing the attitude state. In the embedded clause in (1.15), although the discourse context c_1 supplies the interpretation of the pronoun, the derived context c_2 representing (what is presupposed to be) Tom's beliefs is also available for interpreting the change-of-state verb. In (1.16) the discourse context and the derived context are available for interpreting the positive-form relative gradable adjective 'rich' (where 'o is d-wealthy' abbreviates that o's degree of wealth is at least d). In the unshifted "global" reading the relevant standard for counting as rich is the standard in the discourse, d_{c_1}; in the shifted "local" reading it is the standard in the dream, d_{c_2}.

(1.15)   [Context: We're talking about Bo. It's presupposed that Bo never smoked.]
Alice believes he^{c_1} quit^{c_2} smoking.
>   ≈ "Alice believes that Bo used to smoke and no longer smokes"
>
>   (cf. Swanson 2011: ex. 31)

(1.16)   Alice dreamt that Zoe was rich$^{c_1/c_2}$.
>   ≈ "Alice dreamt that Zoe was d_{c_1}/d_{c_2}-wealthy"

Stalnaker doesn't offer a specific implementation of these ideas. One could perhaps attempt a pragmatic explanation of the shifts in interpretation, say drawing on a general pragmatic account of local context (cf. Schlenker 2010). Or one might treat attitude verbs as context-shifting operators, and introduce mechanisms to capture different ways shifting can occur within a clause (cf. Cumming 2008, Santorio 2010, 2012, Ninan 2012). An alternative approach — the approach I wish to pursue in this book — is to posit variables for the different contexts. The "multiple contexts" with respect to which context-sensitive expressions may be interpreted are represented via object-language variables for assignments.

Adding assignment variables to the object language is far from trivial. Yet we will see how positing representations of context in the syntax can help systematically account for diverse linguistic shifting phenomena, and provide a framework for theorizing about possibilities for (un)shifted readings. The proposed theory affords a unified analysis of the context-sensitivity of expressions such as pronouns, epistemic modals, etc., in the spirit of contextualist theories; yet it improves in compositionally deriving certain recalcitrant shifting data, as desired by revisionary theories. The result will be a novel philosophically informed framework for compositional semantics compatible with the classical paradigm.

An overview of the book is as follows. §2 provides a formal overview of the basic syntax and semantics. §3 motivates a general clausal architecture for an assignment-variable-based theory, drawing on independent work on the syntax–semantics interface. The proposed syntax/semantics standardizes quantification and binding across domains via a generalized (type-flexible, cross-categorial) binder-index feature, which attaches directly to moved expressions. Construction-specific parameters, composition rules, or interpretive principles aren't required. §4 applies the account to several examples with quantifiers and attitude ascriptions. Topics of discussion include quantification in the metalanguage, distinctions between de re vs. de dicto and specific vs. nonspecific readings, binding with pronouns vs. traces, alternative bases for constraints on readings, and a choice-function analysis of names. An improved formalization of assignment modification captures binding relations in examples with long-distance binding.

§§5–9 explore how the assignment-variable-based framework may be extended to other constructions, such as various types of quantified and non-quantified noun phrases (§§5–7), conditionals (§8), and questions (§9). Nominal quantifiers are treated as introducing quantification over assignments, binding pronouns such as relative pronouns in relative clauses, bound-variable pronouns, and donkey pronouns (§§5–6). The assignment-variable-based account of quantifiers and nominal predicates is integrated in a more detailed layered n/v analysis of noun phrases and verb phrases (§7). A semantics with events is briefly considered as a basis for future research. 'If'-clauses are treated as free relatives, interpreted as plural definite descriptions of assignments (possibilities) (§8). Interrogative sentences denote a set of possible answers, with answers conceived as sets of assignments (possibilities) (§9). Compositional derivations of various types of shifting phenomena are provided involving pronoun binding, donkey anaphora, weak vs. strong quantifiers, indexical shift, information-sensitivity, and interrogative flip.

A principal aim of this book is a more cohesive theory of linguistic shifting with improved empirical coverage and explanatory power. Certain features of the treatments of modals, noun phrases, relativization, conditionals, and questions may be of more general interest — e.g., unified analyses of apparent non-c-command anaphora with donkey pronouns, genitive binding, inverse linking, and correlatives; a distinction between trace-binding and pronoun-binding, with applications to weak crossover; parallel phase-based analyses of noun and verb phrases, with applications to specificity, possessive constructions, and existential sentences; uniform compositional semantics for 'if'-clauses in post-nominal, sentence-final, and sentence-initial positions, and in conditionals with declarative or interrogative main clauses, with or without a main-clause modal or 'then'; a unified approach to conditional, correlative, and interrogative clauses; and choice-function analyses of relative words, *wh* words, and certain indefinites and anaphoric proforms. The treatments of quantifier raising, relativization, and questions avoid introducing additional composition rules or interpretive principles (e.g., Predicate Abstraction, Trace Conversion). The semantics is fully compositional.

A methodological remark: The aim of this book isn't to provide a possibility proof; the question isn't whether it is possible to construct a formal syntax/semantics with object-language variables for assignments. I would be surprised if it wasn't. The project is to investigate the prospects for a specific type of syntax/semantics of natural language as a concrete basis for future theory comparison. Contextually determined assignment functions are an already needed theoretical posit. We will see that giving them syntactic representation can help systematically account for diverse linguistic shifting phenomena across syntactic categories and semantic domains. Some of the data will be new, though in many cases the aim will be to provide a new take on old facts — integrating data from diverse literatures in new ways, and systematizing phenomena independently familiar yet often not jointly considered in theorizing. Sustained investigation into a variety of linguistic phenomena is required. One must ensure that particular choice points and analyses generalize across the spectrum of examples, and can be integrated in an overall account that plausibly rivals accounts in more familiar frameworks. The devil is in the details (lambdas, trees). I hope that the preliminary developments in this book illustrate the fruitfulness of an assignment-variable-based framework for linguistic theorizing.

1.2   Parameters and Operators: A (Ptolemaic) Road Not Taken

Recent decades have seen an expansion of resources for capturing different types of linguistic shifting phenomena. Before beginning our constructive project, this section briefly considers how certain of the data might be captured in a familiar operator-based semantics, which analyzes expressions such as modals, attitude verbs, etc. as operators that shift relevant contextual features, construed as parameters of interpretation. To fix ideas I focus on two prominent approaches from the literature — traditional context-index-style frameworks, and recent treatments of indexical shift that introduce assignment-quantification in the metalanguage. The aim isn't to develop the accounts in depth, or to show that no alternative can succeed. The aim is simply to highlight certain prima facie costs so as to further motivate the book's central constructive project. Readers satisfied with the motivations in §1.1 may proceed to §2.

Literatures on epistemic modals have highlighted that the relevant body of information for interpreting epistemic modals under attitude verbs is generally shifted to the subject's information (Stephenson 2007, Silk 2016a, 2017). In quantified epistemic attitude ascriptions the relevant information shifts with the quantificational subject, as reflected in (1.17). There is apparently no reading of (1.17) that ascribes to the contestants a belief about the information i_c accepted in the discourse context.

(1.17)   Every contestant thinks they must be crazy.

      ≈ "for every contestant x, x's beliefs imply that x is crazy"

A prominent (though controversial) approach to capturing this is to add an informational coordinate to the index of evaluation (Stephenson 2007, Yalcin 2007, Hacquard 2010, MacFarlane 2014). A first approximation for a simple epistemic attitude ascription is in (1.18), where $DOX_{x,w}$ is the set of worlds compatible with x's beliefs in w.[2]

(1.18)   Al thinks Bo might win.

     a. [$_S$ Al thinks [might [Bo win]]]

     b. $[\![\text{might } \phi]\!]^{g;w,s} = 1$ iff $\exists w' \in s: [\![\phi]\!]^{g;w',s} = 1$

        $[\![\text{think } \phi]\!]^{g;w,s} = \lambda x_e . \forall w' \in s': [\![\phi]\!]^{g;w',s'} = 1$, where $s' = DOX_{x,w}$

        $[\![S]\!]^{g,s} = 1$ iff $\forall w' \in DOX_{Al,w}: \exists w'' \in DOX_{Al,w}:$ Bo wins in w''

              iff $\exists w'' \in DOX_{Al,w}:$ Bo wins in w''

(1.18) characterizes Al's beliefs as being compatible with Bo winning. The attitude verb obligatorily shifts the informational coordinate in the index to the subject's belief state.

---

[2] For simplicity I treat the informational parameter as a set of worlds, and I bracket details about the compositional semantics for different flavors of modality. For present purposes I assume that worlds are in the index. An abstraction rule such as Heim and Kratzer's (1998) Intensional Function Application can be used in combining modals/attitude verbs with their (type t) complements.

Such a semantics may work well for expressions for which local (shifted) readings are conventionalized. The approach is awkward for expressions permitting both local (shifted) and global (unshifted) readings — that is, most context-sensitive expressions. Recall the standard-sensitivity associated with positive form relative gradable adjectives (cf. (1.16)). The attitude ascription in (1.19) can be used to characterize Al's beliefs about Rita's degree of wealth and/or Al's standard for counting as rich, depending on the context.

(1.19)   Al thinks that Rita is rich.

  a. [Context: We agree that one must be a millionaire to count as rich. We're talking about Al's beliefs about Rita's financial situation. Al thinks Rita is a millionaire.]

    ≈ "Al thinks Rita is at least d_c-rich"

  b. [Context: We accept possibly different standards for richness. Rita's income counts as rich by Al's lights.]

    ≈ "Al thinks Rita is at least d_A-rich"

Since 'rich' is compatible with unshifted readings, it won't do to interpret it directly with respect to an additional coordinate in the index, analogously to the treatment of 'might' in (1.18). So suppose we treat 'rich' as having an argument place which may be filled alternatively by a contextually supplied standard-pronoun **d**, representing global readings, or an element **D** referring to a posited standards coordinate in the index, representing local readings. First-pass analyses are in (1.20)–(1.21), where $DOX^*_{x,w}$ is now a set of world-standard pairs compatible with x's belief state in w (type d for degrees). The truth condition in (1.21b) for the local reading in (1.19b) says, roughly, that for all worlds w' and standards d' compatible with Al's belief state, Rita is d'-wealthy in w'.[3]

(1.20)   a. [$_S$ Al thinks [Rita [rich d_3]]]

  b. [$_S$ Al thinks [Rita [rich D]]]

(1.21) $[\![\text{rich}]\!]^{g;w,s,d} = \lambda d_d.\lambda x_e\,.\,x$ is at least d-rich in w

   $[\![\text{D}]\!]^{g;w,s,d} = d$

   $[\![\text{think } \phi]\!]^{g;w,s,d} = \lambda x_e\,.\,\forall\langle w',d'\rangle \in s^*\colon [\![\phi]\!]^{g;w',s',d'} = 1$,

    where $s^* = DOX^*_{x,w}$ and $s' = \{w'' \mid \exists d''\colon \langle w'',d''\rangle \in DOX^*_{x,w}\}$

  a. $[\![(1.20a)]\!]^{g;w,s,d} = 1$ iff $\forall\langle w',d'\rangle \in DOX^*_{Al,w}\colon$ Rita is $g(3d)$-rich in w'

  b. $[\![(1.20b)]\!]^{g;w,s,d} = 1$ iff $\forall\langle w',d'\rangle \in DOX^*_{Al,w}\colon$ Rita is d'-rich in w'

---

[3] I ignore context-sensitivity from comparison classes, and I bracket issues regarding the internal syntax/semantics of the positive form (Kennedy 2007). An extended version of Intensional Function Application incorporating standards may be used in combining the attitude verb and its complement.

Analogous moves can be made for other expressions optionally taking shifted or unshifted readings. A first approximation for quantifiers and domain variables (von Fintel 1994, Stanley and Szabó 2000, Stanley 2002) is in (1.22)–(1.24), $DOX^*_{x,w}$ now a set of world-standard-domain triples. In (1.22b) the restricted domain is shifted to a set of individuals considered relevant by the attitude subject, as reflected in (1.24b). (For simplicity I treat the domain argument as a set of individuals (type $\langle e, t \rangle$), and I leave 'can-vote' unanalyzed. In lexical entries and derivations I will often use '$f(x)$' to abbreviate '$f(x) = 1$'. I use metalanguage predicates such as '$person_u$' for the set of persons in u.)

(1.22)   Al thinks everyone can vote.

    a.   [Context: We're considering Al's beliefs about the legal status of certain minority groups G, who we think are relevant in questions about voting rights. We know nothing about Al's own moral/legal views.]

       ≈ "Al thinks everyone in G is legally permitted to vote"

    b.   [Context: We're considering Al's moral/legal views. We know he is aware that certain minority groups aren't legally permitted to vote.]

       ≈ "Al thinks everyone in the groups he considers relevant to questions about voting rights is legally permitted to vote"

(1.23)   a.   [$_S$ Al thinks [[everyone P$_5$] can-vote]]

    b.   [$_S$ Al thinks [[everyone G] can-vote]]

(1.24) $[\![everyone]\!]^{g;w,s,d,G} = \lambda P_{et}.\lambda Q_{et} . \forall x: (x \text{ is a person in } w \wedge P(x)) \rightarrow Q(x)$
$[\![G]\!]^{g;w,s,d,G} = G$
$[\![think\ \phi]\!]^{g;w,s,d,G} = \lambda x_e . \forall \langle w', d', G' \rangle \in s^*: [\![\phi]\!]^{g;w',s',d',G'} = 1,$
where $s^* = DOX^*_{x,w}$ and $s' = \{w'' \mid \exists d''\exists G'': \langle w'', d'', G'' \rangle \in DOX^*_{x,w}\}$

    a. $[\![(1.23a)]\!]^{g;w,s,d,G} = 1$ iff $\forall \langle w', d', G' \rangle \in DOX^*_{Al,w}: \forall x: (person_{w'}(x) \wedge g(5et)(x)) \rightarrow x$ can vote in w'

    b. $[\![(1.23b)]\!]^{g;w,s,d,G} = 1$ iff $\forall \langle w', d', G' \rangle \in DOX^*_{Al,w}: \forall x: (person_{w'}(x) \wedge G'(x)) \rightarrow x$ can vote in w'

The preceding semantics captures the relevant shifted readings of context-sensitive expressions by proliferating coordinates in the index. A concern is that such an approach obscures one of the original motivations for distinguishing the index parameter in points of evaluation. Following Lewis (1980), the index consists of those contextual features that can be shifted by operators. If the majority of contextual features can be shifted—arguably even features determining the interpretation of paradigm indexicals such as 'I' (see e.g. Santorio 2012)—one might wonder if a simpler theoretical apparatus and analysis is available.[4]

---

[4] It isn't evident that the approach to (shiftable) contextual domain restrictions will generalize

An alternative approach is to abandon the index parameter and treat expressions such as attitude verbs as assignment-shifters (cf. Cumming 2008, Santorio 2010, 2012, Ninan 2012). Previous accounts have focused on cases of indexical shift with individual pronouns, though the approach can be generalized to shifting with other context-sensitive expressions. Just as the attitudes and circumstances of interlocutors in a concrete discourse are assumed to be representable by an abstract "contextually determined assignment" which determines values for pronouns, quantifier domain restrictions, degree standards, etc. (also Heim and Kratzer 1998, Schlenker 2003, Heim 2008, Silk 2018), so too, we can assume, for concrete attitude states more generally.[5] The attitude verb in (1.25) is now treated as quantifying over assignments compatible with the subject's state of mind.

(1.25) $[\![\text{think } \phi]\!]^{g,a} = \lambda x_e . \lambda w_s . \forall \langle w', a' \rangle \in DOX_{x,w} : [\![\phi]\!]^{g,a'}(w') = 1$

Adapting the semantics from Santorio (2010), suppose that the interpretation function is relativized to an ordinary assignment g as well as an assignment a shifted by (e.g.) attitude verbs. The syntactic indices interpreted with respect to

---

to examples with multiple quantifier phrases. For examples such as (i), one could perhaps represent the index coordinate instead as a function from NP-meanings to domain restrictions, roughly as in (ii), where $[\![G^*]\!]^{g;G^*, \cdots} = G^*$ is type $\langle et, et \rangle$. $G^*(cat_w)$ represents a set of individuals relevant in considering cats, $G^*(dog_w)$ represents a set of individuals relevant in considering dogs, etc. (Following Heim and Kratzer 1998, λ_i is the assumed object-language binder index resulting from QR, interpreted syncategorematically via Predicate Abstraction. We will return to this.)

(i)   Every cat likes every dog.

(ii) $[\![\text{every dog } G^* \lambda_2 [\text{every cat } G^* \text{ likes } t_2]]\!]^{g;w,G^*, \cdots} = 1$ iff $\forall y : (dog_w(y) \land G^*(dog_w)(y)) \rightarrow$
        $(\forall x : (cat_w(x) \land G^*(cat_w)(x)) \rightarrow x \text{ likes } y)$

However, examples such as (iii), where different occurrences of the same quantified expression receive different shifted restrictions, remain problematic.

(iii)   [Context: A panel survey is being conducted to discern sentiments about the fairness of the University's practices in distributing a certain award. The panel members — Alice, Bert, and Chloe — have different views on who should be allowed to be nominated for the award, and who should be allowed to vote in deciding the winner. Alice thinks that the award should be reserved for undergraduates, and that only graduate students and faculty should be allowed to vote for the winner; and she thinks that the award procedure in fact proceeds accordingly. Bert thinks that the award should be open to graduate students too, and that undergrads, grads, and faculty should all be allowed to vote; and he thinks that the award procedure in fact proceeds accordingly. Chloe thinks that the award should be open to all members of the University, but she thinks that faculty are wrongly excluded from being nominated. When asked about how the University is doing regarding sentiments about the award practices, you report:]

        Quite well. Most people think that everyone can vote for everyone.

I won't consider further epicycles here.

[5] We will return to metasemantic issues regarding what it is for an assignment to be compatible with an attitude state in the following chapters.

a can be distinguished accordingly with a [+a] feature. A simplified derivation for the shifted reading in (1.19b) might proceed roughly as in (1.26a).

(1.26)   a. $[_S$ Al thinks [Rita [rich $d_{3[+a]}$]]]

   b. $[\![d_{3[+a]}]\!]^{g,a} = a(3d)$

   $[\![\text{rich}]\!]^{g,a} = \lambda d_d.\lambda x_e.\lambda w_s . x$ is d-rich in w

   $[\![S]\!]^{g,a}(w_c) = 1$ iff $\forall \langle w', a' \rangle \in DOX_{Al,w_c}$: Rita is $a'(3d)$-rich in w'

The embedded adjective 'rich', on the relevant local reading, is interpreted with respect to assignments a' compatible with Al's state of mind.

A challenge for both of the previous types of operator-based accounts comes from intermediate readings, where the interpretation is determined nonlocally but with respect to an environment distinct from the discourse context. Consider (1.27), on the reading where the relevant standard for richness is the standard accepted by the quantificational subject. Identifying the richness-standard argument **d**? in (1.28) as **d**ᵢ would represent the global reading, where the standard is supplied by the contextually determined assignment g; and identifying the variable as **d**ᵢ[+a] (on the assignment-shifting analysis) or **D** (on the context-index analysis) would represent the local reading, where the standard is supplied by the assignment representing the possibility compatible with Zoe's dream state.

(1.27)   [Context: Alice, Bert, and Chip each accepts a particular standard for how rich one must be to count as rich — say, d_A, d_B, d_C, respectively. Alice thinks that Zoe dreamt that Rita was at least d_A-wealthy; Bert thinks that Zoe dreamt that Rita was at least d_B-wealthy; Chip thinks that Zoe dreamt that Rita was at least d_C-wealthy. Talking about Alice's, Bert's, and Chip's beliefs:]

   Everyone thinks Zoe dreamt that Rita was rich.

(1.28)   [everyone P_5 thinks [Zoe dreamt [Alice rich d?]]]

Such examples can be multiplied. On the intermediate reading of 'everyone' in (1.29), the implicit domain restriction represents, for each bigot x, the set of individuals considered relevant by x in matters of voting rights, as reflected in (1.30).

(1.29)   [Context: Arnie, Betty, and Chuck are bigots, prejudiced in favor of their respective groups G_A, G_B, G_C. Arnie thinks Al thinks that all (and only) the G_As (individuals in G_A) can vote; Betty thinks Al thinks that all (and only) the G_Bs can vote; Chuck thinks Al thinks that all (and only) the G_Cs can vote. Talking about Arnie's, Betty's, and Chuck's beliefs:]

   Every bigot thinks that Al thinks everyone can vote.

(1.30) [every bigot P_4 thinks [Al thinks [everyone $P_?$ can-vote]]]

This says that every bigot x is optimistic about Al's beliefs about whether anyone is improperly excluded (by x's lights) from being legally permitted to vote.

Analogous phenomena that have led theorists to posit syntactic world variables and object-language quantification over worlds can thus be observed with features associated with various context-sensitive expressions. This raises a challenge for accounts providing distinct treatments of shifting with worlds and individuals, versus other context-sensitive expressions. One might respond by further complicating the aforementioned sorts of operator-based analyses (see von Fintel and Heim 2011 for related general discussion). I suggest that we put such epicycles to the side.

The traditional framework takes unshifted readings for context-sensitive expressions as paradigmatic. Though such an approach might seem initially plausible for English expressions such as 'I' or 'here', it is awkward when one considers the rich array of shifting phenomena in natural languages — hence the plethora of mechanisms for capturing intensionality, quantification, and local readings across context-sensitive expressions. Indeed Kaplan goes so far as to treat referential readings and bound-variable readings as uses of homonyms (1989: 489–490).[6] The notion of a crosslinguistic class of specialized anaphoric pronouns — pronouns conventionally excluded from receiving their interpretation from the discourse context (§1.1) — is a borderline conceptual impossibility from a classical perspective.

It is time to rethink the foundational assumptions about context-sensitivity motivating the traditional formalism. Our understanding of the richness of

---

[6] Lest one scoff, note that Kratzer's (1998a, 2009) "minimal pronoun" account of apparent bound-variable ("fake indexical") uses of 1st-/2nd-person pronouns is a homonym account. Further, whereas local fake indexicals are treated as minimal pronouns (mere indices) interpreted via an ordinary λ-binder ((i)), long-distance fake indexicals are treated as fully specified pronouns interpreted via distinct context-shifting λ-binders ((ii)), syncategorematically defined as in (iii). The "true" and "fake" indexical uses of the string 'you' in (ii) are homonyms; the local and long-distance fake indexical uses of 'you' in (i) and (ii), respectively, are homonyms; and the binder indices in (i)–(ii) trigger distinct interpretation rules.

(i)   a. Only you got a question that you understood.
      b. [Only [2nd]] λ_2 got a question that $\varnothing_2$ understood

(ii) a. You are the only one who knows somebody who understands your paper.
      b. [2nd] ... $\lambda_{[2nd]}$ know somebody who understands [2nd]'s paper

(iii) a. $[\![[2nd]]\!]^{g,c}$ = addressee(c)
         $[\![\varnothing_n]\!]^{g,c} = g(n)$
      b. $[\![\lambda_n\, \alpha]\!]^{g,c} = \lambda x.[\![\alpha]\!]^{g',c}$, where g' is like g, except possibly that $g'(n) = x$
         $[\![\lambda_{[1st]}\, \alpha]\!]^{g,c} = \lambda x.[\![\alpha]\!]^{g,c'}$, where c' is like c, except possibly that speaker$(c') = x$
         $[\![\lambda_{[2nd]}\, \alpha]\!]^{g,c} = \lambda x.[\![\alpha]\!]^{g,c'}$, where c' is like c, except possibly that addressee$(c') = x$
                                            (cf. Kratzer 1998a: 94–95; 2009: 213–214)

contextual dependencies in natural language — indexicality, intensionality, logophoricity, perspective, projection, local context — has come a long way since Kaplan's (in)famous ban on "monsters." The theory in this book encourages a reorientation in theorizing about context and linguistic shifting. Shiftability for context-sensitive expressions is the default; unshiftability and obligatory shifting on the poles of the spectrum are what call for special explanation. The proposed syntax and semantics with assignment variables provides unified analyses of shifted and non-shifted readings, and a fully compositional standardization of quantification across domains. I encourage the development of alternative overall theories with which the following assignment-variable-based account may be compared.

Part I

2

Preliminaries

2.1 Formal Overview: Semantic Values, Models, Domains, Variables

I begin with formal elements of the basic syntax and semantics.

Instead of using a traditional interpretation function ($[\![\ ]\!]^g)_{g \in G}$ parameterized by assignments (worlds, etc.), we use an unrelativized interpretation function $[\![\ ]\!]$. The semantic values of expressions are given in terms of sets of assignments, included in the model. (I ignore elements such as times and events.)

(2.1)   **Models $\mathcal{M}$**
- E: set of entities
- T: set of truth-values (represented $\{0, 1\}$)
- W: set of worlds
- G: set of assignments

Theoretically, I treat assignments as representing a possibility. This interpretation is in keeping with common appeals to contextually determined assignments representing what world is actual, objects' relative saliences, speaker intentions, etc. (Heim and Kratzer 1998, Schlenker 2003, Heim 2008). For instance, a syntactic representation **it**$_{7e}$ and assignment mapping $\langle 7, e \rangle$ to Fluffy might represent an intention to refer to Fluffy with a token use of 'it' and a possibility in which Fluffy is the center of attention.

Care must be taken in our formalization of assignments and semantic types. Including assignment variables and variables of arbitrary types has the potential for paradox or non-wellfoundedness (cf. Groenendijk and Stokhof 1991, Chierchia 1994). For instance, one cannot have a case where $g(i) = g$, for some assignment-index i, lest there be assignments g in their own codomain. Likewise, we cannot allow ourselves to ask whether an assignment g is in the value it assigns to an index k for a set of assignments, i.e. whether $g \in g(k)$. Given that functions are sets of ordered pairs, a case where $\langle k, S \rangle \in g \wedge g \in S$, for some set of assignments S, would violate standard set-theoretic bans on $\in$-chains.

Let the set of assignments G in the model be a set of ordinary assignments h — functions from typed numerical indices $\langle n, \tau \rangle$, for any non-assignment type τ, to elements of the model. For instance, $h(\langle 4, e \rangle)$ returns an entity $o \in E$, say

Fluffy; $h(\langle 4, et\rangle)$ returns (the characteristic function of) a set of entities in E, say {Fluffy, Fido}; and so on. Ordinary assignments $h \in G$ are undefined for indices for assignments or functions involving assignments. I let the domain of assignments D_g be a set of assignments whose domain also includes indices $\langle n, a\rangle$ for assignments — i.e., where $dom(g) = dom(h) \cup \{\langle n, a\rangle : n \in \mathbb{N}\}$, and $range(g) = range(h) \cup G$. For instance, for some $g \in D_g$, $g(\langle 2, a\rangle)$ is an ordinary assignment $h \in G$; $g(\langle 2, e\rangle)$ is an entity $o \in E$, say Fido; and so on. (Hereafter I will generally omit the brackets in indices, e.g. abbreviating '$\langle i, \alpha\rangle$' with '$i\alpha$'.)

The present system avoids the worries regarding non-wellfoundedness and ϵ-chains. Since assignments g_g return elements in the model, there is no case of an assignment being in its own codomain. For $h \in G$, $h(ia)$ is undefined; and for $g \in D_g$, $g(ia) = h \neq g$. Since high-type assignment indices aren't in the domain of assignments in D_g or G, expressions such as $h(iat)$, $g(iat)$, $g(ia)(iat)$, etc. are undefined. Such a restriction in assignments' domains is motivated by our understanding of assignment-variables as an object-language mechanism for tracking the interpretation of context-sensitive expressions; yet the assumption that there are no pronouns for sets of assignments is ultimately an empirical one. (There may be other expressions of type $\langle a, t\rangle$, etc.; we will return to this.)

It is common to identify basic semantic types with sets in the model. Given our approach to expressions' semantic values, it will simplify our formalism to define semantic types in terms of functions from assignments (cf. Kobele 2010; contrast Sternefeld 1998). For instance, functions from assignments to truth-values in T are type t, and functions from assignments to entities in E are type e. Our semantic types are as follows, where the set of assignments$_M$ G and domain of assignments$_D$ D_g are defined as previously. (For purposes of the present exposition, I will refer to ordinary assignments $h \in G$ as "assignments$_M$" (for assignments in the $\underline{M}$odel), and to the richer assignments $g \in D_g$ as "assignments$_D$" (for assignments in the $\underline{D}$omain). When the distinction is irrelevant I ignore the subscripts; context should disambiguate.)

(2.2)   **Domains/Semantic types**

      $- D_g$ = domain of assignments$_D$
      $- D_e = E^{D_g}$
      $- D_t = \{0, 1\}^{D_g}$
      $- D_s = W^{D_g}$
      $- D_a = G^{D_g}$
      $- D_{\alpha\beta} = D_\beta^{D_\alpha}$

Unlike previous accounts with semantic types for assignments (§1.1), I let the object language include variables for assignments. A natural preliminary idea would be to identify variable denotations with functions from assignments to elements in the model — e.g., treating the denotation of a world-variable $[\![\mathbf{w_i}]\!]$ as $\lambda g_g.g(is)$, where $g(is) \in W$. (I will reserve $\mathbf{g_i}$ for assignment-variables, $\mathbf{w_i}$ for world-variables.) Such a move is unavailable in the system as developed thus far. For instance, an assignment-variable denotation (function $a: D_g \to G$) couldn't combine via function application or function composition with functions $x: D_g \to E$ (individual-variable denotations), $p: D_g \to 2^W$ (proposition-variable denotations), etc.

Instead, I treat non-assignment variables as having an initial argument of type a; semantic composition proceeds via function application. Variables $\mathbf{v_{i\alpha}}$ for basic non-assignment types α denote functions $[\![\mathbf{v_{i\alpha}}]\!] \in D_{a\alpha}$ such that for any $a_a, g_g, [\![\mathbf{v_{i\alpha}}]\!](a)(g) = a(g)(i\alpha)$ — e.g., $[\![\mathbf{w_1}\,\mathbf{g_1}]\!] = [\![\mathbf{w_1}]\!]([\![\mathbf{g_1}]\!]) = \lambda g_g.g(1a)(1s)$. Variables of complex types may be defined via a metalanguage "down"-style operator $^\downarrow$ which maps an element of a domain to an item composed out of associated lowered elements of the model:

(2.3) For γ of (possibly basic) type $\sigma = \langle \sigma_n, \langle \ldots, \sigma_0 \rangle \cdots \rangle$, $^\downarrow\gamma$ is defined by the condition that, for any g_g:
$(^\downarrow\gamma)(g) = $ the (possibly nullary) function $f \in \mathcal{M}$ s.t. for any $\gamma^n_{\sigma_n} \ldots \gamma^1_{\sigma_1}$,
$$\gamma(\gamma^n) \ldots (\gamma^1)(g) = f((^\downarrow\gamma^n)(g)) \ldots ((^\downarrow\gamma^1)(g))$$

For the degenerate case where γ_β is of basic type $\beta \in \{e, s, t, a\}$, $^\downarrow\gamma$ is a function from an assignment$_D$ g_g to the item in the model that is the image under γ of g. For instance, for $x \in D_e$, $(^\downarrow x)(g)$ is the individual (nullary function) $o \in E$ such that $o = x(g)$, i.e. $(^\downarrow x)(g) = x(g)$. For $P \in D_{\langle e,t \rangle}$, $(^\downarrow P)(g)$ is the function $f: E \to T$ such that for any x_e, $P(x)(g) = f((^\downarrow x)(g)) = f(x(g))$; and so on. The denotations of $\mathbf{v_{i\sigma}}$ of complex types $\sigma = \langle \sigma_n, \langle \ldots, \sigma_0 \rangle \cdots \rangle$ can be defined accordingly as functions $[\![\mathbf{v_{i\sigma}}]\!] \in D_{a\sigma}$ such that, for any $g_g, a_a, \gamma^n_{\sigma_n}, \ldots, \gamma^1_{\sigma_1}$, $[\![\mathbf{v_{i\sigma}}]\!](a)(\gamma^n) \ldots (\gamma^1)(g) = a(g)(i\sigma)((^\downarrow\gamma^n)(g)) \ldots ((^\downarrow\gamma^1)(g))$. For instance, a pronoun $[\mathbf{p_{2st}}\,\mathbf{g_1}]$ for a set of worlds denotes a function $[\![\mathbf{p_{2st}}]\!]([\![\mathbf{g_1}]\!]) \in D_{st}$ such that for any $w_s, g_g, g(1a)(2st)((^\downarrow w)(g)) = g(1a)(2st)(w(g))$; a choice-function pronoun $[\mathbf{F_{1ete}}\,\mathbf{g_1}]$ denotes a function $[\![\mathbf{F_{1ete}}]\!]([\![\mathbf{g_1}]\!]) \in D_{\langle\langle e,t \rangle,e \rangle}$ such that for any $P_{\langle e,t \rangle}, g_g$, the individual $g(1a)(1ete)((^\downarrow P)(g)) \in E$ is in (the characteristic set of) $(^\downarrow P)(g)$, where $(^\downarrow P)(g)$ is the function $f: E \to T$ such that $f(x(g)) = P(x)(g)$ for any x_e; and so on. The semantic values of traces lack the initial type a argument, e.g. $[\![\mathbf{t_{1e}}]\!] = \lambda g_g.g(1e)$. For complex type $\sigma = \langle \sigma_n, \langle \ldots, \sigma_0 \rangle \cdots \rangle$, trace $\mathbf{t}$, and pronoun-variable **v** (variables of basic types could be understood degenerately where $n = 0$ and $\sigma_0 \in \{e, s, t, a\}$):[7]

(2.4) $[\![\mathbf{v}_{i\sigma}]\!] = \lambda a_a.\lambda\gamma^n_{\sigma_n} \ldots \lambda\gamma^1_{\sigma_1}.\lambda g_g . a(g)(i\sigma)((\downarrow\gamma^n)(g)) \ldots ((\downarrow\gamma^1)(g))$

    a. For $\alpha \in \{e, s, t\}$, $[\![\mathbf{v}_{i\alpha}]\!] = \lambda a_a.\lambda g_g . a(g)(i\alpha)$ b. $[\![\mathbf{g_i}]\!] = \lambda g_g . g(ia)$

(2.5) $[\![\mathbf{t}_{i\sigma}]\!] = \lambda\gamma^n_{\sigma_n} \ldots \lambda\gamma^1_{\sigma_1}.\lambda g_g . g(i\sigma)((\downarrow\gamma^n)(g)) \ldots ((\downarrow\gamma^1)(g))$

    a. For $\beta \in \{e, s, t, a\}$, $[\![\mathbf{t}_{i\beta}]\!] = \lambda g_g . g(i\beta)$

(Note that variables $\mathbf{g_i}$ for assignments are type a (functions $D_g \rightarrow G$); there are no denotations of type g. For a pronoun $[\mathbf{v}_{i\sigma}\ \mathbf{g_k}]$, I sometimes call $\mathbf{v}_{i\sigma}$ the "pronoun-variable." I use 'pronoun' both in the technical sense for $[\mathbf{v}_{i\sigma}\ \mathbf{g_k}]$, and for vocabulary items such as 'it', 'she', etc.; context should disambiguate.)

2.2   Preliminary Derivation: Pronouns, Quantifiers, Quantification

To get a feel for the basic system it will be instructive to consider a preliminary derivation. Consider (2.6), with a subject-position quantifier and free individual pronoun. (For present purposes I ignore the internal structure and person restriction with 'everyone'. g^- is, intuitively, the counterpart assignment$_M$ $h \in G$ of g. Further intermediate calculations are left to the reader.)[8]

---

[7] I will use traces in representing displacement (cf. Chomsky 1981), though the framework is compatible with a minimalist syntax that rejects traces as theoretical primitives (cf. Chomsky 1995; more on this in §3). The account isn't committed to a fundamental distinction between traces and pronoun-variables. For instance, all variables could be interpreted as in (2.4), and the definition of QR could be adapted so that remnants of movement are sister to an identity function on assignments. A simpler option is afforded by the treatment of indices as features. The rules in (2.4)–(2.5) amount to saying that $[\![\ ]\!]$ returns the values in (i) for number-type feature sets. The pronoun complexes $[\mathbf{v}_{i\sigma}\ \mathbf{g_j}]$ in the main text may thus be understood as representing terminal feature bundles $\{[\langle i, \sigma\rangle], [\langle j, a\rangle]\}$.

(i)   For feature set $F \subseteq \mathbb{N} \times \Theta$, and $\langle i, \sigma\rangle \in F$,

$$[\![F]\!] = \begin{cases} \lambda\gamma^n_{\sigma_n} \ldots \lambda\gamma^1_{\sigma_1}.\lambda g_g . g(i\sigma)((\downarrow\gamma^n)(g)) \ldots ((\downarrow\gamma^1)(g)), & \text{if } |F| = 1 \\ \lambda\gamma^n_{\sigma_n} \ldots \lambda\gamma^1_{\sigma_1}.\lambda g_g . g(ja)(i\sigma)((\downarrow\gamma^n)(g)) \ldots ((\downarrow\gamma^1)(g)), & \text{if } |F| = 2 \wedge [\langle j, a\rangle] \in F \\ \text{undefined otherwise} \end{cases}$$

[8] The asterisk in 'S*' is used to distinguish the different S nodes; it has no theoretical import. I often use 'S' multiply for root sentences, TP, ModP, v*P. I will ignore tense, aspect, voice. In lexical entries and derivations I often write "$\forall x = y: \ldots$" for "$\forall x: (x = y) \rightarrow \ldots$", and abbreviate "$f(x) = 1$" with "$f(x)$." To a first approximation, $g[i/n]$ is the unique assignment g' that maps n to i and is otherwise identical to g; I return to assignment-modification in §4. We will reconsider the semantic types of individual pronouns and the argument structure of nominal and verbal predicates in Part II.

(2.6)   Everyone loves it.

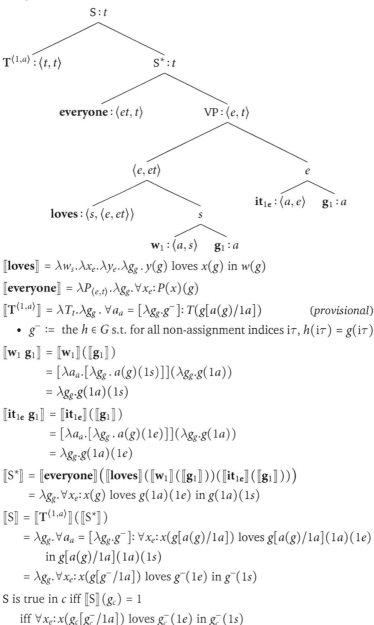

$[\![\mathbf{loves}]\!] = \lambda w_s.\lambda x_e.\lambda y_e.\lambda g_g . y(g) \text{ loves } x(g) \text{ in } w(g)$

$[\![\mathbf{everyone}]\!] = \lambda P_{\langle e,t\rangle}.\lambda g_g. \forall x_e : P(x)(g)$

$[\![\mathbf{T}^{\langle 1,a\rangle}]\!] = \lambda T_t.\lambda g_g . \forall a_a = [\lambda g_g.g^-] : T(g[a(g)/1a])$ *(provisional)*

- $g^- :=$ the $h \in G$ s.t. for all non-assignment indices $i\tau$, $h(i\tau) = g(i\tau)$

$[\![\mathbf{w_1 \; g_1}]\!] = [\![\mathbf{w_1}]\!]([\![\mathbf{g_1}]\!])$

        $= [\lambda a_a.[\lambda g_g . a(g)(1s)]](\lambda g_g.g(1a))$

        $= \lambda g_g.g(1a)(1s)$

$[\![\mathbf{it_{1e} \; g_1}]\!] = [\![\mathbf{it_{1e}}]\!]([\![\mathbf{g_1}]\!])$

        $= [\lambda a_a.[\lambda g_g . a(g)(1e)]](\lambda g_g.g(1a))$

        $= \lambda g_g.g(1a)(1e)$

$[\![S^*]\!] = [\![\mathbf{everyone}]\!]\big([\![\mathbf{loves}]\!]([\![\mathbf{w_1}]\!]([\![\mathbf{g_1}]\!]))([\![\mathbf{it_{1e}}]\!]([\![\mathbf{g_1}]\!]))\big)$

      $= \lambda g_g.\forall x_e : x(g) \text{ loves } g(1a)(1e) \text{ in } g(1a)(1s)$

$[\![S]\!] = [\![\mathbf{T}^{\langle 1,a\rangle}]\!]([\![S^*]\!])$

      $= \lambda g_g.\forall a_a = [\lambda g_g.g^-] : \forall x_e : x(g[a(g)/1a]) \text{ loves } g[a(g)/1a](1a)(1e)$

        $\text{in } g[a(g)/1a](1a)(1s)$

      $= \lambda g_g.\forall x_e : x(g[g^-/1a]) \text{ loves } g^-(1e) \text{ in } g^-(1s)$

S is true in c iff $[\![S]\!](g_c) = 1$

    iff $\forall x_e : x(g_c[g_c^-/1a]) \text{ loves } g_c^-(1e) \text{ in } g_c^-(1s)$

First, pronouns are sister to assignment-variables, which determine their interpretation. I assume that sentences have a topmost assignment-binder $\mathbf{T}^{\langle i,a\rangle}$, which functions to map variables sister to assignment-variables $\mathbf{g_i}$ to the values provided by the input assignment. This anchors intuitively free pronouns to the discourse via the definition of truth-in-a-context (cf. Percus 2000, von Fintel and Heim 2011). The individual pronoun 'it' refers to the contextually relevant individual $g_c^-(1e)$; the implicit world pronoun refers to the contextually relevant world $g_c^-(1s)$. For now one may assume that in the intended interpretation the first-positioned world $g(1s)$ is the world of the possibility represented by g; a more complex clausal architecture and derivation is provided in §3. In §3.5 we will see how the semantic values of binder expressions such as $\mathbf{T}^{\langle i,a\rangle}$ can be derived compositionally from a generalized (cross-categorial, type-flexible) binder-index feature $^{\langle i,\sigma\rangle}$.

Importantly, the outputs of assignments are items in the model. What is loved according to (2.6) isn't a function $y \in D_e$ but an individual $o \in E$—say, Fluffy. Although the quantification in the metalanguage is over functions $x : D_g \rightarrow E$, the items in terms of which the condition is stated are images of the given assignment g under x, i.e. individuals $o \in E$ in the model. The universal quantification over x_e includes functions mapping g to object $o_1 \in E$, functions mapping g to $o_2 \in E$, etc. The quantificational condition $\forall x_e : \ldots$ in (2.6) is satisfied iff regardless of which such function we look at, its value $o \in E$ loves $g_c^-(1e)$ (=Fluffy). If there was an $o_i \in E$ that didn't love Fluffy, then any function $x_i \in D_e$ mapping g_c to o_i would be such that $x_i(g_c)$ doesn't love $g_c^-(1e)$ (=Fluffy), falsifying the condition; and if there was a function $x_j \in D_e$ such that $x_j(g_c)$ doesn't love $g_c^-(1e)$, then there would be an $o_j \in E$, namely $x_j(g_c)$, that doesn't love Fluffy (=$g_c^-(1e)$). In this way the universal quantification over functions $x \in D_e$ makes a claim about every object $o \in E$ in the set of entities (cf. Kobele 2010).

So, the sentence S is true in c iff every $o \in E$ loves the contextually relevant individual $g_c^-(1e) \in E$, Fluffy.

3

Standardizing Quantification

Adding assignment-variables to the object language raises nontrivial issues for the lexical and compositional semantics. This chapter draws on independent work on the syntax–semantics interface to motivate a more complex clausal architecture for an assignment-variable-based theory. §4 applies the account to several examples with attitude ascriptions and modals. The account captures phenomena with intensionality and shifted/unshifted interpretations of context-sensitive expressions via general mechanisms of movement and variable binding, and affords an elegant standardization of quantification across domains (individuals, worlds, assignments).

The treatments of the syntax and semantics in the remainder of the book are of course not the only way of developing a theory with assignment-variables. There will be various choice points, many unforced, along the way. I welcome the development of alternatives with which the account may be compared.

3.1 Preamble

A prima facie worry with frameworks positing syntactic variables for worlds, times, etc. is that they overgenerate readings. The worry might seem especially pressing for a theory with assignment-variables. Absent additional constraints, nothing would seem to exclude the structure and interpretation for (3.1) in (3.2).

(3.1) Alice thinks it cried.

(3.2)
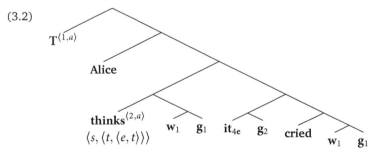

$\approx$ "for every possibility h compatible with Alice's beliefs, the individual o represented with 4 by h ($=h(4e)$) cried in the actual world ($=g_c(1s)$)"

This represents an unattested reading where the embedded individual pronoun receives a local reading (sister to an assignment-variable coindexed with
'think'), and the embedded world pronoun receives a global reading (sister to an
assignment-variable coindexed with the topmost assignment-binder).

It is important not to overstate the explanatory burdens specific to theories
positing object-language variables for worlds, times, assignments. Take 'it'.
Suppose for the sake of argument that the interpretation of 'it' cannot be shifted
in examples such as (3.1). Such a constraint might be formalized, à la Kaplan,
by analyzing 'it' as a variable that receives its interpretation from a contextual
parameter i on the interpretation function, which cannot be shifted by attitude
verbs. An explanatory inquiry isn't far behind. What makes it the case that *that*
formalism correctly represents the conventional meaning and use of the string
'i-t' in the given community? Why can the contextual parameter i not be shifted
in modal contexts, though it can be shifted by elements such as determiner
quantifiers? Why can other pronouns and context-sensitive expressions receive
modally shifted readings? Is the constraint associated with 'it' associated with
analogous pronouns across languages? If so, what general features of human
cognition, sociality, conversation, etc. explain the crosslinguistic universal?

There is much one might say in response. Given the paucity of descriptive
content of 'it', shifted readings under attitude verbs would seem generally
unretrievable. Addressees aren't in general privy to speakers' assumptions about
what some attitude subject takes to be relevantly salient. For frameworks with
unshiftable or selectively shiftable parameters on the interpretation function,
such stories may be understood at the "presemantic" level of what formal objects
represent the shifting possibilities for a given string. Yet all types of theories must
ultimately provide an explanation of tendencies — and in some cases conventionalized constraints — for shifted/unshifted readings across expressions, in English
and crosslinguistically. Of course not all ways of carving up the explanatory
terrain are empirically or theoretically on a par — hence the present project.
We will see that introducing assignment-variables into the syntax and semantics
affords diverse empirical and theoretical advantages. In semantics as in tailoring
(so I'm told), it is often easier to start big and take in.

This chapter focuses on one type of constraint on readings to begin reining
in the system's flexibility: the constraint that the world argument of a clause's
main predicate be bound by the closest world-binder (Percus 2000). The aim is
to derive that the main predicate's world argument receives an obligatory shifted
reading, and to do so in a way that allows other embedded variables to receive
unshifted readings linked to the discourse context. The next chapter applies the

account to shifting phenomena with worlds, individuals, and modals in attitude ascriptions.

3.2 Type-Driven Movement

There is a familiar story about what generates binding relations with object-position quantifiers over individuals. The quantifier undergoes Quantifier Raising because of a type mismatch, and a binder-index binds a coindexed trace. A preliminary implementation in our assignment-variable framework is in (3.3) (n. 7). Roughly put, the binder-index combines with 'everyone' so that the quantifier's scope argument becomes the set of individuals that make the proposition $[\![S^{**}]\!]$ true when returned as the value for $\langle 2, e \rangle$. (For now, I again ignore the person restriction associated with 'everyone', and I treat names as constants. We will examine the compositional semantic details shortly.)[9]

---

[9] Note that the argument of the raised quantifier is type t, rather than property type (cf. Heim and Kratzer 1998, Kobele 2010, Kennedy 2014). The binder-index attaches directly to the moved expression, rather than occupying its own node and triggering a special composition rule such as Predicate Abstraction (Heim and Kratzer 1998). We will return to this. For expository purposes I will use traces in representing displacement (cf. Chomsky 1981), though the framework is compatible with a syntax that rejects treating traces as theoretical primitives. Remnants of movement may be understood as copies of the moved expression, as in a copy theory of movement (Chomsky 1993, 1995, Sauerland 1998, Fox 2000, 2002, Hornstein 2001, Nunes 2004; see Takahashi 2010 for a comparative overview). We can assume that non-semantically-driven movement is undone at LF, and, in a copy theory, that any copies not necessary for semantic composition are deleted. In movement for type reasons, i.e. Quantifier Raising QR (May 1985), the chain might be interpreted via an LF-interface rule that replaces the lowest copy with a coindexed variable, or deletes all parts of the lower copy except its number-type features, as reflected in (i)–(ii) (n. 7; cf. Kratzer 2004). (I use '∧' to indicate binder features.)

(i) QR (alternative): Copy $\alpha^{\langle i, \sigma \rangle}$ from A, and Merge with A.

(ii) a. ⋮
  everyone$^\wedge \langle 5, e \rangle$
  [Alice defeated everyone$^\wedge \langle 5, e \rangle$]
  [everyone$^\wedge \langle 5, e \rangle$ [Alice defeated everyone$^\wedge \langle 5, e \rangle$]]
  b. LF ≈ [everyone$^\wedge \langle 5, e \rangle$ [Alice defeated $\langle 5, e \rangle$]]

The framework is also compatible with different views on the theoretical status of indices, and the representation of chain relations in the narrow syntax and interfaces. Indices could be explicitly represented in lexical item tokens in a lexical array (or a device for identifying complex syntactic objects individuated in terms of such indices), or treated as representing the syntactic relations on which (co)indexing in the interfaces supervenes (see Collins and Stabler 2016, Larson 2016).

(3.3)   Alice likes everyone.

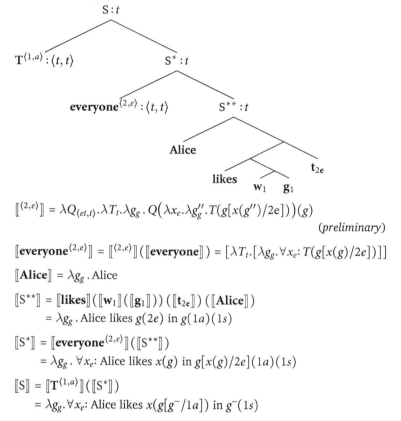

$$[\![^{\langle 2,e\rangle}]\!] = \lambda Q_{\langle et,t\rangle}.\lambda T_t.\lambda g_g\,.\,Q\big(\lambda x_e.\lambda g''_g\,.\,T(g[x(g'')/2e])\big)(g)$$

(preliminary)

$$[\![\mathbf{everyone}^{\langle 2,e\rangle}]\!] = [\![^{\langle 2,e\rangle}]\!]\,([\![\mathbf{everyone}]\!]) = [\lambda T_t.[\lambda g_g.\forall x_e\colon T(g[x(g)/2e])]]$$

$$[\![\mathbf{Alice}]\!] = \lambda g_g\,.\,\mathrm{Alice}$$

$$[\![S^{**}]\!] = [\![\mathbf{likes}]\!]\,([\![\mathbf{w}_1]\!]([\![\mathbf{g}_1]\!]))\,([\![\mathbf{t}_{2e}]\!])\,([\![\mathbf{Alice}]\!])$$
$$\qquad = \lambda g_g\,.\,\mathrm{Alice\ likes}\ g(2e)\ \mathrm{in}\ g(1a)(1s)$$

$$[\![S^{*}]\!] = [\![\mathbf{everyone}^{\langle 2,e\rangle}]\!]\,([\![S^{**}]\!])$$
$$\qquad = \lambda g_g\,.\,\forall x_e\colon \mathrm{Alice\ likes}\ x(g)\ \mathrm{in}\ g[x(g)/2e](1a)(1s)$$

$$[\![S]\!] = [\![\mathbf{T}^{\langle 1,a\rangle}]\!]\,([\![S^{*}]\!])$$
$$\qquad = \lambda g_g.\forall x_e\colon \mathrm{Alice\ likes}\ x(g[g^-/1a])\ \mathrm{in}\ g^-(1s)$$

A hypothesis is that a parallel mechanism is at play in the clausal domain with quantification over worlds. The obligatory local reading of the main predicate's world argument is explained via type-driven movement. Specifically, I treat complementizers such as declarative 'that' as base-generated in the position of the main predicate's world argument, and as raising for type reasons as a quantifier over worlds (cf. Roberts 2001: 144–145, Ritter and Wiltschko 2014, Wiltschko 2014); and I treat semantically modal elements such as attitude verbs as base-generated in an internal assignment argument position of the complementizer, and as raising for type reasons as a quantifier over assignments, as schematized in (3.4) (Z a placeholder for the category of the semantically modal item).[10]

---

[10] I use 'modal' broadly for semantically modal elements of various categories (modal verbs, attitude verbs, **T**), sometimes narrowly for modal verbs; context should disambiguate.

(3.4)

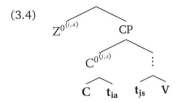

In each case, a binder-index attaches to the quantificational expression due to type-driven movement, leaving a coindexed (individual, world, assignment) trace. Note that the verb's world argument is now a trace, directly bound by the complementizer. The local modal domain for the clause will be determined by the embedding modal.

There are precedents for treating the syntax–semantics interface in this way. von Stechow (2008), following suggestions due to Irene Heim, treats attitude verbs as raising from inside the complement as quantifiers over worlds. Hacquard (2006, 2010) proposes an analogous move for Aspect, treating Aspect as a quantifier over events and moving from the verb's event-argument position (see also Moulton 2015). Heim (2012) treats the question operator as moving from an internal argument of the interrogative complementizer as a quantifier over propositions. Similar semantic effects of head movement have been defended by Lechner (2006), Bruening (2010), Szabolcsi (2011). As we will see in §§5–6, a prominent approach in syntax is to treat quantifiers as raising from their nominal/clausal complement (Campbell 1996, Matthewson 1998, Ihsane and Puskás 2001, Giusti 2002, Luján 2004). In light of crosslinguistic phenomena with nominal tense, Lecarme (1999b, 2004) offers parallel syntax for clauses and noun phrases in terms of verbal/nominal T(ense)-chains (following Guéron and Hoekstra 1995, Campbell 1996). The verbal/nominal predicate's event argument e_i is assumed to be bound by a higher operator OP_i in agreement with Tense$_i$, as reflected in (3.5).

(3.5)   a. $[_{CP} OP_i C [_{TP} T_i ... [_{VP} ... e_i V ...]]]$
         b. $[_{DP} OP_i D [_{TP} T_i ... [_{NP} ... e_i N ...]]]$

Lecarme's focus isn't on compositional semantics. It isn't said what establishes the (obligatory) binding relation between the operator OP_i and e_i, or how the interpretation of the complex construction is derived given the assumed agreement among OP_i, T_i, e_i. Though I will ignore tense, the account developed in what follows can be understood as deriving the relevant operators and chain relations in a precise compositional semantics — e.g., linking the main predicate, complementizer, and an embedding modal via type-driven movement.

The architecture in (3.4) could be refined in light of more detailed analyses of verbal and clausal domains. For instance, the complementizer might be analyzed as raising for type reasons from an internal world argument of Aspect, which, following Hacquard, raises as a quantifier over events from an event argument of the main predicate, as schematized in (3.6) (v a type for events).

(3.6)

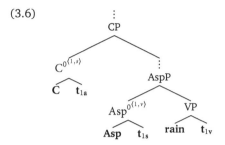

For present purposes I assume the simpler structure in (3.4), where world-binding (intensionality) arises directly from the complementizer, which moves from the world-argument position of the main predicate in the clause.[11]

3.3   Complementizers: World-Binding

In §2 I noted that I would be treating assignments as representing possibilities. It will be useful to define a metalanguage function $@: G \to W$ that maps an assignment h to the world of the possibility represented by h. I offer (3.7) as a lexical entry for declarative complementizers such as 'that' or its unpronounced counterpart, written '$\mathbf{C_d}$' (nn. 8, 11). As we will see, the structure representing 'that it rained' in (3.8) denotes the proposition that it rained in the world, $@(g(1a))$, of the given possibility. The modal element base-generated in C^0 (leaving assignment-trace $\mathbf{t_{1a}}$) determines the modal domain.

(3.7) $[\![\mathbf{that}]\!] = [\![\mathbf{C_d}]\!] = \lambda a_a.\lambda p_{\langle s,t \rangle}.\lambda g_g . \forall w_s = [\lambda g'_g.@(a(g'))] : p(w)(g)$

(3.8)

$$\begin{array}{c}
\vdots \\
\text{CP} \\
\diagup \quad \diagdown \\
C^{0\langle 1,s \rangle} \qquad \text{IP} \\
\diagup \diagdown \qquad \diagup \diagdown \\
\textbf{that} \quad \mathbf{t_{1a}} \quad \mathbf{t_{1s}} \quad \textbf{rained}
\end{array}$$

----

[11] Cf. Koopman 1984 on verbal complementizers crosslinguistically. See Moulton 2015 on further potential complications regarding the syntactic derivation of CP complements. I will ignore independent syntactic differences between overt complementizers (e.g. 'that') and their unpronounced counterparts (e.g. Pesetsky 2017). We will consider base-generated complementizers in §8. I return to events in the syntax/semantics of verb phrases briefly in §7.5.

3.4 Modals, Attitude Verbs: Assignment-Binding

I treat notionally modal elements as introducing quantification over assignments. To fix ideas I focus on the top-level assignment-binder $\mathbf{T}$, doxastic attitude verbs such as 'think', and modal verbs such as 'may'. For $\mathbf{T}$ the quantification is over the assignment a such that $a(g) = g^-$ for any g; with 'may' the quantification is over a such that $a(g)$ is in the set of accessible possibilities; and with 'think' the quantification is over a such that $a(g)$ is compatible with the subject's state of mind.[12]

(3.9) $[\![\mathbf{T}]\!] = \lambda A_{\langle a,t \rangle}.\lambda g_g . \forall a_a = [\lambda g_g . g^-] : A(a)(g)$

(3.10) $[\![\mathbf{may}]\!] =$

    a. $\lambda w_s.\lambda r_{\langle s,at \rangle}.\lambda A_{\langle a,t \rangle}.\lambda g_g . \exists a_a : r(w)(a)(g) \wedge A(a)(g)$
    b. $\lambda A'_{\langle a,t \rangle}.\lambda A_{\langle a,t \rangle}.\lambda g_g . \exists a_a : A'(a)(g) \wedge A(a)(g)$

(3.11) $[\![\mathbf{think}]\!] = \lambda w_s.\lambda A_{\langle a,t \rangle}.\lambda x_e.\lambda g_g . \forall a_a : a(g)$ is compatible with $x(g)$'s state of mind in $w(g) \rightarrow A(a)(g)$

As we will see in the compositional derivations in §4, the set of worlds at which a clause is evaluated is determined by the assignment-quantification introduced by the modal. With $\mathbf{T}$, the main clause is evaluated at a singleton set. The lexical entry for $\mathbf{T}$ ensures that coindexed assignment-variables are mapped to the the assignment g_c^- representing the discourse context, and the modal domain for the main clause is the actual world, $@(a(g_c^-)) = @(g_c^-)$. With modals/attitude verbs, the modal domain is the set of worlds compatible with the modality/attitude. The meaning for the modal verb in (3.10) can be understood as adapting a familiar Kratzer-style semantics, where modals quantify over a set of contextually relevant possibilities (Kratzer 1977, 1981). For simplicity I use a basic accessibility relation r ("modal background"), which maps the world argument to a set of assignments. The alternative entries in (3.10) correspond to alternative argument structures. The (a)-option represents an argument structure where the modal takes the world and modal background pronouns as independent arguments; the (b)-option represents an argument structure where the world and modal-background pronouns combine, yielding a world-indexed set of possibilities which combines with the modal (cf. von Fintel and Heim 2011). To fix ideas I will assume the latter option in (3.10b). As usual, the meaning for 'think' in (3.11) lexically specifies the set of possibilities being quantified over. The complement is evaluated at the worlds $@(a(g))$ of possibilities compatible with the subject's state of mind.

---

[12] We will revisit the argument structure of modals and attitude verbs in §§7–8.

I have said that assignments are theoretically interpreted as representing possibilities — what world is actual, foci of attention, objects' relative saliences, etc. Work in metasemantics may provide additional resources for reining in the system's flexibility. Every account requires metasemantic assumptions — general or specific to particular discourses — about the intended interpretations of syntactic indices and relations among values assigned by shifted assignments. In §2.2 we assumed that the first-positioned world in g_c was identified with the world of the possibility represented by g_c. Or one might require that the first-positioned individual in an assignment h representing an epistemic possibility determined by g_c be an epistemic counterpart of the first-positioned individual in g_c, who is the speaker of c. Generalizing, one might require that the syntactic indexing determined by the concrete discourse be such that, for any relevant index $\langle i, \sigma \rangle$, $h(i\sigma)$ represents an epistemic counterpart of $g_c(i\sigma)$ — more pedantically, that if a concrete discourse c determines that a particular syntactic indexing $\langle i, \sigma \rangle$ and abstract assignment g_c would represent an intention to pick out such-and-such item s in the model with a use in c, then for any assignment h representing an epistemic possibility (or possibility compatible with so-and-so's state of mind), $h(i\sigma)$ is an epistemic (doxastic) counterpart of $g_c(i\sigma) = s$. Any overall theory invoking a notion of the "assignment of the context" g_c, or an "assignment determined by" "the physical and psychological circumstances" (Heim and Kratzer 1998: 243; cf. Schlenker 2003, Cumming 2008, Santorio 2010, 2012, Ninan 2012, Silk 2018) must ultimately address the metasemantics of what makes it the case that an assignment or set of assignments represents a particular content-bearing state, such as a discourse situation, body of information, or state of mind. Yet for purposes of developing the formal syntax and semantics, which takes as given an abstract representation such as an assignment function, I put the metasemantics to the side. Work on indexical shift and concept generators may afford additional grammatical, lexical, and metasemantic resources (cf. §1.2).

3.5 Generalized Binder-Index

The account in this book provides a fully compositional semantics for quantification and binding. This contrasts with prominent analyses of Quantifier Raising (QR) — including implementations in trace theories (e.g. Heim and Kratzer 1998), copy theories (e.g. Fox 2002), and multidominant theories (e.g. Johnson 2012) — which are typically syncategorematic. Following the traditional view in syntax, indices are represented as features on expressions. The binder-index attaches directly to moved expressions, rather than occupying its own node and triggering a specialized interpretation rule (Predicate Abstraction, Trace Conversion). Previous definitions of object-language binder indices have been limited to DPs and binding of individual-variables (Kobele 2010, Kennedy 2014). The syntax/semantics in this chapter affords a means of standardizing quantification via a generalized binder-index, attaching to quantificational expressions of various categories and semantic types, as reflected in (3.12)–(3.15) — where χ_τ is a variable for the type of what is being quantified over, σ is the type of the mother node (i.e. the result of combining the binding expression with its scope argument), and $\gamma_{\sigma_1}^1 \dots \gamma_{\sigma_n}^n$ are variables for any intermediate arguments.

(3.12) *Generalized binder-index feature*

$$[\![^{\langle i,\tau\rangle}]\!] = \lambda \alpha_{\langle\langle\tau,\langle_1\sigma_1\cdots\sigma_n, t\rangle_1\cdots\rangle_n\rangle,\sigma\rangle} \cdot \lambda \beta_{\langle_1\sigma_1\cdots\sigma_n, t\rangle_1\cdots\rangle_n} \cdot$$
$$\alpha\Big(\lambda\chi_\tau.\lambda\gamma_{\sigma_1}^1\cdots\lambda\gamma_{\sigma_n}^n.\lambda g_g.\,\beta(\gamma^1)\cdots(\gamma^n)(g[(^{\downarrow}\chi)(g)/i\tau])\Big)$$

(3.13) $[\![[\text{everything}]^{\langle i,e\rangle}]\!] = [\![^{\langle i,e\rangle}]\!]([\![\text{everything}]\!])$
$$= \lambda T_t.\lambda g_g . \forall x_e : T(g[x(g)/ie])$$

(3.14) $[\![[\text{that } \mathbf{t_{ja}}]^{\langle i,s\rangle}]\!] = [\![^{\langle i,s\rangle}]\!]([\![\text{that } \mathbf{t_{ja}}]\!])$
$$= \lambda T_t.\lambda g_g . \forall w_s = \lambda g_g'.@(g'(ja)): T(g[w(g)/is])$$

(3.15) $[\![[\text{think } \mathbf{t_{js}}]^{\langle i,a\rangle}]\!] = [\![^{\langle i,a\rangle}]\!]([\![\text{think } \mathbf{t_{js}}]\!])$
$$= \lambda T_t.\lambda x_e.\lambda g_g . \forall a_a : a(g) \text{ is compatible with } x(g)\text{'s state of mind}$$
in $g(js) \to T(g[a(g)/ia])$

Roughly put, the binder-index $^{\langle i,\tau\rangle}$ takes an expression α that quantifies over items of type τ, and feeds α the set of τ-type items that verify its sister β when returned as the value for $\langle i,\tau\rangle$.

Important advances in syntax have come from explaining movement operations in terms of more fundamental grammatical principles — e.g., treating QR as an instance of Move α, α any category (Chomsky 1981, May 1985), or analyzing Move in terms of Merge ("remerge," "copy and merge") (Chomsky 1993, 1995, Fox 2000, Collins and Stabler 2016). The assignment-variable-based account developed here follows in the spirit of such developments. The compositional semantics of QR (type-driven movement) proceeds via function application: the expression α undergoing QR combines with the binder-index via function application, and the QR'd expression $\alpha^{\langle i,\tau\rangle}$ combines with its sister via function application. Syntactically, the movement operations in QR proceed via Merge: α merges with the binder-index in its base position, yielding $\alpha^{\langle i,\tau\rangle}$, which is remerged/copied-and-merged later in the derivation.[13] The lower copy may

---

[13] In a model such as that in Groat and O'Neil 1996, type-driven overt vs. covert movements (e.g., with attitude verbs vs. object-position nominal quantifiers) would be distinguished in terms of whether phonological features are moved to the head of the chain. In a theory with local morphophonological spell-out, covert QR would take place after spell-out (cf. Nissenbaum 2000, Cecchetto 2004, Tanaka 2015; more on this in §7.2.4).

be replaced with a coindexed variable directly, as in a trace theory, or via a general replacement/deletion rule in the semantic component (n. 9). The binder-index feature would thus be what triggers QR syntactically, and allows for combination via function application semantically. The result is a syntax and compositional semantics of type-driven movement in terms of feature-driven Merge and function application.[14]

---

[14] Contrast the present simplified derivation for QR in (i) with the trace-theoretic, copy-theoretic, and multidominant alternatives in (ii)–(iv). For concreteness, in (i) I assume a copy theory with a replacement/deletion rule in the semantic component (n. 9). Fox's Trace Conversion in (iii) converts the lower copy to a definite description by replacing the quantifier (here 'every') with 'the' and inserting an identity predicate and coindexed pronoun in the complement, yielding [the [boy [= o_5]] from [every boy]$_5$ (more on this in §5.1.2). In the multidominant syntax in (iv), remerged syntactic objects are literally in both positions — hence Johnson's (2012) need to generate the quantifier (here $\forall$) in the higher position independently. Johnson assumes that, by some morphosyntactic principles, the syntactically displaced $\forall$ and 'the' get pronounced as 'every'. I don't know how such an approach would generalize across varieties of type-driven movement.

(i)   Merge + Function Application
a. [every boy]$^\wedge \langle 5, e \rangle$
   ⋮
   [Alice defeated [every boy]$^\wedge \langle 5, e \rangle$]
   [[every boy]$^\wedge \langle 5, e \rangle$ [Alice defeated [every boy]$^\wedge \langle 5, e \rangle$]]   (by Merge)
b. LF ≈ [[every boy]$^\wedge \langle 5, e \rangle$ [Alice defeated $\langle 5, e \rangle$]]
c. ≈ "for every boy o, Alice defeated o"   (by FA)

(ii) Traces + QR + Predicate Abstraction (PA) (cf. Heim and Kratzer 1998)
a. [every boy]
   ⋮
   SS: [Alice defeated [every boy]$_5$]   (by Merge)
b. LF: [[every boy] [5 [Alice defeated t_5]]]   (by QR)
   • QR: $[\ldots \alpha_i \ldots] \Rightarrow [\alpha_i [\text{i} [\ldots t_i \ldots]]]$
c. ≈ "for every boy o, Alice defeated o"   (by PA, FA)

(iii) Copies + Trace Conversion (TC) + Predicate Modification (PM) + PA* (cf. Fox 2002, 2003)
a. [every boy]$_5$
   ⋮
   [Alice defeated [every boy]$_5$]
   [[every boy]$_5$ [Alice defeated [every boy]$_5$]]   (by Merge)
b. LF: [[every boy]$_5$ [Alice defeated [the [boy [= o_5]]]]]   (by TC)
c. ≈ "for every boy o, Alice defeated the o' s.t. o' is a boy $\wedge$ $o' = o$"   (by PA*, PM, FA)
   • PA*: $[\![DP_i [\ldots DP_i \ldots]]\!]^g = [\![DP]\!]^g (\lambda x. [\![\ldots DP_i \ldots]\!]^{g[x/i]})$

(iv) Multidominance + Decomposed scattered 'every' + Agreement*+ PA* (cf. Johnson 2012)
a. [$_{DP}$ [the* o_5] boy]
   ⋮
   [Alice defeated [$_{DP}$ [the* o_5] boy]]
   [Alice defeated [$_{DP}$ [the* o_5] **NP**]]   [$_{QP}$ $\forall$ **NP**]   (by Merge)
   • **NP**: identical token of [$_{NP}$ boy], sister to both D^0 and Q^0 (multidominance)
b. LF: [[Alice defeated [$_{DP}$ [the* o_5] **NP**]] [$_{QP_5}$ $\forall$ **NP**]]   (by Merge, Agreement*)
   • Agreement*: QP$_i$ must have the same index as the sister to D^0 in the [D^0 o_i] that is sister to the lower occurrence of the NP sister to Q^0.
c. ≈ "for every boy o, Alice defeated o, provided o is a boy"   (by PA*, FA)
   • $[\![\text{the*}]\!] = \lambda x \lambda P : P(x) . x$

4

Attitude Ascriptions

This chapter shows how the derivations of world- and assignment-binding from §3 can capture various types of local/global readings in attitude ascriptions, such as with intensionality (§4.1), nominal predicates (§4.2), modals (§4.3), and names (§4.4).

4.1 Intensionality, Local/Global Readings

Let's start with a simple attitude ascription such as (4.1) (see n. 8). (I abbreviate 'o's state of mind in u' with '$\text{SOM}_{o,u}$'. To improve readability I suppress certain irrelevant assignment modifications, and I omit the explicit quantification over $w \in D_s$ when the modal domain has been derived, both indicated with '$\approx$'. Intermediate calculations are left to the reader.)[15]

(4.1) He thinks it smiled.

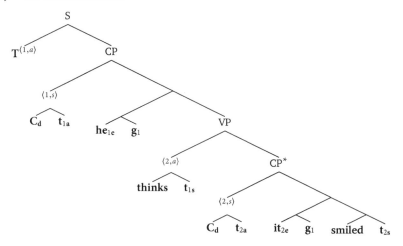

---

[15] I leave open the specific syntactic category of **T**, e.g. whether it raises to Spec,C or heads an extended projection in the CP layer such as ForceP (cf. Rizzi 1997). **C$_d$** is again an unpronounced declarative complementizer. In some languages the complementizer in root sentences may — and in some cases must — be overt (Rizzi 1997, Lecarme 1999a; cf. Chomsky 1995, Franco 2013). I ignore φ-features with individual pronouns.

$\llbracket \text{CP}^* \rrbracket = \lambda g_g \cdot \forall w_s = \lambda g'_g . @(g'(2a)) : g[w(g)/2s](1a)(2e) \text{ smiled in } w(g)$

$\llbracket \text{VP} \rrbracket = \llbracket [\textbf{think t}_{1s}]^{\langle 2,a \rangle} \rrbracket (\llbracket \text{CP}^* \rrbracket)$

$\quad = \lambda x_e . \lambda g_g \cdot \forall a_a : a(g) \text{ is compatible with } \text{SOM}_{x(g),g(1s)} \rightarrow$
$\qquad \forall w_s = \lambda g'_g . @(g'(2a)) :$
$\qquad\quad g[a(g)/2a][w(g)/2s](1a)(2e) \text{ smiled in } w(g[a(g)/2a])$

$\quad \approx \lambda x_e . \lambda g_g \cdot \forall a_a : a(g) \text{ is compatible with } \text{SOM}_{x(g),g(1s)} \rightarrow$
$\qquad g(1a)(2e) \text{ smiled in } @(a(g))$

$\llbracket \text{CP} \rrbracket = \llbracket [\textbf{C}_\textbf{d}\ \textbf{t}_{1a}]^{\langle 1,s \rangle} \rrbracket (\llbracket \text{VP} \rrbracket (\lambda g'_g . g'(1a)(1e)))$

$\quad \approx \lambda g_g \cdot \forall w'_s = \lambda g'_g . @(g'(1a)) :$
$\qquad \forall a_a : a(g) \text{ is compatible with } \text{SOM}_{g(1a)(1e), w'(g)} \rightarrow$
$\qquad g(1a)(2e) \text{ smiled in } @(a(g))$

$\quad \approx \lambda g_g \cdot \forall a_a : a(g) \text{ is compatible with } \text{SOM}_{g(1a)(1e), @(g(1a))} \rightarrow$
$\qquad g(1a)(2e) \text{ smiled in } @(a(g))$

$\llbracket \text{S} \rrbracket = \llbracket \textbf{T}^{\langle 1,a \rangle} \rrbracket (\llbracket \text{CP} \rrbracket) = \lambda g_g \cdot \forall a'_a = \lambda g''_g . g''^- : \llbracket \text{CP} \rrbracket (g[a'(g)/1a])$

$\quad \approx \lambda g_g \cdot \forall a'_a = \lambda g''_g . g''^- : \forall a_a : a(g) \text{ is compatible with } \text{SOM}_{a'(g)(1e), @(a'(g))} \rightarrow$
$\qquad a'(g)(2e) \text{ smiled in } @(a(g))$

$\quad \approx \lambda g_g \cdot \forall a_a : a(g) \text{ is compatible with } \text{SOM}_{g^-(1e), @(g^-)} \rightarrow$
$\qquad g^-(2e) \text{ smiled in } @(a(g))$

Suppose Bert and Fluffy are the contextually relevant individuals represented by 1 and 2, respectively. Then the attitude ascription is true in c according to (4.1), $\llbracket \text{S} \rrbracket (g_c) = 1$, iff Fluffy $(=g_c^-(2e))$ smiled in the world of every possibility compatible with Bert's $(=g_c^-(1e)$'s) state of mind in the actual world $@(g_c^-)$. (Hereafter for readability I will often omit the superscript in 'g_c^-', though it should be understood (§2.2).)

Parallel to the movement of the nominal quantifier in (3.3), the movement of the complementizer from the world-argument position of the clause's main predicate leaves a trace $\textbf{t}_{is}$, and the binder-index attaches to the moved expression $\text{C}^{0\langle i,s \rangle}$. The raised embedding modal elements, $\textbf{T}^{\langle 1,a \rangle}$, $[\textbf{think t}_{1s}]^{\langle 1,a \rangle}$, determine the local modal domain for each clause. The obligatory local reading of the clause's main predicate (§3.1) is captured via general mechanisms of type-driven movement.

Though the world argument in the embedded clause is obligatorily shifted under the attitude verb, being supplied directly by the world-trace $\textbf{t}_{2s}$, the embedded individual pronoun can receive a global reading. The intuitively free reading of 'it' is reflected in being sister to an assignment-variable $\textbf{g}_1$

coindexed with the topmost assignment-binder. This anchors its interpretation to the discourse context via $g_c[a'(g_c)/1a](1a)(2e) = a'(g_c)(2e) = g_c^-(2e)$.[16]

As discussed in §2.2, although the items quantified over are functions — here, functions in D_s, D_g — the conditions are placed on elements (worlds u, assignments h) in the model. The condition placed by the attitude verb is a condition on ways a of mapping the discourse assignment g_c to an assignment $a(g_c) \in G$ representing a possibility compatible with the subject's state of mind. Following Stalnaker (1988, 2014), shifted "contexts" are *derived*, in the sense of being determined by the discourse. Which features of a subject's state of mind are relevant for interpreting embedded material can depend on features of the discourse context. Likewise, the lexical entries for 'think' and C_d/'that' restrict the modal quantification to functions w mapping g_c to worlds $w(g_c) = @(a(g_c))$ of the possibilities compatible with the subject's state of mind. The truth of the attitude ascription requires that $g_c(2e)$ (=Fluffy) smiled in any such world $@(a(g_c)) \in W$.

4.2   De Re/De Dicto, Specific/Nonspecific: Global vs. Local Readings of World Arguments

§4.1 highlights a contrast between pronouns and traces. The trace supplying the world argument of a clause's main predicate is necessarily coindexed with the nearest c-commanding world-binder due to movement of the complementizer. Pronouns, in contrast, receive their interpretation from an assignment-variable. Absent further constraints (§7), world arguments of embedded non-main predicates may receive optional local or global readings, as reflected informally in (4.2)–(4.3) with the world-pronoun associated with 'a friend of mine'. (I leave the predicate unanalyzed.)

(4.2)   Alice thinks[i] that a [friend of mine]$_{i/c}$ laughed.

(4.3)   a.   [$_{DP}$ a [$_{NP}$ friend-of-mine [w$_j$ g$_k$]]]
        b. $[\![a]\!] = \lambda P_{\langle e,t\rangle}.\lambda Q_{\langle e,t\rangle}.\lambda g_g.\, \exists x_e: P(x)(g) \wedge Q(x)(g)$
             $[\![DP]\!] = \lambda Q_{\langle e,t\rangle}.\lambda g_g.\, \exists x_e: x(g)$ is a friend of mine in
             $g(ka)(js) \wedge Q(x)(g)$

Alternative binding configurations with world-pronouns afford a locus for capturing classic contrasts between de re vs. de dicto and specific vs. nonspecific readings. The LF in (4.4), where the embedded world-pronoun [w$_1$ g$_2$] is locally

---

[16] More precisely, an intuitively "free" reading of a pronoun [v$_{i\sigma}$ **g**$_j$] is reflected in an LF where (i) the nearest c-commanding $^{\langle j,a\rangle}$-binder (if any) is **T**$^{\langle j,a\rangle}$, and (ii) there is no $^{\langle i,\sigma\rangle}$-binder c-commanded by the topmost world-binder that c-commands the pronoun.

bound, represents a nonspecific de dicto reading. The LF in (4.5), where the DP 'a friend of mine' raises above the attitude verb, represents a specific de re reading.

(4.4)   *De dicto, Nonspecific*
     ≈ "Alice thinks there is some individual or other who is friend of mine that laughed"

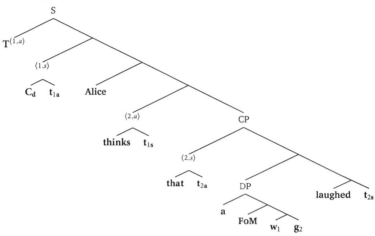

(4.5)   *De re, Specific*
     ≈ "there is some particular individual *o* who is a friend of mine such that Alice thinks *o* laughed"

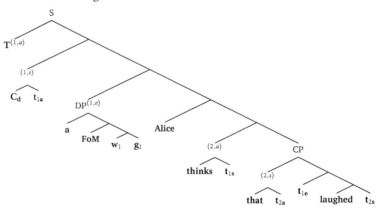

In (4.4) the DP takes narrow scope, and the world-variable receives its interpretation from an assignment-variable g_2 coindexed with the attitude verb. The attitude is about some individual or other who is a friend of mine in the subject's belief-worlds. In (4.5) the DP takes wide scope, and the world-variable receives its interpretation from an assignment-variable g_1 coindexed with the topmost assignment-binder. The attitude is about a particular individual who is a friend of mine in the actual world. (In what follows I will continue to assume that the first-positioned world index $\langle 1, s \rangle$ represents the world of the possibility represented by an assignment, i.e. $h(1s) = @(h)$, for any $h \in G$ (§2.2).)

Fodor (1970) observes that DPs such as 'a friend of mine' in (4.2) may also receive a *nonspecific de re* reading, where the belief ascribed is "nonspecific" in the sense that it isn't about any particular individual, and "de re" in the sense that it is about actual-world friends of mine. The LF in (4.6), where the embedded world-pronoun [$\mathbf{w}_1 \mathbf{g}_1$] is bound long-distance, represents a nonspecific de re reading.

(4.6)   *De re, Nonspecific*
    $\approx$ "there is some group of individuals S who are friends of mine (say, the Sharks) such that Alice thinks some or other $o \in S$ laughed"

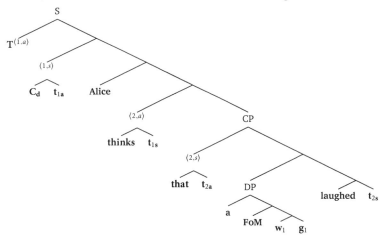

The DP 'a friend of mine' takes narrow scope under the attitude verb, and the predicate's world-variable receives its interpretation from an assignment-variable $\mathbf{g}_2$ coindexed with the topmost assignment-binder. The belief is about some individual or other who is a friend of mine in the actual world.

In these ways, intensionality is diagnosed as a species of local interpretation. Alternative readings are captured in terms of movement and general mechanisms for capturing local/global readings of pronouns, here world-pronouns. Contrasts in possibilities for unshifted readings of predicates in different positions are explained in terms of the treatment of pronouns vs. traces.[17]

---

[17] We will return to contrasts between trace-binding and pronoun-binding, constraints on modally independent readings of noun phrases, and alternative treatments of indefinites in §§5–7.

4.3   Quantified Modal Attitude Ascription

This section works through a more complex example with a quantified modal attitude ascription. Working through this example will help illustrate various features of the account concerning quantification, pronoun binding, and possibilities for local/global readings with context-sensitive expressions. A simplified derivation is in (4.7). (I again ignore the person restrictions associated with 'everyone', 'someone'. I continue to suppress irrelevant assignment modifications and the explicit quantification over $w \in D_s$, indicated with '$\approx$'. Certain equivalences from assignment modification are underlined for comment below. I will use 'r/$\mathbf{r}$' in indices/pronouns for type $\langle s, at \rangle$.)[18]

(4.7)   Everyone thinks they might love someone.

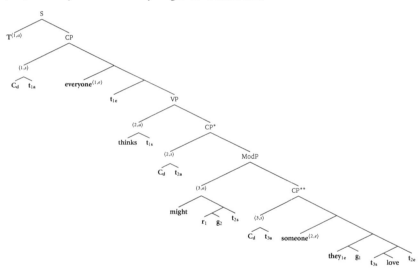

---

[18] I represent the nonfinite clausal complement of the modal as CP. (See Bhatt 2006 on modally interpreted nonfinite CPs more generally; cf. Kayne 1994, Mavrogiorgos 2010. I don't assume that all nonfinite clauses need be CPs.) We will reconsider the approach to bound individual pronouns in §6.3. Sample intermediate calculations are as follows:

$[\![\text{CP}^{**}]\!] \approx \lambda g_g . \exists x_e : g[w(g)/3s][x(g)/2e](1a)(1e) \text{ loves } x(g[w(g)/3s]) \text{ in } @(g(3a))$

$\begin{aligned}
[\![[\mathbf{r}_1 \ \mathbf{g}_2]]\!] &= [\![\mathbf{r}_1]\!]([\![\mathbf{g}_2]\!]) \\
&= [\lambda a'_a . [\lambda w_s . [\lambda a_a . [\lambda g_g . a'(g)(1r)(w(g))(a(g))]]]](\lambda g_g . g(2a)) \\
&= [\lambda w_s . [\lambda a_a . [\lambda g_g . g(2a)(1r)(w(g))(a(g))]]]
\end{aligned}$

$[\![\text{ModP}]\!] = [\![[\mathbf{might} \ [[\mathbf{r}_1 \ \mathbf{g}_2] \ \mathbf{t}_{2s}]]^{\langle 3, a \rangle}]\!]([\![\text{CP}^{**}]\!])$
$\qquad \approx \lambda g_g . \exists a_a : g(2a)(1r)(g(2s))(a(g)) \wedge \exists x_e : g(1a)(1e) \text{ loves } x(g) \text{ in } @(a(g))$

$[\![\text{VP}]\!] = [\![[\mathbf{think} \ \mathbf{t}_{1s}]^{\langle 2, a \rangle}]\!]([\![\text{CP}^{*}]\!])$
$\qquad \approx \lambda y_e . \lambda g_g . \forall a_a : a(g) \text{ is compatible with } \text{SOM}_{y(g), g(1s)} \rightarrow$
$\qquad\qquad \exists a'_a : a(g)(1r)(@(a(g)))(a'(g)) \wedge \exists x_e : g(1a)(1e) \text{ loves } x(g) \text{ in } @(a'(g))$

$$\llbracket S \rrbracket \approx \lambda g_g . \forall a''_a = \lambda g_g . g^- :$$
$$\forall y_e \forall a_a : a(g) \text{ is compatible with } SOM_{y(g), @(a''(g))} \rightarrow$$
$$\big(\exists a'_a : a(g)(1r)(@(a(g)))(a'(g)) \wedge$$
$$\exists x_e : g[a''(g)/1a][y(g)/1e](1a)(1e) \text{ loves } x(g) \text{ in } @(a'(g)))$$
$$\approx \lambda g_g . \ldots \quad \exists x_e : a''(g[y(g)/1e])(1e) \text{ loves } x(g) \text{ in } @(a'(g))$$
$$\approx \lambda g_g . \ldots \quad \exists x_e : g[y(g)/1e]^-(1e) \text{ loves } x(g) \text{ in } @(a'(g))$$
$$\approx \lambda g_g . \forall y_e \forall a_a : a(g) \text{ is compatible with } SOM_{y(g), @(g^-)} \rightarrow$$
$$\exists a'_a : a(g)(1r)(@(a(g)))(a'(g)) \wedge \exists x_e : y(g) \text{ loves } x(g) \text{ in } @(a'(g))$$

Roughly put, this says that (4.7) is true iff every individual o is such that for every possibility h compatible with o's beliefs, there is a possibility h' accessible from h such that there is some individual o' whom o loves in the world of h'.

4.3.1 Standardizing Quantification: Binding with Pronouns and Traces

Bound readings of pronouns, shifting under modal expressions, and context-sensitivity are captured in a unified way via quantification over individuals, worlds, and assignments. First, obligatory binding relationships may be established by movement. The cross-categorial binder-index combines via function application with expressions raising for type reasons. The complementizer moves from the main predicate's world argument position, leaving a coindexed world-trace, and a modal element moves from the complementizer's assignment argument position, leaving a coindexed assignment-trace. This coindexing-via-movement derives the local reading of each clause's main predicate: the "loving" occurs in worlds $@(a'(g_c))$ compatible with the relevant information; the relevant information is determined relative to worlds $@(a(g_c))$ compatible with the subject's attitude state; the subject's attitude state is assessed at the world $@(g_c)$ of the discourse context.

In contrast, the optional bound reading of 'they' is represented via the pronoun complex $[\mathbf{they}_{1e} \, \mathbf{g}_1]$. Coindexing between $\mathbf{they}_{1e}$ and $\mathbf{everyone}^{\langle 1, e \rangle}$ requires that the pronoun be interpreted with respect to the input assignment modified to take $\langle 1, e \rangle$ to $y(g)$, the individuals being quantified over. Although embedded under multiple assignment shifters, the pronoun is linked to individuals in the actual world via the assignment-variable $\mathbf{g}_1$ coindexed with $\mathbf{T}^{\langle 1, a \rangle}$. Analogously, the variable $\mathbf{r}_1$ in the modal verb's epistemic modal background pronoun receives its interpretation from an assignment-variable $\mathbf{g}_2$ coindexed with the attitude verb. The shifted modal background $a(g_c)(1r)$ represents a doxastic counterpart of the modal background $g_c(1r)$ that would be determined by the discourse — i.e., an epistemic modal background determined by the possibility $a(g_c)$. The set of accessible possibilities is determined relative to the worlds $@(a(g_c))$ compatible with the subject's beliefs. Although 'might' quantifies over functions $a' : D_g \to G$, the modal background $a(g_c)(1r)$ is a function from worlds $u \in W$ to a set of possibilities $h' \in G$, and the quantified condition is a condition on a possibility in this set.

4.3.2 Assignment Modification and Bound Pronouns

It is standard to introduce the notion of a modified assignment by saying something to the effect that $g[x/i]$ is the unique assignment which is just like g except that i is mapped to x. A question rarely, if ever, addressed is how to interpret expressions "$g[...g.../i]$" in the metalanguage, where the description of what i gets mapped to includes 'g'. This issue becomes pressing in derivations such as (4.7) in which modified assignments are further modified. Consider the final steps in (4.7) when $g[y(g)/1e]$ is modified to $g[a''(g)/1a][y(g)/1e]$. Given the standard characterization of modified assignments, $g[y(g)/1e]$ is the assignment g' that is just like g except that $1e$ is mapped to $y(g)$; and this modified assignment is modified to the assignment g'' that is just like g' except that $1a$ is mapped to $a''(g)$. So, feeding $1a$ to g'' would seem to return $a''(g) = [\lambda g'_g.g'^-](g) = g^-$. However, the desired result of then feeding $1e$ isn't whatever happens to be returned by (the counterpart in G of) the original assignment g, i.e. $g^-(1e)$, but rather what is returned by g as modified by the initial modification, i.e. $g[y(g)/1e]^-(1e) = y(g)$. What we need—and as yet fail to have—is a sort of dynamic updating, so that references to "g" in later modifications pick out assignments as modified in earlier steps.[19]

To capture this, I treat assignment modifiers as operators on assignments, and combine repeated modifications via function composition. The definitions in (4.8) derive the equivalence $g[a''(g)/1a][y(g)/1e](1a)(1e) = y(g)$ in (4.7), reflected in (4.9). The metalanguage description '$\cdots$' of what $i\tau$ gets mapped to in (4.8a) may or may not include reference to the assignment-variable g being abstracted over. In (4.9), the modifier $[a''(g)/1a]$ maps $m = g[y(g)/1e]$ to an assignment m' that is just like m except for mapping $1a$ to the image of the *modified* assignment m under a''.[20]

---

[19] The only place I've seen this issue addressed is Sternefeld 1998: 16–17. Sternefeld cheats in the way mentioned in the main text.

[20] For readability I abbreviate the right conjunct in (4.8a) as '$m(j\sigma_{\neq i\tau}) = g(j\sigma_{\neq i\tau})$':

(i) $[a''(g)/1a] = \lambda g_g . \iota m_g : m(1a) = a''(g) \land m(j\sigma_{\neq 1a}) = g(j\sigma_{\neq 1a})$
      $[y(g)/1e] = \lambda g_g . \iota m_g : m(1e) = y(g) \land m(j\sigma_{\neq 1e}) = g(j\sigma_{\neq 1e})$

   $g[a''(g)/1a][y(g)/1e](1a)(1e)$
      $= ([a''(g)/1a] \circ [y(g)/1e])(g)(1a)(1e)$
      $= [\lambda g_g . [a''(g)/1a]([y(g)/1e](g'))](g)(1a)(1e)$

(4.8) Assignment modification

    a. $[\cdots/i\tau] := \lambda g_g . \iota m_g : m(i\tau) = \cdots \wedge m(j\sigma) = g(j\sigma)$, for all $j\sigma \neq i\tau$

    b. $g[\cdots]_1 \ldots [\cdots]_n := [\cdots]_1 \circ \ldots \circ [\cdots]_n(g)$

(4.9) $g[a''(g)/1a][y(g)/1e](1a)(1e) = g[a''(g[y(g)/1e])/1a](1a)(1e)$

The remainder of the derivation proceeds straightforwardly: feeding $1a$ to $g[a''(g)/1a][y(g)/1e]$ thus returns $a''(g[y(g)/1e]) = g[y(g)/1e]^-$, which, given $1e$, returns $y(g)$. The pronoun receives a bound reading under the quantifier, as desired.

4.3.3 *Context-Sensitive Expressions and Local/Global Readings*

Many paradigm context-sensitive expressions may at least optionally receive their interpretation from the context of utterance in embedded contexts. A principal challenge for contextualists about epistemic modals has been to capture the contrasting behaviour of epistemic modals, which seem obligatorily linked to the attitude subject (§1). The obligatory subject-linking can be observed with quantificational subjects, apparently reflecting a kind of binding. There is no reading of (4.10) which characterizes Bert as ascribing to every contestant o the belief that it's compatible with Alice's or Bert's evidence that o is the winner.

(4.10) *Alice:* Bert thinks that every contestant thinks they might be the winner.

The syntax/semantics in (4.7) compositionally derives local and bound readings of embedded epistemic modals; and it does so while maintaining the core contextualist idea of modeling the context-dependence in the same kind of way as the context-dependence of paradigm context-sensitive expressions — via binding with assignment-variables. The account may thus be of interest to theorists who are compelled by the thought that the interpretation of epistemic modals

---

$= [a''(g)/1a]\big([y(g)/1e](g)\big)(1a)(1e)$

$= [a''(g)/1a]\big(\iota m_g : m(1e) = y(g) \wedge m(j\sigma_{\neq 1e}) = g(j\sigma_{\neq 1e})\big)(1a)(1e)$

$= \Big(\iota m'_g : m'(1a) = a''\big(\iota m_g : m(1e) = y(g) \wedge m(j\sigma_{\neq 1e}) = g(j\sigma_{\neq 1e})\big)$

        $\wedge\, m'(j\sigma_{\neq 1a}) = \big(\iota m_g : m(1e) = y(g) \wedge m(j\sigma_{\neq 1e}) = g(j\sigma_{\neq 1e})\big)(j\sigma_{\neq 1a})\Big)(1a)(1e)$

$= a''\big(\iota m_g : m(1e) = y(g) \wedge m(j\sigma_{\neq 1e}) = g(j\sigma_{\neq 1e})\big)(1e)$

$= a''(g[y(g)/1e])(1e)$

$= g[y(g)/1e]^-(1e)$

$= y(g)$

depends, in some sense, on context, but have reservations with foundational innovations introduced by revisionary theories (relativism, expressivism).

There is substantial variation among expressions in tendencies for local vs. global readings (§1; see also Silk 2016a, 2017 and references therein). For expressions compatible with local and global readings, conversational explanations may be given regarding patterns in readings. Such explanations can be understood at the presemantic level of what LFs are determined by token utterances. Not all LFs may be equally likely representations of speaker intentions in uttering a given string. For certain types of epistemic uses of modals, where local readings are arguably conventionalized, a locality principle may filter out LFs in which the modal-background pronoun isn't coindexed with the closest c-commanding assignment-binder.[21] Such a principle would be no more ad hoc than a globality principle for (say) English gendered pronouns or conventionalized referential pronouns, as in (4.11)–(4.12) (see also §1).

(4.11) [Context: Al incorrectly believes that Bert is female. Talking about Bert:]
        #Al thinks she is smart.

(4.12) [Mékw' ye   swíyeqe]$_i$ kw'ákw'ets-et-es   te   stóles-s
        every   DET.PL man   looking-TRANS-3SBJ DET wife-3POSS
        tú-tl'òlem$_{c/*i}$.
        DET-3PL
        'All men$_i$ are looking at their$_{c/*i}$ wives.'
                                (cf. Déchaine and Wiltschko 2002: ex. 10; Halkomelem (Salish))

An elegant picture emerges regarding the landscape of readings — to a first approximation: (i) classical indexicals with conventionalized global readings, lexically required to be bound by **T**; (ii) shifty expressions with conventionalized local readings, lexically required to be bound by the nearest c-commanding assignment-binder; (iii) specialized anaphoric expressions with conventionalized non-global readings, lexically required to be bound by an element other than **T**;[22] and (iv) the majority of context-sensitive expressions, conventionally compatible with both shifted and unshifted readings. The assignment-variable framework affords a unified analysis of the context-sensitivity of the different classes of expressions, along with a principled basis for distinguishing patterns

---

[21] See Silk 2016a, 2017 on characterizing the relevant type of uses ("endorsing uses"), and discussion of the putative conventionalization of local readings.

[22] I ignore discourse anaphora. I consider potential complications due to interrogatives in §9. Conventionalized anaphoric pronouns requiring local antecedents — pronouns with obligatory local+non-global readings — are also possible, as with the Russian possessive *svoj* in (i), or the specialized correlative proform in (1.6).

(i)   Vanja$_i$ znaet čto Voledja$_k$ ljubit svoju$_{k/*i}$ sestru.
        'Vanja$_i$ knows that Volodja$_k$ loves his$_{k/*i}$ sister.'   (Rappaport 1986: ex. 13)

of readings. (We will examine other types of conventionalized constraints on shifted/unshifted readings throughout the following chapters.)

4.4 Pierre and Friends

A natural application of the assignment-variable framework is to classic cases of shifted interpretations of proper names. §1.1 mentioned Stalnaker's (1988) "multiple context" approach to attitude ascriptions as a possible informal precedent for the project in this book. Swanson (2011) suggests extending Stalnaker's approach to the interpretation of the two occurrences of 'London' in (4.13), where the proposition presupposed and not realized by "Puzzling Pierre" (Kripke 1979) isn't necessarily true.

(4.13)   Pierre doesn't realize that London is London.   (Swanson 2011: ex. 34)

Though Stalnaker and Swanson don't offer specific formal implementations, recent work provides various mechanisms, such as variables for "guises" or "concept generators," for capturing shifted interpretations of referential expressions (Uriagereka 1998, Percus and Sauerland 2003, Cumming 2008, Santorio 2010, Ninan 2012, Charlow and Sharvit 2014). Such machinery could be layered into the assignment-variable framework developed thus far. Since the terrain is already well trod, it may be more interesting to explore a novel approach.

To fix ideas, consider a predicativist account on which a name 'N', qua lexical item, denotes the property of being called N (see Geurts 1997, Elbourne 2005, Matushansky 2006, Ghomeshi and Massam 2009, Fara 2015; cf. Hawthorne and Manley 2012).[23] The names in (4.14) appear in frames used for predicates. For ordinary bare singular uses such as (4.15) predicativists posit that the name is the complement of an implicit determiner (cf. (4.15a)). In many languages the determiner may be pronounced (Longobardi 1994, Borer 2005a, Ghomeshi and Massam 2009). The overt determiners in (4.16) are obligatory.[24]

(4.14)   a.   The Alice I know is brilliant.
        b.   Some Alfreds are crazy; some are sane.   (Burge 1973: 429)
        c.   There are at least two Tylers with philosophy degrees from Princeton.
                                    (Fara 2015: ex. 8)

(4.15)   Alfred is crazy.
        a. $[_{DP} \varnothing_D [_{NP} \text{Alfred}]]$ is crazy
        b.   ≈ "the relevant individual called Alfred is crazy"

---

[23] See Cumming 2008 on names as variables; for treatments of names as constants, see Kripke 1980, Salmon 1986, Soames 2002. See Hawthorne and Manley 2012 for critical discussion and a tentative treatment of bare singular uses as akin to specific existentials.

[24] Apt: Burge 1973 / Longobardi 1994.

(4.16) a. *(Der) Hans hat den   Hasen gesehen.
            DET.M Hans has DET.M rabbit seen
            'Hans saw the rabbit.'
                                    (Ghomeshi et al. 2009a: ex. 18; Austrian German)
        b. áts'x-en-ts-as   *(kw-s) Rose.
            see-TRANS-1SG.O-3ERG DET-NOM Rose
            'Rose saw me.'
                                    (Matthewson 1998: 77; St'át'imcets (Lillooet Salish))

It is common among predicativists to treat the implicit element in bare singular uses as a definite article or demonstrative. Since such moves are familiar, let's consider a variant approach in which names in bare singular uses are sister to an implicit *choice-function pronoun* — a pronoun for a function F_{cf} which selects a particular individual from a set of individuals, as reflected in (4.17)–(4.18).[25] (I will use 'cf' in indices to indicate items of type $\langle et, e \rangle$ that are choice functions, e.g. F_{1cf}. I use (e.g.) '$Alfred_u$' for the characteristic function of the set of individuals $o \in E$ such that o is called Alfred in u. Recall $\downarrow$ which "lowers" an item in a domain to an item composed out of associated elements of the model (§2).)

(4.17) $F:[X \to T] \to X$ is a *choice function* iff for all nonempty $S \subseteq X$, $F(^XS) \in S$
        (where ^XS is the characteristic function of S)

(4.18) a. $[_{DP} F_{1cf} g_1 [_{NP} \text{Alfred } w_1 g_1]]$
        b. $[\![\textbf{Alfred}]\!] = \lambda w_s.\lambda x_e.\lambda g_g . x(g)$ is called Alfred in $w(g)$
            $[\![\textbf{F}_{1cf} \textbf{g}_1]\!] = \lambda P_{et}.\lambda g_g . g(1a)(1cf)((^{\downarrow}P)(g))$
            $[\![DP]\!] = \lambda g_g . g(1a)(1cf)\big(\text{the function } f \text{ such that}$
            $\qquad \forall y_e{:} f(y(g))$ iff $y(g)$ is called Alfred in $g(1a)(1s)\big)$
            $\qquad = \lambda g_g . g(1a)(1cf)(Alfred_{g(1a)(1s)})$

---

[25] Appeals to choice functions and choice-function pronouns are prominent in semantics for various types of (specific) indefinite and definite expressions (e.g., Egli and von Heusinger 1995, Dayal 1996, Kratzer 1998b, Cowper and Hall 2009, von Heusinger 2011). See Egli and von Heusinger 1995, Winter 1997 for discussion of choice functions defined for empty sets. I ignore complications from Skolemizing choice-function variables (cf. Kratzer 1998b, von Heusinger 2002) and definiteness. I consider a combined definite+choice-function analysis briefly in n. 62.

The implicit choice-function pronoun $[\mathbf{F}_{1cf}\ \mathbf{g}_1]$ denotes a function $g(1a)(1cf)$ which selects a particular individual $o \in E$ from the set of individuals called Alfred in the given world $(=Alfred_{g(1a)(1s)})$.

Like variabilist accounts and other predicativist accounts, we capture the context-sensitivity of unembedded uses, as in (4.19).

(4.19) [Context: from an advertising campaign in which the character Freddo is standing next to a Freddo cookie]

Freddo met Freddo.

a. $[_S\ T^{\langle 1,a\rangle}\ [[C_d\ t_{1a}]^{\langle 1,s\rangle}\ [[_{DP}\ F_{1cf}\ g_1\ [_{NP}\ \text{Freddo}\ w_1\ g_1]]$
$[_{VP}\ \text{met}\ t_{1s}\ [_{DP}\ F_{2cf}\ g_1\ [_{NP}\ \text{Freddo}\ w_1\ g_1]]]]$

b. $[\![S]\!] \approx \lambda g_g . g^-(1cf)(Freddo_{g^-(1s)})$ met $g^-(2cf)(Freddo_{g^-(1s)})$ in $@(g^-)$

The first use of 'Freddo' is interpreted with respect to a choice-function pronoun $[\mathbf{F}_{1cf}\ \mathbf{g}_1]$ that denotes a choice function $g_c(1cf)$ which selects the Freddo character from the set of individuals called Freddo in the world of the discourse, $g_c(1s) = @(g_c)$ (§§2.2, 4.2). The second use of 'Freddo' is interpreted with respect to a choice-function pronoun $[\mathbf{F}_{2cf}\ \mathbf{g}_1]$ that denotes a choice function $g_c(2cf)$ which selects the Freddo cookie in the ad.

Turning to attitude ascriptions, let's consider first an example with a global reading of a name, as in (4.20), adapted from an example from Jennifer Saul. I can use 'Bob Dylan' to characterize Glenda's belief, even though she wouldn't "put it that way," since what matters for our purposes is Glenda's belief about the individual whom we associate with 'Bob Dylan' (see also Jaszczolt 1997). An analysis is in (4.21) (I leave 'sings beautifully' as an unanalyzed predicate).

(4.20) [Context: We're talking about people's views on Bob Dylan's singing abilities. I know that Glenda, one of his childhood friends, knows him only under the name 'Robert Zimmerman'. Since you know him only under the name 'Bob Dylan', I say:]

Glenda believes that Bob Dylan has a beautiful voice.

(cf. Saul 1998: 366)

(4.21)

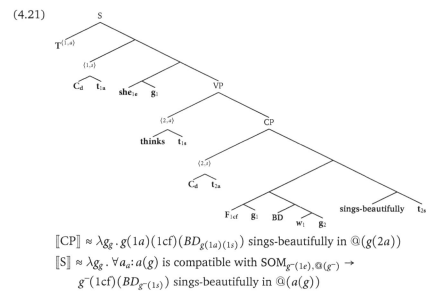

$$[\![CP]\!] \approx \lambda g_g \,.\, g(1a)(1cf)(BD_{g(1a)(1s)}) \text{ sings-beautifully in } @(g(2a))$$

$$[\![S]\!] \approx \lambda g_g \,.\, \forall a_a \colon a(g) \text{ is compatible with } SOM_{g^-(1e),@(g^-)} \to$$
$$g^-(1cf)(BD_{g^-(1s)}) \text{ sings-beautifully in } @(a(g))$$

The choice-function pronoun $[F_{1cf}\,\mathbf{g_1}]$ is bound by the topmost assignment-binder $T^{\langle 1,a\rangle}$, anchoring its interpretation to the discourse assignment g_c. The contextually supplied value $g_c(1cf)$ selects the relevant individual $o \in E$ called Bob Dylan. The attitude ascription is true iff for every possibility h compatible with Glenda's ($=g_c(1e)$'s) state of mind, the selected individual o — the individual with whom we in the discourse context associate the name — has a beautiful voice in $@(h)$. Whether o is called Bob Dylan in the subject's belief-worlds $@(h)$ is irrelevant.

As those with anti-Millian intuitions may be keen to point out, the sentence in (4.20) can also have a reading on which it seems false. Consider the alternative context in (4.22). An analysis for the true reading of (4.22b) is in (4.23).

(4.22)   [Context: Gwen attends an afternoon reunion where she hears her childhood friend going by the name 'Robert Zimmerman' sing a dedication song. Feeling nostalgic she says 'I love Robert; he always sang so beautifully'. Later that evening she attends a concert of a man named 'Bob Dylan'. She can't stand big public events and says 'This is awful; this Bob Dylan guy has a terrible voice'. Since Bob Dylan is excellent at keeping his star status concealed to his childhood friends, Gwen doesn't realize that the man singing at the concert is her childhood friend who also sang at the reunion. We're talking about how factors such as kinship, environment, etc. can affect people's perceptions; you say:]

a. Gwen thinks Robert Zimmerman has a beautiful voice.
b. Gwen thinks Bob Dylan has a terrible voice.

(4.23)

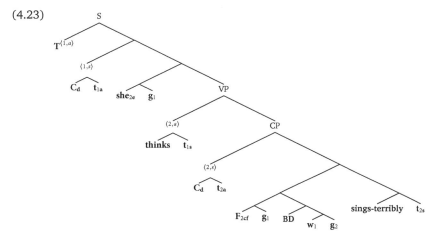

$$[\![S]\!] \approx \lambda g_g . \forall a_a : a(g) \text{ is compatible with } SOM_{g^-(2e),@(g^-)} \rightarrow$$
$$g^-(2\text{cf})(BD_{a(g)(1s)}) \text{ sings-terribly in } @(a(g))$$

Each of Gwen's ($=g_c(2e)$'s) belief-worlds u includes two epistemic counterparts of the actual individual Bob Dylan (=Robert Zimmerman) — a childhood friend named 'Robert Zimmerman' who sings beautifully, and a distinct celebrity named 'Bob Dylan' who sings terribly. In the context in (4.22) the contextually relevant choice function $g_c(2\text{cf})$ selects from $\{o' : o' \text{ is called Bob Dylan in } u\}$ ($=BD_{a(g_c)(1s)}$) the individual o who is the singer-counterpart in u of BD/RZ. The attitude ascription is true insofar as for every such world u compatible with Gwen's beliefs, the selected individual o sings terribly.

The preceding analysis captures how the embedded choice-function pronoun receives its interpretation from the discourse, while the world-pronoun for the name-qua-predicate receives a local reading shifted by the attitude verb. The discourse context determines the basis for selecting the individual $o \in BD_u$ in each of Gwen's belief-worlds u, while each such set BD_u is determined on the basis of Gwen's beliefs. The contextually relevant choice function in the context in (4.22) selects, from any set of Bob Dylans in Gwen's belief-worlds, a particular epistemic counterpart o of BD/RZ, namely the singer-celebrity counterpart. The use of the name is represented as having a *specific de dicto* reading — "specific" in the sense that every o is identical to one another (or a metaphysical counterpart of one another), and "de dicto" in the sense that the selected terrible singer is conceptualized as being called Bob Dylan. Indeed (4.22b) could be used to characterize Gwen's state of mind even if the "Bob Dylan" craze was an elaborate hoax and there is no such individual. Santorio (2013) argues that capturing specific de dicto readings of indefinite DPs requires overhauling the semantics for descriptions; some have even expressed doubt about the possibility of specific de dicto readings (von Fintel and Heim 2011). The interpretation of names in contexts such as (4.22) follows from a basic predicativist semantics with choice functions, implemented in an assignment-variable framework.

Recall the "Puzzling Pierre" example in (4.13), where the uses of 'London' under the attitude verb receive different interpretations. In Kripke's (1979) case, Pierre is a native French speaker who has heard wonderful things about a beautiful distant city named *Londres*. Later, he moves to an unattractive part of London and learns that it is named 'London'; finding it ugly, he says 'London isn't pretty'. Not realizing that the city he currently lives in is the same city as the city he heard about while in France, he continues to accept the French sentence *Londres est jolie*. Hence:

(4.13)   Pierre doesn't realize that London is London.

There are various formalizations that would derive how the use of 'London is London' in (4.24) may fail to characterize Pierre's state of mind. A sample LF and semantic value is as follows. (For the sake of argument I assume an "is-of-identity" reading for 'is'.)

(4.24)   He thinks London is London.

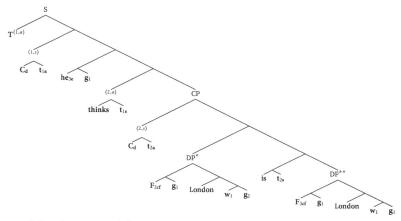

$$[\![S]\!] \approx \lambda g_g \,.\, \forall a_a \colon a(g) \text{ is compatible with } SOM_{g^-(3e),@(g^-)} \rightarrow$$
$$g^-(2cf)(London_{a(g)(1s)}) = g^-(3cf)(London_{g^-(1s)}) \text{ in } @(a(g))$$

Roughly put, this says that the attitude ascription in (4.24) is true, on the relevant reading, iff for every possibility h compatible with Pierre's ($=g_c(3e)$'s) state of mind, the city $o_1 = F'(London_{@(h)})$ selected among the things called London in Pierre's belief-worlds $(=a(g_c)(1s))$ is identical to the city $o_2 = F''(London_{@(g_c)})$ selected from among the things called London in the actual world $(=g_c(1s))$.

Pierre's state of mind is such that each of his belief-worlds includes a city called Londres which is pretty, and a dreary city called London where he lives. The occurrence of 'London' in DP* receives a local reading, picking out the city called London as Pierre conceives it; the occurrence of 'London' in DP** receives a global reading, picking out the actual city of London — though perhaps not so-called in Pierre's belief-worlds. In the second occurrence, the contextually determined value for the choice-function pronoun, $F'' = g_c(3cf)$, selects the present capital city of England from any set which includes it; hence $F''(London_{g_c(1s)}) = o_2 =$ London, an entity that includes areas believed pretty by Pierre. In contrast, the world-pronoun in the first occurrence of 'London' receives a local reading. The contextually determined choice function $F' = g_c(2cf)$ selects the dreary city o_1 where Pierre lives from any set of things called London in his belief-worlds $@(h)$. Hence the belief ascribed isn't necessarily true; indeed (4.24) is correctly derived as false: the selected objects o_1, o_2 are non-identical in (some if not all of) Pierre's belief-worlds. The entirety of o_2 is ugly and named 'London' throughout the worlds $@(h)$; not so for o_1, which includes areas that are pretty and named 'Londres'.

Our assignment-variable-based framework formally implements the Stalnakerian idea that "multiple contexts" can be available for interpretation in a single embedded clause. Devices such as names can be used both to characterize an individual's "psychological semantic representation of a word" (Partee 1979: 11), and also "to pick out individuals in the basic context, and … express propositions that alter the derived context" representing a subject's state of mind (Stalnaker 1988: 158–159). These dual functions come together vividly in Puzzling Pierre cases such as (4.13)/(4.24). It isn't evident how to capture such examples in an operator-based variabilist semantics, where names are analyzed as simple variables (e.g. Cumming 2008), without treating the names as ambiguous. By contrast, the lexical item 'London' in (4.24) has the same semantic value in both occurrences. Alternative shifted and unshifted readings are derived from how individuals are selected (via the choice-function pronoun) and which individuals are candidates for selection (via the name-qua-predicate's world-pronoun).

In these ways, various classic puzzles of names in attitude ascriptions can be assimilated to phenomena with local and global readings of context-sensitive expressions. The spectrum of readings is derived from independently motivated resources from the literature — choice-function pronouns and predicativism — and our general assignment-variable-based syntax and semantics. Further mechanisms specific to names (e.g., substitutional quantification, guises) aren't required.[26]

The account outlined in this section maintains features motivating various types of semantics for names. With predicativists, we give a uniform semantics for names in predicative and bare singular uses. In both environments the lexical item 'N' denotes the property of being called N. Second, like many non-Millian accounts, the account captures the context-sensitivity of uses of names without treating names as systematically ambiguous. The uses of the string 'Freddo' in (4.19) are uses of the same lexical item. The different interpretations are derived from the contextually determined values for the choice-function pronouns. Third, the semantics is compatible with certain uses of names being "rigid designators," roughly in the sense of being used to designate the same individual across worlds. In a bare singular use, context may determine a value for the choice-function pronoun that is defined only for sets including a particular individual o, and that selects o from every such set.

(4.25) A choice-function $F \colon [E \to T] \to E$ is *rigid* iff for some $o \in E$ and every nonempty $S \subseteq E \colon F(S) = o$ if $o \in S$, else undefined.

However, rigidity isn't encoded in the conventional meaning of names themselves. This is for the better in light of descriptive uses such as (4.26) (see also Cumming 2008).

(4.26) [Context: Bert has been receiving daily unsigned letters ostensibly from a secret admirer. Bert doesn't know whom they're from, and even wonders whether they're all from the same individual. We, who deliver the letters, deliver them without the envelopes, which we see are in each case addressed from "Ernie." We see Bert walking excitedly to the mailbox; you say:]

Bert thinks Ernie sent him another letter.

The use of 'Ernie' in (4.26) is appropriate even if (it's presupposed that) the individual $o \in E$ who sends Bert a letter varies across Bert's belief-worlds.

Many variabilist and predicativist accounts are motivated by non-purely-referential uses of names. Any overall account must also address apparent

---

[26] Contrast: "it is impossible to make substantial claims about the semantics of names without making quite fundamental assumptions about the status and aims of semantic theory" (Geurts 1997: 343).

differences in shiftability between names and context-sensitive expressions such as pronouns, definite descriptions, etc., as in (4.27)–(4.28).

(4.27)   a.   Every professor invited *Alice* to class.

  $\neq$ "every professor x invited the relevant individual x knows called Alice to x's class"

   b.   Every professor made *the final exam* as hard as possible.

  $\approx$ "every professor x made the final exam for x's class as hard as possible"

   c.   The contestant answered every question before *the question* was finished.

  $\approx$ "the contestant answered every question x before x was finished"

   d.   Every guitarist thinks *they* play the fastest.

  $\approx$ "every guitarist x thinks x plays the fastest"

(4.28)   a.   Only Alfred did *Alfred's* homework.

  $\neq$ "only Alfred $= o$ is such that $[\lambda x.x$ did x's homework$](o) = 1$"

   b.   Only you did *your* homework.

  $\approx$ "only you $= o'$ are such that $[\lambda x.x$ did x's homework$](o') = 1$"

This isn't the place to provide a binding theory for names. Suffice it to say that binding phenomena with names are less than straightforward. Copy reflexive languages readily use names with bound-variable readings, as in (4.29)–(4.30) (see also Lasnik 1989, Mortensen 2003, Boeckx et al. 2007).

(4.29)   John$_i$ koonnuat khong John$_i$ lae Peter$_k$ ko muankan.
    John shave   of   John and Peter the same
    'John$_i$ shaved himself$_i$, and Peter$_k$ did too (~~shave himself$_k$~~).'

  (Lee 2003; Thai)

(4.30)   R-ralloh Gye'eihlly$_i$ r-yu'làaa'z-ënn Gye'eihlly$_i$ chiru' zë'cy cahgza'
    think   Mike   like.1PL   Mike   also likewise
    Li'eb$_k$.
    Felipe
    'Mike$_i$ thinks we like him$_i$, and so does Felipe$_k$ (~~think we like him$_k$~~).'

  (Lee 2003; Zapotec)

Even in English, bound-variable readings are perhaps possible in certain contexts. After a surge of presidential apery one might say (4.31).

(4.31) ?Every Donald thinks Donald is the best.

  $\approx$ "every person x called Donald thinks x is the best"

Or suppose that in response to a wave of familial scorn, several Donalds change their ways and begin telling others they are called Ronald. Characterizing their families' states of mind, one might say (4.32), and later (4.33).

(4.32) ?Every family with a Donald thinks Donald should grow up.

(4.33) ?Every partner of a Donald thinks Donald is called Ronald.

> ≈ "every x such that x is the partner of some y called Donald thinks y is called Ronald"

It isn't immediately evident how such examples might be captured in existing variabilist or predicativist accounts.[27] The implementation with choice functions in this section would provide a natural account, as reflected schematically in (4.34) for (4.31). The bound shifted reading of the embedded 'Donald' is represented analogously to the bound shifted reading of the embedded epistemic 'might' in (4.7). (Assume that in the intended interpretation the index 2cf represents, roughly, a "bestness" choice function.)

(4.34)   ... [[$_{DP}$ every Donald-w_1-g_1] [[thinks t_{1s}]$^{\langle 2,a \rangle}$ ...

[$_{DP}$ F_{2cf}-g_2 Donald-w_1-$g_{1/2}$] ...

I leave refinements in light of crosslinguistic binding phenomena with names for future work. (Hereafter I put the complications in this section with names aside; unless otherwise noted I will treat names as constants.)

4.5   Recap: Next Steps

Let's take stock. Various linguistic phenomena have led theorists to posit linguistic reference to different parameters of interpretation in the syntax. This book investigates the prospects for a linguistic theory which posits syntactic variables for assignment functions — variables for the sort of item responsible for interpreting context-sensitive language generally. Contextually determined assignments are a substantial, already needed theoretical posit. Giving them syntactic representation affords diverse theoretical advantages. The proposed assignment-variable-based account standardizes quantification across domains, and it systematizes a range of linguistic shifting phenomena in which the relevant context for interpreting certain expressions seems to shift within a sentence, such as with quantifiers, intensionality, epistemic vocabulary, and local/global read-

---

[27] If the reader finds (4.32)–(4.33) to bear an uncanny resemblance to donkey sentences: indeed. We will revisit issues with pronoun binding and donkey anaphora throughout the following chapters.

ings of context-sensitive expressions. The syntax and semantics affords a unified analysis of the context-sensitivity of pronouns, epistemic modals, etc., in the spirit of contextualist theories. Yet it improves in compositionally deriving certain recalcitrant shifting phenomena, as desired by revisionary theories. Compositional semantic values are treated systematically in terms of sets of assignments, conceived as representations of possibilities. Binding with individuals, worlds, assignments is derived uniformly from a generalized binder-index feature, which attaches directly to expressions moving for type reasons. Quantification-specific composition rules and added parameters of interpretation aren't required.

On the assignment-variable-based account developed here, world-binding arises from the complementizer, which moves from the world-argument position of the clause's main predicate; assignment-binding arises from (e.g.) modal elements, which move from the assignment-argument position in C^0. A distinction between trace-binding and pronoun-binding, desirable for independent reasons (Büring 2004, 2005), falls out. An improved formalization of assignment modification helps capture binding relations in examples with repeated modifications. Additional sources of constraints on readings — e.g., in the syntax, lexical and compositional semantics, metasemantics — call for more thorough investigation. (We will return to these issues throughout the following chapters.)

§§2–4 applied the assignment-variable framework to certain phenomena with quantifiers and attitude ascriptions. The remainder of the book examines how the framework and treatments of the syntax–semantics interface may be extended to other types of expressions. I focus primarily on local/global readings in various types of noun phrases (§§5–7), conditionals (§8), and questions (§9). §5 uses the assignment-variable framework to develop an improved head-raising analysis of restrictive relative clauses. Nominal quantifiers are treated as introducing quantification over assignments, binding relative words and pronouns such as donkey pronouns. §6 generalizes the assignment-quantificational syntax/semantics from §5 to non-relativized quantifier phrases, and applies it to further phenomena with specificity, restrictive modification, and pronoun binding. §7 integrates the account in a more detailed general analysis of noun phrases. An alternative matching analysis of relative clauses is provided (§7.4), which improves on the §5-account. A semantics with events is briefly explored in a parallel layered v analysis of verb phrases (§7.5). §§8–9 explore how the assignment-variable-based treatments of relativization and pronominal anaphora in noun phrases may be extended to shifting phenomena in conditionals and questions. §8 develops an analysis of 'if'-clauses and individual and conditional correlatives as plural definite descriptions of assignments. §9 develops an approach to questions as sets of possible answers, with answers construed as sets of assignments. The account affords a unified choice-function analysis of relative words, *wh* words, and certain indefinites and anaphoric proforms, and a fully compositional semantics for relativization in nominal, verbal, and clausal domains.

Part II

5

Relative Clauses (I)

This chapter begins to apply the assignment-variable framework to certain types of relative clauses and linguistic anaphora. I focus here on headed restrictive relative clauses such as in (5.1)–(5.2), in which a nominal is modified via a (possibly implicit) relative word ('which', 'who') or complementizer ('that'). (I will use 'relative clause' informally for expressions such as the bracketed material, 'relative phrase' for the combination of the relative word and nominal ('which puppy'), and 'nominal head' for the nominal in the relative phrase ('puppy'). This terminology doesn't presuppose particular analyses of the syntax or semantics.)

(5.1) a. Every [puppy that __ jumped] is cute.
       b. Every [puppy which Alice likes __] is cute.

(5.2) Every [baby who Alice gave a toy to __] liked it.

§5.1 motivates an account of nominal quantifiers in headed relative clauses as introducing quantification over assignments. Individual- and assignment-binders are derived from independently motivated D-complement and raising analyses of relative clauses. The semantics is fully compositional. §5.2 applies the treatment of relative clauses from §5.1 to several types of donkey anaphora. The syntax/semantics of nominal quantifiers and donkey pronouns avoids the proportion problem, and allows for alternative universal and existential readings of donkey pronouns. §§6–7 explore ways of extending the approach to the syntax/semantics from this chapter to other types of noun phrases, restrictive modification, and pronoun binding; a revised analysis of headed relative clauses is provided. §§8–9 extend the approach to relativization in this chapter to 'if'-clauses, correlatives, and interrogatives.

5.1 Head Raising: Syntax and Semantics

5.1.1 Syntax (Preliminary)

Informally, the restrictive relative in (5.1a) functions to restrict the domain of 'every' to the set of puppies o such that o jumped. How to derive this intuitive interpretation in the syntax and compositional semantics is controversial.

A common idea, following Heim and Kratzer (1998), is that the relative word triggers Predicate Abstraction, and the nominal head and relative clause combine by Predicate Modification, roughly as in (5.3).

(5.3)   a. LF $\approx$ [$_{NP}$ puppy [$_{CP_{rel}}$ which$_i$ [t$_i$ jumped]]]
         b. $[\![CP_{rel}]\!] \approx \{o : o$ jumped$\}$
             $[\![NP]\!] \approx \{o : o$ is a puppy$\} \cap \{o : o$ jumped$\}$
             $\approx \{o : o$ is a puppy $\wedge o$ jumped$\}$

It is worth exploring whether we can develop a syntax/semantics without requiring additional composition rules or a syncategorematic treatment of relativization and quantification.

A prominent approach in syntax is to treat the nominal head as having a representation inside the relative clause. One compelling source of evidence comes from languages with circumnominal relatives — relative constructions in which the relative phrase is pronounced inside the relative clause (de Vries 2002, Hiraiwa 2017). To fix ideas, in this chapter I follow head-raising analyses in treating the head NP as base-generated inside the relative CP; and I assume that the relative CP is the complement of the matrix determiner, reflected schematically in (5.4) (cf. Åfarli 1994, Kayne 1994, Bianchi 1999, Bhatt 2002, de Vries 2002, Sportiche 2017).[28]

(5.4)   "Head-raising" + D-complement
         [$_{DP}$ D [$_{CP_{rel}}$ ... [REL NP] ...]]

The following sections examine how our assignment-variable framework may provide a basis for an improved head-raising analysis of relative clauses. (An alternative "matching" analysis (Lees 1960, Sauerland 1998, 2003) is developed in §7.4 in the context of a more general syntax/semantics for noun phrases.)

5.1.2 Trace Conversion?

Treating the head NP as interpreted inside the relative clause raises a challenge for the compositional semantics. This challenge is at times underappreciated in syntactic accounts.[29] Here is Bianchi (typos corrected; emphasis added):

---

[28] Given our purposes we can leave open how the pronounced form is derived from the narrow syntax in different languages. I ignore syntactic differences between postnominal relatives in languages such as English and left-headed circumnominal relatives; and I ignore differences between D+CP analyses in which the head NP is in Spec,C, and D+XP analyses in which the NP raises further to a nominal projection which takes the relative CP as its complement (see Bhatt 2002, de Vries 2002, Hiraiwa 2005, 2017, Donati and Cecchetto 2015).

[29] Contrast McCloskey (2002: 219) in concluding his extensive discussion of the syntax of relativization in Irish: "The semantic system of natural language is clearly one that is rich enough and powerful enough to allow for the construction of arbitrarily complex properties... But the locality

[I]n LF the relative DP is reconstructed in the trace position ... [In (5.5b)] the *relative DP within IP has an open position and is bound by a higher operator*, namely the external D^0... [T]he whole structure is c-commanded by the higher determiner, and hence constitutes its restrictive term rather than its nuclear scope [(5.5c)].

[(5.5)] a. $[_{DP}$ *the* $[_{CP}$ $[_{DP}$ *boy* $[_{DP}$ *who* $t_{NP}]]$ $[_{IP}$ *I met* $[_t$ *who boy*]]]]
  b. $[_{DP}$ the $[_{CP}$ $[_{IP}$ *I met* $[_{DP}$ *who boy*]]]]$
  c. the x such that (x is a boy) & (I met x)

(Bianchi 1999: 81)

Deriving the intuitive interpretation in (5.5c) from the LF in (5.5b) is nontrivial. The verb 'met' requires an object argument of type *e*. So, simply reconstructing type $\langle e, t \rangle$ 'boy' into the "gap" (trace) position, or reconstructing the relative phrase (as in (5.5b)) and treating 'who' as vacuous would yield a type mismatch. An alternative semantics for the relative word might yield a type *e* argument (or a type $\langle et, t \rangle$ generalized quantifier to QR and leave a type *e* trace). However, such a semantics would seem to render the relative clause as type *t*. Assuming 'the' requires an argument of type $\langle e, t \rangle$, a type mismatch is again in the offing. The compositional challenge is to capture both that the IP-internal predicate can combine with whatever fills the gap position (yielding, say, a type *t* denotation for the relative IP), and that the relative clause CP_{rel} is of a type suitable to combine with the matrix determiner (say, type $\langle e, t \rangle$).

The principal attempt to address this compositional semantic challenge for head-raising analyses comes from Bhatt 2002, which resorts to noncompositional operations for interpreting traces and effects of reconstruction (see also Elbourne 2005, Moulton 2015). On Bhatt's analysis, the relative phrase 'REL NP' reconstructs in the gap position in IP_{rel}; and a mechanism of Trace Conversion (Fox 2000, 2002) replaces the relative phrase with a definite description, roughly "the NP identical to x_i," where the variable x_i is bound by a binder-index posited in the position of the highest copy of the relative phrase. The derivation proceeds from a full chain such as (5.6a) to (5.6b), where deleting the non-lowest copies leaves a binder index in the position of the highest copy; and from (5.6b) to (5.6c) by Trace Conversion (Quantifier Replacement + Variable Insertion).

---

requirements that are an integral part of the syntactic system mesh poorly with this power, and there is, as a consequence, a certain awkwardness in the fit between syntactic and semantic representations. The ungainly morphosyntax of the complementizer system (which Irish gives us an uncommonly clear glimpse of) can, perhaps, be viewed as a response to this mismatch."

(5.6)   every puppy which Alice thinks that Bert likes

    a. every [[which puppy] Alice thinks [[which puppy] that Bert likes [which puppy]]]

    b. every λx [Alice thinks [that Bert likes [which puppy]]]

    c. every λx [Alice thinks [that Bert likes [the puppy $=x$]]]

(cf. Bhatt 2002: exs. 35–38)

These operations are not compositional. In order to generate the λ-binder Bhatt "assume[s] that when a copy is deleted, the λ abstraction created as part of the movement is retained" (2002: 64). Consistently applied, such an assumption would require retaining the λ-binder above the deleted intermediate copy as well, as in (5.7). (I use the object-language binders 'λ_i' to distinguish the syntactic basis for the assumed semantic λ-abstraction (§1.2). Strikethrough here indicates syntactic deletion. 'Puppy' and '$=o_1$' combine by Predicate Modification; $[\lambda_i \, \alpha]$ is interpreted by Predicate Abstraction (Heim and Kratzer 1998).)

(5.7)   a. every [~~[which puppy]~~$_T$ λ_1 Alice thinks [~~[which puppy]~~$_T$ λ_1 that Bert likes [which puppy]$_1$]]

    b. every [λ_1 Alice thinks [λ_1 that Bert likes [which puppy]$_1$]]

    c. every [λ_1 Alice thinks [λ_1 that Bert likes [the [[puppy] [$=o_1$]]]]]

The LF in (5.7c) is uninterpretable. The complement of 'thinks' in (5.7c) denotes $[\lambda x_e \, . \, \text{Bert likes the puppy identical to } x]$. This isn't what Lewis (1979) had in mind in treating properties as the objects of belief. Even if the type-mismatch were resolved, the highest binder index doesn't bind the variable in the position of the lowest copy. The predicted denotation of the relative clause is a constant function.

    In response one might stipulate different effects at LF of deleting copies in different positions. Such a principle would have to be construction-specific; it isn't in general the case that retaining the binder-index of the highest copy in a chain yields an interpretable structure. As Bhatt and Pancheva (2006) argue, drawing on Iatridou 1991, some sentence-initial 'if'-clauses must reconstruct — e.g., in (5.8a) under the attitude verb, and in (5.8b) under the quantifier. The anomalousness of the examples in (5.9) are thus explained as Condition C violations. Yet it would be unattractive to posit that 'if' conditionals are ambiguous based on whether the 'if'-clause is reconstructed and interpreted in a trace position (cf. (5.10)).

(5.8)   a. [If it rains]$_i$, Bert thinks (t_i) the party should be canceled.

    b. [If his$_k$ teacher is out sick]$_i$, every boy$_k$ will be happy (t_i).

(5.9)   a. *[If Bert$_k$ is sick]$_i$ he$_k$ thinks [if Bert$_k$ is sick]$_i$ the party should be canceled

b. *[If Alice$_j$ gives his$_k$ teacher food poisoning]$_i$ every boy$_k$ will be grateful to <u>her</u>$_j$ [if <u>Alice</u>$_j$ gives his$_k$ teacher food poisoning]$_i$

(5.10) a. Chloe said that [if his$_k$ teacher is out sick]$_i$, every boy$_k$ will be happy (t_i).

b. Chloe said that every boy$_k$ will be happy if his$_k$ teacher is out sick.

A seemingly simple Copy operation in the syntax of movement yields "copy and delete along with any binder indices, unless at the base, in which case reinterpret via Trace Conversion, and unless a relative phrase with no higher copies, in which case delete but retain the binder index" at the syntax–semantics interface.

One way of alleviating some of these concerns would be to treat the relative phrase as partially reconstructing (cf. Chomsky 1995, Moulton 2015). Compare the derivation in (5.12) where the intermediate copy is erased at LF, the relative word is interpreted in the highest copy position, and the nominal head is interpreted in the gap position; the modified version of Trace Conversion in (5.11) yields the interpretable LF in (5.12e).

(5.11) Trace Conversion (modified)

a. Binder Insertion: DP$_i$ [... DP$_i$ ...] $\rightsquigarrow$ DP λ_1 [... DP$_i$ ...]

b. Determiner Insertion/Replacement: [$_{DP}$ (D) NP] $\rightsquigarrow$ [$_{DP_i}$ THE NP]

c. Variable Insertion: [$_{DP_i}$ THE NP] $\rightsquigarrow$ [$_{DP}$ THE [NP =o$_i$]]

(5.12) a. every [[which puppy]$_1$ Alice thinks [[which puppy]$_1$ that Bert likes [which puppy]$_1$]]

b. every [[which ~~puppy~~] λ_1 Alice thinks [[~~which puppy~~] λ_T that Bert likes [~~which~~ puppy]$_1$]]

c. every [which λ_1 Alice thinks [that Bert likes [puppy]$_1$]]

d. every [which λ_1 Alice thinks [that Bert likes [THE puppy]$_1$]]

e. every [which λ_1 Alice thinks [that Bert likes [THE [puppy =o$_1$]]]]

Supposing the relative word denotes the identity function $\lambda P_{et}.P$, the relative clause denotes (roughly) $[\lambda x.$ Alice thinks Bert likes the puppy identical to $x]$.

The LF in (5.12e) yields an intuitively correct denotation for the relative clause. Consider the needed array of assumptions: (i) The highest copy of 'puppy' and the intermediate copy of the relative phrase are erased at LF, whereas the deleted lowest copy of 'which' is replaced at LF with an interpreted definite determiner. (ii) A variable 'o$_1$' coindexed with the relative phrase is inserted with an identity predicate inside the position of the lowest copy — i.e., inside the DP originally represented with the relative phrase, the movement of which created a coindexed λ-binder. (iii) The identity predicate '=o$_1$' (type $\langle e, t \rangle$) combines with 'puppy' (type $\langle e, t \rangle$) via Predicate Modification. (iv) The semantic λ-abstraction is derived syncategorematically via a Predicate Abstraction rule; the node $[\lambda_1]$ isn't given a denotation. (v) There is no constituent for the relative phrase at LF; 'which puppy' doesn't receive a semantic value.

The operations in (5.6) and (5.12) formalize what ought to be explained.[30] For purposes of comparison, the remainder of this section examines one way in which our assignment-variable-based framework may help yield an improved compositional semantics for head-raising analyses. §5.2 begins to apply the account to cases of pronominal anaphora (more on which in the following chapters). As we will see, there are reasons to think that the account of relativization cannot be right for the general case. However, the following discussion will be instructive in illustrating resources for extending the system from §§3–4.

5.1.3 Assignment Quantification and Choice-Function Pronouns

Research into parallels between nominals and clauses has a rich history in diverse areas of syntax and semantics. As noted in §3.2, positing DP-internal

---

[30] The previous discussion followed Bhatt 2002 (following Fox 2000, 2002) in treating Trace Conversion as a syntactic rule. The points carry over to semantic implementations of Trace Conversion. For instance, one might treat the narrow syntax as delivering (i-a), which is converted to the LF (i-b) by copy deletion and semantically interpreted via the rule in (ii) (cf. Fox 2003: ex. 52). The interpretation of the relative clause in (i-b) may be derived roughly as in (iii) (again assuming scattered copy deletion and treating the relative word as denoting the identity function).

(i)   a.   every $[_{\mathrm{CP_{rel}}}$ $[_{\mathrm{DP_1}}$ which ~~puppy~~] Alice thinks $[_{\overline{\mathrm{DP_1}~\mathrm{which}~\mathrm{puppy}}}$ Bert likes $[_{\mathrm{DP_1}}$ ~~which~~ puppy]]]

        b.   every $[_{\mathrm{CP_{rel}}}$ $[_{\mathrm{DP_1}}$ which] Alice thinks [Bert likes $[_{\mathrm{DP_1}}$ puppy]]]

(ii)   *Trace Conversion (semantic)*
        Let α be a structure of the form: DP_i $[_\beta \ldots \mathrm{DP}_i \ldots]$. $[\![\alpha]\!] = [\![\mathrm{DP}]\!]\,(\lambda x. [\![\beta'_{x/i}]\!])$, where

        a. $\beta'_{x/i}$ is the structure derived from replacing the (possibly empty) head of every i-indexed constituent in β with **the**$_x$, where

        b. $[\![\mathbf{the}_x]\!] = \lambda P_{et}. [\![\mathbf{the}]\!]\,(\lambda y. y = x \wedge P(y))$

(iii) $[\![\mathrm{CP_{rel}}]\!] = (\lambda Q_{et}.Q)(\lambda x. [\![[\ldots \text{Bert likes } [_{\mathrm{DP}} \text{ puppy}]_1]'_{x/1}]\!])$

        $= \lambda x. [\![\ldots \text{Bert likes } [\text{the}_x \text{ puppy}]]\!]$

        $= \lambda x. \ldots \text{Bert likes } [\![\mathbf{the}]\!]\,(\lambda y. y = x \wedge y \text{ is a puppy })$

        $\approx \lambda x. \text{Alice thinks Bert likes the unique puppy identical to } x$

The formalization of Trace Conversion in (ii) encodes the series of syntactic operations considered in the main text in a compositional semantic rule. (See also the accounts in Safir 1999, which analyzes certain lower copies like pronouns, and Sportiche 2006, which analyzes the lower copies as demonstratives. Given their purposes, Safir and Sportiche don't offer compositional semantic derivations.)

operator movement has independent precedents in syntactic work on quantifica-tional/definite noun phrases. So, we can try saying, just as modal elements raise for type reasons from inside the complement clause (§3), the matrix determiners in headed relative clauses raise for type reasons from inside the relative clause. An assignment-variable-based syntax/semantics for relativization along these lines may contribute to the long tradition of linguistic work on linguistic parallels between nominal and verbal categories and individual and modal domains.[31]

There are various ways of formally implementing such an approach. To help motivate a particular response I take a brief detour to examine indefinites. It is well known that the interpretation of indefinites and expressions linguistically dependent on them can shift, not only in "shifty" contexts such as conditionals and attitude ascriptions, but under ordinary quantifiers. For instance, certain indefinites can exhibit apparent "intermediate" readings — readings intermediate between nonspecific readings ((5.13)) and specific readings about a particular individual ((5.14)), in which the indefinite is specific relative to (e.g.) an attitude state or quantificational subject, as in (5.15)–(5.16) (Farkas 1981, Kratzer 1998b, von Heusinger 2011). The intermediate reading of (5.16) says that for every baby o there is a specific toy o' of o's such that o petted every dog that licked o' (for Annie it was the clown, for Timmy the jack-in-the-box, etc.).

(5.13) Alice thinks a friend of mine died in the fire.

- *Nonspecific reading* ≈ "Alice thinks I had some friend or other who died in the fire"

(5.14) If a friend of mine from Texas had died in the fire, I would have inherited a fortune. (Fodor and Sag 1982: ex. 60)

- *Specific reading* ≈ "there is some particular friend of mine (say, Tex) such that I would have inherited a fortune if he had died in the fire"

(5.15) Bert might think some stalker is out to get him.

- *Intermediate reading* ≈ "it's possible that there is some particular stalker o such that Bert thinks o is out to get him" (*might* > *indef* > *think*)

[31] For discussion and further examples of DP-internal movement, see Tellier 1991, Longobardi 1994, Campbell 1996, Alexiadou and Wilder 1998, Matthewson 1998, Bhattacharya 1999a,b, Lecarme 1999b, Bernstein 2001, Ihsane and Puskás 2001, Giusti 2002, Luján 2004, Hiraiwa 2005, Laenzlinger 2005, Larson 2014, Ilkhanipour 2016. For general discussion on syntactic and semantic parallels across domains, see also Partee 1984, Fukui and Speas 1986, Abney 1987, Szabolcsi 1994, Guéron and Hoekstra 1995, Bittner and Hale 1996, Lecarme 1996, 2008, Siloni 1997, Stone 1997, Kratzer 1998a, Rijkhoff 2002, 2008, Bhat 2004, Svenonius 2004, Koopman 2005, Alexiadou et al. 2007, Aikhenvald 2008, Megerdoomian 2008, Wiltschko 2014. We will return to parallels between nominal and verbal extended projections in §7.

(5.16)   Every baby petted every dog that licked a/some toy of hers.

(every baby > indef > every dog)

In donkey sentences the interpretation of the pronoun varies as a function of the indefinite and a supposition or quantificational subject.

(5.17)   a.   If a baby gets a toy, they like it.
        b.   Most babies who got a toy for their birthday liked it.

(5.17b) isn't true simply if most baby–toy pairs $\langle x, y \rangle$ are such that x liked y, or if most toy-owning babies liked someone else's toy. The truth of (5.17b) requires that most babies x liked some birthday present toy of x's. The interpretation of the donkey pronoun varies with the subject and value for the indefinite in the quantifier's restriction.

A hypothesis is that the interpretations of pronouns may be shifted by modal as well as nominal quantifiers. I suggest that we treat the matrix determiners in headed relative clauses as quantifying over assignments, and as raising for type reasons from inside the relative clause. Choice points for developing this idea include the relation between relative words and interrogative *wh* words, and binding relations among the relative phrase, relative complementizer, and gap position. For purposes of this section I assume, following (e.g.) Sternefeld (2001) and Gračanin-Yuksek (2008), that the relative phrase originates in Spec,C_{rel}. So, just as the declarative complementizer raises for type reasons from the clause's verbal head, the relative complementizer in an individual relative clause raises for type reasons from the nominal gap position. And just as a modal quantifier raises from an internal argument of the declarative complementizer, the matrix determiner raises from an internal argument of the relative complementizer. A schematic LF is in (5.18) (I use 'wh' for relative words).[32]

---

[32] Free relatives in argument positions might be treated analogously (though see Caponigro 2003, Gračanin-Yuksek 2008). Adapting Comp accounts of free relatives, the relative phrase in (i) is in a specifier position, and what raises from C_{rel}^0 is a definite-like element, which picks out the maximal (possibly plural) individual in the relevant domain that satisfies the property denoted by the relative clause (cf. Jacobson 1995, Rullmann 1995, Dayal 1996, Grosu and Landman 1998, Caponigro 2003, 2012).

(i)   *Free relative as DP:* $D_\emptyset$ CP_{rel} (schematic)

$\iota_o^{\langle i,a \rangle}$ [$_{CP_{rel}}$ wh-g$_i$ P$_{et}$-g [[C_{rel} t$_{ia}$]$^{\langle j,e \rangle}$ ... t$_{je}$ ...]]

An interesting precedent for the analyses in (5.18)/(i) is Rullmann 1995: 149–150; in Rullmann's (ii), the relative complementizer also binds a variable occupying the gap position and the relative word is in Spec,C. Rullmann stipulates that the empty complementizer is parsed as a lambda abstractor and coindexed with the variable in the gap position. Rullmann treats the relative word as a maximality operator; the account isn't applied to restrictive (non-maximalizing) relatives.

(ii)   [$_{CP}$ what [$_{\overline{C}}$ e_i [$_{IP}$ John ordered t_i]]]   (Rullmann 1995: 150)

Compare also Caponigro 2003, which treats DP-like free relatives as CPs with the covert maximalizing operator in an adjoined position. The approach in (i) could be adapted accordingly. Caponigro treats

(5.18) *Headed restrictive relative DP: D CP$_{rel}$* (schematic)

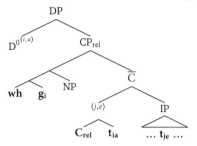

It is crosslinguistically common for relative forms to be synchronically or diachronically related to indefinites. In some languages the relativizing element may be a specific indefinite determiner, as in (5.19) (see also Williamson 1987, Hiraiwa 2005, Hiraiwa et al. 2017).

(5.19) a. [saan-**so** n ni puhl] la
stranger-SPEC.INDEF I C greeted D
'the stranger who I greeted'
 b. m puhi saan-so.
I greeted stranger-SPEC.INDEF
'I greeted a certain stranger.'

(cf. Peterson 1974: 77; Dagbani (Niger-Congo))

A prominent approach is to treat specific indefinites as introducing a variable for a choice function (see von Heusinger 2011). Drawing on data such as (5.19) I suggest that we treat relative words as *choice-function pronouns*. A choice function F_{cf} of individuals, recall (§4.4), selects an individual $o \in E$ from a nonempty set of individuals. Informally put, a relativized DP such as 'every puppy which Alice likes' can be treated as quantifying over the set of individuals which could be chosen from among the puppies and which verify a correct answer to the question what Alice likes. I offer the following lexical entry for the relative complementizer C_{rel}, and preliminary assignment-quantificational entry for (e.g.) 'every'.[33]

---

relative determiners in free relatives as raising from the gap position to Spec,C via *wh*-movement, leaving a λ-binder in C; the $[_{\overline{C}} \lambda_i \text{ IP}]$ node is interpreted via a noncompositional abstraction rule. I am not aware of precedents for such an implementation of QR/*wh*-movement. Caponigro is careful to restrict his analysis to free relatives. It isn't evident how the analysis might apply to headed relatives or *wh* interrogatives. An analogous treatment of headed relatives would need to assume that in headed relatives with an overt complementizer ('baby that Bert likes'), the complementizer is deleted prior to *wh*-movement. Such an assumption would raise issues for interrogatives, which require the presence of the interrogative complementizer throughout the derivation (e.g., to trigger *wh*-movement and satisfy selection requirements of question-embedding expressions). I revisit comparisons between relative words and interrogative *wh* words in §9.

[33] Dayal (1996: 191–193) also offers a substantive semantic value for the relative complementizer. The relative complementizer is treated as type $\langle et, \langle et, \langle et, t \rangle \rangle \rangle$; the relative clause CP

(5.20) $[\![\mathbf{C_{rel}}]\!] = \lambda a_a.\lambda P_{et}.\lambda y_e.\lambda x_e.\lambda g_g.x(g) = y(g) \wedge P(x)(g)$

(5.21) $[\![\mathbf{every}]\!] = \lambda P^+_{\langle a,et\rangle}.\lambda Q^+_{\langle a,et\rangle}.\lambda g_g.\forall x_e \forall a_a : P^+(a)(x)(g) \rightarrow Q^+(a)(x)(g)$

A relative clause CP_{rel} denotes a singleton set of individuals — the singleton of individuals $x(g) \in E$ which have property $^\downarrow P$ and are identical to a selected individual $y(g)$. The property is supplied by the complement of $\mathbf{C_{rel}}$; the individual is supplied by the relative phrase. The assignment-quantification introduced by the matrix quantifier shifts what individual is selected and determines the domain.

The derived semantic value of a simple sentence with a free pronoun and headed relative is in (5.22). (I continue to use 'cf' in indices to indicate items of type $\langle et, e\rangle$ that are choice functions; and I use (e.g.) '$puppy_u$' for the characteristic function of the set of individuals $o \in E$ such that o is a puppy in u. I continue to assume that in the intended interpretation $h(1s)$ is the world of the possibility represented by h, i.e. $h(1s) = @(h)$.)[34]

'wh-NP C IP' is a type-$\langle et, t\rangle$ plural definite description, denoting the set of properties of the unique maximal individual that is NP and has the property resulting from abstracting over the gap position in IP. Though such a semantics may be suitable for certain free relatives in argument positions, it won't apply to relatives combining with a determiner quantifier. Dayal is forced to treat relative expressions as ambiguous. Treating relative clauses themselves as maximizing may also be problematized by relatives that are incompatible with definite interpretations. Regarding examples such as (i) Williamson (1987: 182) remarks, "the speaker has no particular apple … in mind (and, indeed, these objects may not even exist)."

(i)   [[Thaspą wą-ži tąyą yužaža pi] cha]   wachį.
       apple   a-IRR well wash   PL INDIC I-want
       'I want an apple that is well washed.'   (Williamson 1987: 182; Lakota (Siouan))

The entry in (5.20) generalizes to headed and free relative clauses. In both cases the relative CP denotes a set of individuals. Definiteness effects associated with free relatives may be captured, not via a distinctive determiner-like relative complementizer, but via an implicit maximalizing operator, analogous to the matrix determiner in restrictive relatives (n. 32).

[34] In the general definition of the binder-index: with **every**, $\tau = a, \sigma = \langle\langle a, et\rangle, t\rangle, \sigma_1 = e$; with DP: D CP_{rel}, $\tau = a, \sigma = t, \sigma_1 = e$. I assume that the relative word must have the same assignment-variable as the local relative complementizer, e.g. due to agreement (Chung 1998, Kratzer 2009).

(5.22) Every puppy which she likes jumped.

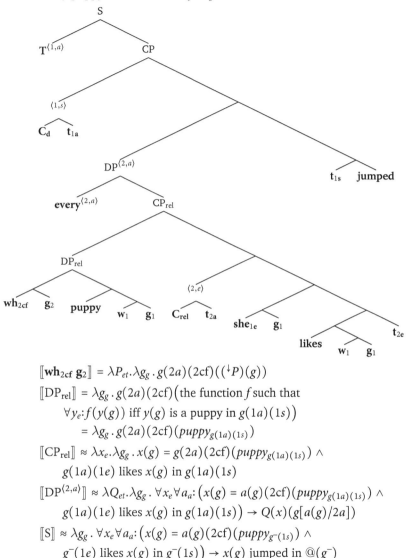

$$[\![\mathbf{wh}_{2cf}\ \mathbf{g}_2]\!] = \lambda P_{et}.\lambda g_g\,.\,g(2a)(2cf)((^\downarrow P)(g))$$

$$[\![\mathrm{DP}_{rel}]\!] = \lambda g_g\,.\,g(2a)(2cf)\big(\text{the function } f \text{ such that}$$
$$\forall y_e{:}f(y(g)) \text{ iff } y(g) \text{ is a puppy in } g(1a)(1s)\big)$$
$$= \lambda g_g\,.\,g(2a)(2cf)(puppy_{g(1a)(1s)})$$

$$[\![\mathrm{CP}_{rel}]\!] \approx \lambda x_e.\lambda g_g\,.\,x(g) = g(2a)(2cf)(puppy_{g(1a)(1s)}) \,\wedge$$
$$g(1a)(1e) \text{ likes } x(g) \text{ in } g(1a)(1s)$$

$$[\![\mathrm{DP}^{\langle 2,a\rangle}]\!] \approx \lambda Q_{et}.\lambda g_g\,.\,\forall x_e \forall a_a{:}\big(x(g) = a(g)(2cf)(puppy_{g(1a)(1s)}) \,\wedge$$
$$g(1a)(1e) \text{ likes } x(g) \text{ in } g(1a)(1s)\big) \to Q(x)(g[a(g)/2a])$$

$$[\![\mathrm{S}]\!] \approx \lambda g_g\,.\,\forall x_e \forall a_a{:}\big(x(g) = a(g)(2cf)(puppy_{g^-(1s)}) \,\wedge$$
$$g^-(1e) \text{ likes } x(g) \text{ in } g^-(1s)\big) \to x(g) \text{ jumped in } @(g^-)$$

The derived truth condition says that for every individual $o \in E$ and assignment $h \in G$, if o is the individual selected from the puppies by the choice function $h(2cf)$ and is liked by the contextually relevant female $g_c(1e)$, then o jumped. Roughly put, the DP 'every puppy which she likes' quantifies over those individuals that are chosen by some choice function or other from among the puppies and are liked by $g_c(1e)$. The sentence is true iff every such individual jumped.

For instance, suppose there are four individuals $o_{1\text{-}4}$; only $o_{1\text{-}3}$ are puppies; only $o_{1\text{-}2}$ are liked by $g_c(1e)$; and only o_1 jumped. And suppose that $h_1(2\text{cf})$ selects o_1 from the set of puppies $\{o_1, o_2, o_3\}$; $h_2(2\text{cf})$ selects o_2; and $h_3(2\text{cf})$ selects o_3. So, for individual o_2 and assignment h_2, the restrictor condition is satisfied: $o_2 = h_2(2\text{cf})(puppy_{g_c(1s)})$ and $g_c(1e)$ likes o_2; but o_2 didn't jump. So (5.22) is false.

The previous analysis derives an intuitively correct interpretation for the relative clause without additional composition rules or principles for interpreting reconstructed phrases (e.g. Predicate Abstraction, Trace Conversion). The syntax is co-opted from head-raising and D-complement analyses of headed relatives. Semantic composition again proceeds via function application. The treatment of the syntax–semantics interface parallels the treatment with verbal quantifiers from §§3–4. Just as a declarative clause predicates a property of a world identical to a world in a domain determined by an embedding modal, a relative clause predicates a property of an individual identical to an individual in a domain determined by an embedding determiner quantifier. Semantically modal elements raise from inside their complement clause as quantifiers over assignments, determining the relevant modal domain; analogously, the nominal quantifier 'every' in (5.22) raises from inside the complement CP_{rel}, determining the relevant domain of individuals. The basic $\langle aet, \langle aet, t\rangle\rangle$ type for 'every' in (5.21) parallels the basic $\langle at, \langle at, t\rangle\rangle$ type for modals in §3.

5.2 Donkey Pronouns

5.2.1 *Pronouns, Copies, and Nominal Complements*

This section begins to examine how the assignment-variable-based treatment of nominal quantifiers can help capture certain shifted interpretations of pronouns. I start with standard cases of donkey anaphora[35] such as (5.23). The indefinite 'a toy' embedded under 'every' doesn't c-command the pronoun 'it', yet their interpretations covary; (5.23) says, intuitively, that every puppy that got a toy liked the toy that they got.

(5.23) Every puppy which got *a toy* liked *it*.

---

[35] I use 'anaphora', 'anaphoric', etc. informally for phenomena in which an expression seems to receive its interpretation directly from the linguistic context (local or nonlocal). My usage doesn't presuppose that pronouns with "anaphoric" or "intuitively bound" readings are to be analyzed as syntactically or semantically bound by their felt linguistic antecedents.

Approaches to donkey anaphora are diverse. One could layer resources from one's preferred theory into the assignment-variable framework — e.g., adding unselective binders and revising the treatment of indefinites (Kamp 1981, Heim 1982), or treating donkey pronouns as E-type definite descriptions (Evans 1977, Heim 1990, Büring 2004, Elbourne 2005). Yet it is worth exploring how the assignment-quantificational semantics from §5.1.3 might be exploited in an account of donkey anaphora. (We will turn to other types of (non-)c-command anaphora in the following chapters.)

Following our treatment of relative words, suppose we represent the relevant uses of indefinites such as 'a' also as choice-function pronouns (cf. Reinhart 1997, Kratzer 1998b, von Heusinger 2011). To a first approximation, I suggest representing donkey pronouns as *copies of their linguistic antecedent*. There are various ways of implementing this idea. One option is to represent the anaphoric pronoun as a copy of the interpreted material of the antecedent (refinements to follow). A donkey pronoun such as 'it' in (5.23) is spelled out at LF with a coindexed choice-function pronoun and elided nominal complement, as in (5.24) (cf. Postal 1969, Elbourne 2005).[36] (In what follows, unless indicated otherwise the strikethrough indicates material that is interpreted at LF but unpronounced.)

---

[36] The present approach could perhaps be understood as an assignment-variable analogue of the NP-deletion E-type theory developed prominently by Elbourne (2005, 2013) (though see below); see Postal 1969, Radford 1997, Wiltschko 1998, Déchaine and Wiltschko 2002, Baltin 2012, Patel-Grosz and Grosz 2017 for "X+elided-complement" analyses of other pro-forms crosslinguistically. I don't assume that all indefinites or pronouns need be analyzed with choice functions. Free readings of pronouns could be represented with simplex type e pronouns, or with choice-function pronouns coindexed with $\mathbf{T}$ and an implicit (possibly trivial) property-type pronoun ($\approx$ "which relevant thing"). For unified theories of pronouns (free, bound, anaphoric), see Heim and Kratzer 1998, Panagiotidis 2002, Elbourne 2005, 2013; for contrasting approaches, see Noguchi 1997, Hornstein 2001, 2007, Bhat 2004, Déchaine and Wiltschko 2002, 2017, Cowper and Hall 2009, Kratzer 2009. See Kratzer 1998b for a lexical ambiguity account of indefinites which maintains a choice-function analysis of specific indefinites and a quantificational analysis of nonspecific indefinites (cf. Fodor and Sag 1982). I leave open the syntactic category of the relevant English pronouns, and I ignore projections for φ-features (see Déchaine and Wiltschko 2002, 2015, 2017, Bhat 2004, Alexiadou et al. 2007, Baltin 2012, Grosz and Patel-Grosz 2016, Patel-Grosz and Grosz 2017 on structural differences among pronouns crosslinguistically). The analysis is compatible with apparent φ-feature mismatches such as in (i). Such examples may be assimilated to independent phenomena in which pronouns' φ-features are uninterpreted, as in "fake indexical" and "split binding" cases such as (ii) (cf. von Stechow 2003, Heim 2008, Kratzer 2009, Sudo 2012, Déchaine and Wiltschko 2015, Wiltschko 2016).

(i)   Every freshman who met a senior hoped that they would become friends.

(ii)   a. I'm the only one around here who will admit that I could be wrong. (Partee 1989a: fn. 3)
        b. Only you remember our first appointment.   (Kratzer 2009: ex. 87)

I focus exclusively on intrasentential anaphora where the pronoun has a linguistic antecedent. I put aside cases of "paycheck pronouns," such as 'it' in (iii), where the relation determining the pronoun's covarying interpretation is contextually determined.

(iii)   [Context: A new faculty member picks up her first paycheck from her mailbox. Waving it in the air, she says to a colleague:]
        Do most faculty members deposit it in the Credit Union?   (Jacobson 2000: 89n.12)

(5.24) Every puppy which got a toy liked it.

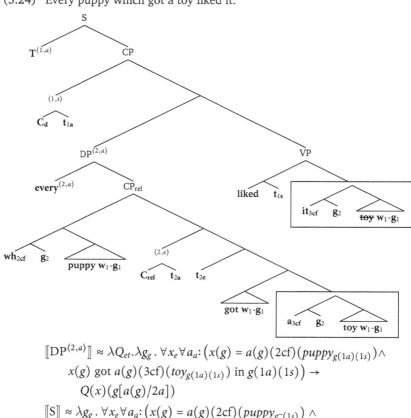

$$[\![DP^{\langle 2,a\rangle}]\!] \approx \lambda Q_{et}.\lambda g_g . \forall x_e \forall a_a \colon \big(x(g) = a(g)(2\mathrm{cf})(puppy_{g(1a)(1s)})\wedge$$
$$x(g) \text{ got } a(g)(3\mathrm{cf})(toy_{g(1a)(1s)}) \text{ in } g(1a)(1s)\big) \rightarrow$$
$$Q(x)(g[a(g)/2a])$$

$$[\![S]\!] \approx \lambda g_g . \forall x_e \forall a_a \colon \big(x(g) = a(g)(2\mathrm{cf})(puppy_{g^-(1s)}) \wedge$$
$$x(g) \text{ got } a(g)(3\mathrm{cf})(toy_{g^-(1s)}) \text{ in } g^-(1s)\big) \rightarrow$$
$$x(g) \text{ liked } a(g)(3\mathrm{cf})(toy_{g^-(1s)}) \text{ in } @(g^-)$$

The anaphoric connection between 'a toy' and 'it' is captured by the syntactic representation of the donkey pronoun in terms of its antecedent $[\mathbf{a}_{3\mathrm{cf}}\text{-}\mathbf{g}_2 \ \mathbf{toy}\text{-}\mathbf{w}_1\text{-}\mathbf{g}_1]$, and the assignment-binder introduced from type-driven movement of the matrix quantifier. As usual in syntax, the binder-index feature attaching to the D head 'every' projects to the DP. This assignment-binder binds the assignment-variable in the (c-commanded) choice-function pronoun $[\mathbf{it}_{3\mathrm{cf}} \ \mathbf{g}_2]$ representing the donkey pronoun.[37] Roughly put, the subject 'every puppy which got a toy'

---

[37] See Büring 2004 for a situation-based E-type analysis that also denies a binding relation between the donkey pronoun and indefinite. For discussion of alternative approaches to "indirect binding" phenomena, see Büring 2011. I return to other types of apparent binding out of DPs in §6.4. As in the general case, index features not necessary for interpretation may be deleted in the interfaces.

universally quantifies over those individuals $o \in E$ and choice functions F, F' such that F $(= a(g)(2\mathrm{cf}))$ selects o from among the puppies, F' $(= a(g)(3\mathrm{cf}))$ selects some o' from among the toys, and o got o' — i.e., puppies o that got some toy or other o'. The sentence is true iff, for every such o, o liked o'.

Treating donkey pronouns as copies of their linguistic antecedent captures the prominent idea that "there is a pairing of indefinite antecedents with donkey-pronouns that is *purely syntactic* (as expected under the unselective binding approach, but not available under the E-type approach)" (von Fintel 1994: 176, drawing on Kratzer 1995, emphasis mine; see also Elbourne 2005, Patel-Grosz and Grosz 2010). However, treating certain anaphoric pronouns as "copies" of their linguistic antecedents shouldn't be conflated with copies in the sense of the copy theory of movement (see n. 9). Copies of movement are identical to the moved expression (or at least identical with respect to φ-features, [wh] features, Case; cf. Nunes 2004, van Koppen 2007). The donkey pronoun, in contrast, need only be equivalent to its antecedent with respect to features interpreted at LF. The present usage leaves open whether a given anaphoric "copy" is the result of a syntactic Copy operation.

If donkey pronouns are syntactically complex in the proposed way, one should expect to find evidence for this complexity in other languages. In some languages donkey-anaphoric expressions can be complete pronounced copies of their antecedents. Using a reduced or alternative form in (5.25)–(5.26) is ungrammatical.

(5.25) a. ni   xihuan **shei**$_i$ wo piping   **shei**$_i$.
          you like   who I   criticize who
          'If you like X, I will criticize X' / 'Whoever you like, I will criticize them.'

       b. *ni   xihuan shei$_i$ wo piping
          you like   who I   criticize
          pro$_i$/ta$_i$/na-ge-ren$_i$/shenme ren$_i$.
          Ø/him/her/that-CL-person/what person
                              (Cheng and Huang 1996: exs. 14, 17; Mandarin Chinese)

(5.26) a. **Tug twg**$_i$ pum *pro*$_j$ los **tug twg**$_i$ yeej   nyam *pro*$_j$.
          CLF which see   Ø   TOP CLF which always like   Ø
          'Whoever sees him will surely like him.'

       b. *Tug twg$_i$ pum *pro*$_j$ los nwg$_i$/*pro*$_i$ yeej   nyam *pro*$_j$.
          CLF which see   Ø   TOP 3SG/Ø   always like   Ø
                              (Mortensen 2003: ex. 35; Hmong)

In Hindi donkey sentences, the anaphoric expression can be realized as a copy of the antecedent nominal, as in (5.27) with bare anaphoric *gadheKO* 'donkey'.

The representation of the Hindi donkey anaphor in (5.28) (using English glosses) is the mirror image of the representation of 'it' in (5.24). In both cases the anaphoric expression is spelled out via a copied choice-function pronoun and NP complement; what distinguishes them is which material is pronounced.[38]

(5.27) har   aadmii jis ke paas **koii   gadhaa**$_i$ hotaa hai **gadheKO**$_i$
        every man REL with   some donkey   has   donkey-ACC
        maartaa hai.
        beats
        'Every man who has a donkey beats it.' (Srivastav 1991: ex. 45a; Hindi)

(5.28) ... [$_{DP^{(2,a)}}$ ... a$_{3cf}$-g$_2$ donkey-w$_1$-g$_1$ ...] [$_{VP}$ ... ~~F$_{3cf}$-g$_2$~~ donkey-w$_1$-g$_1$] ...

There is also independent evidence for analyzing certain pronouns used in donkey sentences as syntactically complex in the relevant way. For instance, Wiltschko (1998) argues on independent grounds that German *d*-pronouns are DPs with an elided nominal complement (see also Schwarz 2009, Patel-Grosz and Grosz 2017). Though *d*-pronouns are generally incompatible with bound-variable readings, they can be used as donkey pronouns, as in (5.29) with *den*. A similar pattern can be observed with Halkomelem pro-DPs, as in (5.30) with the independent pronoun *t(h)ú-tl'ò*. With Halkomelem independent pronouns the nominal complement can be pronounced ((5.30b)).[39]

---

[38] The ostensibly bound names from (4.32)–(4.33) could perhaps be represented analogously to the Hindi donkey anaphor in (5.28), with an elided choice-function pronoun and pronounced NP, schematically:

(i)   a. ?Every family with a Donald thinks Donald should grow up.
      b. ... [[$_{DP^{(2,a)}}$ ... a$_{2cf}$-g$_2$ Donald-w-g] [$_{VP}$ ... ~~F$_{2cf}$-g$_2$~~ Donald-w-g ...]]

An alternative hypothesis regarding (5.27) is that the donkey expression includes a covert demonstrative, and that this demonstrative captures the felt anaphoric connection. (5.27) would be relevantly analogous not to (5.23), but to (ii) (cf. Abbott 2002).

(ii)   Every child who got a toy will bring that toy for show-and-tell.

Simply positing a covert demonstrative is insufficient. Compare (5.27), where the bare nominal can function as the anaphoric expression, with the correlative in (iii-a), where omitting the demonstrative is ungrammatical. Though correlatives generally require a demonstrative correlate in the main clause, the ungrammaticality of (iii-a) without the demonstrative cannot be due to the lack of an overt correlate. (iii-b), where the correlate is implicit, is acceptable (cf. Lipták 2012 on Hungarian).

(iii) a. [jo laRkii khaRii hai] *(vo) laRkii lambii hai.
        REL girl standing is DEM girl   tall   is
        lit. 'Which girl is standing, that girl is tall.'
        'The girl who is standing is tall.'   (Srivastav 1991: exs. 13a, 17a; Hindi)
      b. [jo laRkii khaRii hai] lambii hai.
        REL girl standing is tall is
        lit. 'Which girl is standing is tall.'
                                                        (Bhatt 2003: ex. 69; Hindi)

If a covert demonstrative could capture the anaphoric connection in (5.27), one might wonder why it couldn't do so in (iii-a).

[39] Pronouns licensing overt nominal complements are well attested crosslinguistically (e.g. English 'we students'; see also Postal 1969, Collins 1993, Déchaine and Wiltschko 2002). Overtly

(5.29) Wenn ein Bauer einen Esel$_i$ hat, dann schlägt er den$_i$.
      if   a   farmer a   donkey has then beats he D-PRON
      'If a farmer owns a donkey, then he beats it.'

                                                (Wiltschko 1998: ex. 57; German)

(5.30) a. te tál-s   tl'   Strang$_i$ mamáy-t-em   tú-tl'ò$_i$.
           D mother-3POSS D.OBL Strang help.REDUP-TRANS-INTRANS D-3SG
           'Strang's mother is helping him.'
        b. su me   ts'tl'ém [thú-tl'ò   só:seqwt].
           so come jump   D.FEM-3SG youngest.sister
           'So the youngest sister came to jump.'

                        (Wiltschko 2002: 167–168, 179; Halkomelem (Salish))

Second, in some languages certain pronouns freely allow overt modifiers, even full restrictive relative clauses, as in (5.31)–(5.32) (see also Luján 2004). Like the Halkomelem independent pronoun in (5.30)–(5.31), the Norwegian pro-forms in (5.32) can be used in donkey sentences, as in (5.33).

(5.31) tú-tl'ò la   xwmékwàth-et the Martina
      D-3SG AUX kiss-TRANS   D   Martina
      'him who kissed Martina' (Wiltschko 2002: 186; Halkomelem (Salish))

(5.32) a. det som   jeg spiste
           it   which I   ate
        b. han med rød hatt
           he   with red hat   (Hestvik 1992: exs. 27, 29; Norwegian)

(5.33) Hvis en mann eier   et esel,   slår   han det.
      if   a   man   owns a donkey beats he   it

The position of the NP posited in the representation of the donkey pronoun can be overtly modified.[40]

---

prenominal uses of English 'it' are attested in toddler speech, as in the naturally occurring example in (i-a). Following Radford, such uses reflect a developmental stage where the child hasn't yet learned that 'it' in English selects for a phonetically unrealized complement (unlike e.g. 'we').

(i)   a. Get it ladder!   (McNeill 1970: 29; toddler English)
      b. [$_{DP}$ [$_D$ it] [$_{NP}$ ladder]]   (Radford 1997: ex. 81)

Synchronic and diachronic morphosyntactic connections among third-person pronouns, determiners, and relative words are crosslinguistically common (Wiltschko 1998, 2002, Gair et al. 1999, Lyons 1999, Heine and Kuteva 2002, Bhat 2004, Luján 2004, Thurgood and LaPolla 2017).

[40] For the Norwegian pronouns in (5.32), an alternative hypothesis might be that they are pro-NPs (pro-forms with the syntax of nouns), which can also take overt modifiers, as in (i) with anaphoric 'one' and Japanese *kare* (Postal 1969, Déchaine and Wiltschko 2002, Falco and Zamparelli 2016):

5.2.2 Asymmetric, Universal, and Existential Readings

Although the entry for 'every' in (5.21) introduces quantification over assignments, the semantics is still a selective quantification that relates sets of individuals. The account avoids the "proportion problem" (Kadmon 1987) facing unselective binder analyses which treat the quantification fundamentally as relating sets of assignments (Lewis 1975, Kamp 1981, Heim 1982). Consider an asymmetric reading with 'most' in (5.35), assuming an LF parallel to (5.24). (Assume a simple "more than half" semantics for 'most', and an off-the-shelf semantics for the plural where *puppies$_u$* is the (characteristic function of the) set of puppy pluralities in u — formally, the closure under sum formation of the set of atomic puppies in u.)[41]

(5.34) $[\![\textbf{most}]\!] = \lambda P^+_{\langle a,et\rangle}.\lambda Q^+_{\langle a,et\rangle}.\lambda g_g$.

$\quad\quad \#o\big[\exists a_a\colon P^+(a)(\lambda g_g.o)(g) \;\wedge\; Q^+(a)(\lambda g_g.o)(g)\big]$

$\quad\quad \div \#o'\big[\exists a'_a\colon P^+(a')(\lambda g_g.o')(g)\big] > 1/2$

- $\#o\big[\ldots o \ldots\big]$:= the cardinality of the set of atoms o s.t. $\ldots o \ldots$

(5.35) a. Most puppies which got a toy liked it.

   b. $[\![S]\!] \approx \lambda g_g \,.\, \#o\big[\exists a_a\colon o = a(g)(2\text{cf})(puppies_{g^-(1s)}) \;\wedge\;$

$\quad\quad o \text{ got } a(g)(3\text{cf})(toy_{g^-(1s)}) \text{ in } g^-(1s) \;\wedge\;$

$\quad\quad o \text{ liked } a(g)(3\text{cf})(toy_{g^-(1s)}) \text{ in } @(g^-)\big]$

$\quad\quad \div \#o'\big[\exists a'_a\colon o' = a'(g)(2\text{cf})(puppies_{g^-(1s)}) \;\wedge\;$

$\quad\quad o' \text{ got } a'(g)(3\text{cf})(toy_{g^-(1s)}) \text{ in } g^-(1s)\big] > 1/2$

(i)   a. tiisai kare
            small   he
            'he who is small'   (Noguchi 1997: 777; Japanese)
        b. small one

However, such a hypothesis can be excluded. Unlike the forms in (5.32), pro-NPs are generally incompatible with bound-variable readings (Déchaine and Wiltschko 2002).

(ii)   a. *Daremo$_i$-ga kare$_i$-no hahaoya-o aisite-iru.
            everyone   he-GEN mother   love
            'Everyone loves his mother.'   (Noguchi 1997: 770; Japanese)
        b. *Everybody$_i$ thinks one$_i$ is better than average.

(iii)   Hver eneste gutt$_i$ løftet hatten hans$_i$.
        every   boy   lifted hat.DEF his
        'Every boy lifted his hat.'   (Hestvik and Philip 2000: 185; Norwegian)

Pro-forms such as those in (5.32)–(5.33) thus arguably have at least the structure of a φP (if not DP), which also take nominal complements (Patel-Grosz and Grosz 2017). The modifiers in (5.32) modify the implicit NP.

[41] Following Link 1983, E is structured to include sums of atomic individuals. An atomic individual — the referent of a singular DP — is an individual whose only atomic part is itself. Note that atoms are included in *puppies$_u$* (Krifka 1989). We will return to number in §7.

Suppose there are three puppies b_{1-3}; b_1 got four toys and liked them; and neither b_2 nor b_3 liked the unique toy they got. So, b_2 and b_3 satisfy the restriction that there are choice functions which select them from among the puppies and select a toy they got; however, b_2 and b_3 fail to satisfy the scope condition since they don't like the selected toy. Hence (5.35) is correctly predicted to be false.

The semantics for 'every' in (5.21) derives a so-called "universal reading" for donkey sentences: the truth condition in (5.24) is falsified if there is a puppy o' and choice function F' such that o' got $F'(toy)$ and o' didn't like $F'(toy)$. Although many theories predict only universal readings for donkey sentences (Kamp 1981, Heim 1982, Groenendijk and Stokhof 1991, Elbourne 2005), it has been observed that some donkey sentences have existential readings. (5.36b) is intuitively true if every person who has a dime will put some dime that she has in the meter.

(5.36) a. Yesterday, every person who had a credit card paid his bill with it.
            (R. Cooper)
        b. Every person who has a dime will put it in the meter.
            (Pelletier and Schubert 1989)
        c. Every person who submitted a paper had it rejected once.
            (Chierchia 1995: 63)

One way of capturing existential readings is to weaken the semantics of the quantifier. Consider the following alternative entry for 'every' and semantic value for (5.24).

(5.37) $[\![\mathbf{every_2}]\!] = \lambda P^+_{\langle a,et\rangle}.\lambda Q^+_{\langle a,et\rangle}.\lambda g_g . \forall x_e : \big(\exists a_a : P^+(a)(x)(g)\big) \rightarrow$
        $\big(\exists a'_a : P^+(a')(x)(g) \wedge Q^+(a')(x)(g)\big)$

(5.38) $[\![(5.24)]\!] \approx \lambda g_g . \forall x_e : \big(\exists a_a : x(g) = a(g)(2\mathrm{cf})(puppy_{g^-(1s)}) \wedge$
        $x(g)$ got $a(g)(3\mathrm{cf})(toy_{g^-(1s)})$ in $g^-(1s)\big) \rightarrow$
        $\big(\exists a'_a : x(g) = a'(g)(2\mathrm{cf})(puppy_{g^-(1s)}) \wedge$
        $x(g)$ got $a'(g)(3\mathrm{cf})(toy_{g^-(1s)})$ in $g^-(1s) \wedge$
        $x(g)$ liked $a'(g)(3\mathrm{cf})(toy_{g^-(1s)})$ in $@(g^-)\big)$

The derived truth condition requires, roughly, that for any $o \in E$ for which there are choice functions F, F' such that $o = F(puppy)$ and o got $F'(toy)$, there is a choice function F'' that selects a toy that o got and liked. There is universal quantification over puppies o, but existential quantification in the scope condition over toys liked by o — more precisely, over assignments which determine choice functions that select a toy that o liked from the toys o received. The condition "$P^+(a')(x)(g)$" in (5.37) ensures that the choice function F'' selects a toy received by *o*. (5.24) is still predicted false in a scenario where a puppy liked some toys or other but hated all the toys it received. (5.24) isn't equivalent to (5.39) .

(5.39)　Every farmer who owns a donkey beats a donkey.

It is controversial whether some donkey sentences conventionally have both existential and universal readings. I leave open whether all universal readings can be derived conversationally, or positing some sort of ambiguity is necessary (see e.g. Brasoveanu 2007). Hereafter for simplicity I will assume "universal reading" entries such as (5.21).

5.3　Recap: Features and Bugs

This chapter developed an assignment-variable-based compositional semantics for head-raising analyses of restrictive relative clauses, and applied the account to certain types of pronominal anaphora. The syntax/semantics advances our project of standardizing quantification across domains. The treatment of quantificational DP: D CP is effectively a nominal counterpart of the treatment of modal elements from §§3–4. The semantics is again fully compositional. Additional composition rules or principles for interpreting reconstructed phrases aren't required. The assignment-quantificational semantics for nominal quantifiers helps capture linguistic shifting data in universal, existential, and asymmetric readings of donkey sentences. The analysis of donkey pronouns as copies of their linguistic antecedents is supported by independent crosslinguistic data.

Yet there are reasons to be dissatisfied. First, the analysis from §5.1.3 treats the relative complementizer as raising for type reasons from the "gap" position; yet there is syntactic and semantic evidence that, in at least some cases, the relative phrase originates in the gap position. In languages with circumnominal relative clauses, the relative phrase can be pronounced in this position, as in (5.40) (de Vries 2002, Hiraiwa 2005, 2017). Relative phrases in DP-like free relatives can also appear inside the relative IP, as in (5.41).

(5.40)　[$_{CP_{rel}}$ Atia n da'　　**bua seka** da'a　　zaam]　　la bɔi　　mɛ.
　　　　　　　Atia c buy.PERF goat REL　market yesterday D lose.PERF PRT
　　　　　　　(lit. 'The [Atia bought which goat at the market yesterday] got lost.')
　　　　　　　'The goat that Atia bought at the market yesterday got lost.'
　　　　　　　　　　　　　　　　　(Hiraiwa et al. 2017: 5; Gurenɛ (Niger-Congo))

(5.41)　[$_{CP_{rel}}$ Mary **taku**　　kağe] ki　ophewathų.
　　　　　　　Mary something make the I.buy
　　　　　　　'I bought what Mary made.'　(Williamson 1987: 188; Lakota (Siouan))

It is hard to see how relative clauses such as these could be derived if the relative phrase originated in Spec,C_{rel} (or outside CP_{rel}, as in head-external analyses). In (5.40) the relative clause subject is pronounced in this position.

Even in English there are semantic reasons for thinking that the relative phrase can have a representation in the gap position. Consider (5.42) (the indices are used informally to indicate the interpretation of the predicate's world argument).

(5.42) Callie wants to hug every unicorn$_i$ which Timmy thinks^i he found.

Roughly put, the relevant reading of (5.42) says that Callie wants to hug every o such that for every possibility h compatible with Timmy's beliefs, o is a unicorn in h and Timmy found o in h. (5.42) needn't imply that there are unicorns. It is hard to see how the world argument of 'unicorn' could be linked to 'thinks' if the relative phrase 'which unicorn' originates above 'thinks' in Spec,C_{rel}. Alternative local and intermediate readings of the nominal head's world argument are also possible. In (5.43) the world argument of 'monster' is intuitively associated with the intensional predicate 'is afraid' in the relative clause. (5.43) says, roughly, that Timmy gets nightmares from every o such that for every possibility h compatible with Alice's beliefs and every possibility h' compatible with what Timmy fears in h, o is a monster in h'. In (5.44) the world argument of 'monster' is linked to the attitude verb 'thinks' in the relative clause.

(5.43) [Context: Alice doesn't believe in monsters.]
Every monster$_k$ which Alice thinks^i Timmy is afraid^k of gives him nightmares.

(5.44) [Context: Timmy thinks that his mother doesn't believe in monsters, and that the noises she's scared of are actually monsters.]
Every monster$_i$ which Timmy thinks^i his mother is afraid^k of gives him nightmares.

In some manner to be explained, the nominal head needs to be able to receive shifted readings under modal elements inside the relative clause, while still being targeted by the matrix quantifier for determining the domain of quantification, as reflected informally in (5.45).

(5.45) a. every^j [$_{CP_{rel}}$ ... Timmy thinks^i he found [wh unicorn$_i$]$_j$]
b. every^j [$_{CP_{rel}}$ ... Alice thinks^i Timmy is afraid^k of [wh monster$_k$]$_j$]
c. every^j [$_{CP_{rel}}$ ... Timmy thinks^i Alice is afraid^k of [wh monster$_i$]$_j$]

Intensional gap readings (as we might call them) raise a challenge for any account in which the nominal head isn't represented in the gap position.

One needn't assume that restrictive relative clauses in all languages are formed from the same underlying structure (Carlson 1977, Åfarli 1994, Sauerland 1998, Bhatt 2002, Grosu 2002, Hastings 2004, Gračanin-Yuksek 2008; contrast Cinque 2013, 2015, Sportiche 2017). The analysis in this chapter might be correct for certain types of relative clauses. (Indeed the analyses of correlative clauses, 'if'-clauses, and interrogative clauses in §§8–9 will be modeled after the treatment of free relatives mentioned in n. 32.) Yet it is worth investigating the prospects for a compositional semantics applicable to both circumnominal and overtly head-external relativization strategies. §7.4 develops an alternative "matching" analysis (Lees 1960, Sauerland 2003) of restrictive relative clauses which maintains the features of the head-raising account and treatment of donkey sentences in this chapter while giving the relative phrase an IP_{rel}-internal representation. Before returning to relative clauses, it will be useful to have on the table a more detailed understanding of the syntax and semantics of noun phrases more generally. The next chapter begins by extending the assignment-quantificational approach to quantifier phrases with non-relativized complements.

6

Quantifiers

§5 developed an assignment-variable-based compositional semantics for head-raising analyses of restrictive relative clauses. The assignment binding resulting from type-driven movement of the matrix determiner helped capture the link between the relative phrase and gap position in the relative clause, and various linguistic shifting phenomena with donkey sentences. This chapter extends the approach to quantifier phrases with non-relativized complements. The proposed generalized assignment-quantificational syntax/semantics for quantifier phrases captures various phenomena concerning specificity (§6.1), possessives and restrictive modification (§6.2), pronoun binding (§6.3), and weak crossover (§6.4). §7 integrates the account in a more detailed general analysis of noun phrases.

6.1 "Specificity" (I)

The account in §5.1.3 treated quantifier words in headed relative constructions as type $\langle\langle a, et\rangle, \langle\langle a, et\rangle, t\rangle\rangle$, and as raising for type reasons from inside the relative clause. A pressing question is how this syntax/semantics relates the syntax/semantics with non-relativized noun phrases, as in (6.1).

(6.1)   Every baby laughed.

One response would be to treat quantifiers as systematically ambiguous between items taking arguments of type $\langle e, t\rangle$ vs. type $\langle a, et\rangle$. LFs with the "wrong" homonym would be filtered out due to a type mismatch. However, parsimony worries and Ziff's (1960) "Occam's Eraser" aside, there are reasons to treat quantifier phrases with non-relative complements as also introducing assignment-quantification. Relative clause donkey sentences aren't the only case of apparent "binding out of DP" (Büring 2004). In genitive binding and inverse linking examples such as (6.2)–(6.3), the interpretation of the pronoun 'him' intuitively depends on the embedded quantifier phrase 'every boy', though the quantifier phrase doesn't c-command the pronoun at LF.

(6.2)   a. Every boy$_i$'s cat likes him$_i$.
        b. ≈ "for every boy b, the cat owned by b likes b"

(6.3)   a. Some cat of every boy$_i$ likes him$_i$.
         b. ≈ "for every boy b, some cat owned by b likes b"

It is worth examining the prospects for an assignment-quantificational analysis of quantifier phrases so as to provide a unified account of such cases (more on which in §6.4).

One approach is to analyze quantifier phrases in general as having internal structure relevantly analogous to structure in a relative clause. Headed relative constructions aren't the only case of determiners taking clausal complements crosslinguistically.[42] In some languages, determiners in headed relative constructions can be used with factive clauses or root clauses, as in (6.4) with *la*.

(6.4)   a. naa bu la
             COW CL DEM
             'that cow'
         b. Amoak nya [[$_{CP}$ Atim ale sua naa buui] la].
             Amoak saw   Atim c own cow REL   DEM
             'Amoak saw the cow that Atim owned.'
         c. [[$_{CP}$ Atim ale dɛ mango-kú] la] tɛ   Amoak po   pienti.
             Atim c ate mango-D   DEM gave Amoak stomach whiten
             'That Atim ate the mango pleased Amoak.'
         d. [[$_{CP}$ Atim nagi Amoak] la].
             Atim hit Amoak DEM
             'Atim hit Amoak, as I said.'
             (Hiraiwa 2005: 31, Hiraiwa et al. 2017: 5–6; Bùlì (Niger-Congo))

In light of crosslinguistic phenomena with nominal tense marking, Lecarme (2008, 2012) and Chang (2012) treat DPs as taking tensed TP complements, yielding a structure for DPs analogous to that for sentences (§3.2; see also Hiraiwa 2005, Ilkhanipour 2016). Following Kayne (1994), generalized D+CP analyses of DPs have been defended by various researchers (see Campbell 1996, Koopman 2003, 2005, Luján 2004). In Campbell's and Luján's accounts, the main operator is analyzed as moving from inside the complement of the determiner, schematically as in (6.5) (cf. also Matthewson 1998, Ihsane and Puskás 2001, Giusti 2002, Laenzlinger 2005, Larson 2014).

(6.5)   a. [$_{DP}$ D$_i$ [$_{CP}$ ... t$_i$ ...]]   (Luján 2004)
         b. [$_{DP}$ OP$_i$ [D [$_{CP}$ ... t$_i$ ...]]]   (Campbell 1996)

---

[42] See Kayne 1994, Uriagereka 1998, Caponigro 2002, de Vries 2002, Koopman 2003, 2005, Larson 2003, Hiraiwa 2005, Law 2011, Hankamer and Mikkelsen 2012, Himmelmann 2016.

The focus in the preceding accounts is on matters of syntax. A generalized assignment-quantificational account of DPs, as pursued here, may be conceived as deriving the relevant movement operations and binding relations in a specific compositional semantics.

Treating determiner quantifiers as taking complements with structure analogous to a relative clause doesn't require identifying the complement as a relative construction. In the D+CP structure for 'every baby' in (6.6), the [F NP] constituent needn't be identified as a relative phrase (irrelevant numerical indices omitted).

(6.6)   every$^{\langle i,a \rangle}$ [$_{CP}$ F$_{cf}$-g$_i$ baby-w-g [[C t$_{ia}$]$^{\langle j,e \rangle}$ [t$_{je}$ P$_{et}$-g]]]

The complement of the quantifier needn't even be a CP. In (6.7) the relevant structure is integrated in an extended nominal projection XP.[43] Here the quantifier raises for type reasons from inside the FP (perhaps identified as a Focus Phrase).

(6.7)   every$^{\langle i,a \rangle}$ [$_{XP}$ (YP) X [$_{FP}$ F$_{cf}$-t$_{ia}$ baby-w-g]]

With headed relative clauses there was a clear basis for positing the constituent with the choice-function pronoun: the relative phrase. It is worth pausing to consider independent linguistic evidence for the relevant structure in quantificational DPs generally. This section focuses primarily on morphosyntactic and semantic evidence for a choice-function element. §6.2 argues that data with genitive constructions may favor an analysis such as (6.7), with a reduced XP complement, over a generalized D+CP analysis such as (6.6). §§6.3–6.4 examine how the resulting assignment-quantificational syntax/semantics for quantifier phrases captures further linguistic shifting data with pronominal anaphora.

First, there is morphological evidence for the extra structure in other languages. It is crosslinguistically common for quantifier words to be diachronically or synchronically related to a relative/*wh* form or determiner/demonstrative — e.g., with German *jeder* 'every' as *je* 'ever' + *der* 'that'/'the'/'which', or Romanian *fiecare* 'every' as *fie* 'be' + *care* 'which' (cf. Haspelmath 1995, 1997, Heine and Kuteva 2002, Thurgood and LaPolla 2017). Choice-function pronouns will also be exploited in our analyses of *wh* words and certain demonstrative proforms in §§8–9. In many languages quantified expressions are overtly realized with a quantifier word and a distinct determiner phrase. The overt determiner is obligatory in (6.8)–(6.12).[44]

---

[43] Cf. Matthewson 1998, Bhattacharya 1999b, Zamparelli 2000, Adger 2003, Aboh 2004, Hiraiwa 2005, Bhatt 2006, Lecarme 2008, Megerdoomian 2008. We will examine the nature of the extended projections in due course.

[44] See also Löbel 1989, Giusti 1991, 1992, 1997, Santelmann 1993, Lecarme 1996, 2004, Matthewson 1998, 2001, 2008, 2013, Zamparelli 2000, Hiraiwa 2005, Julien 2005, Alexiadou et al.

(6.8) léxlex   [tákem **i**=smelhmúlhats=**a**].
       intelligent all   DET.PL=woman.PL=EXIS
       'All (the) women are intelligent.'
                              (Matthewson 2013: exs. 6–7; St'át'imcets (Lillooet Salish))

(6.9) Namaky   [**ny** boky roa] [**ny** mpianatra tsirairay].
       PAST.AT.read DET book two DET student   each
       'Each student read two books.'
                              (Paul and Travis 2006: 323; Malagasy (Austronesian))

(6.10) rov   **ha**-sfarim
       most DET-books
       'most books'   (Danon 1996: 25; Hebrew)

(6.11) ibn xald n   istakšaf-a   [ʔakθar-/kull-a l-žibāl-i].
       ibn khaldun explored-3MS most-/all-ACC   DET-mountains-GEN
       'Ibn Khaldun explored most/all (of the) mountains.'
                              (Hallman 2016: 2–3; Standard Arabic)

(6.12) [ardáy-**d**ii   kúlli-g-ood]   wáy   gudbeen.
       students-DET+PAST whole-DET+POSS.3PL DECL.3PL succeeded
       'All (the) students succeeded.'   (Lecarme 1999b: ex. 35b; Somali)

In (6.11)–(6.12) each element of the XP complement from (6.7) is overt: the quantifier word, the choice-function pronoun via the article, the X head via the genitive marker, and the nominal predicate. Expressing quantification via a genitive construction is attested in various language families (see also Franks 1994, Bošković 2006, Hartmann and Milićević 2009, Francez and Goldring 2012).

Second, extending our syntax/semantics along the lines in (6.6)–(6.7) may give precise expression to ideas about the "specificity" (Enç 1991) of quantificational DPs. Here is Enç (Enç's NP corresponds to our DP):

2007, Keenan and Paperno 2012, Cardinaletti and Giusti 2017. Matthewson (1998, 1999, 2013) shows that the determiners in St'át'imcets quantifier phrases cannot be assimilated to a definite article on the model of explicit partitives ('all of the women'). For instance, the determiners can take a singular range, and they are unmarked for definiteness. St'át'imcets has a distinct structure corresponding to English-style partitives in which a Case-assigning element is overt and the choice-function pronoun is semantically definite, as in (i) (cf. also Gillon 2013).

(i)   [zí7zeg' lhél=ki=smúlhats=a]   ít-em.
       each   from=DET.PL=woman=EXIS sing-INTR
       'Each of the women sang.'   (Matthewson 2013: ex. 15; St'át'imcets)

> [Q]uantifiers in natural languages quantify over contextually given sets … For example, [(6.13) entails] only that [Sally] danced with every contextually relevant man …
>
> [(6.13)] Sally danced with every man.
>
> If universal quantification is over contextually relevant sets of individuals, it follows that NPs that quantify universally are specific. This account also ensures that universally quantifying NPs presuppose existence … [T]he specificity requirement is not restricted to universally quantifying NPs … All quantifiers are specific. (Enç 1991: 11)

Lecarme draws on Enç's notion of specificity in her account of nominal tense. What distinguishes "strong" — and tense-marked — noun phrases in Somali (e.g. 'every/most N', compared to 'many/three N'), according to Lecarme, is the "referentiality" of the Determiner category (2008: 204; cf. Chomsky 2007: 25, Hartmann 2008: 111, 131, 139). The inherent "definiteness" of D (Lyons 1999, Déchaine and Wiltschko 2002, 2015, Paul et al. 2015) is treated by Déchaine and Wiltschko as capturing differences in binding possibilities among pronouns:

> Assuming D to be the locus of specificity, DPs … are directly connected to the discourse, given their intrinsic deictic properties.
> [T]he tense morpheme in Somali nominals … links the reference of DP to a discourse-identified set of possible referents. Specificity is thus understood as "D(iscourse)-linking" (Pesetsky 1987). (Lecarme 1999a: 301, 1996: 16)
>
> This view [locates] DP's specific/anaphoric reference and discourse function directly in its head Determiner … Accordingly, determiners may be described as discourse-linking functions. (Luján 2004: 130)
>
> D, the locus of indexicality, is responsible for assigning reference. … Person in D is intrinsically deictic … Consequently, fake indexicals are analyzed as instantiating φ rather than D. (Déchaine and Wiltschko 2017: 68, 80n.10)

It isn't always manifest how authors take the above notions — specificity, indexicality, presuppositionality, definiteness, deixis, discourse linking — to be relevantly related. Plainly understood, the appeals to notions such as referentiality may seem puzzling. One wouldn't typically expect to find quantificational determiners in a list of indexicals. On the face of it, definite noun phrases and quantifiers can be bound ((6.14); see also von Fintel 1998b). The weak/cardinal noun phrases in (6.15) would seem to be interpreted with respect to "relevant sets of individuals" as much as 'every man' in (6.13). (6.15a) can be true even if Alice is satisfied with universal cookie production; pointing out in (6.15b) that many players were congratulating members of their own team likely won't earn one points with the referee.

(6.14) a. Every first-year intern was mistreated by the hospital administrator.
                                                            (Williams 1997: ex. 34a)
        b. In every music school, most guitar students wanted to play like the head instructor.

(6.15) a. Alice gave Timmy a brownie because she thought there weren't many cookies.
        b. I regret to inform you that your teams didn't meet the required standards for sportsmanship: The referee didn't observe three players congratulate three players. So you won't be advancing to the next round.

It is a substantive question to what extent the various syntactic and semantic properties track one another — e.g., being unbindable or referential, triggering an existence presupposition, being associated with implicit domain restriction, exhibiting notional definiteness (familiarity, maximality, uniqueness), etc.[45]

The choice-function-based analyses developed here may provide loci for representing certain notions of specificity. Consider the D+CP/XP analyses of (6.1) in (6.16)–(6.18). (Assume $[\![C]\!] = [\![C_{rel}]\!]$.)

(6.16) Every baby laughed.
        a. $[_S \ T^{\langle 1,a\rangle} \ [[C_d \ t_{1a}]^{\langle 1,s\rangle}$
            $[[_{DP^{\langle 2,a\rangle}} \ \text{every}^{\langle 2,a\rangle} \ [_{CP} \ F_{2cf}\text{-}g_2 \ \text{baby-}w_1\text{-}g_1 \ [[C \ t_{2a}]^{\langle 2,e\rangle} \ [t_{2e} \ P_{1et}\text{-}g_1]]]]$
            $t_{1s} \ \text{laughed}]]]$
        b. $[_S \ T^{\langle 1,a\rangle} \ [[C_d \ t_{1a}]^{\langle 1,s\rangle}$
            $[[_{DP^{\langle 2,a\rangle}} \ \text{every}^{\langle 2,a\rangle} \ [_{XP} \ P_{1et}\text{-}g_1 \ [X \ [F_{2cf}\text{-}t_{2a} \ \text{baby-}w_1\text{-}g_1]]]]]$
            $t_{1s} \ \text{laughed}]]]$

(6.17) $[\![X]\!] = \lambda x_e.\lambda P_{et}.\lambda y_e.\lambda g_g \, . \, y(g) = x(g) \wedge P(y)(g)$

(6.18) $[\![(6.16a)]\!] = [\![(6.16b)]\!] \approx \lambda g_g \, . \, \forall x_e \forall a_a : \big(x(g) = a(g)(2cf)(baby_{g^-(1s)})$
        $\wedge \, g^-(1et)(x(g)) \big) \rightarrow x(g) \text{ laughed in } @(g^-)$

---

[45] See e.g. Enç 1991, Szabolcsi 1994, de Hoop 1995, Lecarme 1996, 1999b, Giusti 1997, 2002, Matthewson 1998, 2013, Bhattacharya 1999a,b, Cardinaletti and Starke 1999, Lyons 1999, Danon 2001, Ihsane and Puskás 2001, von Heusinger 2002, 2011, Aboh 2004, Alexiadou et al. 2007, Faller and Hastings 2008, Hartmann 2008, Cowper and Hall 2009, Schwarz 2009, Gorrie et al. 2010, Gillon 2013, Paul et al. 2015, Sabbagh 2016, Türker 2019.

The derived semantic value treats 'every baby' as quantifying over individuals in the contextually relevant domain that could be chosen from among the babies — roughly, $\{o : o \in g_c(1et) \land o = F_{cf}(baby_{g_c(1s)})$, for some $F_{cf}\}$. First, "true" (Lecarme 2008: 204) quantificational DPs such as 'every baby' "presuppose existence" (Enç 1991: 11) insofar as the denotation of the choice-function pronoun is undefined for empty sets of individuals. If there are no babies, $h(2cf)(baby_{g_c(1s)})$ is undefined, and the sentence fails to receive a semantic value.[46] Second, the connection to a contextually relevant set of individuals — "D(iscourse)-linking" (Pesetsky 1987) — may be captured as a species of implicit domain restriction. The domain pronoun $[\mathbf{P}_{1et}\ \mathbf{g}_1]$ restricts the quantification to a topical subdomain of babies in $g_c(1et)$.[47]

Although D-linking is commonly understood as linking to a set of individuals relevant in the discourse, we have seen that the element providing the restriction may be shifted in modal environments (cf. §1.2). (6.19) needn't presuppose the existence of trolls or any contextually familiar set of trolls. The domain- and world-pronouns associated with 'every troll' receive local readings under the attitude verb, as reflected in (6.20). (For simplicity assume the D+XP analysis, and leave 'can-vote' as an unanalyzed predicate.)

(6.19) [Context (cf. (1.22)): Alice thinks there are magical trolls. She thinks that some groups of them aren't legally permitted to vote (e.g., baby trolls), but that no group with a moral right to vote is legally excluded from voting.]

Alice thinks every troll can vote.

≈ "Alice thinks there are trolls and that every troll in the groups she considers relevant in matters of voting rights is legally permitted to vote"

(6.20) a. $[_S\ T^{\langle 1,a \rangle}\ [[C_d\ t_{1a}]^{\langle 1,s \rangle}\ [Alice\ [[thinks\ t_{1s}]^{\langle 3,a \rangle}\ [[C_d\ t_{3a}]^{\langle 2,s \rangle}$
$[[_{DP^{\langle 2,a \rangle}}\ every^{\langle 2,a \rangle}\ [_{XP}\ P_{2et}\text{-}g_3\ [X\ [F_{2cf}\text{-}t_{2a}\ troll\text{-}w_1\text{-}g_3]]]]$
$t_{2s}\ can\text{-}vote]]]]]]$

---

[46] Lexical entries for $\mathbf{C}/\mathbf{C_{rel}}$ and $\mathbf{X}$ such as (i) would make the connections with presuppositionality even more explicit.

(i)   Presuppositional CP/XP (variant)
   a. $[\![\mathbf{C}]\!] = [\![\mathbf{C_{rel}}]\!] = \lambda a_a.\lambda P_{et}.\lambda x_e.\lambda y_e.\lambda g_g : x(g) = y(g) . P(y)(g)$
   b. $[\![\mathbf{X}]\!] = \lambda x_e.\lambda P_{et}.\lambda y_e.\lambda g_g : x(g) = y(g) . P(y)(g)$

[47] The domain pronoun could be world-indexed, type $\langle s, et \rangle$, to capture intensionality. I ignore this complication. For general discussion, see von Fintel 1994, Stanley and Szabó 2000, Martí 2002, Stanley 2002, Gillon 2013.

b. $[\![S]\!] \approx \lambda g_g . \, \forall a'_a : a'(g)$ is compatible with $\text{SOM}_{Alice, @(g^-)} \to$
$\left(\forall x_e \forall a_a : x(g) = a(g)(2\text{cf})(troll_{a'(g)(1s)}) \wedge a'(g)(2et)(x(g)) \to \right.$
$\left. x(g) \text{ can-vote in } @(a'(g)) \right)$

The attitude ascription is true iff for all possibilities h compatible with Alice's state of mind, every $o \in h(2et)$ that could be selected from the trolls in $@(h)$ can vote. The shifted domain $h(2et)$ represents a doxastic counterpart of the domain that would be determined by the discourse—here, say, the set of individuals to be considered in matters of voting rights. The local reading of the domain pronoun is captured analogously to the local readings of the pronouns in our examples from §4.

Positing a functional element such as a choice-function pronoun in of quantificational DPs has precedents in work on D-linking. Holmberg (1993) and Rullmann and Beck (1998) distinguish D-linked noun phrases in terms of an additional determiner or demonstrative (see also Santelmann 1993, Bhattacharya 1999a,b, Zamparelli 2000, Giusti 2002, Boeckx and Grohmann 2004). In some theories the specificity element is also treated as having an internal argument, such as a situation variable, which figures in determining the relevant domain (cf. von Fintel 1994, Büring 2004, Elbourne 2005, 2013, Schwarz 2009, Patel-Grosz and Grosz 2017). Our choice-function pronoun $[_{FP} \, [_{F^0} \, \mathbf{F_{cf}} \, \mathbf{g}] \, NP]$ in the extended NP layer might be understood analogously.

Some accounts positing an additional DP-internal element identify it as a definite article or deictic demonstrative.[48] Such identifications should be regarded with caution. Our identifying the choice-function pronoun in quantificational DPs with, say, a semantically definite determiner would be no more warranted for the general case than our identifying it with a relative word on the basis of examples with headed relative clauses. In the headed relative clause examples in §5 the choice-function pronoun is realized with a relative word; in quantifier phrases such as 'every baby' it is implicit; in St'át'imcets quantifier phrases it is realized with an overt determiner; in Somali quantifier phrases it is realized with syntactic definiteness marking. As Matthewson (1998, 1999, 2013) and Lecarme (1996, 1999b) are careful to point out, the determiners in St'át'imcets/Somali quantified expressions needn't exhibit semantic definiteness (see Gillon 2013 on Squamish Salish; cf. also Giusti 1992, 1997, 2002, Lyons 1999, Danon 2001, Kupisch and Koops 2007, Hallman 2016). Choice-function pronouns in F needn't be notionally definite in the sense of presupposing that the selected individuals have been previously introduced in the discourse. Additional constraints may be

---

[48] Cf.: "Since both types of pronouns denote individuals, the most plausible assumption is that both contain a definite determiner" (Patel-Grosz and Grosz 2017: 272).

associated with particular (types of) expressions — e.g., a feature restricting to choice functions whose domain/range is restricted to individuals in a particular discourse-determined domain. Such lexical or construction-specific differences may yield a more refined typology of the spectrum of "specificity" effects within and across languages (more on this in §§7, 9.3).

For simplicity I have assumed that quantifier words occupy D; this is inessential. For instance, Chomsky (2007) gives syntactic arguments for reviving the idea that the head of the noun phrase is a nominal element n, rather than a functional determiner per the DP hypothesis (see also Bruening 2009, Satık 2017). For definite/specific nominals Chomsky suggests in passing an analysis as $[_{n^*P}\ n^*\ DP]$, with n^* parallel to v^* in complete verb phrases (2007: 25–26).[49] The D+XP-style analysis in (6.7) could be adapted in developing an nP account of noun phrases along these lines — e.g., identifying X with n^*, and F with Chomsky's D.[50] In quantified noun phrases the quantifier would raise from the internal assignment-argument position of D^0, analogously to how modal elements raise from the internal assignment-argument position of C^0. In (6.21a) the quantifier is treated as raising to the n^*P layer; in (6.21b) it heads its own projection QP. Representing the domain pronoun as an internal argument of the quantifier in Q^0 would bring the parallels with modals even closer.

(6.21) a. n^*P: Q n^*P (variant)

   $[_{n^*P}\ Q^{0^{\langle i,a\rangle}}\ [_{n^*P}\ (YP)\ X\ [_{DP}\ F_{cf}\text{-}t_{ia}\ NP]]]$

   b. QP: Q n^*P (variant)

   $[_{QP}\ Q^{0^{\langle i,a\rangle}}\ [_{n^*P}\ (YP)\ X\ [_{DP}\ F_{cf}\text{-}t_{ia}\ NP]]]$

§7 develops the syntax/semantics in precisely this way.

6.2 Genitives and Restrictive Modification

The previous discussion focused primarily on independent morphosyntactic and semantic evidence for including a choice-function element in quantifier phrases. This section examines how analyses such as (6.6)–(6.7) can help capture certain other forms of restrictive modification, in particular in genitive constructions.

The D+XP/CP treatments of implicit domain restriction in (6.16)–(6.20) can be extended to certain overt restrictive modifiers (cf. Kayne 1994, Campbell

---

[49] On layered v analyses of verb phrases, see Kratzer 1996, Rackowski 2002, Hiraiwa 2005, Pylkkänen 2008, Harley 2013, 2017, Legate 2014, D'Alessandro et al. 2017, Wood and Marantz 2017. We will return to this in §6.2 and in detail in §7.

[50] Compare also the QP: Q+DP analysis of St'át'imcets quantifier phrases developed by Matthewson (1999, 2001, 2013). Matthewson also treats the NP as complement of a choice-function pronoun, which she represents as occupying D. However, Matthewson assimilates the contribution of the determiner qua choice-function pronoun with domain restriction (contrast (6.16), (6.20)).

1996, Alexiadou 2003, Koopman 2003, 2005, Luján 2004). In (6.22) 'girl' is given its usual $\langle e, t \rangle$ meaning; a lifted type or composition rule such as Predicate Modification (Heim and Kratzer 1998) isn't required.[51]

(6.22)   Every girl baby (laughed)

     a. every$^{\langle 2,a \rangle}$ [$_{CP}$ F_{2cf}-g_2 baby-w_1-g_1 [[C t_{2a}]$^{\langle 2,e \rangle}$ [t_{2e} girl-w_1-g_1]]]

     b. every$^{\langle 2,a \rangle}$ [$_{XP}$ girl-w_1-g_1 [X [F_{2cf}-t_{2a} baby-w_1-g_1]]]

     c. $[\![CP]\!] = [\![XP]\!] = \lambda x_e.\lambda g_g . x(g) = g(2a)(2cf)(baby_{g(1a)(1s)}) \wedge x(g)$ is a girl in $g(1a)(1s)$

The modified phrase 'every girl baby' quantifies over the set of individuals that are girls and could be chosen from the babies.

It is common following Partee (1983) to distinguish modifier readings vs. argument readings of genitives *X's Y*.[52] Informally put, in modifier ("free *R*") readings the relevant relation for interpreting the genitive is contextually supplied, whereas in argument ("inherent *R*") readings the relation is linguistically supplied by the nominal *Y* (see also Barker 1995, Partee and Borschev 2003, Badulescu and Moldovan 2008, Lichtenberk et al. 2011, van Rijn 2017).

(6.23)   "Inherent *R*" (argument) reading

     a. Alice's mother

     b. ≈ "the *o* such that *o* bears the *is a mother of* relation to Alice"

---

[51] I remain neutral regarding the base positions of different restrictive modifiers; the compositional semantics is compatible with (e.g.) positions left- or right-adjoined to $\overline{X}$/XP, or in Spec of X or some intermediate projection (see Cinque 2013: chs. 7, 13 on treating all modifiers of lexical heads as merged left of the head; see Alexiadou et al. 2007: part III and references therein on word-order differences crosslinguistically). I will ignore additional domain pronouns in examples with overt modifiers. Examples with multiple restrictive modifiers could be represented via iterated specifiers/adjuncts in the XP layer and a type-flexible lexical entry for X heads, as in (i)–(ii). (Analogous moves could be made in a D+CP analysis.) Alternatively, one could follow Cinque 1995 and treat apparent modifier iteration as asyndetic coordination (cf. Gil 2013). In some languages the coordination is overt, as in (iii).

(i)   every$^{\langle 2,a \rangle}$ [$_{XP}$ P_{1et} g_1 [freshman-w_1-g_1 [student-w_1-g_1 [X [F_{2cf}-t_{2a} athlete-w_1-g_1]]]]]

(ii)   *Polymorphic* X^0
     $[\![\mathbf{X}]\!] = \lambda x_e.\lambda P_{et}^1 \ldots \lambda P_{et}^n.\lambda y_e.\lambda g_g . y(g) = x(g) \wedge P^1(y)(g) \wedge \cdots \wedge P^n(y)(g)$

(iii)   a. xaashí-da yar **ee** cád
         paper-DET small and white
         'the small white sheet of paper'   (Lecarme 2008: ex. 6, Somali)
      b. May malaki-**ng** disyerto-**ng** nasa   Australya.
         exist big-LNKR desert-LNKR PRED.LOC Australia
         'There is a big desert that is in Australia' (Sabbagh 2009: 694; Tagalog (Austronesian))

[52] I will use 'genitive (DP)' for complex phrases such as *X's Y*. I use 'possessor' for *X*, though the relevant relation needn't be possession narrowly construed (more on which shortly); I sometimes use 'structural possessor/possessee' or scare quotes to highlight this point. I use 'genitive morpheme' for elements such as **'s**.

(6.24) "Free *R*" (restrictive modifier) reading

    a. Alice's cat

    b. ≈ "the *o* such that *o* is a cat and *o* bears R_c (e.g. *is a pet of*) to Alice"

In many languages the presence of the further relation in free *R* readings is overtly marked, as in (6.25). In some cases the additional element used in free *R* readings is historically derived from a relational noun (e.g., 'hand', 'home') or preposition, or an element expressing other thematic relations.[53] (I will use 'POSS$_{fr}$' in glosses for free *R* genitive markers.)

(6.25)   a.   qatu-ku

             head-1SG.GEN

             'my head'

---

[53] See Dixon 1980: ch. 10, 2010: ch. 16, Merlan 1982, Lichtenberk 1985, 2002, 2009b, Chappell and McGregor 1989, Heine et al. 1991: §6.1, Koptjevskaja-Tamm 1996, 2001, Heine 1997: chs. 2–3, Song 1997, Aikhenvald 2000, 2013, Heine and Kuteva 2002, Sato 2009, Frajzyngier 2013, Sabbagh 2016, van Rijn 2017. For instance, in (i) the first occurrence of *la-* expresses a general possession relation, the second occurrence a benefactive relation; the free *R* marker *a* in (ii-a) is used to introduce the agentive subject in (ii-b). In languages with multiple free *R* markers, some markers may be subspecialized for different sorts of relations, e.g. that "x is food for y" as in (iii-c)–(iii-d).

(i)   Sohn el   mole-lah [ik **la**-l   Sepe ah] [**la**-l   Sru].

         John 3SG.SBJ buy-ASP fish POSS$_{fr}$-3SG.POSS Sepe DET POSS$_{fr}$-3SG.POSS Sru

         'John has bought Sepe's fish for Sru.'   (Song 1997: 33; Kusaiean (Austronesian))

(ii)   a.   nga kur [**a**   Mere]

           ART dog POSS$_{fr}$ Mere

           'Mere's dogs'

      b.   ka whakamau [**a**   Mere] i   te   taura.

           T/A fasten   POSS$_{fr}$ Mere ACC ART rope

           'Mere is fastening the rope.'

                           (Harlow 2007: 166, Chung 1973: 652; Maori (Austronesian))

(iii)   a.   sina-gu

           mother-my

           'my mother'

      b.   **e**-gu   udo

           POSS$_{fr}$-my taro

           'my taro'

      c.   **a**-gu   udo

           POSS$_{fr.edib}$-my taro

           'my taro (to eat)'

      d.   [Context: a man who contracts to eat parts of a motor-car in a sideshow says:]

           a-gu   motoka

           POSS$_{fr.edib}$-my car

           'my car (to eat)'   (Lynch 1973: 71, 87, 99n.18; Suau (Austronesian))

These patterns, in which the forms used in free *R* readings are at least as morphologically complex or marked as the corresponding forms used in inherent *R* readings, are crosslinguistically robust (see previous references, also Seiler 1983a, Haiman 1985: 130–136, Nichols 1988, Chappell and McGregor 1996, Stolz et al. 2008, Helmbrecht 2016: §4, Haspelmath 2017).

b. **no**-ku   qatu

   POSS$_{fr}$-1SG.GEN head

   'my head (e.g. pig's head)'

                                    (Hyslop 2001: 170, 183; Lolovoli (Austronesian))

This contrast in readings can be given a structural basis — namely, in whether the "possessor"+relation is supplied by the NP, with the relation given by the head noun (inherent R readings), or is represented in a position for restrictive modifiers, with the relation supplied by an implicit pronoun (free R readings).[54]

Consider first a D+CP implementation in which the genitive morpheme 's is treated as the head determiner, as in (6.28); an assignment-quantificational def-

---

[54] As may be anticipated, iterated free R possessor modifiers and free R modifiers with saturated relational nouns are attested, as in (i)–(ii), respectively (see also Partee and Borschev 2003: 83, 100, Lichtenberk 2009b: 396–397, Sato 2009: 358–361).

(i)   il-kotba   ta'   Pietru ta'   l-awtur   favorit tieghi
        DEF-books POSS$_{fr}$ Peter POSS$_{fr}$ DEF-author favorite my
        'Peter's books by my favorite author'   (Koptjevskaja-Tamm 1996: 266; Maltese)

(ii)   nək-k   nelk-n
        POSS$_{fr.edib}$-1SG leg-3SG.GEN
        'my leg of its (e.g., of chicken, to eat)'   (Lynch 1973: 91; Lenakel (Austronesian))

Uniform analyses of free/inherent R readings are also possible — e.g., reducing inherent R readings to free R readings in which the supplied relation is identified with the relation expressed by the head noun, or reducing free R readings to inherent R readings in which the head noun is coerced to having a relevant relational meaning (e.g. *is a TV owned by*) (Jensen and Vikner 1994; cf. von Prince 2016). Though the latter sort of shift in argument structure certainly occurs, Partee and Borschev (2003) conclude that a uniform approach of either type is incorrect for English. Interestingly, the distinction between argument vs. modifier "possessors" can be reflected in the distribution of tense morphemes in languages with nominal tense. Lecarme (1996, 1999b, 2004) observes that tense morphemes in Somali typically cannot appear on the head nominal in genitives with partitive, kinship, and body-part nouns, as in (iii). Data such as (iv) from Pomak support the hypothesis that the distribution of tense features correlates with the distinction between free R vs. inherent R readings. The body-part noun in the free R reading in (iv-a) bears interpretable tense features (cf. Adamou 2011). (Thanks to Evangelia Adamou.)

(iii)   macallimád-ood-íi   iyo habár-tood(*-ii)
        teacher-DET.POSS3PL-PAST and mother-DET.POSS3PL-PAST
        'their teacher and their mother'   (Lecarme 2004: ex. 32; Somali)

(iv)   [Context: We're medical students practicing on cadavers (=(6.29))]
        a. ören'ciete   ra'kota
           student-DEF.PAST hand-DEF.PAST
           'the student's hand (was broken)'   (free R reading, cf. (6.29a); tense on head noun)
        b. ören'civata   'roka
           student-DEF.PAST hand
           'the student's hand (was broken)'   (inherent R reading, cf. (6.29b); tense on possessor)
                                               (Evangelia Adamou, p.c.; Pomak (Slavic))

The contrasting analyses for free R vs. inherent R genitives in what follows may support a "purely structural" (Lecarme 2004: 15) basis for the distribution of tense morphemes, without requiring questionable semantic or metaphysical assumptions about the (a)temporality of certain relations or fundamental appeals to notions of "alienable" vs. "inalienable" possession (as in Lecarme 1996, 1999b, 2004).

inite semantics is in (6.26), for now assuming $[\![\text{'s}]\!] = [\![\iota_o]\!]$. (For readability I introduce the metalanguage ι operator, to be understood as in (6.26). I will use 'R'/'$\mathbf{R}$' in indices/pronouns for type $\langle e, et\rangle$. Assume that structures such as (6.27b)–(6.28b) are situated in LFs of the form $[_S \mathbf{T}^{\langle 1,a\rangle} [[\mathbf{C_d} \, \mathbf{t_{1a}}]^{\langle 1,s\rangle} \ldots \mathbf{V} \, \mathbf{t_{1s}}]].)$[55]

(6.26) $\quad [\![\iota_o]\!] = \lambda P^+_{\langle a,et\rangle}.\lambda Q^+_{\langle a,et\rangle}.\lambda g_g . \exists x_e \exists a_a \colon P^+(a)(x)(g) \wedge$

$\qquad \quad \big(\forall y_e \colon P^+(a)(y)(g) \to y(g) = x(g)\big) \wedge Q^+(a)(x)(g)$

$\qquad = \lambda P^+_{\langle a,et\rangle}.\lambda Q^+_{\langle a,et\rangle}.\lambda g_g . \exists x_e \exists a_a \colon \big(x(g) = \text{the } o \text{ s.t. } ({}^{\downarrow}P^+)(a(g))(o)\big)$

$\qquad \quad \wedge Q^+(a)(x)(g)$

$\qquad = \lambda P^+_{\langle a,et\rangle}.\lambda Q^+_{\langle a,et\rangle}.\lambda g_g . \big[\iota x(g)\exists a_a \colon P^+(a)(x)(g)\big] Q^+(a)(x)(g)$

(6.27) D+CP "free R" (modifier) reading LF

    a. Bert's TV is broken.

    b. ... 's$^{\langle 2,a\rangle}$ $[_{CP}$ $[F_{2cf}$-g_2 TV-w_1-$g_1]$ $[[C \, t_{2a}]^{\langle 1,e\rangle}$ $[t_{1e} \, [R_1$-g_1 Bert]$]]]$ ...

    c. $[\![S]\!] \approx \lambda g_g . \big[\iota x(g)\exists a_a \colon x(g) = a(g)(2cf)(TV_{g^-(1s)}) \wedge$

        $g^-(1R)(\text{Bert})(x(g))\big]\, x(g)$ is broken in $@(g^-)$

    d. $\approx$ "the o such that there is a choice function that selects o from the TVs and o bears the relevant relation $g_c(1R)$ to Bert, is broken"

(6.28) D+CP "inherent R" (argument) reading LF

    a. Bert's hand is broken.

    b. ... 's$^{\langle 2,a\rangle}$ $[_{CP}$ $[F_{2cf}$-g_2 [hand-w_1-g_1 Bert]] $[[C \, t_{2a}]^{\langle 1,e\rangle}$ $[t_{1e} \, P_{1et}$-$g_1]]]$ ...

    c. $[\![S]\!] \approx \lambda g_g . \big[\iota x(g)\exists a_a \colon x(g) = a(g)(2cf)(hand\text{-}of\text{-}Bert_{g^-(1s)}) \wedge$

        $g^-(1et)(x(g))\big]\, x(g)$ is broken in $@(g^-)$

    d. $\approx$ "the o such that there is a choice function that selects o from the hands of Bert and o is in the relevant set of entities $g_c(1et)$, is broken"

The domain pronoun $[\mathbf{P_{1et}} \, \mathbf{g_1}]$ in (6.28) captures how the inherent R reading can be felicitous even if Bert has more than one hand (cf. Jespersen 1924: 110–111). If the contextually relevant domain $g_c(1et)$ includes only one of Bert's hands, the uniqueness condition is satisfied. Likewise for the felicitous free R and inherent R readings of 'Bert's hand' in (6.29):

---

[55] I will ignore intensionality with the relation pronoun, and I leave open the category of the possessor+relation-pronoun constituent in free R readings. In §7.5 I will suggest analyzing it as a Case phrase $[_{KP}$ K DP], with the general function of (non-vacuous) K heads being to introduce thematic arguments (cf. n. 53). I revisit the argument structure for relational predicates in §7.1. See den Dikken 1995, Heine 1997, Larson and Cho 2003 for precedents in treating possessor phrases in free R readings as having a predicative syntax/semantics. See Kayne 1994, Alexiadou 2003 for D+CP analyses of free R readings. Note that X's isn't a constituent on either type of reading, e.g.:

(i)   a. *What boy's were you rooting for a team of?

       b. *What boy's were you talking to a brother of?

(6.29)   [Context: We're medical students practicing on cadavers.]

    a.   Bert's hand is broken. It's obvious, but I bet he won't notice and will get the diagnosis wrong.   (*free R*)

    b.   Bert's hand is broken. There's no way he'll be able to pass the practice exam with his cast on.   (*inherent R*)

The relevant value for the relation pronoun in (6.29a) associates Bert with the body part(s) he is currently practicing on.

The previous D+CP implementation captures the specificity of prenominal genitives in the semantics of the genitive morpheme, treated as occupying D. Such an analysis is awkward for predicate-position uses, such as with the postnominal genitives in (6.30).

(6.30)   a.   every cat/sister of Alice's

    b.   The winner was a cat/sister of Alice's.

More promising is to distinguish the genitive morpheme from the head determiner in argument-position uses. Following Partee (1983) the prenominal genitive can be treated along the lines of a postnominal genitive with a higher (possibly implicit) definite element, i.e. roughly *A's B* ≈ *the B of A('s)*. A D+XP syntax affords a natural implementation. The genitive morpheme occupies X. Overt articles in predicative uses such as (6.31) can be understood as realizing the choice-function element. (Thanks to Miklós Rédei.)

(6.31)   Ez   a   kalap [Mari-nak **a**   kalap-ja]$_{\text{PRED}}$.
       this DET hat   Mari-DAT DET hat-POSS
       'This hat is Mary's hat/a hat of Mary's.'   (Hungarian)

D+XP analyses of free *R* and inherent *R* readings are in (6.34)–(6.35). It isn't uncommon crosslinguistically for genitive markers to be diachronically or synchronically related to markers of restrictive modification,[56] as in (6.32) with *ge*; the revised entry for **'s** in (6.33) directly implements such a function.

(6.32)   a. a^{33}-faay^{55} ge^{33} piŋ^{11}-guo^{35}
         Ah Fai   ASSOC apple
         'Ah Fai's apple'
    b.   hooŋ^{11} ge^{33} piŋ^{11}-guo^{35}
         red   ASSOC apple
         'red apple'

---

[56] See Dixon 1969, 1980: ch. 10, Matisoff 1972, Heine 1997: 149–150, Heine and Kuteva 2002, Heath 2008, Lichtenberk 2009b, Aikhenvald 2013, Frajzyngier 2013, Gil 2013, Nikolaeva and Spencer 2013, van Rijn 2017, Thurgood and LaPolla 2017.

c. a^{33}-faay^{55} maai^{13} ge^{33} piŋ^{11}-guo^{35}

   Ah Fai   buy   ASSOC apple

   'apple that Ah Fai bought'   (Gil 2013: ex. 3; Cantonese)

(6.33) $\llbracket$'s$\rrbracket = \lambda x_e.\lambda P_{et}.\lambda y_e.\lambda g_g \cdot y(g) = x(g) \wedge P(y)(g)$

(6.34) D+XP free R prenominal/postnominal genitive LFs

a. Alice's cat / every cat of Alice's (jumped)

b. ι_o/every$^{\langle 2,a\rangle}$ [$_{XP}$ [R$_1$-g$_1$ Alice] ['s [F$_{2cf}$-t$_{2a}$ cat-w$_1$-g$_1$]]]

c. $\llbracket$XP$\rrbracket \approx \lambda x_e.\lambda g_g \cdot x(g) = g(2a)(2cf)(cat_{g(1a)(1s)}) \wedge$

     $g(1a)(1R)(\text{Alice})(x(g))$

d. [$_S$ T$^{\langle 1,a\rangle}$ [[C$_d$ t$_{1a}$]$^{\langle 1,s\rangle}$ [[every$^{\langle 2,a\rangle}$ XP] t$_{1s}$ jumped]]]

    $\llbracket$S$\rrbracket \approx \lambda g_g \cdot \forall x_e \forall a_a \colon \big(x(g) = a(g)(2cf)(cat_{g^-(1s)}) \wedge$

     $g^-(1R)(\text{Alice})(x(g))\big) \to x(g)$ jumped in @(g^-)

(6.35) D+XP inherent R prenominal/postnominal genitive LFs

a. Alice's brother / every brother of Alice's (jumped)

b. ι_o/every$^{\langle 2,a\rangle}$ [$_{XP}$ [P$_{1et}$ g$_1$] ['s [F$_{2cf}$ t$_{2a}$ [brother-w$_1$-g$_1$ Alice]]]]

c. $\llbracket$XP$\rrbracket \approx \lambda x_e.\lambda g_g \cdot x(g) = g(2a)(2cf)(bro\text{-}of\text{-}A_{g(1a)(1s)}) \wedge$

     $g(1a)(1et)(x(g))$

d. [$_S$ T$^{\langle 1,a\rangle}$ [[C$_d$ t$_{1a}$]$^{\langle 1,s\rangle}$ [[every$^{\langle 2,a\rangle}$ XP] t$_{1s}$ jumped]]]

    $\llbracket$S$\rrbracket \approx \lambda g_g \cdot \forall x_e \forall a_a \colon \big(x(g) = a(g)(2cf)(bro\text{-}of\text{-}A_{g^-(1s)}) \wedge$

     $g^-(1et)(x(g))\big) \to x(g)$ jumped in @(g^-)

As previously, in the inherent R reading in (6.35) the structural "possessor" is an argument of the head noun; in the free R reading in (6.34) the possessor+relation-pronoun in the XP layer functions as a restrictive modifier (cf. Tellier 1991, Kayne 1993, Español-Echevarría 1997, Alexiadou 2003, van Rijn 2017). In both cases the XP constituent representing the genitive construction is type $\langle e, t\rangle$ ((6.34c)–(6.35c)). This XP is suitable to combine with an overt quantifier, as in postnominal genitives (cf. (6.34d)–(6.35d)), or an implicit definite, as in English prenominal genitives. Additional resources aren't required for the compositional semantics of postnominal genitives.[57]

---

[57] See Taylor 1989: 682–683, Partee and Borschev 2003, Storto 2003, Dixon 2010: 295–296 on apparent interpretive restrictions with postnominal genitives of the form *B of A's* in English. I leave open how the pronounced forms of prenominal and postnominal genitives are derived in the narrow syntax and morphophonolological components. For prenominal inherent *R* readings, 's and the "possessor" DP could fuse via Local Dislocation (Embick and Noyer 2001), yielding e.g. [[Alice+'s] brother] directly from ['s [$_{NP}$ [Alice] brother]]. In English *B of A's* constructions the head noun may then raise to Spec of a (semantically vacuous) higher functional head, arguably realizing 'of'. For relevant discussion see Szabolcsi 1983, Tellier 1991, Kayne 1993, 1994, Barker 1995, den Dikken 1995, Español-Echevarría 1997, Siloni 1997, Alexiadou and Wilder 1998, Bhattacharya 1999b, Alexiadou 2003, Kim et al. 2004, Lecarme 2004, Nunes 2004, Bernstein and Tortora 2005, Boneh and Sichel 2010.

The analyses in (6.27)–(6.28) and (6.34)–(6.35) both maintain a uniform semantics for 's. The intuitive contrast between free R and inherent R readings needn't require positing a lexical ambiguity in the genitive morpheme, systematic lexical coercion, or type shifting (as in e.g. Partee 1983, Jensen and Vikner 1994, Vikner and Jensen 2002, Partee and Borschev 2003). The distinction between "possessors" as arguments vs. restrictive modifiers can be captured in terms of general features of the structure of DPs.

Like many other pronouns, the implicit relation pronoun in free R readings may receive alternative local or global readings. Suppose Bert and Ernie are former roommates, and there is a dispute about who is to be responsible for which of their pet ducks, Ducky and Fluffy. Bert was the original owner of Ducky, and Ernie was the original owner of Fluffy; but Bert's lifestyle is more conducive to Fluffy's general welfare, and Ernie's lifestyle is more conducive to Ducky's general welfare (perhaps Fluffy dislikes the water). Suppose we all agree that the rightful owner is the one who would be in the duck's best interest (Bert and Ernie aren't party to our conversation). In such a context we can felicitously say (6.36) to describe Chip's beliefs about Ducky, even if we assume Chip isn't acquainted with Ernie and may have no idea about Ducky's relation to Ernie. The value for the relation pronoun determined by the discourse assignment maps $\langle \text{Ernie}, y \rangle$ to True iff y = Ducky.

(6.36)　Chip thinks^k Ernie's$_i$ duck is brown, but that's because it was really dirty when Chip saw it.

Alternatively, if we are talking about Bert and how he wants to keep Ducky for himself, we might say (6.37). If Bert has been confused in his biology, we might say (6.38). The local reading of the relation-pronoun comes apart from the global reading of the head noun's world-pronoun.

(6.37)　Bert wants^k his$_k$ duck to be Ducky (but his$_i$ duck is really Fluffy).

(6.38)　Bert thinks^k his$_k$ duck$_i$ is a loon$_k$.

Suppose that Ernie mistakes Fluffy for a loon, yet is more altruistic, willing to yield Fluffy to Bert. We might characterize the unfortunate state of affairs with the quantified attitude ascription in (6.39). The bound reading of the relation pronoun is derived analogously to the bound reading of the modal background pronoun in the quantified modal attitude ascription from §4.3.

(6.39) Everyone thinks Bert's duck is a loon.

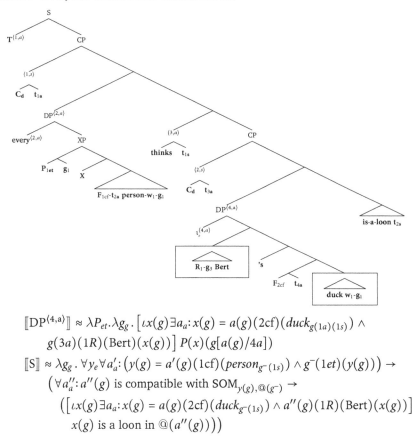

$$\llbracket DP^{\langle 4,a\rangle}\rrbracket \approx \lambda P_{et}.\lambda g_g . \big[\iota x(g)\exists a_a : x(g) = a(g)(2cf)(duck_{g(1a)(1s)}) \wedge$$
$$g(3a)(1R)(Bert)(x(g))\big] P(x)(g[a(g)/4a])$$

$$\llbracket S\rrbracket \approx \lambda g_g . \forall y_e \forall a'_a : \big(y(g) = a'(g)(1cf)(person_{g^-(1s)}) \wedge g^-(1et)(y(g))\big) \rightarrow$$
$$\big(\forall a''_a : a''(g) \text{ is compatible with } SOM_{y(g),@(g^-)} \rightarrow$$
$$\big(\big[\iota x(g)\exists a_a : x(g) = a(g)(2cf)(duck_{g^-(1s)}) \wedge a''(g)(1R)(Bert)(x(g))\big]$$
$$x(g) \text{ is a loon in } @(a''(g))\big)\big)$$

This says, roughly, that for every relevant o—every $o \in g_c(1et)$ selectable from the persons—for every possibility h compatible with o's state of mind, the o' such that o' bears $h(1R)$ to Bert and o' is identical to some actual duck or other, is a loon in $@(h)$. The domain pronoun $[\mathbf{P}_{1et}\,\mathbf{g}_1]$ restricts the quantification to the contextually relevant individuals, say $g_c(1et) = \{\text{Bert, Ernie, Ducky, Fluffy}\}$. The relation-pronoun $[\mathbf{R}_1\,\mathbf{g}_3]$ in the representation of 'Bert's duck' receives a local reading under the attitude verb. Roughly put, the shifted value for the pronoun relates Bert to individuals determined to be properly in Bert's charge; per §§3.4, 4, the shifted value represents the quantificational subject's epistemic counterpart of the relation $g_c(1R)$ that would be determined by the discourse assignment. For every possibility h' compatible with Bert's state of mind, Ducky $\in h'(1R)(\text{Bert})$, and for every possibility h'' compatible with Ernie's state of mind, Fluffy $\in h''(1R)(\text{Bert})$. By contrast, the world-pronoun $[\mathbf{w}_1 \, \mathbf{g}_1]$ associated with 'duck' receives a global reading. The truth of (6.39) requires that Fluffy and Ducky are selectable from the set of actual ducks, and that Bert thinks Ducky is a loon and Ernie thinks Fluffy is a loon.

A D+XP analysis helps capture connections between individual quantification and genitive modification, often ignored in compositional semantic accounts. An attractive hypothesis is that the nominal XP projection posited in quantificational DPs just is the projection headed by the genitive morpheme in genitive constructions. As we have seen, in various languages individual quantification is expressed via a genitive construction (cf. (6.11)–(6.12)). Our X arguably corresponds to the head posited for assigning genitive Case in quantifier complements in certain Slavic languages, as in (6.40) (see also Bošković 2006, 2014).[58]

(6.40) Mnogo (nekih)   ljudi   želi pravdu.
        many some.GEN people.GEN want justice
        'Many (different) people want justice.'
                    (Hartmann and Milićević 2009: exs. 14, 23; Serbian)

In light of her extensive work on nominal tense in genitives, Lecarme even concludes that "genitive constructions universally involve a form of quantification" (2004: 17; cf. Borschev et al. 2008, Hartmann and Milićević 2009, Peters and Westerståhl 2013).

The semantics for the genitive morpheme in (6.33) is equivalent to the semantics for **X** in (6.17). X heads may of course differ with respect to other syntactic and semantic features. For instance, there may be morphosyntactic differences such as regarding case and EPP properties. In English prenominal genitives, X is overt and an overt structural "possessor" in Spec,X is required. In English quantifier phrases such as (6.41a), X is implicit. As we have seen, in some languages the (genitive) Case assigned by X may have morphological content in ordinary quantifier phrases. In explicit partitives such as (6.41b), the definite article spells out the choice-function pronoun, and the Case-assigning element may be pronounced. A first-pass analysis of the partitive falls out of

---

[58] As is common, we can regard morphological case marking as generally accompanying abstract Case assignment even if the two are conceptually distinct (Marantz 1991, Harley 1995). Notably, the layered DP syntax developed in Bhattacharya 1999a,b and Hiraiwa 2005 also identify distinct heads for Case/agreement and a specificity element under D, roughly as in (i) (Bhattacharya 1999a, 1999b: 85–98, Hiraiwa 2005: 201, 213–214; I use neutral category labels F_1, F_2 for consistency; cf. also Zamparelli 2000, Megerdoomian 2008, 2009, Himmelmann 2016). Bhattacharya's and Hiraiwa's nominal shell under D is essentially the same XP structure posited in this section: the (implicit) choice-function pronoun instantiates F_2, and X corresponds to F_1.

(i)   D $[_{F_1P} F_1 [_{F_2P} F_2 \text{ nP}]]$

the general D+XP structure; special semantic operations such as type shifting (Ladusaw 1982, Giannakidou 2004) aren't required.

(6.41)   a.   'all puppies'
         $\text{all}^{(i,a)}$ [$_{XP}$ P$_{et}$ g [X [F$_{cf}$-t$_{ia}$ puppies-w-g]]]
    b.   'all (of) the puppies'
         $\text{all}^{(i,a)}$ [$_{XP}$ P$_{et}$ g [X(of) [the$_{cf}$-t$_{ia}$ puppies-w-g]]]

In some languages partitives can also be realized with a genitive construction. In addition to the prenominal strategy in (6.42a), genitive partitives in Somali can be realized via a "construct state" construction, as in (6.42b). Somali genitives of the latter form require linear adjacency without preposition or case (Lecarme 1996, 1999b, 2004).

(6.42)   a.   macallimín-tii   qaar-k-óod   (baa la   xeray).
          professors-DET+PAST part-DET+POSS.3PL DECL one put-in-jail
    b.   qáar macállimín-tii   ká mid ah (baa la   xeray).
          part professors-DET+PAST one from be DECL one put-in-jail
          'Some of the professors (have been put in jail)'
                                     (Lecarme 1999b: ex. 35; Somali)

In (6.42a) X is overt; in (6.42b) it is implicit.

X heads may also differ with respect to semantic features such as thematic roles. As Partee and Borschev put it, "an argument [inherent *R*] genitive is most like a direct object, an 'internal argument' ... A 'possessor' [free *R*] genitive, on the other hand, is most subject-like, agent-like, less like an internal argument, more independent" (2003: 100; cf. Haiman 1985: 130–136, Nichols 1988, 1992: 116–122, Heine 1997: §3.4, Alexiadou 2003). In various language families this distinction is reflected in the morphology. The contrasting readings of 'my story' in (6.43a)–(6.44a) are reflected in constructions introducing the possessor on the model of an object (cf. (6.43b)) vs. an agentive subject of a deverbal (cf. (6.44b)). In (6.45), only in the free *R* reading can the possessor be introduced with the transitive-subject marker.[59]

(6.43)   a.   nounage ín   Titoga
         story   TRANS Titoga
         'Titoga's story (i.e. the story about Titoga)'

---

[59] See also Chung 1973, Seiler 1983a,b, Mosel 1984, Lichtenberk 1985, 2009a,b, Chappell and McGregor 1989, Koptjevskaja-Tamm 1996, Sato 2009, Dixon 2010: ch. 16, Aikhenvald 2013, von Prince 2016, Haspelmath 2017, van Rijn 2017.

    b. i-ak-am-ɨgn-ín   uus aan
       1EXCL-CONCURR-CONT-afraid-TRANS man that
       'I am afraid of that man.'

(6.44) a. nounage **taha** Titoga
         story   POSS$_{fr}$ Titoga
         'Titoga's story (i.e. the one he told)'
       b. n-arɨk-aan   **taha**-mar   le   nauanu uk
         NOMZ-stay-NOMZ POSS$_{fr}$-1EXCL.PL LOC village this
         'our staying in this village'
                              (Lynch 1978: 31, 86, 111; Lenakel (Austronesian))

(6.45) thau na   vanua/*ama
       I   TRANS.SBJ village/father
       'my village/father'   (cf. Lynch 1973: 74, 86; Aroma (Austronesian))

Such structural differences may correspond to semantic differences. As Mosel notes, the "very same" range of relations expressed in free R marked possessives — "relationships which presuppose activity, control or voluntariness on [the] part of the possessor" — "is expressed by the agent noun phrase and the verb in active ... clauses" (1984: 36–37; cf. Harlow 2007: 163–170). Unlike inherent R readings, free R readings are often associated with a "default preference ... for a genitive relation in the family of 'owns', 'possesses', 'controls'" (Partee and Borschev 2003: 70). In some languages, modifier genitives obligatorily receive possession readings, as with Russian prenominal possessives such as (6.46). Although the range of relations under the heading of "possession" can be broad, it is more constrained than the range of relations potentially associated with argument genitives generally.[60]

(6.46) Petin   ubijca
       Petja-POSS-M.SG murderer-M.SG
       a.#'Petja's murderer' / 'the murderer of Petja'
       b. 'a murderer Petja has hired'   (Partee and Borschev 2003: ex. 25b)

The proposed D+XP analyses reflect these distinctions. In free R readings the possessor originates in Spec,X — a position analogous to the position of agentive subjects in Spec,v*, as mentioned in §6.1 (more on this in §7). The geni-

---

[60] See Seiler 1983a, Nichols 1988, Chappell and McGregor 1989, 1996, Taylor 1989, Barker 1995: ch. 2, Langacker 1995, Koptjevskaja-Tamm 1996, Heine 1997, Marantz 1997, Partee and Borschev 2003, Storto 2003, Lee-Schoenfeld 2006, Badulescu and Moldovan 2008, Payne 2009, Dixon 2010: ch. 16, Lichtenberk et al. 2011, Aikhenvald 2013.

tive morpheme can be treated as assigning a broadly possessional θ-role—
optionally in English, obligatorily in certain genitive constructions in other
languages. In inherent *R* readings the structural "possessor" originates as the
object argument of a relational noun. Though the possessor nominal may
receive (genitive) Case assignment from X, its θ-role is assigned in its base
position.[61]

Let's recap. The previous sections examined several ways of extending the
assignment-variable-based syntax/semantics for headed relative constructions
in §5 to quantifier phrases with non-relative complements. I argued that a
generalized D+CP/XP account is motivated by crosslinguistic diachronic, morphological, and syntactic data, and it helps capture a range of independent linguistic phenomena, including semantic connections with notions of "specificity"
(broadly construed), non-relative restrictive modification, and the distinction
between free *R* (modifier) and inherent *R* (argument) readings of genitives.
The assignment-quantificational semantics is compatible with different ways of
filling out the syntactic details. Yet I speculated that a D+XP implementation for
non-relativized quantificational DPs may have advantages over a D+CP implementation. The posited XP projection is independently motivated by connections between individual quantification and genitive constructions, and parallels
between nominal and verbal domains. The D+XP analyses afford a common basic
structure for prenominal and postnominal genitives, and capture the distinction
between free *R* and inherent *R* readings in terms of a more general treatment of
restrictive modification. The independent features of the proposed analyses provide further motivation for the LFs used in capturing the linguistic shifting data,
which constitute the project's primary focus. The remainder of the chapter applies
our generalized assignment-variable syntax/semantics of quantifier phrases to
several additional phenomena with pronominal anaphora and binding.

6.3 Bound Pronouns

Many accounts of semantic binding require $\overline{\text{A}}$-movements such as QR in order to
capture bound readings (cf. May 1985, Heim and Kratzer 1998, Kayne 2002). In
Heim and Kratzer's (1998) account, although the subject-position quantifier in
(6.47a) needn't raise for type reasons, it must QR in order to generate the binder
index that binds the pronoun, as in (6.47b). (Assume a simplified "the-N-of-o"
analysis of the possessive pronoun.)

---

[61] It might be tempting to compare the checking of genitive Case on the object of the relational
noun by X/n* with the checking of accusative Case on the direct object of an active transitive verb by
v*, e.g. via Agree (Chomsky 2000, 2001). Like how active v* assigns an agent θ-role to the external
argument generated in its specifier, possessive X/n* assigns a broadly possessor θ-role. We will return
to syntactic/semantic parallels between noun phrases and verb phrases in detail in §7.

(6.47) a. Every puppy likes its owner.

         b. [$_S$ every puppy [2 [t_2 likes the-owner-of-it$_2$]]]

                                        (cf. Heim and Kratzer 1998: 262–264)

Drawing on the treatment of donkey pronouns from §5.2, suppose we represent the bound pronoun as a copy of the antecedent FP in the quantifier phrase. The assignment-binding introduced by the quantifier derives the bound reading, as reflected in (6.48) (again assuming the ad hoc analysis of 'its').

(6.48) a. [$_S$ T$^{\langle 1,a \rangle}$ [[C$_d$ t$_{1a}$]$^{\langle 1,s \rangle}$

              [[$_{DP^{\langle 2,a \rangle}}$ every$^{\langle 2,a \rangle}$ [$_{XP}$ P$_{1et}$-g$_1$ X [F$_{2cf}$-g$_2$ puppy-w$_1$-g$_1$]]]

              [$_{VP}$ likes t$_{1s}$ [the-owner-of-it$_{2cf}$-g$_2$-~~puppy~~-w$_1$-g$_1$]]]]]

         b. $[\![S]\!] \approx \lambda g_g \,.\, \forall x_e \forall a_a \colon \big(x(g) = a(g)(2cf)(puppy_{g^-(1s)}) \wedge$

              $g^-(1et)(x(g))\big) \to$

              $x(g)$ likes the-owner-of-$a(g)(2cf)(puppy_{g^-(1s)})$ in $@(g^-)$

Non-type-driven QR of the subject-position quantifier isn't required.

    Support for (6.48) may come from languages in which bound readings can be overtly realized with a pronounced copy of the antecedent, as in (6.49).[62]

(6.49) **Aajarn**$_i$ khit   waa puak rua chob **aajarn**$_i$.

        teacher think that all   we like teacher

        'The teacher$_i$ thinks we like him$_i$.'   (Lee 2003: ex. 38; Thai)

Interestingly, whereas complex donkey-anaphoric copies are possible in some languages, as we saw in §5.2.1, bound-pronoun copies with morphologically complex antecedents are generally excluded, as in (6.50) (see Lee 2003, Mortensen 2003, Nunes 2004, Boeckx et al. 2007).

---

    [62] Copied bound-variable readings with names are also possible in such languages, as in (i). A D+XP adaptation of the choice-function-based predicativist account from §4.4, say along the lines in (ii), would provide a straightforward account.

(i)   R-ralloh   Gye'eihlly$_i$ r-yu'làáa'z-ënn Gye'eihlly$_i$ chiru' zë'cy cahgza' Li'eb.

       HAB-think Mike   HAB-like-1PL Mike   also likewise   Felipe

       'Mike$_i$ thinks we like him$_i$, and so does Felipe$_j$ (think we like him$_j$)'

                                    (cf. Lee 2003: ex. 49; Zapotec)

(ii)   a. ... $\iota_o^{\langle 2,a \rangle}$ [$_{XP}$ P$_{1et}$ g$_1$ [X [F$_{2cf}$-t$_{2a}$ Mike-w$_1$-g$_1$]]] ...

       b. $\approx$ "the relevant $o \in g_c(1et)$ such that o is called Mike in $g_c(1s)$"

(6.50) **Yra'ta' zhyàa'p**$_i$ r-càaa'z   g-ahcnèe' *pro*$_i$/***yra'ta' zhyàa'p**$_i$ Lia
        every girl   HAB-want IRR-help Ø/every   girl   FEM
        Paamm.
        Pam
        'Every girl wants to help Pam.'   (Lee 2003: exs. 103–104; Zapotec)

This restriction at PF is mirrored at LF on the present analysis. The quantificational subject is represented with a more richly articulated D+XP structure in contrast to the reduced FP syntax of the bound pronoun.

Finally, consider reflexives — dedicated local-domain forms/devices for expressing reflexive relations.[63] A prominent approach in movement theories of reflexivization is to analyze reflexives as pronounced copies of movement (Hornstein 2001, 2007, Boeckx et al. 2007, Bošković and Nunes 2007, Drummond et al. 2011; cf. Lebeaux 1983, Chomsky 1993, Kratzer 2009). The reflexive pronoun in (6.51a), on this view, is the realization of a copy of movement in an A-chain (specifically, a chain spanning multiple θ-positions). In explicit copy reflexive languages the lower copy can in some cases be pronounced, as in (6.52) (Lasnik 1989, Lee 2003, Mortensen 2003, Boeckx et al. 2007).

(6.51) a. Everyone likes herself.

        b. [*everyone*$_i$ [$_{VP}$ likes *everyone*$_i$-self]]

(6.52) Quas-dlev$_i$ pum quas-dlev$_i$.
        IND-dog   see IND-dog
        'The dog sees itself.'   (Mortensen 2003: ex. 16a; Hmong)

A straightforward implementation would be to analyze the reflexive forms in such examples as (reduced) copies of their antecedent at LF.[64] Whereas certain

---

[63] Hereafter I will omit this restriction to dedicated local-domain forms/devices, but it should be understood (see Zribi-Hertz 2008, Déchaine and Wiltschko 2017).

[64] Unlike in cases of QR, the lower copy would be partially deleted in the narrow syntax (cf. n. 9). The reduced FP delivered by the syntax can be interpreted straightway at LF; in English it would be converted to a reflexive pronoun in the morphophonological component.

differences may be possible in the representations of a donkey pronoun or bound pronoun and its antecedent (§5.2), no such differences would be possible with reflexives qua copies of movement. The LF representation of the reflexive in (6.53a) is an identical copy for purposes of interpretation of the FP in the antecedent quantifier phrase. (I ignore any semantic contribution of '-self'.)

(6.53) Every puppy likes itself.

a. $[_S \ T^{\langle 1,a \rangle} \ [[C_d \ t_{1a}]^{\langle 1,s \rangle}$

$[[_{DP^{\langle 2,a \rangle}} \ \text{every}^{\langle 2,a \rangle} \ [_{XP} \ P_{1et}\text{-}g_1 \ X \ [F_{2cf}\text{-}g_2 \ \text{puppy-}w_1\text{-}g_1]]]$

$[_{VP} \ \text{likes} \ t_{1s} \ it_{2cf}\text{-}g_2\text{-}\text{~~puppy~~}\text{-}w_1\text{-}g_1]]]]$

b. $[\![S]\!] \approx \lambda g_g . \ \forall x_e \forall a_a \colon \big(x(g) = a(g)(2cf)(puppy_{g^-(1s)}) \land$

$g^-(1et)(x(g))\big) \rightarrow$

$x(g) \ \text{likes} \ a(g)(2cf)(puppy_{g^-(1s)}) \ \text{in} \ @(g^-)$

Roughly put, the sentence is true iff for all relevant $o \in g_c(1et)$ selected by some choice function or other F from the puppies, o likes o $(=F(puppy_{@(g_c)}))$. Like with the bound pronoun in (6.48), the bound reading of the reflexive is derived without a special abstraction principle, non-type-driven QR, or an ad hoc binder index (Heim and Kratzer 1998, Büring 2005, Kratzer 2009).

The extensions in this section to other types of pronominal anaphora have been speculative. I don't assume that individual pronouns across languages constitute a unified syntactic or semantic class (n. 36). There are interesting crosslinguistic differences among bound pronouns and reflexives — e.g., in their relative distributions, internal and external syntax, and binding-theoretic properties (Hornstein 2001, Déchaine and Wiltschko 2002, 2015, 2017, Bhat 2004, Zribi-Hertz 2008, Drummond et al. 2011). Comparisons with movement analyses of other anaphoric expressions may provide fruitful avenues to explore (e.g., with resumptive pronouns or doubled clitic pronouns; cf. Kayne 2002, Boeckx 2003, Mavrogiorgos 2010, Rouveret 2011).

6.4 Donkey Crossings: Weak Crossover, Inverse Linking, Genitive Binding

Our discussion has focused on examples with subject-position quantifiers. Consider (6.54) with an object-position quantifier undergoing QR. As in the subject-position examples, the assignment binder-index feature on D projects to the DP. An individual binder-index attaches to the QR'd quantifier phrase, yielding the feature set $\{\langle 2, a \rangle, \langle 2, e \rangle\}$.

(6.54)   Alice petted every puppy.

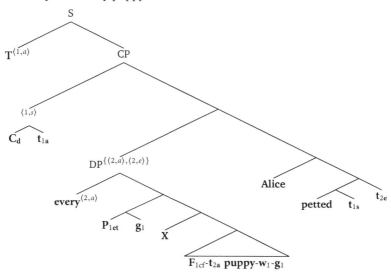

However, a prima facie worry comes from crossover.

Following Reinhart (1983) a prominent generalization of weak crossover is that an expression β can bind a pronoun only if β is in an A-position (argument position) that c-commands the pronoun at LF. This allows for trace-binding from $\overline{\text{A}}$-positions (non-argument positions), such as positions derived from QR or *wh*-movement, but excludes pronoun-binding from such positions, as in (6.55). (6.55b) cannot mean that every puppy is liked by its owner.

(6.55)   a.   Every puppy$_i$ likes its$_i$ owner.
         b.   *Its$_i$ owner likes every puppy$_i$.

Reinhart's generalization has also been applied to donkey pronouns in cases of "donkey crossover" (Haïk 1984, Reinhart 1987, Büring 2004), as in (6.56). (6.56b) cannot mean that every child who petted a puppy was thanked by the puppy's owner; the indefinite 'a puppy' cannot provide an intuitive antecedent for the pronoun from inside the QR'd quantifier phrase.

(6.56)   a.   Every child who petted a puppy$_i$ thanked its$_i$ owner.
         b.   *Its$_i$ owner thanked every child who petted a puppy$_i$.

A worry is that, absent additional constraints, nothing would seem to exclude LFs for (6.55b)/(6.56b) as schematized in (6.57a)/(6.58a). The derived semantic values represent the unattested readings where the interpretation of the pronoun covaries with the raised DP. (Assume again an ad hoc "the-N-of-o" analysis of the possessive pronoun.)

(6.57) a. ... [[every$^{\langle 2,a\rangle}$ [$_{XP}$ ... F$_{3cf}$-g$_2$ puppy-w$_1$-g$_1$]]$^{\{\langle 2,a\rangle,\langle 3,e\rangle\}}$
[the-owner-of-it$_{3cf}$-g$_2$-~~puppy~~-w$_1$-g$_1$ likes-t$_{1s}$ t$_{3e}$]]

    b. $\approx \lambda g_g.\forall x_e \forall a_a\colon \big(x(g) = a(g)(3\mathrm{cf})(puppy_{g^-(1s)}) \wedge g^-(1et)(x(g))\big) \rightarrow$
the-owner-of-$a(g)(3\mathrm{cf})(puppy_{g^-(1s)})$ likes $x(g)$ in @(g^-)

(6.58) a. ... [[every$^{\langle 2,a\rangle}$ [$_{CP}$ ... a$_{3cf}$-g$_2$ puppy-w$_1$-g$_1$]]$^{\{\langle 2,a\rangle,\langle 3,e\rangle\}}$
[the-owner-of-it$_{3cf}$-g$_2$-~~puppy~~-w$_1$-g$_1$ thanked-t$_{1s}$ t$_{3e}$]]

    b. $\approx \lambda g_g.\forall x_e \forall a_a\colon \big(x(g) = a(g)(2\mathrm{cf})(child_{g^-(1s)}) \wedge$
$x(g)$ petted $a(g)(3\mathrm{cf})(puppy_{g^-(1s)})$ in $g^-(1s)\big) \rightarrow$
the-owner-of-$a(g)(3\mathrm{cf})(puppy_{g^-(1s)})$ thanked $x(g)$ in @(g^-)

One response would be to treat Reinhart's generalization as a basic principle in the grammar (cf. Safir 2004: §3.3). LFs such as (6.57a)/(6.58a) would be excluded because they violate Reinhart's generalization: the pronoun [it$_{3cf}$ g$_2$] is bound by the assignment-binder from the QR'd DP in an $\overline{\mathrm{A}}$-position. Yet it would be preferable to derive generalizations such as Reinhart's from more basic features of the syntax/semantics.

Suppose we posit a principle that no expression may "bind" distinct variables, in some relevant sense of binding — call it *s-binding*. A first approximation of such a principle is in (6.59). (I will at times be sloppy about distinguishing expressions/variables (qua types) from occurrences.)

(6.59) *Variable Binding Constraint:* An occurrence of an expression in a tree γ may s-bind occurrences of at most one variable at LF.

    a. An occurrence of an expression β *s-binds* an occurrence of a variable $\mathbf{v}_{i\sigma}$ in γ iff the sister of β is the largest subtree of γ in which $\mathbf{v}_{i\sigma}$ is s-free.

    b. $\mathbf{v}_{i\sigma}$ is *s-free* in γ iff there is no occurrence in γ of an expression with binder-index feature $^{\langle i,\sigma\rangle}$ that c-commands $\mathbf{v}_{i\sigma}$.

A diagnosis of weak crossover follows. The QR'd DP$^{\{\langle 2,a\rangle,\langle 3,e\rangle\}}$ in (6.57a) s-binds two variables: the assignment-variable in the pronoun [it$_{3cf}$ g$_2$], and the individual trace t$_{3e}$. This violates the constraint in (6.59). The pronoun cannot be bound by the raised DP at LF because the DP's binding capacities are exhausted from binding the trace left from QR (cf. n. 9). Hence a string such as (6.55b) can be acceptable, but only with an intuitively free reading of 'its'.

The previous explanation carries over to cases of donkey crossover. The QR'd DP$^{\{\langle 2,a\rangle,\langle 3,e\rangle\}}$ in (6.58a) s-binds both the trace t$_{3e}$ derived from QR and the assignment-variable g_2 in the representation of the donkey pronoun, violating (6.59). No such constraint excludes an anaphoric reading of the donkey pronoun in (6.56a). The (A-position) DP may s-bind the pronoun.

In this way, a unified treatment of weak crossover and donkey crossover falls out of the assignment-quantificational syntax/semantics for quantifiers, the representation of the anaphoric pronouns as copies of their antecedents, and a general variable-binding constraint such as (6.59). That a unified account is made available provides independent support for extending the assignment-variable-based treatments of headed relative constructions and donkey anaphora from §5 to quantifier phrases and bound-variable anaphora more generally. The remainder of the chapter applies the account to two additional recalcitrant cases of apparent binding out of DPs: *genitive binding* and *inverse linking* (see Büring 2004).

Consider donkey-style anaphora and crossover with genitives:

(6.60) a. Every boy$_i$'s puppy likes him$_i$.

b. *His$_i$ cat likes every boy$_i$'s puppy.

In (6.60a) the embedded DP 'every boy' can provide an antecedent for 'him' even though it doesn't c-command the pronoun at LF. However, the interpretation of the pronoun cannot covary with the quantifier in (6.60b) when the genitive DP is in a raised position from QR. (6.60b) cannot mean that every boy b's puppy is liked by b's cat.

In (6.60a) the quantificational possessor 'every boy' QRs for type reasons, as reflected in (6.61) (cf. May 1985). Thus far our compositional semantics has proceeded solely via function application. Suppose that we allow a principled role for function composition in deriving the semantic values of certain adjunction structures, such as complex DPs formed from DP-internal movement (cf. Kobele 2010).[65] Combining DP* of type $\langle et, t \rangle$ and the raised DP** of type $\langle t, t \rangle$ in (6.61) by function composition yields the complex subject DP of type $\langle et, t \rangle$. (For simplicity assume that the implicit domain pronoun in DP** is trivial, contextually identified with E.)[66]

---

[65] Kobele's (2010) account of inverse linking also appeals to function composition and introduces assignments into the model and type system. Kobele doesn't incorporate assignment-variables into the syntax, or consider assignments or binder indices for variables of types other than e. We will examine additional uses of function composition in §8 with adjoined 'if'-clauses.

[66] I assume that, like with [WH] features, binder-index features on or c-commanding a head Z in a ZP project/percolate to the ZP. The asterisks are used here to distinguish the different DP nodes; they have no theoretical import.

(6.61)   Every boy$_i$'s puppy likes him$_i$.

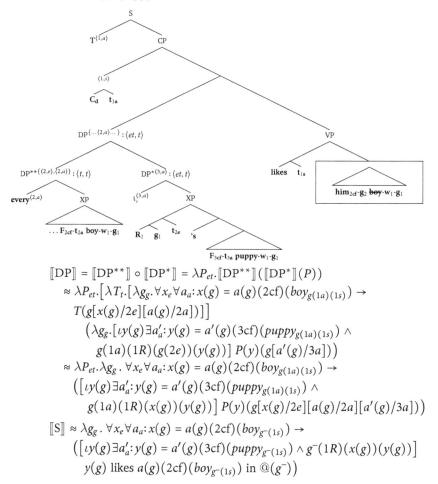

$$[\![DP]\!] = [\![DP^{**}]\!] \circ [\![DP^*]\!] = \lambda P_{et}.[\![DP^{**}]\!]([\![DP^*]\!](P))$$
$$\approx \lambda P_{et}.\Big[\lambda T_t.\big[\lambda g_g. \forall x_e \forall a_a: x(g) = a(g)(2\mathrm{cf})(boy_{g(1a)(1s)}) \to$$
$$T(g[x(g)/2e][a(g)/2a])\big]\Big]$$
$$\Big(\lambda g_g.[\iota y(g)\exists a'_a: y(g) = a'(g)(3\mathrm{cf})(puppy_{g(1a)(1s)}) \wedge$$
$$g(1a)(1R)(g(2e))(y(g))]\, P(y)(g[a'(g)/3a])\Big)$$
$$\approx \lambda P_{et}.\lambda g_g . \forall x_e \forall a_a: x(g) = a(g)(2\mathrm{cf})(boy_{g(1a)(1s)}) \to$$
$$\Big([\iota y(g)\exists a'_a: y(g) = a'(g)(3\mathrm{cf})(puppy_{g(1a)(1s)}) \wedge$$
$$g(1a)(1R)(x(g))(y(g))]\, P(y)(g[x(g)/2e][a(g)/2a][a'(g)/3a])\Big)$$
$$[\![S]\!] \approx \lambda g_g . \forall x_e \forall a_a: x(g) = a(g)(2\mathrm{cf})(boy_{g^-(1s)}) \to$$
$$\Big([\iota y(g)\exists a'_a: y(g) = a'(g)(3\mathrm{cf})(puppy_{g^-(1s)}) \wedge g^-(1R)(x(g))(y(g))]$$
$$y(g) \text{ likes } a(g)(2\mathrm{cf})(boy_{g^-(1s)}) \text{ in } @(g^-)\Big)$$

The donkey pronoun 'him' is again represented as a copy of its linguistic antecedent — here, the FP in DP** representing 'every boy'. The assignment-binder projected to the DP binds the choice-function pronoun, yielding the covarying interpretation. Roughly put, the sentence is true iff for every $o \in E$ that could be chosen from among the boys, the unique $o' \in E$ that could be chosen from among the puppies and that bears the relevant relation $g_c(1R)$ (e.g. "is a pet of") to o, likes o.

The preceding account of weak crossover and donkey crossover carries over to cases of "genitive crossover" such as (6.60b), reproduced in (6.62). (Assume again a trivial domain pronoun in DP**.)

(6.62) *His cat$_i$ likes every boy$_i$'s puppy.

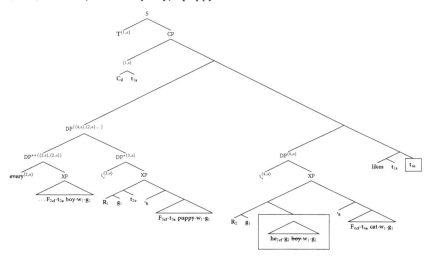

The object quantifier 'every boy's puppy' has a set of binder-index features including an individual binder from QR, and an assignment binder projecting from DP**. The individual binder-index binds the coindexed trace t_{4e}. On the unattested covarying reading, the assignment binder-index also binds g_2 in the representation of the pronoun 'his', violating (6.59).

Finally, let's turn to inverse linking readings. The relevant reading of (6.63a) says that every child has some friend or other who high-fived her. Like 'every boy' in (6.60a), the embedded 'every child' QRs for type reasons within the subject DP (May 1985, Heim and Kratzer 1998). The interpretation of 'her' covaries with the quantificational subject even though the pronoun isn't c-commanded by its intuitive antecedent 'every child'. However, as in cases of donkey crossover, the covarying interpretation is excluded when the embedding DP 'some child of every parent' is in a raised position derived from QR. (6.63b) cannot mean that every child o has a friend who was high-fived by o's cat.

(6.63) a. Some friend of every child$_i$ high-fived her$_i$.
    b. *Her$_i$ cat high-fived some friend of every child$_i$.

As with the quantified genitive in (6.61), DP** and D* of types of types $\langle t, t \rangle$ and $\langle et, t \rangle$, respectively, combine by function composition to yield the quantificational subject of type $\langle et, t \rangle$, reflected in (6.64). The assignment binder-index feature projected from DP** to the DP binds the donkey pronoun. (Assume again that the domain pronouns in the XPs are trivial.)

(6.64)   Some friend of every child$_i$ high-fived her$_i$.

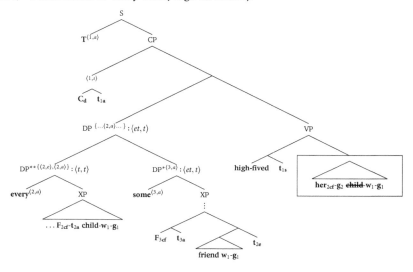

$$\llbracket \textbf{some} \rrbracket = \lambda P^+_{\langle a,et \rangle}.\lambda Q^+_{\langle a,et \rangle}.\lambda g_g \, . \, \exists x_e \exists a_a \colon P^+(a)(x)(g) \wedge Q^+(a)(x)(g)$$

$$\llbracket \text{DP} \rrbracket = \llbracket \text{DP}^{**} \rrbracket \circ \llbracket \text{DP}^* \rrbracket = \lambda P_{et}.\llbracket \text{DP}^{**} \rrbracket (\llbracket \text{DP}^* \rrbracket(P))$$

$$\approx \lambda P_{et}.\lambda g_g \, . \, \forall x_e \forall a_a \colon x(g) = a(g)(2\text{cf})(child_{g(1a)(1s)}) \rightarrow$$
$$\big(\exists y_e \exists a'_a \colon y(g) = a'(g)(3\text{cf})(friend\text{-}of\text{-}x(g)_{g(1a)(1s)}) \wedge$$
$$P(y)(g[x(g)/2e][a(g)/2a][a'(g)/3a])\big)$$

$$\llbracket \text{S} \rrbracket \approx \lambda g_g \, . \, \forall x_e \forall a_a \colon x(g) = a(g)(2\text{cf})(child_{g^-(1s)}) \rightarrow$$
$$\big(\exists y_e \exists a'_a \colon y(g) = a'(g)(3\text{cf})(friend\text{-}of\text{-}x(g)_{g^-(1s)}) \wedge$$
$$y(g) \text{ high-fived } a(g)(2\text{cf})(child_{g^-(1s)}) \text{ in } @(g^-)\big)$$

This says, roughly, that for every $o \in E$ selectable from the children, there is an $o' \in E$ selectable from the friends of o such that o' high-fived o. However, the variable binding constraint in (6.59) excludes the covarying interpretation when 'every child' is embedded in a QR'd object DP, as in (6.65).

(6.65) *Her cat$_i$ high-fived some friend of every child$_i$.

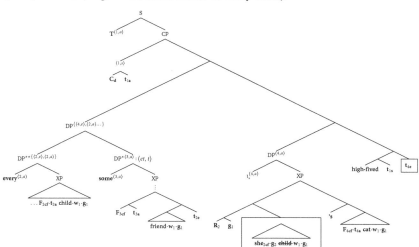

The QR'd object DP s-binds its coindexed trace t_{4e} and the assignment-variable g_2 in the representation of the pronoun 'her'.

§§6.3–6.4 have examined how the assignment-variable-based approach to donkey pronouns from §5.2 might be extended to other types of pronominal anaphora and apparent binding out of DPs. The D+XP syntax captures how complex expressions such as 'every boy's puppy' and 'some friend of every child' form constituents at LF (contrast May 1977). The covarying readings in genitive binding and inverse linking examples ((6.61), (6.64)) follow from the analysis of certain anaphoric pronouns as copies of their linguistic antecedent (§§5.2, 6.3), the generalized assignment-quantificational syntax/semantics for nominal quantifiers (§§6.1–6.2), and a principled use of function composition in the compositional semantics.

A worry with many accounts of Reinhart's generalization — or what excludes pronouns from receiving covarying interpretations with antecedents in or embedded in QR-derived positions — is that they end up formalizing what needs to be explained: the distinction between trace-binding and pronoun-binding. Contrasts such as in (6.55) may be captured via stipulations on admissible indexings (Haïk 1984, Reinhart 1987), or ad hoc syntactic/semantic distinctions between traces and pronouns (Büring 2004, Safir 2004, Elbourne 2005, Schlenker 2005). For instance, Büring 2004 — arguably the most extensive account in the literature — introduces distinct syntactic categories for traces and pronouns, distinct binders and domains for assignments corresponding to the two categories, and distinct principles regarding admissible LFs for traces and pronouns and their respective binding operators. The assignment-variable-based framework developed in §2 independently distinguishes pronouns and traces. Pronouns $[v_i \; g_j]$ include an assignment-variable from which the element receives its interpretation. No assignment-variable is included in the representation of traces t_i; the binder-index attaching to the moved expression binds the variable directly. This distinction may be exploited in an account of weak crossover.

I suggested explaining data such as Reinhart's generalization and its extension to varieties of donkey crossover via a general principle excluding expressions from binding distinct variables, in the sense defined in (6.59). Since a raised expression is coindexed with its trace, the assignment-variable in the representation of a pronoun cannot be bound by a QR'd DP — in standard weak crossover configurations ((6.55b)), donkey sentences ((6.56b)), genitive binding ((6.60b)), and inverse linking ((6.63b)) alike. There is no analogous obstacle to covarying readings when the quantifier is in subject position — hence Reinhart's generalization that bound pronouns, unlike traces, must be bound from A-positions.[67] Additional binding operators or constraints on admissible indexings aren't required.

---

[67] The last inference was too quick. Nothing has been said about weak crossover with *wh* interrogatives, e.g.:

(i) a. Who$_i$ (t_i) high-fived her$_i$ friend?
     b. *Who$_i$ did her$_i$ friend high-five (t_i)?

There are independently attested contrasts between *wh*-chains and QR-chains regarding the interpretation of traces and pronouns (e.g. Safir 1999, Cecchetto 2004). How to extend the approach will depend on one's views on the syntactic/semantic status of *wh*-movement, reconstruction, pied piping. A more general binding theory is needed. I return to *wh* interrogatives briefly in §9.3.

7

Noun Phrases

§§5–6 began developing an assignment-variable-based theory of different types of quantificational noun phrases. In §6.1 we saw how the account captures certain effects associated with "specificity" (Enç 1991), such as existence presuppositions and contextual domain restriction. Not all quantifier words exhibit these effects. A critical question is how the framework developed thus far might be applied to other types of noun phrases, such as those with (so-called) "weak" quantifiers — to a first approximation, quantifiers that can be used in existential 'there' sentences such as (7.1) (Milsark 1974), and can be used nonpresuppositionally, as in (7.2) (using 'sm' for unstressed 'some').[68]

(7.1)   a.   There is a/*every/*the book on the table.

  b.   There are no/sm/many/two/*all/*most books on the table.

---

[68] By 'presuppositional uses' I mean uses associated with existence implications and contextual domain restriction. Uses of "strong" quantifiers are "presuppositional" in this sense, though this is something to be explained rather than definitional. We will revisit the utility of these classifications later in the chapter. I will use 'quantifier word' informally for words/strings that may be used to express quantification, including 'every', 'no', etc. as well as numerals ('three') and articles ('the'). I use 'quantifier' multiply for quantified expressions, for quantifier words as types, and for particular tokens. Crucially, my usage doesn't presuppose that the item has the syntax or semantics of a generalized quantifier. All examples with 'there' sentences will be with existential 'there', not locative or presentational 'there' (cf. (i)). See McNally 1997, Zamparelli 2000, Francez 2007 on uses of strong quantifiers with kind/amount nominals. There are notable variations in acceptability with different quantifiers, noun phrases, and modifiers, e.g. in (ii)–(vi):

(i)   a.   There was/wasn't a child in the room.
  b.   There was/*wasn't a certain child in the room.
  c.   There appeared/*didn't appear a child in the room.

(ii)   a.   There was every kind/#tub of ice cream (on sale/available/in the store).
  b.   There were all kinds/#tubs of ice cream (on sale/available/in the store).

(iii) a.   There was every/??each kind of ice cream (on sale/available/in the store).
  b.   There were all/??most kinds of ice cream (on sale/available/in the store).
  c.??There were all/most of the kinds of ice cream (on sale/available/in the store).

(iv)   a.   There was every dessert we wanted on the menu.
  b.#There were all/most desserts we wanted on the menu.
  c.??There were all/most of the desserts we wanted on the menu.

(v)   a.#There was every/each kind of ice cream being eaten.
  b.   There were all/#most kinds of ice cream being eaten.

(vi)   a.   There is every/#all/#most reason to believe that Alice will win.
  b.   There is ?#every/#all/#most chance/probability/possibility that Alice will win.

(7.2)   I have no idea yet whether there are any mistakes in the manuscript, but we definitely can't publish it if some/two/#most/#both mistakes are found.   (adapting von Fintel 1998a: ex. 9)

This chapter begins to examine the varieties of expressions and uses in a more general assignment-variable-based syntax/semantics for noun phrases.

§7.1 situates the D+XP analysis of quantifier phrases developed in §6 in a general layered n analysis for noun phrases. §§7.2–7.3 reexamine how various "specificity" phenomena can be understood in terms of the proposed architecture — e.g., presuppositional vs. nonpresuppositional uses, weak vs. strong quantifiers and existential 'there' sentences, and modal independence. §7.4 revisits the challenges facing the head-raising analysis of restrictive relative clauses from §5; an improved matching analysis is layered into the syntax/semantics developed thus far. §7.5 briefly outlines how events might be incorporated in a parallel layered v analysis of verb phrases.

I want to flag that parts of this chapter are more syntactically oriented than the previous chapters. Certain of the syntactic developments may be of general interest, independent of the assignment-variable-based framework; yet the discussions aren't tangential. It is critical in developing our compositional semantics with assignment-variables that the sources of linguistic shifting and (un)shiftability be derived from independently motivated syntactic structures. We will see that a general assignment-variable-based syntax/semantics for noun phrases can be motivated by diverse crosslinguistic data and integrated in a broadly phase-based model from current syntactic theories.

7.1   A Layered n Analysis of Noun Phrases

I begin with the following basic nP syntax for nominals:

(7.3)

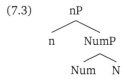

As usual, NumP is a projection for number and certain uses of numerals and non-definite determiners; it provides the locus of cardinal and "specified quantity" interpretations, e.g. distinguishing 'a/two book(s)' from mass nominals such as 'water' (Ritter 1991, Bernstein 2001, Borer 2005a, Megerdoomian 2008, Cowper and Hall 2009). Number features can be treated semantically as modifiers (cf. Ionin and Matushansky 2006), as in (7.4).[69] (Following Link 1983, components of the model such as E are structured to include plural objects, or sums of atomic objects (n. 41). I use 'count' as a metalanguage predicate for whatever the relevant properties are for being in a plural or count denotation, where 'count(o)' implies at least that o has atomic parts; hence 'atom(o)' implies 'count(o)'.)

(7.4) a. $[\![\,\text{SG}\,]\!] = \lambda P_{\langle s,et\rangle}.\lambda w_s.\lambda y_e.\lambda g_g : \text{atom}(y(g)) . P(w)(y)(g)$
  b. $[\![\,\text{PL}\,]\!] = \lambda P_{\langle s,et\rangle}.\lambda w_s.\lambda y_e.\lambda g_g : \text{count}(y(g)) . P(w)(y)(g)$

Little n is a light noun parallel to v in a verb phrase (e.g. 'do'). Following Marantz 1997 it is common to treat n and v as distinguishing nominal and verbal environments. In some languages, nominalizers and verbalizers with lexical roots can be overt, as in (7.5)–(7.6) (Heine and Kuteva 2002, Rackowski 2002, Levinson 2007, Pylkkänen 2008, Harley 2009, 2013, 2017, Legate 2014, Julien 2015, D'Alessandro et al. 2017).

(7.5) a. $[_\text{nP} [_\text{n} /\text{u}/] \sqrt{barg}] \rightsquigarrow$ *bargu* ('work' (n.))
  b. $[_\text{vP} [_\text{v} /\text{a}/] \sqrt{barg}] \rightsquigarrow$ *bargat* ('work' (v.))
      (Julien 2015: 6; North Sámi (Uralic))

(7.6) Aman kari-te-wa.
    there house-v^0-PASS
    'Houses are being built there.' (Harley 2013: 53; Hiaki (Uto-Aztecan))

I propose that we treat n^0 and v^0 as the locus of world variables. The argument structure for nominal and verbal predicates can be adapted accordingly — e.g., treating relational 'like'/'sister' as type $\langle e, \langle s, et\rangle\rangle$, 'think' as type $\langle at, \langle s, et\rangle\rangle$, etc., as in (7.7). The world-variable of the clause's main predicate is again determined by type-driven movement of the complementizer, now represented as originating in v^0, as in (7.8).[70]

---

[69] The relative positions of number words and number features is inessential for our purposes. I leave open whether number features are realized in Num or in an independent head between Num and N (cf. Rijkhoff 2002, Borer 2005a). In some languages numerals may occupy an adjectival position in NP (Franks 1994, Aboh 2004, Tănase-Dogaru 2007). Given the parallels between number and aspect, the modificational treatment of number words/features might be compared to treatments of aspectual heads as modifiers of the verb in a verb phrase (more on this in §7.5).

[70] In the definition of the binder-index (§3.5), now for 'think': $\tau = a$, $\sigma = \langle s, et\rangle$. I put aside issues regarding the base position of direct objects (e.g., Comp of V, or Spec of an intermediate functional head such as Aspect). For now I continue to ignore v^* for introducing external arguments; we will revisit this in §7.5.

(7.7)   a. $[\![\textbf{like}]\!]$ = $\lambda x_e.\lambda w_s.\lambda y_e.\lambda g_g \,.\, y(g)$ likes $x(g)$ in $w(g)$

        b. $[\![\textbf{think}]\!]$ = $\lambda A_{\langle a,t \rangle}.\lambda w_s.\lambda x_e.\lambda g_g \,.\, \forall a_a\colon a(g)$ is compatible with $x(g)$'s
           state of mind in $w(g) \rightarrow A(a)(g)$

(7.8)   ... $[_{vP}\ t_{1s}\ [_{VP}\ \text{think}^{\langle 2,a \rangle}\ [_{CP}\ [C_d\ t_{2a}]^{\langle 2,s \rangle}\ [\text{Percy}\ [_{vP}\ t_{2s}\ [_{VP}\ \text{likes Colin}]]]]]]$

The D+XP structure for quantifier phrases from §6 is thus now conceived as in
(7.9). As discussed in §§6.1–6.2, F is a position for certain specificity elements
and choice-function pronouns; n* is the category of elements such as **X** or the
genitive morpheme, parallel to v* in complete verb phrases.[71]

(7.9)

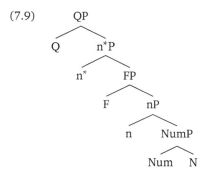

7.2   "Specificity" Revisited (II)

7.2.1   *Presuppositional and Nonpresuppositional Uses*

This section suggests a structural basis for presuppositional vs. nonpresuppositional readings. Presuppositional uses of quantifiers can be analyzed as in
§§6.1–6.2: specificity elements in F above the (world-indexed) nP select an
individual from the given world; and the quantifier raises from an internal

---

[71] The present layered analysis builds on developments — primarily in the verbal domain — which
delineate categories for N/V (the root or head noun/verb), n/v (a functional projection identifying
nominal/verbal environments), and n*/v* (a functional projection closing off complete noun/verb
phrases) (cf. Rackowski 2002, Lecarme 2004, 2008, Collins 2005, Levinson 2007, Megerdoomian
2008, Pylkkänen 2008, Harley 2009, 2013, 2017, Merchant 2013, Legate 2014, Julien 2015,
D'Alessandro et al. 2017, Wood and Marantz 2017). I will continue to use **X** for the implicit lexical
item, now identifying n* as the category. I leave open whether v* is to be equated with Voice (Kratzer
1996; see Ramchand 2017 for critical discussion). Adapting ideas from the "supercategorial theory"
in Hiraiwa 2005, n and v might be treated as different manifestations of a single "supercategory"
w. We will examine constraints on world-variables in the nP area and substantive lexical entries for
certain nominalizing/verbalizing heads in the following sections. I consider an alternative F position
under n in §§7.4–7.5. I represent some quantifier words as projecting a QP, but this is inessential
(§6.1). I leave open where other φ-features and classifiers may be located. For general discussion on
structural differences among (non-)quantificational noun phrases crosslinguistically, see Cardinaletti
and Starke 1999, Zamparelli 2000, Bernstein 2001, Matthewson 2001, Giusti 2002, Lecarme 2004,
2012, Borer 2005a, Cowper and Hall 2009, Gil et al. 2013, Paul et al. 2015, Türker 2019.

assignment-argument position to a position above n*. The presuppositional reading of the weak quantifier 'some' in (7.11) is derived parallel to (7.10) with 'every'.[72] (Unless otherwise noted I will ignore the contributions of number features from (7.4). As previously, I use e.g. '*people$_u$*' for the set of (possibly plural) people $o \in E$ in u.)

(7.10) The editor didn't find every mistake (#...because there weren't any)

    a. [S T$^{\langle 1,a \rangle}$ [$_{CP}$ [C$_d$ t$_{1a}$]$^{\langle 1,s \rangle}$ -n't

        [[every$^{\langle 2,a \rangle}$ [$_{n^*p}$ P$_{1et}$ g$_1$ [X [$_{FP}$ F$_{2cf}$ t$_{2a}$ [$_{nP}$ w$_1$-g$_1$ mistake]]]]]$^{\{\langle 2,a \rangle, \langle 2,e \rangle\}}$

        [the-editor [$_{vP}$ t$_{1s}$(did) [find t$_{2e}$]]]]]]

    b. $[\![S]\!] \approx \lambda g_g . \neg \big(\forall x_e \forall a_a \colon \big(x(g) = a(g)(2\text{cf})(mistake_{g^-(1s)}) $

        $\wedge\, g^-(1et)(x(g)) \big) \big) \rightarrow$ the-editor found $x(g)$ in $@(g^-) \big)$

(7.11) Some (#sm) people are jackasses.   (Milsark 1977: 54–55)

    a. [$_S$ T$^{\langle 1,a \rangle}$ [$_{CP}$ [C$_d$ t$_{1a}$]$^{\langle 1,s \rangle}$

        [[some$^{\langle 2,a \rangle}$ [$_{n^*p}$ P$_{1et}$ g$_1$ [X [$_{FP}$ F$_{2cf}$ t$_{2a}$ [$_{nP}$ w$_1$-g$_1$ people]]]]]$^{\langle 2,a \rangle}$

        [vP t$_{1s}$ (are) jackasses]]]]

    b. $[\![S]\!] \approx \lambda g_g . \exists x_e \exists a_a \colon x(g) = a(g)(2\text{cf})(people_{g^-(1s)}) \wedge g^-(1et)(x(g))$

        $\wedge\, x(g)$ are jackasses in $@(g^-)$

In (7.10) the choice-function pronoun selects an entity that is a mistake in the world of the discourse ($g_c(1s) = @(g_c)$). So the quantification presupposes that there are mistakes in the manuscript — hence the infelicity of continuations implying that there weren't any mistakes. As Milsark puts it regarding (7.11):

> [T]he only sense of *some* which can be understood felicitously ... is the ... 'some' sense ..., that some members of the human race, as opposed, presumably, to others, are jackasses. Substitution of destressed *sm* and its reading of an indefinite number of people, nothing more, yields nonsense. (Milsark 1977: 55)

Indeed, the quantifier existentially quantifies over those individuals o who are potentially selectable among actual people and in the contextually relevant domain ($=g_c(1et)$). The sentence is true iff some such o are jackasses.

Uses with genitives provide key data regarding the source of presuppositional vs. nonpresuppositional readings. Although quantifiers such as 'no', 'few', 'many' are generally compatible with nonpresuppositional readings, they seem

---

[72] For now I ignore any additional semantic contribution of 'be', and I leave open the category of the copula in different languages (see Partee 1986a, den Dikken 1995, Harley 1995, Dixon 2002, Folli and Harley 2007, Moro 2017). We will return to this in §7.5.

to become presuppositional with genitive complements. It is hard to hear uses of 'Q_{wk} Ns of X's' as failing to imply that there Ns, as reflected in (7.12)–(7.13).

(7.12) There are no friends of Bert's in the audience (??because he doesn't have any friends).

(7.13) Alice found no/few mistakes of the author's,

   a. so she's going to get fired.
   b.??so the author must have been super careful.

Modifiers don't in general produce such an effect. The continuations in (7.14b)–(7.15b) are felicitous.

(7.14) a. Alice found no mistakes (…because there aren't any)
   b. Alice found no mistakes in the manuscript (…because there aren't any)

(7.15) a. There are no monsters.
   b. There are no monsters under Timmy's bed (…because there's no such thing as monsters)

Indeed adding the modifiers in (7.16b)–(7.17b) improves the (a)-examples with postnominal genitives. In a null context, existential 'There are Q_{wk} Ns of X's' is generally marked in comparison to 'There are Q_{wk} N's of X's ZP'. The contrasts in (7.16)–(7.17) are analogous in this respect to observed contrasts with explicit partitives, as in (7.18).

(7.16) a.??There are no friends of Bert's.
   b. There are no friends of Bert's in the audience.

(7.17) a.??There are no monsters of your brother's.
   b. There are no monsters of your brother's under your bed.
       ((b)-examples ok only if Bert has friends, your brother has monsters)

(7.18) a. *There were two of the Beethoven sonatas.
   b. There were two of the Beethoven sonatas on the program.
                                             (cf. Stockwell et al. 1973: 119)

One could imagine saying (7.17b) as a way of allaying a child's fears before bed while accommodating an assumption that there are monsters in the brother's charge.

   We noted in §6.1 that it is common to treat D as the locus of "specificity" phenomena such as existence presuppositions (D-linking, etc.). Data such as (7.12)–(7.18) suggest that the key position is rather n^* — the position occupied by the genitive morpheme (or other Case-assigning element (§6.2)). The presuppositional effects with genitives in (7.12)–(7.13) and (7.16)–(7.17) can be observed in the absence of a definite determiner or strong quantifier.

I suggest that what distinguishes nonpresuppositional uses of weak quantifiers (indefinites, numerals) is that they are interpreted below n in NumP, the position associated with number and specified quantity. A key feature of weak quantifiers is that their meanings can be given in cardinal terms, as in (7.19) (where '$a \sqsubseteq b$' says that a is a (possibly improper) part of b). Treating number words as type $\langle\langle s, et\rangle, \langle s, et\rangle\rangle$, yielding type $\langle e, t\rangle$ denotations for the nPs, coheres with ideas in syntax about the predicative status of weak quantifiers and number phrases.[73] A derivation for a predicative use is in (7.20) (I leave 'the-winners' unanalyzed; nn. 69, 72).

(7.19)   Cardinal lexical entries (schematic)

$$[\![\delta_\#]\!] = \lambda P_{\langle s,et\rangle}.\lambda w_s.\lambda y_e.\lambda g_g.\,\#x(g)\big[P(w)(x)(g) \wedge x(g) \sqsubseteq y(g)\big]\, R_\delta\, n_\delta$$

  • $\#o\big[\ldots o \ldots\big]$:= the cardinality of the set of atoms o s.t. $\ldots o \ldots$

(7.20)   The winners were three women.

  a. $[_S\, T^{\langle 1,a\rangle}\, [[C_d\, t_{1a}]^{\langle 1,s\rangle}\, [\text{the-winners}\, [t_{1s}\, [_{\text{NumP}}\, \text{three}_\#\, [[\text{PL}]\, \text{woman}]]]]]]$

  b. $[\![\mathbf{three}_\#]\!] = \lambda P_{\langle s,et\rangle}.\lambda w_s.\lambda y_e.\lambda g_g.\,\#x(g)\big[P(w)(x)(g) \wedge x(g) \sqsubseteq y(g)\big] \geq 3$

  $[\![\text{NumP}]\!] = \lambda w_s.\lambda y_e.\lambda g_g : \text{count}(y(g))\,.$

  $\#x(g)\big[x(g) \text{ is a woman in } w(g) \wedge x(g) \sqsubseteq y(g)\big] \geq 3$

  $[\![S]\!] \approx \lambda g_g.\,\#x(g)\big[x(g) \text{ is a woman in } @(g^-) \wedge x(g) \sqsubseteq \text{the-winners}\big] \geq 3$

The entry in (7.20b) treats cardinal 'three' as taking a property P and returning the property true of (plural) individuals with at least three P-atoms. The sentence is true iff the cardinality of the set of atomic individuals o such that o is a woman and o is in the group of winners is at least 3, i.e. iff there are three women among the winners.

Denotations in predicative vs. non-predicative environments can be systematically related via a general lexical rule for number words or an analogous type shift at the level of the nP, as in (7.22)–(7.23), adapting a Partee-style $\langle e, t\rangle$-to-$\langle et, t\rangle$ shift for a plural domain (Partee 1986b, 1989b). To simplify the definitions, (7.21) defines a metalanguage operator MAX, which maps a set of individuals to the singleton set of its maximal element, if any. In both options the upshot at the level of the nP is, in effect, a mapping from a set of individuals S' to the set of sets

---

[73] See Partee 1986b, Giusti 1991, 1992, 1997, Diesing 1992, Cinque 1995, Lyons 1999, Zamparelli 2000, Landman 2003, Ionin and Matushansky 2006, Cowper and Hall 2009.

of individuals S'' such that the maximal element of S'' is in S'. A sample derivation with the type-shift option is in (7.24). (For clarity I represent the type shift with an element in the nP layer, though there are plausibly reasons for treating it as a semantic type-shifter that applies on demand (see Partee 1986a,b, Chierchia 1998, Landman 2003). In the lexical rule option, LFs with the "wrong" entry would be filtered out for type reasons. I won't distinguish singular and plural predicates; we can understand our metalanguage in such a way that a condition such as that o laughed is satisfied iff every atomic part of o laughed. I will often leave number features implicit in what follows.)

(7.21) For any x_e, F_{et}, g_g: $\text{MAX}(F)(x)(g)$ iff $F(x)(g) \wedge \forall x'_e: F(x')(g) \rightarrow x'(g) \sqsubseteq x(g)$

(7.22) Lexical rule option: For $[\![\delta_\#]\!] \in D_{\langle\langle s,et\rangle, \langle s,et\rangle\rangle}$,

$$[\![\delta]\!] = \lambda P_{\langle s,et\rangle}.\lambda w_s.\lambda F_{et}.\lambda g_g \, . \, \forall z_e: \text{MAX}(F)(z)(g) \rightarrow [\![\delta_\#]\!](P)(w)(z)(g)$$

(7.23) Type shift option (σ): For any F'_{et},
$$sigma(F') = \lambda F_{et}.\lambda g_g \, . \, \forall z_e: \text{MAX}(F)(z)(g) \rightarrow F'(z)(g)$$

(7.24) Bert found no unicorns (…because there aren't any)   *(to be revised)*

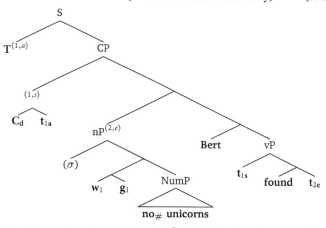

$$[\![\mathbf{no}_\#]\!] = \lambda P_{\langle s,et\rangle}.\lambda w_s.\lambda y_e.\lambda g_g \, . \, \#x(g)\big[P(w)(x)(g) \wedge x(g) \sqsubseteq y(g)\big] = 0$$
$$[\![\text{NumP}]\!] = \lambda w_s.\lambda y_e.\lambda g_g \, . \, \#x(g)\big[x(g) \text{ is a unicorn in } w(g) \wedge x(g) \sqsubseteq y(g)\big] = 0$$
$$sigma\big([\![\text{NumP}]\!]([\![\mathbf{w}_1 \, \mathbf{g}_1]\!])\big) = \lambda F_{et}.\lambda g_g \, . \, \forall z_e: \text{MAX}(F)(z)(g) \rightarrow$$
$$\#x(g)\big[x(g) \text{ is a unicorn in } g(1a)(1s) \wedge x(g) \sqsubseteq z(g)\big] = 0$$
$$[\![S]\!] \approx \lambda g_g \, . \, \forall z_e: \text{MAX}(\lambda z_e.\lambda g_g.\text{Bert found } z(g) \text{ in } @(g^-))(z)(g) \rightarrow$$
$$\#x(g)\big[x(g) \text{ is a unicorn in } g^-(1s) \wedge x(g) \sqsubseteq z(g)\big] = 0$$

$$\approx \lambda g_g \,.\, \forall z_e \colon \big(\text{Bert found } z(g) \text{ in } @(g^-) \wedge$$
$$\forall y_e \colon \text{Bert found } y(g) \text{ in } @(g^-) \rightarrow y(g) \sqsubseteq z(g)\big) \rightarrow$$
$$\#x(g)\big[x(g) \text{ is a unicorn in } g^-(1s) \wedge x(g) \sqsubseteq z(g)\big] = 0$$

The NumP 'no unicorns' denotes the property of having no unicorn as a part; this property is shifted by *sigma* at the level of the nP to a generalized quantifier — roughly, the set of sets of individuals whose maximal element has no unicorn as a part. The sentence is true iff for any o, if Bert found o and o includes everything Bert found as a part, then the number of o' such that o' is a unicorn and o' is a part of o is zero — i.e., iff there is no unicorn among the things, if any, that Bert found. The derived truth condition can be satisfied even if there are no unicorns; indeed (7.24) is guaranteed to be true on the intended reading if there are no unicorns. The rules in (7.22)–(7.23) also allow for the truth of sentences such as (7.25a). If Bert didn't find anything, the universal quantification in (7.25b) is vacuously satisfied.[74]

(7.25) a. Bert found nothing.

  b. $\approx \lambda g_g . \forall z_e \colon$ Bert found $z(g)$ in $@(g^-) \wedge \ldots \rightarrow$
  $$\#x(g)\big[x(g) \text{ is a thing in } g^-(1s) \wedge x(g) \sqsubseteq z(g)\big] = 0$$

Nonpresuppositional argument-position uses needn't imply the existence of anything satisfying their restriction or their scope.

The previous account derives the denotations of nonpresuppositional uses from modificational cardinal lexical entries. The account derives the following correspondence: The only "true" quantifiers — occurrences with the syntax and semantics of a restricted quantifier — are quantifiers introducing assignment quantification; and all true quantifiers are presuppositional (cf. (7.10)–(7.11)).[75]

Treating nonpresuppositional uses in this way doesn't forfeit the features of the assignment-quantificational accounts from §§5–6. For instance, the matrix quantifier in the headed relative construction in (7.27) is still base-generated in an assignment-argument position and thus requires an assignment-quantificational lexical entry, as in (7.26). The treatment of the donkey pronoun proceeds as in §5.2.

---

[74] *sigma* is in this respect like a total version of the composition of Partee's *iota* and *lift* adapted for pluralities.

[75] I will continue to use 'quantifier word' informally for strings that may be used to express quantification. I occasionally use small caps Q for the abstract quantificational concept, whether or not the item expressing that concept has a quantificational semantics. So, e.g., talk of "the quantifier word 'three'" or "the quantifier THREE" is compatible with 'three' having associated lexical entries, one of which is modificational.

(7.26) $[\![\mathbf{no}_Q]\!] = \lambda P_{\langle a,et \rangle}.\lambda P'_{\langle a,et \rangle}.\lambda g_g . \neg \exists x_e \exists a_a : P(a)(x)(g) \wedge P'(a)(x)(g)$

(7.27) No puppy which got a toy liked it.

However, the account does predict, surprisingly, that covarying interpretations in other "binding out of DP" (genitive binding, inverse linking) configurations from §6.4 should be marked with nonpresuppositional uses. This prediction appears to be borne out, as reflected in (7.28a)–(7.29a) with unstressed 'sm'.

(7.28) [*A*: "My cat doesn't like me because cats don't like boys." *B*: "No, it's you; …]

    a. #sm boys$_i$' cats like them$_i$.

    b. Some/SOME/Most boys$_i$' cats like them$_i$.

(7.29) [*A*: "My students don't like me because no teachers are popular with their students." *B*: "No, it's you; …]

    a. #Most students of sm teachers$_i$ like them$_i$.

    b. Most students of some/SOME/most teachers$_i$ like them$_i$.

The nPs representing nonpresuppositional 'sm boys/teachers' in (7.30) don't introduce an assignment binder-index. The donkey pronoun cannot be represented as a copy of an antecedent [F nP] since there isn't one. Hence an anaphoric reading is unavailable.

(7.30) a. $[_{\text{QP}^{\langle 3,a \rangle}} [_{\text{nP}^{\langle 2,e \rangle}} \ldots \text{sm boys}] [\iota_o^{\langle 3,a \rangle} [_{\text{n*P}} \ldots t_{2e} \ldots]]]$ like ???

     b. $[_{\text{QP}^{\langle 3,a \rangle}} [_{\text{nP}^{\langle 2,e \rangle}} \ldots \text{sm teachers}] [\text{most}^{\langle 3,a \rangle} [_{\text{n*P}} \ldots t_{2e} \ldots]]]$ like ???

(We will return to donkey pronouns in §7.4.3.)

7.2.2 Sources of "Specificity" and the Nominal Spine

The previous analysis of (non)presuppositional noun phrases distinguishes the following key ingredients: Num, which modifies the NP by specifying number or cardinality, e.g. mapping a property *P* to the property of having *n* *P*-individuals as atomic parts; a nominalizer little n, which may supply the world argument for the nP; F, which selects an individual from the set denoted by the nP in the world supplied by n; n*, which provides a locus of contextual domain restriction, and may project an external argument; and "true" quantifiers, which raise for type reasons from inside the noun phrase, and provide the locus of proportional readings and assignment-quantification.

(7.31) Prototypical properties

    • nP ('sm toys'): nonspecific, predicative

- FP ('a certain toy'): specific, existence implication
- n*P ('toy of Timmy's'): domain restriction
- QP ('every/no$_Q$ toy'): assignment-quantification, proportional

Delineating the sources of "specificity"-related phenomena (§6.1) in this way has several further features.

First, the account again makes no essential reference to syntactic or semantic definiteness or a word class of determiners. As discussed in §§6.1–6.2, there is variation within and across languages in how definiteness may be realized. The overt determiners in F in St'át'imcets quantifier phrases needn't be associated with semantic definiteness (maximality, uniqueness, familiarity); likewise in Somali, where the determiner in genitives and quantified expressions can be used without an intuitively specific or referential reading (§6.1). Although I treated F as a position for specific indefinites, I suggested that the position may also be realized by a definite article in explicit partitives such as 'all the babies' (§6.2). In languages such as Gungbe, the lexically distinct indefinite specificity marker and definite specificity marker compete for the same position — on our analysis, F — as reflected in (7.32c).

(7.32) a. Kókú xɔ̀   távò **ɖé**   lέ.
            Koku bought table SPFC$_{[-DEF]}$ PL
            'Koku bought some specific tables.'

    b. Kókú xɔ̀   távò **lɔ́**   lέ.
        Koku bought table SPFC$_{[+DEF]}$ PL
        'Koku bought the specific tables.'

    c. *Kókú xɔ̀   távò **ɖé**   lɔ́   (lέ).
        Koku buy.PERF table SPFC$_{[-DEF]}$ SPFC$_{[+DEF]}$ PL

                        (Aboh 2004: 76–77; Gungbe (Niger-Congo))

English quantifier phrases such as 'every baby' are "presuppositional" in the sense of implying the existence of babies and a relevant domain. Whereas the contextual domain restriction with (e.g.) anaphoric 'both babies' or an explicit partitive is to a set of previously introduced individuals in the context, no such "familiarity" presupposition need be associated with 'every baby'. Additional implications may be associated with particular expressions or occurrences, though I don't assume that syntactic or semantic definiteness is criterial of any of the positions delineated in (7.9). The structure in (7.9) may also apply to languages without articles or determiners. The account is compatible with elements such as quantifier words or choice-function-expressing words realizing different syntactic categories. What is essential in the general architecture are the functional heads n, n*, criterial of noun phrases; a position for specificity elements (e.g., specific indefinites, relative words); and a position for number.

Although an FP may pick out an individual in the world supplied by the nP, not all uses of expressions with at least the structure of an FP need have intuitively specific readings or imply existence in the world of the discourse. Assignment-binders inside or outside the noun phrase may generate local readings of a choice-function pronoun, domain pronoun, or world pronoun, yielding nonspecific interpretations or existence implications in a shifted domain (§§5.1, 6.1; more on this in §7.4). In quantifier phrases the selected individual varies with the assignment-quantification introduced by the quantifier. For this reason in what follows I will reserve 'specific' for readings about a particular individual or group of individuals.

7.2.3 Sources of Specificity II: "Weak" vs. "Strong" Quantifiers and Existential 'There' Sentences

The account in §7.2.1 derives the contrast between nonpresuppositional and presuppositional readings in terms of structural complexity. In a nonpresuppositional use of a string Q N, Q has the syntax/semantics of a modifier in NumP; in a presuppositional use, Q has the syntax/semantics of a restricted quantifier in a complete n*P. Logical properties such as being symmetric or intersective haven't played a fundamental explanatory role (contrast Keenan 1987). However, there may still be interesting connections between the presuppositional properties of quantifier words and the kinds of quantification intuitively expressed. Notably, the account predicts that quantifier words expressing quantificational concepts Q that cannot be defined in cardinal terms to be incompatible with nonpresuppositional readings (n. 75). Given that such quantifiers can only have quantificational lexical entries (type $\langle aet, \langle aet, t \rangle \rangle$), they can only be generated in a complete Q+n*P—the sort of structure generally associated with existence implications and "contextually given sets" (Enç 1991: 11), as in (7.10)–(7.11). That is, we expect the class of "strong" quantifiers across languages to include quantifier words expressing concepts with an inherently relational or proportional seman-tics—quantifiers whose semantics can only be given in terms of a relation between a restriction and scope—such as positive universal quantifiers ('all', 'every', 'each') and proportional quantifiers such as 'most' (cf. Partee 1995, Keenan 2002). To the best of my knowledge this prediction is borne out. I am not aware of languages with quantifier words for 'all', 'most', etc. that can be used nonpresuppositionally.[76]

---

[76] I think it is sometimes underappreciated just how surprising this crosslinguistic tendency (if not generalization) is. Enç's response is representative (Enç's NP corresponds to our DP):

The abstract semantics of quantifier words such as 'some', 'no', etc. renders them compatible with both modifier/cardinal uses and quantificational/proportional uses (§7.2.1). Yet we should expect there to be languages with words expressing SOME, NO, etc. that lexically specify a particular type of use. That is, we should expect there to be quantifier words expressing such concepts which only have a type $\langle\langle s, et\rangle, \langle s, et\rangle\rangle$ denotation — hence can only be used nonpresuppositionally as modifiers (cf. (7.20), (7.24)–(7.25)) — or only have a type $\langle\langle a, et\rangle, \langle\langle a, et\rangle, t\rangle\rangle$ denotation — hence can only be used presuppositionally as (assignment) quantifiers (cf. (7.10)–(7.11)). This prediction is also borne out.

Unstressed 'sm' is of the former kind. As we saw in §7.2.1, 'sm' can receive only the nonpresuppositional "reading of an indefinite number of people ..., yield[ing] nonsense" (Milsark 1977: 55) in examples such as (7.11)/(7.34). Unlike 'some', 'sm' is associated exclusively with a modifier entry such as (7.33b). ('sm N' needn't have a count meaning in the manner suggested by (7.33b) (e.g. 'sm water'); but for present purposes I give the entry following the schema in (7.19). I assume the *sigma* type shift option in (7.34).)

(7.33) a. $[\![\mathbf{some_Q}]\!] = \lambda P^+_{\langle a,et\rangle}.\lambda Q^+_{\langle a,et\rangle}.\lambda g_g\,.\,\exists x_e \exists a_a{:}\,P^+(a)(x)(g) \wedge Q^+(a)(x)(g)$

   b. $[\![\mathbf{some}_{\#}]\!] = \lambda P_{\langle s,et\rangle}.\lambda w_s.\lambda y_e.\lambda g_g\,.\,\#x(g)\big[P(w)(x)(g) \wedge x(g) \sqsubseteq y(g)\big] \geq 1$

(7.34) #sm people are jackasses. (cf. (7.11); *to be revised*)

   a. $[_S T^{\langle 1,a\rangle}\ [_{CP}\ [C_d\ t_{1a}]^{\langle 1,s\rangle}\ [[_{nP}\ (\sigma)\ w_1\text{-}g_1\ \text{sm people}]\ [t_{1s}\ (\text{are})$
       jackasses]]]]

   b. $[\![\mathbf{sm}]\!] = [\![\mathbf{some}_{\#}]\!]$

       $[\![nP]\!] = \lambda F_{et}.\lambda g_g\,.\,\forall z_e{:}\,\mathrm{MAX}(F)(z)(g) \to$
       $\#x(g)\big[x(g)\ \text{is a person in}\ g(1a)(1s) \wedge x(g) \sqsubseteq z(g)\big] \geq 1$

Why should universally quantifying NPs be specific? ... It has often been noted that universal quantifiers in natural languages quantify over contextually given sets... *If* universal quantification is over contextually relevant sets of individuals, it follows that NPs that quantify universally are specific ... The characterization of universally quantifying NPs as specific guarantees [that they presuppose existence]. (Enç 1991: 11; emphasis added)

There are reasons to be dissatisfied here. The question is why universal quantification must be over "contextually given sets," and why other types of quantification need not be. It would be striking if no language lexicalized a nonpresuppositional universal quantifier *all** (≈ 'all if any') felicitous in uses such as (i).

(i)   I have no idea whether there are aliens, but if many/*all** aliens attack us, it will be a bad day.

On the present account, the general absence of such quantifier words follows from the general structure of noun phrases and logical properties of the relevant quantificational concepts.

$$[\![S]\!] \approx \lambda g_g \,.\, \forall z_e \colon \mathrm{MAX}(\lambda z_e \lambda g_g . z(g) \text{ is a jackass in } @(g^-))(z)(g) \rightarrow$$
$$\#x(g)\big[x(g) \text{ is a person in } g^-(1s) \wedge x(g) \sqsubseteq z(g)\big] \geq 1$$
$$\approx \big|\{o \colon \mathrm{atom}(o) \wedge \mathrm{person}_@(o) \wedge o \sqsubseteq \text{the-maximal-jackass}_@\}\big| \geq 1$$

"Nonsense" indeed.

On the flip side, quantifier words which correspond to paradigmatic "weak" quantifiers in English, yet can only be used with existence implications, are attested across language families. Faller and Hastings (2008) show that *wakin* 'some' in Cuzco Quechua functions as a strong quantifier; it cannot be used predicatively, in existential 'there' sentences, or nonpresuppositionally ((7.35)). In some languages the distinction between presuppositional and nonpresuppositional 'some' is lexicalized with different words (see also Enç 1991, Matthewson 1998, 2009, Türker 2019).

(7.35) #Tari-sqa-ku-raq   **wakin** dodo-kuna-ta.

find-NX.PAST-PL-CONT some   dodo-PL-ACC

'They found some dodos.' (Surprisingly, given we had believed them extinct.)

(Faller and Hastings 2008: 308; Cuzco Quechua)

Unlike English 'some', expressions such as *wakin* can be understood as lexically specifying an assignment-quantificational entry such as (7.33a). (7.35) with *wakin* can only be represented with a Q+n*P structure such as (7.36c), yielding a presuppositional interpretation.

(7.36) a. $[\![\textit{\textbf{wakin}}]\!] = [\![\textbf{some}_Q]\!]$

      b. $[_{\mathrm{NumP}} \textit{wakin} \text{ dodos}] \notin [\![\ ]\!]$

      c. $\ldots \textit{wakin}^{\langle 2,a \rangle} [_{\mathrm{n^*P}} P_{1et} \, g_1 \, [_X \, [_{\mathrm{FP}} F_{2cf}\text{-}t_{2a} \, [_{\mathrm{nP}} w_1\text{-}g_1 \text{ dodos}]]]]$

Special semantic conditions or primitive "specificity markers" needn't be required to capture the properties of *wakin*, etc. characteristic of strong quantifiers. Quantifier words such as 'every', 'most' are incompatible with a modificational syntax/semantics in NumP (hence nonpresuppositional use) by virtue of the kind of quantificational concepts they express. Expressions such as *wakin* pattern this way as a quirk of their lexical semantics.

So, our syntax/semantics predicts an asymmetry with weak vs. strong quantifiers. On the one hand, the account predicts that we should find languages which lexicalize strong quantifier words expressing intuitively nonproportional quantificational concepts—e.g., SOME-words that are incompatible with nonpresuppositional or predicative uses. This prediction is confirmed in various language families. On the other hand, the account predicts that we should not expect to find languages which lexicalize weak quantifier words expressing inherently relational/proportional quantificational concepts — e.g., MOST-words that are compatible with nonpresuppositional or predicative uses. If only crosslinguistic generalizations weren't so dangerous.

Languages with lexicalized presuppositional quantifiers provide a key insight into the distinction between quantifiers which can vs. cannot be used in existential sentences. The existential sentences in (7.37) with lexicalized presuppositional SOME-words are ungrammatical.

(7.37) a. ***Wakin** llama-kuna chakra-pi ka-n.
    some llama-PL field-LOC be-3
    'There are some llamas in the field.'
         (Faller and Hastings 2008: 283; Cuzco Quechua)
   b. *Bahçe-de **bazı** çocuk-lar var.
    garden-LOC some child-PL exist
    'There are some children in the garden.' (Enç 1991: 15; Turkish)

A prominent approach is to explain felicity in existential sentences in terms of presuppositionality (Enç 1991, Diesing 1992, Zucchi 1995, Faller and Hastings 2008). In light of data such as (7.37), Faller and Hastings conclude by

> identifying presuppositionality as the key factor which excludes strongly quantified noun phrases from existential environments. That is, universal quantifiers … as well as other strong quantifiers like *wakin* 'SOME' … are felicitous only when it is understood that their restrictions are non-empty. (Faller and Hastings 2008: 285–286)

The account in this section suggests, rather, a common cause underlying the connection between presuppositional quantifiers and incompatibility with existential 'there': the non-predicative syntax/semantics of the noun phrase.

The analysis of existential 'there' sentences is controversial. Suppose that the syntax corresponds to the surface form — i.e., where an element such as 'there' (if any) is the grammatical subject and *(be)* Q N is the main predicate (cf. Williams 1984, Chung 1987, Hazout 2004, Francez 2007, Sabbagh 2009, Villalba 2013, Creissels 2014). The distribution of quantifier words falls out: Q N can be used in existential sentences only if Q N is predicative. Lexicalized presuppositional quantifiers are excluded ((7.37)) for the same reason that quantifier words expressing inherently relational quantificational concepts are excluded ((7.1)), and for the same reason that both types of quantifier words are excluded from predicative environments generally: they lack the cardinal entry that would allow them to be used as modifiers in the nP. The structure in (7.38) is uninterpretable.

(7.38) $[_{vP}$ (t_{is}) $[_{nP}$ every/most/*wakin* llama(s)]] $\notin \llbracket \; \rrbracket$

The problem of quantifier words in existential 'there' sentences is fundamentally a problem not of presupposition, syntax (Safir 1985), or logic (Keenan 1987), but of compositional semantics.

Following work by Partee and Borschev and Francez, suppose that existential 'there' sentences include a plural/locational pronoun representing a relevant domain (Borschev and Partee 2002, Francez 2007, 2010; see also Hartmann 2008, McCloskey 2014, Irwin 2018). A preliminary derivation is in (7.39).[77]

---

[77] We will revisit the syntax/semantics of the nominal predicate and contextual domain element in §7.5. See Francez 2007, 2009, 2010 for possible further structure in the element determining the relevant domain restriction. I ignore potential complications from distinguishing sorted variables for locations (cf. Kracht 2002). I bracket questions about the relation between the interpreted plural/locational pronoun and overt grammatical subjects such as 'there'. Interestingly, whereas standard English exploits the otherwise-locative marker 'there', Appalachian English uses the plural pronoun 'they':

(i)   They is something bad wrong with her.
                            (Montgomery and Hall 2004: lxii; Appalachian English)

Distinguishing the grammatical subject and the type-*e* pronoun may afford an analysis of existential constructions in languages that use both an expletive subject and a locative marker, as in (ii) with French *il y a*. Another candidate for an element realizing the type-*e* pronoun might be the German locative *da* in existentials with *sein* 'be' ((iii)). Unlike *es*, *da* isn't merely a syntactic expletive merged in Spec,C to license V2 (Czinglar 2000, 2002, Hartmann 2008); in (iv), where the coda phrase serves as the V2-licenser, *da* can still follow the tensed verb. 'Be' existentials where *da* and *es* co-occur are also possible ((v)); the expletive *es* is merged in Spec,C, and *da* remains in situ. Hartmann (2008) reports that although *da*'s locative meaning is largely bleached in existential sentences, *da* still makes a semantic contribution. Unlike in French, an alternative impersonal existential construction is available (*es gibt*), and *da* retains a broadly locational flavor ((vi)). (Thanks to Maja Spener and Merten Reglitz for assistance with the data.)

(ii)   Il y   a   trois enfants.
        it LOC has three children
        'There are three children.'

(iii)   Da sind viele Elefanten.
        DA are many elephants
        'There are many elephants.'

(iv)   Im   Zoo sind da/*es viele Elefanten.
        in.the zoo are DA/it many elephants
        'There are many elephants in the zoo.'

(v)   Es sind da bewährte Strategen am   Werk, mit denen Merkel sich   umgibt.
        it are DA proven   strategist at.the work with whom Merkel herself surrounds
        'There are proven strategists at work with whom Merkel surrounds herself.'
                            (www.heise.de/tp/features/Die-Bundeskuemmerin-4116705.html)

(vi)   ??Da ist (/^{ok}Es gibt) genau eine gerade Primzahl.
        DA is   it gives only   one even prime-number
        'There is only one even prime number.'   (Hartmann 2008: 208, Czinglar 2000: 57)

(7.39) There are three pillows.

    a. $[_S \, T^{\langle 1,a \rangle} \, [[C_d \, t_{1a}]^{\langle 1,s \rangle} \, [_{vP} \, o_{3e} \, g_1 \, [t_{1s} \, [three_{\#} \, pillows]]]]]$

    b. $[\![S]\!] \approx \lambda g_g \, . \, \#x(g)[x(g) \text{ is a pillow in } @(g^-) \wedge x(g) \sqsubseteq g^-(3e)] \geq 3$

(to be revised)

This says, roughly, that (7.39) is true iff the number of pillows in the contextually relevant domain — pillows that are part of the plurality/location $g_c(3e)$ — is at least three. The derived truth condition is equivalent to the intuitive quantificational condition that there are three o such that o is a pillow $\wedge \dots$ Yet there is no existential quantification, no "existence predicate," no implication of property instantiation (contrast Milsark 1974, McNally 1997, 2016, Chung and Ladusaw 2004, Hartmann 2008, Sabbagh 2009, Law 2011, McCloskey 2014, Irwin 2018). This is for the better. No innovations are required for examples with nominals expressing downward entailing ('no/few Ns') or non-monotone ('exactly three Ns') quantificational concepts. The compositional semantics of (7.40) with 'no' proceeds as in (7.39).

(7.40) There are no pillows (… so we should go buy some)

    a. $[_S \, T^{\langle 1,a \rangle} \, [[C_d \, t_{1a}]^{\langle 1,s \rangle} \, [_{vP} \, o_{2e} \, g_1 \, [t_{1s} \, [no_{\#} \, pillows]]]]]$

    b. $[\![S]\!] \approx \lambda g_g \, . \, \#x(g)[x(g) \text{ is a pillow in } @(g^-) \wedge x(g) \sqsubseteq g^-(2e)] = 0$

'(be) no pillows' is given the syntax/semantics of a main predicate. The property expressed is predicated of the plurality/location $g_c(2e)$ representing the contextually relevant domain. (7.40) is true iff the number of pillows in $g_c(2e)$ is zero. In (7.41) the relevant domain $g_c(4e)$ might be the set of entities E. E might even be empty (cf. 'There are no unicorns, because nothing exists', possibly true, never truly uttered).

(7.41) There are no unicorns.

    a. $[_S \, T^{\langle 1,a \rangle} \, [[C_d \, t_{1a}]^{\langle 1,s \rangle} \, [_{vP} \, o_{4e} \, g_1 \, [t_{1s} \, [no_{\#} \, unicorns]]]]]$

    b. $[\![S]\!] \approx \lambda g_g \, . \, \#x(g)[x(g) \text{ is a unicorn in } @(g^-) \wedge x(g) \sqsubseteq g^-(4e)] = 0$

There is nothing distinctly "existential" about so-called existential 'there' sentences.

The account of nonpresuppositional uses in §7.2.1 derives a non-predicative meaning for argument-position nPs from a general lexical rule or semantic type shift. Although type shifts are sometimes assumed to be universal, Partee herself

---

It would be interesting to examine whether other locative clitics in certain Romance existentials might also be analyzed as realizing the type-e pronoun (e.g., Italian *ci*, Catalan *hi*, Borgomanerese *ghi*); see also n. 100 on Irish *ann* 'in it'. We will consider additional motivations for a contextual domain element in §7.5, drawing on crosslinguistic connections between existential and possessive sentences.

was careful not to make such an assumption (e.g., 1986b: 208). A natural question is whether there are languages which lack type-shifting operations such as (7.22)–(7.23). Argument-position uses of quantifier words in such languages would have exclusively non-cardinal readings. Interestingly, Matthewson (1998) reports that quantifiers in St'át'imcets have obligatory cardinal readings in predicative uses, and obligatory proportional readings in non-predicative uses, as reflected in (7.42).

(7.42) a. [cw7it plísmen]$_{PRED}$ i=úxwal'=a
            many policemen   DET.PL=go.home=EXIS
            'The ones who went home were many policemen.'
                                                    (*cardinal reading obligatory*)
        b. [cw7it i=plísmen=a]   úxwal'
            many DET.PL=policeman=EXIS go.home
            'Many (of the) policemen went home.'
                                                (proportional reading obligatory)
                          (Matthewson 1998: 329, 321; St'át'imcets (Lillooet Salish))

If St'át'imcets lacks the operations in (7.22)–(7.23), then there isn't a *sigma* type shift to convert the predicative nP to type $\langle et, t\rangle$, or a lexical rule to derive a type-$\langle\langle s, et\rangle, \langle s, \langle et, t\rangle\rangle\rangle$ entry for the quantifier word. The only structure in which a cardinal use can appear is an nP of type $\langle e, t\rangle$ — hence the unavailability of a cardinal reading of *cw7it* 'many' in (7.42b). The only interpretable structure for (7.42b) is the structure with the complete n*P and quantificational proportional entry for 'many', as reflected in (7.43)–(7.44) (n_i a number-variable supplying a relevant threshold *n* for what counts as "many").[78]

(7.43) a. $[[_{nP} w_1 g_1 [[cw7it_\# n_1\text{-}g_1] \text{ police}]] [_{vP} t_{1s} \text{ went-home}]]$
        b. $[\![cw7it_\#]\!](n) = [\![\mathbf{many}_\#]\!](n) = \lambda P_{\langle s,et\rangle}.\lambda w_s.\lambda y_e.\lambda g_g .$

            $\#x(g)[P(w)(x)(g) \wedge x(g) \sqsubseteq y(g)] \geq n(g)$
            $[\![nP]\!] = \lambda y_e.\lambda g_g . \#x(g)[x(g) \text{ is a policeman in } g(1a)(1s) \wedge x(g) \sqsubseteq y(g)]$
            $\geq g(1a)(1n)$
            (7.43a) $\notin [\![\ ]\!]$

(7.44) a. $[_S T^{\langle 1,a\rangle} [_{CP} [_{C_d} t_{1a}]^{\langle 1,s\rangle}$
            $[[_{QP^{\langle 2,a\rangle}} [cw7it_Q n_1\text{-}g_1]^{\langle 2,a\rangle} [_{P_{1et}} g_1 [X [_{FP} F_{2cf} t_{2a} [_{nP} w_1\text{-}g_1 \text{ police}]]]]]$
            $[_{vP} t_{1s} \text{ went-home}]]]]$

---

[78] See Matthewson 1998: 353–358 on the specific proportional conditions associated with quantificational *cw7it*; see Partee 1989b on English 'many'.

b. $[\![cw7it_Q]\!](n) = [\![\mathbf{many}_Q]\!](n) = \lambda P_{\langle a,et\rangle}.\lambda P'_{\langle a,et\rangle}.\lambda g_g$.

$$\#o\big[\exists a_a\colon P(a)(\lambda g_g.o)(g) \wedge P'(a)(\lambda g_g.o)(g)\big]$$
$$\div \#o'\big[\exists a'_a\colon P(a')(\lambda g_g.o')(g)\big] \geq n(g)$$

(7.44a) $\in [\![\ ]\!]$

Insofar as St'át'imcets quantifier words in argument-position uses can only appear in QPs, our account predicts that such uses will invariably carry an existence implication. In (7.44a), as in (7.10)–(7.11), the choice-function pronoun selects an individual in the given world; structures such as (7.24) yielding nonpresuppositional readings are unavailable. Indeed Matthewson (1998) glosses the enclitic portion ...*a* of the determiner in St'át'imcets quantifier phrases as encoding "assertion of existence."

7.2.4 *Sources of Specificity III: Modal (In)dependence*

The syntax/semantics for noun phrases developed in these chapters delineates phenomena often associated with "specificity" and weak vs. strong quantifiers, such as existence implications, domain restriction, definiteness, cardinal and proportional readings, and compatibility with existential 'there' sentences. This section considers one further connection regarding modal independence.

A key advance came from Musan (1995), who observed that temporally independent readings — readings in which the temporal interpretation of the noun phrase is independent of the temporal interpretation of the clause's main predicate — are generally unavailable with nonpresuppositional noun phrases. (7.45) needn't have the perhaps surprising implication that (7.46) has.

(7.45) In the sixties, every senator was a child.

    a. ≈ "in the sixties, everyone who was a senator at that time was a child"
                (*temporally dependent reading*)

    b. ≈ "in the sixties, everyone who is now a senator was then a child"
                (*temporally independent reading*)

(7.46) In the sixties, (sm) senators were children.

    a. ≈ "in the sixties, some senators at that time were children"
                (*temporally dependent reading*)

    b. ≉ "in the sixties, some people who are now senators were then children"   (*temporally independent reading*)
                (cf. Musan 1995: 74–76)

Although Musan, following Enç, focused primarily on tense and temporal interpretations, she notes that contrasts analogous to those in (7.45)–(7.46) may be observed with worlds (1995: 219–220).[79] Examples such as (7.47)–(7.48) support Musan's generalization. Unlike (7.47), (7.48) cannot receive the (non-sadistic) reading in which the world of 'murderer' is independent of the world of the supposition. In (7.49) Alice has a superior tactical strategy; Bert is confused.

(7.47)   It would be better if every murderer was a priest.

    a.   ≈ "for all worlds u in which every murderer in u is a priest in u, things are better in u"   (*modally dependent reading*)

    b.   ≈ "it would be better if everyone who is actually a murderer was a priest"   (*modally independent reading*)

(7.48)   It would be better if sm murderers were priests.

    a.   ≈ "for all worlds u in which some murderers in u are priests in u, things are better in u"   (*modally dependent reading*)

    b.   ≉ "it would be better if some people who are actually murderers were priests"   (*modally independent reading*)

(7.49)   [Context: Alice and Bert are watching their team in a match. Players are assigned either an offensive position or a defensive position.]

    a.   *Alice:* The team would play better if everyone on offense was on defense.

    b.   *Bert:* The team would play better if there were (sm) players on offense on defense.

In (7.49a) Alice is saying that the team would play better if all the players who are actually playing on offense played defense instead. (7.49b) can only be interpreted as saying that the relevant better worlds are worlds in which offensive players are (also? simultaneously?) on defense; the world relevant for interpreting 'players on offense' can only be the world of the counterfactual possibility.

The distribution of modally (temporally) independent noun phrases — noun phrases with nonlocal readings of world (time) arguments — cannot be characterized simply at the level of quantifier words. Whereas in (7.50a) 'no one on offense' can receive a modally independent reading, (7.50b) with the existential 'there' construction is incoherent.

---

[79] Lecarme (1996, 1999b, 2004, 2008) shows that in nominal tense languages such as Somali these interpretive possibilities are reflected in the morphology. Indefinite noun phrases in Somali are incompatible with interpreted tense morphemes, which would supply an independent temporal interpretation. In some languages modally independent readings can also be overtly marked, e.g.:

(i)   oko   jibotee-**ne**   o-katomi-ne
          1SG.POSS spouse-IRR.F 1SG.AGT-fight.with-CONTIN.F
       'I fight with (and kill) one who could have been my wife (he said)'
                                (Dixon 2004: ex. 10.68; Jarawara (Arawan))

In what follows I will continue to ignore tense.

(7.50) The team would play better…

     a. if no one on offense was on offense.   ($\approx$ (7.49a))

     b.#if there was no one on offense on offense. ($\not\approx$ (7.49a))

What relevantly distinguishes (7.50b) is that the existential 'there' construction forces a nonpresuppositional reading — a structure in which the quantifier word is in NumP (§§7.2.1–7.2.3). This suggests that the possibility of receiving a modally independent reading depends on having at least the structure of an FP: F nP. The distinction between uses of quantifier words that can have modally independent interpretations vs. uses that cannot corresponds to the distinction between structurally non-defective vs. structurally defective noun phrases.

§4.2 applied the assignment-variable framework to classic de re vs. de dicto ambiguities in attitude ascriptions. The distinction between de re and de dicto readings was diagnosed as a distinction between global and local readings of world arguments. We can now see that not all noun phrases can receive de re readings in this sense. World-variables in nP noun phrases ((7.48), (7.49b), (7.50b)) have obligatory local (de dicto, modally dependent) readings.[80]

The relevant generalization is that world-variables in nP noun phrases must be coindexed with the world-variable in the closest v (cf. Rizzi 1990). No such constraint applies if the nP is embedded in a larger noun phrase. Given that indices are features, the generalization amounts to the claim that index-features in n agree with the index-feature in the closest v unless n is "blocked off" (in some sense to be made precise) by a relevant intervening head. These generalizations can be derived from the current architecture and agreement mechanisms in contemporary syntax.

For purposes of illustration consider a general phase-based framework (Chomsky 2000, 2001, 2008) in which syntactic derivations take place in small chunks — *phases* — which provide the window for syntactic operations, such as

---

[80] In §4.2 we also considered examples with nonspecific de re readings such as (i), where the noun phrase takes narrow scope and its world argument receives a global reading:

(i)   Alice thinks a friend of mine will win.

        • *nonspecific de re* $\approx$ "there is some group of individuals who are friends of mine (say, the Sharks) such that Alice thinks some or other of them will win"

Unlike noun phrases with 'a', noun phrases with 'sm' are exclusively nPs. So, we should expect nonspecific de re readings to be generally unavailable with 'sm' and other nonpresuppositional uses of weak quantifiers. This prediction appears to be borne out. Nonspecific de re readings in (7.48)–(7.50), where nonspecificity is forced by the scope island, are apparently unavailable. The attitude ascription in (ii) is similarly strained.

(ii)   [Context: There's a group of friends of mine, the Sharks, and Bert thinks some or other of them are after him, but he doesn't know who. Bert doesn't think I have any friends.]

     #Bert thinks there are sm friends of mine after him.

feature matching/transmission (also e.g. Cecchetto 2004, Hiraiwa 2005, Kratzer 2009). Phases are characterized by various types of syntactic, semantic, and morphophonological independence. In the clausal case the phases have been argued to be (at least) v*P and CP.[81] Arguments from the literature for treating DP as a phase, such as regarding island constraints, can be reframed as applying to the spread of functional projections above nP (e.g. Adger 2003: ch. 10, Svenonius 2004, Hiraiwa 2005, Lee-Schoenfeld 2007). Extraction is degraded from the specific indefinites, definites, and presuppositional quantifier phrases in (7.51).[82]

(7.51) a. Who did Alice say you saw sm/several/more than three pictures of?
        b.*?Who did Alice say you saw the/a certain picture of?
        c. *Who did Alice say you saw Bert's/most picture(s) of?

                                                    (cf. Diesing 1992: 97–98)

As we have seen, specific indefinites, genitives, and presuppositional quantifiers can also receive modally/temporally independent interpretations. The apparent gradation in unacceptability in (7.51b)–(7.51c) may support positing multiple nominal phases (cf. Svenonius 2004, Kazuhiro 2010, Jiménez-Fernández 2012). For present purposes we can assume that at least FP: F nP is a phase.[83]

The modal dependence of nP noun phrases on the closest v, and the modal independence of noun phrases larger than nP, can be derived from feature transmission and the locality of phases. The definitions in (7.52)–(7.53) will suffice (see also Richards 2007, Heim 2008, Kratzer 2009, Gallego 2010).

(7.52) *Phase Impenetrability Condition* (PIC)

        At the phase ZP containing phase HP, the domain of H is not accessible
        to operations; only H and its edge [i.e. specifier(s)/adjunct(s)] are
        accessible to such operations.   (cf. Chomsky 2001: 14, 2004: 108)

---

[81] Recall that v* is the verbal functional head closing off complete verb phrases. Thus far I have ignored v* in the compositional semantics; we will return to this in §7.5.

[82] As Diesing (1992: 98) notes: "Thus, the 'specificity' effect is not due to a contrast between the definite and indefinite determiners, or even between strong and weak determiners. Although extraction from an NP with a strong determiner is generally bad, the acceptability of extraction from an NP with a weak determiner hinges on their being no presuppositional reading available (or required) in the given context."

[83] Alternatively the relevant minimal nominal phase could be treated as n*P, where the apparent phasal status of FP noun phrases such as specific indefinites is due to an n*P shell. Unlike in genitives, quantifier phrases, etc., the n* head would be semantically empty (thus maintaining the contrast between specific indefinites of type e and n*Ps such as postnominal genitives of type $\langle e, t \rangle$). Such an analysis would make the parallels between noun phrases and verb phrases even more transparent: nP/vP are defective noun/verb phrases, and n*P/v*P are nominal/verbal phases (cf. Chomsky 2007: 25–26). The talk of "FP phases" in what follows could be understood as short for $[_{n*P} n^* [_{FP} F nP]]$ structures with semantically vacuous n*. We will return to these issues in §§7.4–7.5.

(7.53) *Feature Checking* (FC) (application to worlds)

The features of a world argument $w[s]$ agree with (match, unify with) the features of the verbal functional head $W[s]$, if any, that it is in the domain of.

The Phase Impenetrability Condition (PIC) encodes the idea that the complement of a phase is accessible to syntactic operations (e.g. agreement) only from positions inside the phase.[84] Feature Checking (FC) states that world-index features in a verbal domain agree, where "verbal domains" are understood broadly as domains headed by elements with world features.

The possibility of modally independent readings with FPs (n^*Ps, QPs) follows from the PIC. The world-pronoun in the nP is inside the complement of a nominal phase; it is thus inaccessible to feature-matching operations from outside the phase, as reflected in (7.54) (where H is the relevant nominal phase head; I use the large parentheses to indicate inaccessibility at the higher phase ZP).

(7.54) $[_{ZP}$ Z ... $[_{HP}$ H $\Big($ ... $[_{nP}$ $[w_k\ g_j]$ ...

The interpretation of the world-pronoun might be contextually identified with the interpretation of the world-variable of the clause's main predicate. Yet since the nominal phase head renders n invisible from the positions of higher verbal functional heads, no coindexing or interpretive equivalence is required.

Turning to nPs, there are two relevant positions to consider. If the nP originates in the vP, agreement in world-index features with v is ensured in the next v^*P/CP phase, as illustrated in (7.55) (I will use underlining to indicate results of FC). The world-variable in n is visible for syntactic operations from v; hence the feature sets agree by FC, yielding the coindexed variables with features $[i], [s]$.

(7.55) $[_{ZP}$ ... $[_{vP}$ $\underline{v^0_{is}}$ ... $[_{nP}$ $\underline{n^0_{is}}$ ...

If the nP is generated as an external argument in Spec,v^*, then the agreement in world-index features is ensured (at minimum) by the complementizer in the CP phase. By the PIC, the n in the edge of the v^*P phase is visible for syntactic operations from the local C position. Given that the complementizer raises for type reasons from v, C has feature s. Hence the feature sets agree by FC, yielding the coindexed variable with features $[i], [s]$, as reflected in (7.56).

---

[84] A syntactic constraint such as the PIC needn't raise concerns for familiar top-down compositional semantic derivations and LF representations. Although it is often assumed that the complements of phases are shipped to the phonological and semantic components simultaneously, a phase-based theory with local morphophonological spell-out is compatible with treating the semantic component as accessed one-off when the syntactic derivation completes (Nissenbaum 2000, Cecchetto 2004, Tanaka 2015).

(7.56) $[_{CP} \; \underline{C^{0^{\langle i,s \rangle}}} \; ... \; [_{v^*P} \; [_{nP} \; \underline{n_{is}^0} \; ...] \; [v^* \; \big(\; ... \; v_{is}^0 \; ...$

In either configuration, since FC applies at the phase-level, n's index cannot be determined via agreement from a higher clause, as reflected in (7.57) (order of the embedded n and v irrelevant).

(7.57) $[_{ZP} \; ... \; v_{ks}^0 \; ... \; [_{CP} \; C^{0^{\langle i,s \rangle}} \; \big(\; ... \; n_{is}^0 \; ... \; v_{is}^0 \; ...$

The locality of phases and type-driven movement of C from v ensure that the world-variable in n is coindexed with the closest v.

So, for a vP-internal dependent nP in the domain of v*P, FC applies with v_{is}^0 in the v*P phase; and for a dependent nP in the domain of CP, FC applies with $C^{0^{\langle i,s \rangle}}$ in the CP phase. In both cases the result is a world-variable in n_{is}^0 coindexed with the local $C^{0^{\langle i,s \rangle}}$ and v_{is}^0.[85]

A derivation for a modally dependent nonspecific de dicto nP is in (7.58). The boxes indicate the result of agreement by FC in the lower CP phase. (For now I continue to ignore v* in the semantics. I assume the *sigma* type-shift option and simplified cardinal entry for 'sm' from §7.2.1.)

---

[85] A syntactic account of modally dependent readings of nPs along these lines is compatible with alternative theories of agreement, e.g. understanding agreement in terms of feature matching, copying, or merging/unification. Although agreement construed as unification is neutral regarding the direction of feature transmission, our compositional semantics would severely constrain the possible nP noun phrases that can enter the syntactic derivation. Given that the complementizer raises for type reasons from v, v will be fully specified for world-index features, say v_{is}^0. If n enters the derivation with a feature-set including $[d]$, for some number $d \neq i$ or type $d \neq s$, then n won't be interpretable after FC since variables with multiple numerical or type indices aren't interpretable (§2). The only options are (a) for n to enter the structure with a matching feature-set, n_{is}^0; (b) for n to enter the structure minimally specified for type, n_s^0; (c) for n to be empty (ignoring e.g. category features). In (a), FC amounts to checking; in (b), n receives its numerical index from v or C and becomes an interpretable variable syntactically/semantically bound by C; and in (c), n lacks a world feature and thus isn't recognized as a target for FC. Case (c) might be understood as applying to '(be) nP' predicate nominals, where the nominal supplies the clause's main predicate ((7.20), (7.39)–(7.41)), as reflected in (i). Alternatively, the complementizer might be treated as raising directly from n^0, as in (ii). In (ii) the predicate nominal is "nominal" in having the category of the root determined by n (and having interpretable φ-features), and "predicative" in having its world features determined directly by the (type-driven) movement of the complementizer. The upward φ-feature propagation to the verbal/clausal domain discussed in Hazout 2004 follows straightway.

(i) $C^{0^{\langle i,s \rangle}} \; ... \; [_{vP} \; v_{is}^0 \; [_{nP} \; n_\varnothing \; NumP]]$

(ii) $C^{0^{\langle i,s \rangle}} \; ... \; [_{vP} \; v \; [_{nP} \; [_{n^0} \; n_\varnothing \; t_{is}] \; NumP]]$

(7.58) Bert thinks sm friends of mine smoke.

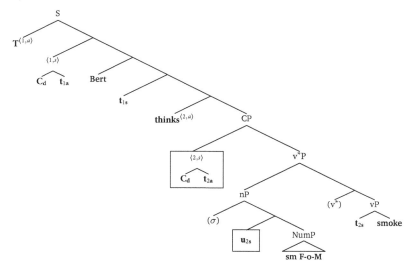

$$\llbracket v^*P \rrbracket \approx \lambda g_g . \forall z_e \colon \text{MAX}(\lambda z_e.\lambda g_g.z(g) \text{ smokes in } g(2s))(z)(g) \rightarrow$$
$$\#x(g)\big[x(g) \text{ is a friend-of-mine in } g(2s) \wedge x(g) \sqsubseteq z(g)\big] \geq 1$$

$$\llbracket S \rrbracket \approx \lambda g_g . \forall a_a \colon a(g) \text{ is compatible with Bert's state of mind in } @(g^-) \rightarrow$$
$$\big(\forall z_e \colon \text{MAX}(\lambda z_e.\lambda g_g.z(g) \text{ smokes in } @(a(g)))(z)(g) \rightarrow$$
$$\#x(g)\big[x(g) \text{ is a friend-of-mine in } @(a(g)) \wedge x(g) \sqsubseteq z(g)\big] \geq 1 \big)$$

This says, roughly, that for all possibilities h compatible with Bert's state of mind, the number of $o \in E$ that are friends of mine in $@(h)$ and included among the smokers in $@(h)$ is at least one. The embedded subject nP 'sm friends-of-mind' is in the edge of the lower v^*P phase. The n with feature $[s]$ is thus visible from the position of the embedding complementizer and accessible to operations such as FC. The nominal's world-variable is coindexed with C's binder-index by agreement, and so, by extension, with the world-trace in the clause's main predicate due to type-driven movement of the complementizer.

The account in this section provides a purely syntactic basis for obligatory modally dependent readings of certain uses of noun phrases. One might wonder whether the obligatory local reading of the clause's main predicate might be captured by a similar general agreement mechanism. The answer is "no." In clauses with complete verb phrases, the main predicate's world argument in the vP is embedded in the complement of the v^*P phase, and thus inaccessible to operations such as FC from the position of the complementizer or an embedding modal element.

(7.59) MOD $[_{CP}$ C ... $[_{v^*P}$ v* $\Big($ $[_{vP}$ ...

A purely agreement-based approach is inadequate for the general case.

Our syntax/semantics with (overt, type-driven) movement of the complementizer obviates this issue. The complement of a phase becomes inaccessible to further syntactic operations when the next higher phase is assembled (e.g. Chomsky 2001: 13–14). Hence a vP becomes inaccessible only after the movement of the complementizer is triggered (§3.5) and the complementizer is again merged to the structure, yielding $[_{CP}$ C$^{0^{\langle i,s\rangle}}$ ... $[_{v^*P}$ v* $\Big($ ... t$_{is}$ ....[86] The complementizer is coindexed with the world-variable of the main predicate by type-driven movement, and with the world-variables of any dependent nPs in the clause by agreement, as described previously.

A key feature of our assignment-variable-based framework has been its ability to capture various types of local and global readings. Yet just as important for an overall theory is an account of readings which are obligatory or unavailable. We have seen that different mechanisms may apply in different cases. For the obligatory local reading of the world argument of a clause's main predicate, §3 offered a movement-based explanation. The complementizer is base-generated in the main predicate's world-argument position, and moves for type reasons as a quantifier over worlds; and the interpretation of the world-variable is determined by an embedding modal element, which raises as a quantifier over assignments from an internal argument in C^0. For the modal dependence of nonpresuppositional noun phrases — the obligatory local readings of world arguments in nPs — this section has offered an agreement-based syntactic explanation. Obligatory local/global readings of particular expressions may also be determined by lexical constraints — e.g., that an associated assignment-variable be bound by the local or topmost assignment-binder (cf. §4.3.3). For some expressions, the relevant lexical constraints might be explainable in terms of the truth-conditional content and general features of contexts of use (cf. Blutner 2004, Leckie 2013, Silk 2016a, 2017); for other expressions, the constraints may be language-specific and idiosyncratic (cf. §7.2.3). Appealing to multiple explanatory mechanisms in these ways needn't be a defect. Indeed we should expect the different parts of the theory — narrow syntax, lexical and compositional semantics, pragmatics — to constrain interpretation in different ways. A linguistic theory with assignment-variables can provide compositional derivations of the varieties of local and global readings, while offering principled bases for reining in the flexibility of the system.

---

[86] In a copy theory of movement, the lower copy would be converted to the coindexed variable in the semantic component (nn. 9, 84).

7.3 Taking Stock

Let's recap. §§5–6 applied the assignment-variable framework to different types of quantifier phrases and linguistic shifting phenomena with relativization and pronominal anaphora. This chapter has examined the internal syntax and compositional semantics more carefully in developing a more general assignment-variable-based theory of noun phrases. The proposed analysis is motivated by crosslinguistic data, coheres with current syntactic theories, and provides precise derivations of various phenomena often associated with "specificity" and the weak vs. strong quantifier distinction — e.g., existence implications, contextual domain restriction, predicative uses and existential 'there' sentences, and modal independence. I hope that these features may provide a fruitful contribution to broader crosslinguistic work on the syntax and compositional semantics of noun phrases and quantifier words.

Noun phrases and verb phrases are given a parallel basic layered N/V, n/v, n^*/v^* structure. First, nP noun phrases represent nonpresuppositional readings and provide the nominal analogue of "defective" vPs. Their syntax/semantics is fundamentally predicative. Nonproportional (cardinal) readings of quantifier words are represented as modifiers in NumP, yielding a property-type denotation. The nominalizer/verbalizer n/v provides the locus of world-variables. In predicate nominals the world argument may be supplied directly by the world-trace derived from type-driven movement of the complementizer. In argument-position uses the world-variable in n is determined by agreement with the local v in the v^*P phase or with the local C in the CP phase. In both cases the world argument for the noun phrase is derived to be coindexed with the world argument of the clause's main predicate. The modal dependence of nonpresuppositional noun phrases — the obligatory local (de dicto) reading of the nominal predicate's world argument — follows from the proposed nP analysis, the general clausal architecture from §3, and independent syntactic mechanisms (e.g., feature transmission, PIC).

Contrasts between nonpresuppositional and presuppositional uses are captured in terms of the structural complexity of the noun phrase. We delineated three relevant heads above nP (perhaps among others): F, for elements such as specific indefinites, relative words, and certain uses of pronouns, articles, and other determiners; n^*, for elements such as the genitive morpheme and certain (possibly implicit) Case-assigning elements; and Q, for certain uses of quantifier words. Various "specificity"-related phenomena are derived from the syntax/semantics of elements in the larger structure.

The analysis delineates the sources of specific readings, existence implications, and notional definiteness. In FP: F nP structures the F head may select an nP-individual from the world supplied by n, giving rise to specific readings and existence implications. In embedded environments such as attitude ascriptions, the existence implication may be relative to a local domain. Quantification introduced in more complex noun phrases can lead to readings that aren't intuitively specific, in the sense of being about a particular individual. The n*P layer may provide a source of contextual domain restriction. Absent further semantic definiteness features or lexical constraints, the individual(s) denoted by an FP or in the denotation of an n*P may or may not be "familiar," in the sense of having been previously introduced in the discourse.

The modal independence of specific indefinites, definites, genitives, and pre-suppositional uses of quantifier words — the possibility of nonlocal (de re) read-ings of the nominal's world argument — is an instance of the syntactic/semantic independence of the nominal phase. The world-argument position in n is inac-cessible to syntactic operations such as agreement with a verbal head out-side the phase. The interpretation of the supplied world-pronoun might be contextually identified with the world of the clause's main predicate, but it need not be.

"True" quantifiers — quantifiers with the syntax/semantics of a restricted quantifier — provide the locus of proportional readings and assignment quantifi-cation. I suggested that the distinction between "weak" vs. "strong" quantifiers corresponds to a distinction between quantifier words that can vs. cannot function as modifiers in NumP. Strong quantifiers across languages are predicted to be those which express inherently relational quantificational concepts, such as 'all', 'each', 'most'. The quantifiers' abstract semantics, along with the general syntactic architecture, predict that they can only be used in QPs, and thus that they invariably exhibit properties such as presuppositionality, proportional readings, independence, etc. Weak quantifiers, in contrast, express quantifica-tional concepts that can be represented with modifier entries such as (7.19). Insofar as they can be used in nP phrases, such quantifiers are compatible with predicative, nonpresuppositional, and cardinal uses. Although a quantifier's abstract semantics may be compatible with modifier and quantificational entries, languages may have forms which are only associated with a particular entry — e.g., a form expressing SOME that is exclusively modificational and thus can only be used in nPs with nonpresuppositional, cardinal, dependent readings, or a form that is exclusively quantificational and thus can only be used in QPs with presuppositional, proportional readings. Some languages may lack type-shifting operations for non-predicative uses of nPs, leading to systematic correlations between predicative/non-predicative environments and cardinal/proportional readings of quantifiers.

7.4 Relative Clauses, Revised: Internal Heads and Intensional Gaps

§5.1 applied the assignment-variable framework to develop an improved compositional semantics for head-raising analyses of relative clauses. On the proposed analysis, the relative phrase originates in Spec,C_{rel}, and the relative complementizer raises from the "gap" position as a quantifier over individuals. §5.3 raised critical syntactic and semantic issues for an account developed along these lines. It is hard to see how an analysis in which the relative phrase originates outside IP_{rel} could apply to circumnominal relative constructions such as (7.60), or how it could capture *intensional gap readings*, where the interpretation of the nominal predicate's world argument is apparently shifted by an IP_{rel}-internal element, as reflected in (7.61).

(7.60)   [$_{CP_{rel}}$ Atia n da'   **bua seka** da'a   zaam]   la bɔi   mɛ.
         Atia C buy.PERF goat REL   market yesterday D lose.PERF PRT
         (lit. 'The [Atia bought which goat at the market yesterday] got lost.')
         'The goat that Atia bought at the market yesterday got lost.'
                                (Hiraiwa et al. 2017: 5; Gurenɛ (Niger-Congo))

(7.61)   Callie wants to hug every unicorn$_i$ which Timmy thinks^i he found.

This section shows how an improved "matching" analysis of relative clauses can be layered into the general syntax/semantics for noun phrases developed in this chapter. The account generalizes to languages with circumnominals and captures linguistic shifting data with donkey sentences and intensional gap readings.

7.4.1   A Matching Account of Relative Clauses

In §6.2 we saw how certain types of restrictive modification could be captured in the n*P layer. A natural idea would be to extend the approach to restrictive relative clauses. Like with the n*Ps in (7.51c), extraction from the nominal head of a relative clause is generally degraded — even when the noun phrase occurs with a nonpresuppositional quantifier, as reflected in (7.62). As noted in §6.2, in some languages the same markers used in introducing free *R* possessors are used in introducing restrictive relative clauses, as in (7.63). The restrictive relative clause in (7.65) would function analogously for purposes of compositional semantics to the restrictive free *R* possessor modifier in (7.64).

(7.62)   a.*?Who did you say there are sm/three pictures of which Alice likes?
       b.   Who did you say there are sm/three pictures of (in the newspaper)?

(7.63)   a.   a^{33}-faay^{55} ge^{33} piŋ^{11}-guo^{35}
           Ah Fai   ASSOC apple
           'Ah Fai's apple'

b. a^{33}-faay^{55} maai^{13} ge^{33} piŋ^{11}-guo^{35}
   Ah Fai   buy   ASSOC apple
   'apple that Ah Fai bought'   (Gil 2013: ex. 3; Cantonese)

(7.64) cat of Alice's

a. [$_{n^*P}$ [R$_1$-g$_1$ Alice] ['s [F$_{2cf}$-t$_{2a}$ w$_1$-g$_1$-cat]]]

b. $[\![n^*P]\!] = \lambda x_e.\lambda g_g \, . \, x(g) = g(2a)(2cf)\big(cat_{g(1a)(1s)}\big)\wedge$
$$g(1a)(1R)(\text{Alice})(x(g))$$

(7.65) cat that Alice bought

[$_{n^*P}$ [$_{CP_{rel}}$ … F$_{2cf}$-t$_{2a}$ w$_1$-g$_1$-cat…] [X [F$_{2cf}$-t$_{2a}$ w$_1$-g$_1$-cat]]]

The structure schematized in (7.65) is essentially a matching structure. Matching analyses agree with head-raising analyses that the relative phrase originates inside the relative clause; however, matching analyses posit that the nominal head also has an independent representation outside CP$_{rel}$, not related by movement (Lees 1960, Carlson 1977, Sauerland 1998, 2003, 2004, Bhatt 2002; see also Cinque 2013, 2015). Although one of the "internal" and "external" heads is generally deleted in the phonological component, both are semantically interpreted. In languages with double-headed circumnominal relative constructions (de Vries 1993, Dryer 2005, Heath 2008, Cinque 2013: ch. 17, 2017), the structure in (7.65) may correspond to the pronounced form. In Jamsay (7.66) the particle mediating the relative clause and external head is a genitive morpheme.

(7.66) [ìjè   è   íjɛ́   bèrɛ̂:]   mà   ìjɛ́
        position 2PL stand can.IMPF-PPL.NONHUM POSS position
        'the position (/situation) where you stand'
                                    (Heath 2008: 481; Jamsay (Niger-Congo))

Each of the internal and external nominal heads and n* is overtly realized.

  Let's start by considering the internal structure of the relative clause. In light of the data with circumnominal relatives, suppose the relative phrase originates in the gap position inside the relative clause. One option would be to treat the world argument of the relative clause's main predicate as a world-pronoun, as in §5. The world argument of 'failed' in (7.67) can be interpreted independently of the (shifted) world of the supposition.

(7.67) It would be better if sm students who failed didn't fail.

An alternative is to unify the analysis of the relative complementizer with the analysis of the declarative complementizer, as raising from v as a quantifier over worlds. Examples such as (7.68)–(7.69) provide preliminary support for the latter option. (7.68b) is sad; (7.68a) is disturbing.

(7.68) a. In the sixties, few children who sm senators bullied were invited to their birthday parties.
   b. In the sixties, few children who most senators bullied were invited to their birthday parties.

(7.69) [Context: Bert doesn't think there are spies, but we know better.]
   Bert thinks that if people who most/#sm spies are friends with come to the party, it will be fun.

Like in the examples from §7.2.4, the modal/temporal interpretation of the subject-position nonpresuppositional noun phrase is obligatorily linked to the relative clause's main predicate. This follows from the §7.2.4-account if the relative complementizer has world-index features: the world argument of the nP in Spec,v^* is determined by feature transmission FC in the CP_{rel} phase, as reflected in (7.70) (again using underlining to indicate the result of FC).

(7.70) ... $[_{CP_{rel}} \underline{C^{0^{(2,s)}}_{rel}} [_{v^*P} [_{nP} \underline{u_{2s}} \text{ sm spies}] v^* \big(vP \ldots$

What distinguishes individual relative clauses from clauses in verbal environments is that the local modal domain isn't determined by type-driven movement of an immediately embedding modal element.

The relative complementizer's internal assignment argument can be supplied instead by an assignment-variable representing the relevant local/global reading. A revised structure for the n*P is in (7.71).[87]

(7.71) a. cat which meowed
   b. $[_{n^*P} [_{CP_{rel}} [C_{rel} \, g_1]^{(2,s)} [[wh_{2cf}\text{-}t_{2a} \, w_1\text{-}g_1\text{-cat}] \, t_{2s} \text{ meowed}]]$
      $[X [F_{2cf}\text{-}t_{2a} \, w_1\text{-}g_1\text{-cat}]]]$

The relative phrase is a copy for purposes of interpretation of the external FP (see Sauerland 2004, Cinque 2013: ch. 17 for potential complications). The modal interpretation of the relative clause's main predicate (and any dependent noun phrases) is determined by the assignment-variable in C^0_{rel}. The CP_{rel} modifier is layered into the general structure of n*P noun phrases.

---

[87] I put aside which of the internal/external nominal heads represents the elided head. It is often assumed in matching accounts that the elided head is the head inside the relative clause; see Cinque 2013 for arguments that which head is pronounced can vary across within and across languages (cf. Law 2014). To fix ideas I follow Cinque 2003, 2013 in representing the relative clause as merged left of n*, though the compositional semantics is compatible with right- or left-adjoined positions.

The present matching account affords a unified syntax/semantics for relativized and non-relativized quantifier phrases. In both cases the quantifier raises from the internal assignment argument of the choice-function pronoun and takes a nominal complement.[88] A preliminary derivation is in (7.72).

(7.72)   Every cat which meowed jumped.

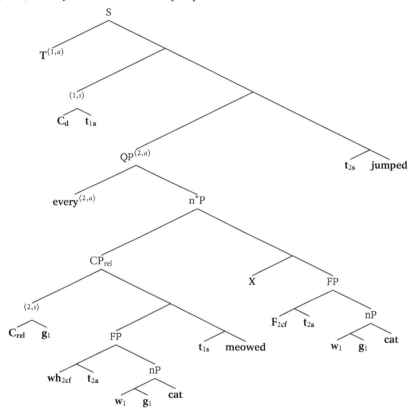

---

[88] If the relative clause is merged cyclically and the relative phrase is formed by a Copy operation, the embedding assignment quantifier (here 'every') may raise by ATB movement (perhaps via sideward movement (Nunes 2004) of the external head to the relative clause). Such an analysis may provide an independent basis for *wh*/Op-movement in relative clauses. The relative phrase would need to move to the edge of the CP$_{rel}$ phase in order to be accessible for operations such as the movement of the higher assignment quantifier (cf. Iatridou et al. 2001). Alternatively, if the relative clause is constructed and merged countercyclically, the relative phrase would be formed after the movement of the assignment-quantifier. Perhaps differences in this respect could help explain intralinguistic and crosslinguistic differences in island-sensitivity for different types of relative clauses (Chomsky 1977, Williamson 1987, Grosu 2002, de Vries 2002, Hastings 2004, Hiraiwa 2005, 2017). To fix ideas I will represent the assignment-variables in the internal and external choice-function pronouns as traces, and assume that the assignment quantifier raises by ATB movement.

$$[\![\mathbf{C_{rel}}]\!] = \lambda a_a.\lambda p_{st}.\lambda x_e.\lambda g_g . \forall w_s = [\lambda g'_g.@(a(g'))]:p(w)(g)$$

$$[\![CP_{rel}]\!] \approx \lambda x_e.\lambda g_g . g(2a)(2cf)(cat_{g(1a)(1s)}) \text{ meowed in } @(g(1a))$$

$$[\![n^*P]\!] \approx \lambda x_e.\lambda g_g . x(g) = g(2a)(2cf)(cat_{g(1a)(1s)}) \wedge$$
$$g(2a)(2cf)(cat_{g(1a)(1s)}) \text{ meowed in } @(g(1a))$$

$$[\![S]\!] \approx \lambda g_g . \forall x_e \forall a_a: \big(x(g) = a(g)(2cf)(cat_{g^-(1s)}) \wedge a(g)(2cf)(cat_{g^-(1s)})$$
$$\text{meowed in } @(g^-)\big) \to x(g) \text{ jumped in } @(g^-)$$

The assignment-variable $\mathbf{g}_1$ in C_{rel}^0 is bound by the topmost assignment-binder, anchoring the interpretation of the relative clause's main predicate 'meowed' to the world of the discourse. Roughly put, the matrix quantifier quantifies over those individuals o for which there is some choice function F that selects o from the set of cats $(=cat_{g_c(1s)})$, and $F(cat_{g_c(1s)})$ $(=o)$ meowed. Given the parallel representations of the relative phrase and external FP, both conditions are derived as conditions on the same individual. The sentence is true iff every such $o = F(cat_{g_c(1s)})$ jumped.

7.4.2 Intensional Gap Readings

Let's return to intensional gap readings. The target reading of (7.73) ascribes to Callie a belief that the thing o which is a monster and found by Alice in Timmy's belief-worlds ate Fluffy. (7.73) can be true even if there are no monsters and Callie doesn't think that there are.

(7.73) Callie thinks that the monster$_i$ which Timmy thinks^i Alice found ate Fluffy.

The challenge is to capture how the world argument for the internal head receives a local reading under the CP_{rel}-internal attitude verb anchored to Timmy's beliefs, while maintaining that the condition placed on the selected individual is a condition on the individual being quantified over, i.e. the individual in Callie's belief-worlds that ate Fluffy.

In §5 we noted that it is crosslinguistically common for relative words to be morphologically related to indefinites (e.g., de Vries 2002, Bhat 2004). Thus far we have represented the relative phrase parallel to specific indefinites with an independent world-pronoun. However, just as there are indefinite words in phasal and non-phasal noun phrases, so too, we might expect, for relative words. Let's suppose as a working hypothesis that the relative phrase in intensional gap readings is an nP. For present purposes we can leave open what specific position the choice-function element occupies above Num. One option is to posit an alternative F(ocus) position under n, reflected in (7.74).[89]

---

[89] Cf. Harley 2009, 2013, 2017, Ramchand 2017 on functional projections FP between v and v*, and between v and V in verb phrases. In circumnominals such as (i) the number word occurs between the noun and relative morpheme:

(7.74)

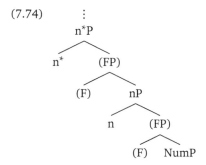

Semantically, choice-function elements under n can be analyzed as (what we might call) *intensional choice function pronouns* — pronouns $[\mathbf{F_{cf*}}\ \mathbf{g}]$ for functions $F^*: [W \to [E \to T]] \to E^W$ from properties P to individual concepts o^* that manifest P. Formally, an individual concept is a function from worlds to individuals. We can assume that, in the intended interpretation, the denotations F^* map properties P to relevant "transworld" lines — functions from worlds u to individuals $F^*(P)(u)$ such that the manifestations of $F^*(P)$ in the worlds in $F^*(P)$'s domain are relevant counterparts of one another; i.e., for any u, v on which $F^*(P)$ is defined, $F^*(P)(u)$ is a relevant counterpart of $F^*(P)(v)$ (cf. Ojeda 1993). (Hereafter I will use 'cf*' in indices for items of type $\langle set, et \rangle$ that are intensional choice functions in this sense.)

Since nP noun phrases aren't phases, their world-variable is determined by feature transmission FC with the local verbal head (§7.2.4). In (7.75), for (7.73), the world-variable for the relative phrase is $\mathbf{u_{3s}}$, determined via agreement with the local v in the v*P phase. The world associated with the internal head is anchored by agreement to the attitude state representing Timmy's beliefs.

(7.75) $[_{CP_{rel}}\ [C_{rel}\ g_2]^{\langle 4,s \rangle}$ Timmy $[thinks\ t_{4s}]^{\langle 3,a \rangle}$
        $[_{CP}\ [C_d\ t_{3a}]^{\langle 3,s \rangle}$ Alice $[_{vP}\ \underline{t_{3s}}$ found $[_{nP}\ \underline{u_{3s}}\ wh_{2cf*}\text{-}t_{4a}$ monster$]]]]$

(i)   Amok ale da   [mango-ta ŋa-nu   tii] diem   la
       Amok c   bought mango-PL CL.PL-five REL yesterday DEM
       'the five mangos that Amok bought yesterday'   (Hiraiwa 2005: 221; Bùlì)

The world argument for the external head can be supplied by a world-pronoun.[90] The resulting LF and semantic value is in (7.76).

(7.76)

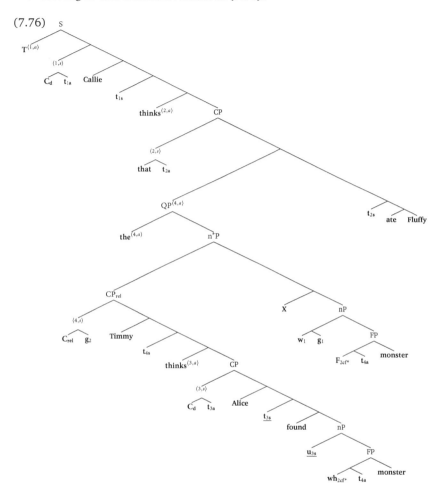

---

[90] Absent further constraints, treating the world argument in the external nP as a world-pronoun allows for the possibility of modally independent interpretations of the external head in intensional gap readings. Examples such as (i) provide preliminary support for such a prediction. Callie's utterance implies that there is a certain actual monster *o*, and that things would be better if *o* wasn't a monster; yet the belief ascribed to Timmy is still de dicto and nonspecific.

(i) [Context: Callie believes in monsters. She thinks that Timmy thinks Alice found some monster or other. Callie says:]

It would be better if the monster which Timmy thinks Alice found wasn't a monster.

The world-pronoun in the external nP is bound nonlocally by the topmost assignment-binder.

$$[\![S]\!] \approx \lambda g_g \, . \, \forall a_a \colon a(g) \text{ is compatible with } \mathrm{SOM}_{\mathrm{Callie}, @(g^-)} \to$$
$$\big(\big[\iota x(g) \exists a''_a \colon x(g) = a''(g)(2\mathrm{cf}^*)(monster)(a(g)(1s)) \wedge$$
$$\big(\forall a'_a \colon a'(g) \text{ is compatible with } \mathrm{SOM}_{\mathrm{Timmy}, @(a(g))} \to$$
$$\text{Alice found } a''(g)(2\mathrm{cf}^*)(monster)(@(a'(g))) \text{ in } @(a'(g)) \big) \big]$$
$$x(g) \text{ ate Fluffy in } @(a(g)) \big)$$

Roughly put, this says that (7.73) is true iff for all possibilities h compatible with Callie's state of mind, Fluffy was eaten by the o such that: for some individual concept of a monster $F^*(monster)$, o is identical to the manifestation of $F^*(monster)$ in $@(h)$, and for all possibilities h' compatible with Timmy's state of mind in $@(h)$, Alice found the manifestation of $F^*(monster)$ in $@(h')$.

As in (7.72), the relative phrase is constructed a copy of the external FP. Rather than selecting an individual in a given world, the FP under n selects an individual concept — an individual concept of a monster $F^*(monster)$. The local intensional reading of the relative phrase follows from the general feature transmission mechanisms from §7.2.4. The world argument for the internal head is supplied by the world-variable $\mathbf{u}_{3s}$ anchored to Timmy's belief-worlds. The relative clause $\mathrm{CP}_{\mathrm{rel}}$ requires that, for all possibilities h' compatible with Timmy's state of mind, Alice found the individual o who is the manifestation of $F^*(monster)$ in $@(h')$.

Although the FPs denote an individual concept, the account avoids ascribing to Callie a belief that Fluffy was eaten by an individual concept. The world argument for the external head is supplied by the world-pronoun $[\mathbf{w}_1 \, \mathbf{g}_2]$ anchored to Callie's belief-worlds. The external nP picks out the manifestation of $F^*(monster)$ in the world $@(h)$ of the given possibility h compatible with Callie's state of mind. The entities which ate Fluffy and Alice found are ordinary concrete individuals.

Similarly, the derived truth condition doesn't imply a commitment to transworld eating. The internal and external FPs denote the same individual concept, yet the supplied world arguments differ. The subject noun phrase picks out the individual o in $@(h)$ that manifests some individual concept $F^*(monster)$ of a monster, and is such that for all of Timmy's belief-worlds $@(h')$, Alice found the relevant counterpart of o, $F^*(monster)(@(h'))$. The attitude ascription is true, on the intended reading, iff for each such $@(h)$, o ate Fluffy in $@(h)$.

The metasemantics suggested above delimits the class of intensional choice functions $F^* \in D_{\langle set, se \rangle}$ by a requirement that, for property P, the individuals selected by $F^*(P)$ across worlds be relevant counterparts of one another. A stronger condition would require also that $F^*(P)(u) \in P(u)$, for any $u \in W$ (cf. Chierchia 1998), as in (7.77). The value of an intensional choice-function pronoun, on this approach, associates a property P with a part of the maximal $P(u)$-individual.

(7.77) For any property $P: W \rightarrow E \rightarrow T$ and world $u \in W$ such that $P(u) \neq \varnothing$:
$$P(u)\big(F^*(P)(u)\big)$$

There are reasons to avoid treating a principle such as (7.77) as a general requirement on $\langle set, se \rangle$ denotations in [n FP] noun phrases. The intensional gap reading of (7.78) needn't imply a commitment to monsters. Indeed (7.78) would typically be interpreted as saying that the object which you think you saw wasn't a monster, as you believe, but a shadow. A rough LF and semantic value is in (7.79) (cf. n. 90).

(7.78) The monster$_i$ which you think^i you saw was a shadow.

(7.79) $[_S \, T^{\langle 1,a \rangle} \, [_{CP} \, [C_d \, t_{1a}]^{\langle 1,s \rangle} \, [[_{QP^{\langle 3,a \rangle}} \, \text{the}^{\langle 3,a \rangle}$
  $[_{n^*P} \, [_{CP_{rel}} \, [C_{rel} \, g_1]^{\langle 2,s \rangle} \, \text{you}_{2e}\text{-}g_1 \, t_{2s} \, \text{think}^{\langle 2,a \rangle}$
    $[_{CP} \, [C_d \, t_{2a}]^{\langle 3,s \rangle} \, \text{you}_{2e}\text{-}g_1 \, \underline{t_{3s}} \, \text{saw} \, [_{nP} \, \underline{u_{3s}} \, \text{wh}_{2cf^*}\text{-}t_{3a} \, \text{monster}]]]$
  $[X \, [_{nP} \, w_1\text{-}g_1 \, F_{2cf^*}\text{-}t_{3a} \, \text{monster}]]]]$
  $[t_{1s} \, \text{a-shadow}]]]]$
  $[\![S]\!] \approx \lambda g_g \, . \, \big[\iota x(g) \exists a_a : x(g) = a(g)(2cf^*)(monster)(@(g^-)) \wedge$
    $\big(\forall a' : a'(g) \text{ is compatible with SOM}_{g^-(2e), @(g^-)} \rightarrow$
      $g^-(2e) \text{ saw } a(g)(2cf^*)(monster)(@(a'(g))) \text{ in } @(a'(g))\big) \big]$
    $x(g) \text{ was a shadow in } @(g^-)$

The subject noun phrase picks out the o such that, for some individual concept of a monster $F^*(monster)$, o is the manifestation of $F^*(monster)$ in the actual world, and for all possibilities h compatible with your state of mind, you saw the counterpart of o in $@(h)$, $F^*(monster)(@(h))$. Though the manifestations of $F^*(monster)$ throughout your belief-worlds may be monsters, so that $F^*(monster)(@(h)) \in monster_{@(h)}$, the "world-line" may include worlds in which the manifestation isn't a monster but a (monster-looking) shadow. (7.78) is true, according to (7.79), if the actual world $@(g_c)$ is such a world—i.e., if $F^*(monster)(@(g_c))$, the counterpart of the monsters $F^*(monster)(@(h))$ you saw in your belief-worlds, was a shadow in $@(g_c)$. That said, for interpretive reasons $\langle set, se \rangle / cf^*$ indices may often represent intensional choice functions that satisfy (7.77). Compare (7.78) with the anomalous (7.80).

(7.80) ??The monster which you think you saw hit Bert.

Absent substantial contextual setup it is hard to imagine a plausible non-monster counterpart of the monsters in your belief-worlds that would be the sort of thing that would hit Bert.[91]

7.4.3 Donkey Pronouns in Intensional Contexts

The account of donkey anaphora from §5.2 carries over to the matching analysis in this section. The donkey pronoun in (7.81) is represented as a copy of its linguistic antecedent at LF. The assignment-binding introduced by the quantifier captures the apparent anaphoric connection. (For simplicity, unless otherwise noted I will represent relative phrases with an [F nP] structure.)

(7.81)   Every puppy which got *a toy* liked *it*.

---

[91] I have suggested that some relative and individual pronouns may be represented in alternative F positions above/below n. A possible interesting connection may be to relative constructions with resumptive pronouns. Doron 1982 observes that resumptive pronouns in languages such as Hebrew are incompatible with certain sorts of intensional readings. The "highly preferred reading" (Sharvit 1999: 593) of (i-b) with the resumptive pronoun is the reading implying the existence of a salient woman who is the object of Dani's seeking. (i-b) lacks the possible reading of (i-a) on which Dani is merely "looking for a woman with certain properties" — e.g., a woman to lead his team — "but does not know who such a woman might be" (Sells 1987: 288).

(i)   a. Dani yimca   et   ha-iša   še   hu mexapes.
          Dani find.FUT ACC the-woman that he seeks
      b. Dani yimca   et   ha-iša   še   hu mexapes **ota**.
          Dani find.FUT ACC the-woman that he seeks   her
          'Dani will find the woman he is looking for.'   (Doron 1982: 25; Hebrew)

Suppose that resumptive pronouns are pronounced realizations of the (lowest copy of the) relative phrase with an elided noun (cf. §§5.2, 6.3, 6.4). If Hebrew resumptive pronouns are [F nP] noun phrases, they will be incompatible with structures such as (7.76)/(7.79) representing intensional gap readings. The world arguments for the internal and external heads will be world-pronouns, as in (ii).

(ii)   ... the$^{\langle 3,a \rangle}$ [[$_{CP_{rel}}$ [C$_{rel}$ g$_1$]$^{\langle 2,s \rangle}$ Timmy t$_{2s}$ thinks$^{\langle 2,a \rangle}$

       [$_{CP}$ [C$_d$ t$_{2a}$]$^{\langle 3,s \rangle}$ Alice t$_{3s}$ found [$_{FP}$ *ota*$_{2cf}$-t$_{3a}$ w$_1$-g$_{1/2}$-monster]

       [X [$_{FP}$ F$_{2cf}$-t$_{3a}$ w$_1$-g$_{1/2}$-monster]]]]

This represents the readings according to which Timmy's belief is about a certain actual monster ([w$_1$ g$_1$]) or an individual that Callie thinks is a monster ([w$_1$ g$_2$]). (Sells 1987 characterizes the distinction in readings with/without the resumptive pronoun as a distinction between specific vs. nonspecific readings — e.g., readings which do/don't imply that there is a particular woman *o* such that Dani is looking for *o* (1987: 288). Sharvit 1999 characterizes the distinction as a distinction between de re vs. de dicto readings — e.g., readings which do/don't imply the existence of a (salient) woman (1999: 593). Doron 1982 labels the distinction as de re/de dicto, but glosses examples in terms specificity/nonspecificity (1982: 305). Bianchi 2011 uses the distinctions interchangeably (2011: 320). Further data would be needed to tease apart precisely which distinction is operative (see also Boeckx 2003). Thanks to Anya Saliy and Amit Ginbar for helpful feedback.)

a. $[_S T^{\langle 1,a\rangle} [_{CP} [_{C_d} t_{1a}]^{\langle 1,s\rangle} [[_{OP^{\langle 2,a\rangle}}$ every$^{\langle 2,a\rangle}$
$[_{n^*P} [_{CP_{rel}} [_{C_{rel}} g_1]^{\langle 2,s\rangle} [[_{FP}$ wh$_{2cf}$-t$_{2a}$ w$_1$-g$_1$-puppy]
$[_{vP} t_{2s}$ got a$_{3cf}$-g$_2$ w$_1$-g$_1$-toy]]]
$[X [_{FP} F_{2cf}$-t$_{2a}$ w$_1$-g$_1$-puppy]]]]
$[_{vP} t_{1s}$ liked it$_{3cf}$-g$_2$ w$_1$-g$_1$-t̶o̶y̶]]]]

b. $[\![S]\!] \approx \lambda g_g . \forall x_e \forall a_a : \big(x(g) = a(g)(2cf)(puppy_{g^-(1s)}) \wedge$
$a(g)(2cf)(puppy_{g^-(1s)}) \wedge$ got $a(g)(3cf)(toy_{g^-(1s)})$ in $@(g^-)\big) \rightarrow$
$x(g)$ liked $a(g)(3cf)(toy_{g^-(1s)})$ in $@(g^-)$

The derived truth condition is equivalent to the truth condition derived with the head-raising analysis in (5.24). Roughly put, the sentence is true iff for all individuals o and choice functions F, F' such that F selects o from the puppies and o got the toy o' selected by F', o liked o'.

King (2004) appeals to examples such as (7.82) in objecting to prominent approaches to donkey anaphora such as DRT and dynamic theories. Insofar as they treat donkey pronouns as semantically bound variables, King argues that these approaches predict a specific reading for 'he', attributing to each relevant star a belief about a particular individual. However, the attitude ascription can also receive a nonspecific reading that "can be true even though the [stars] in question don't know who their secret admirers are" (King 2004: 105).

(7.82) Every star who has a secret admirer$_i$ thinks he$_i$ is stalking him.

(cf. King 2004: ex. 18)

Or imagine, à la Dretske, that a trickster sent each zoo-owning epistemologist a letter that some or other of the zebra-looking animals in their latest delivery is a cleverly painted mule. Which mule ruined epistemology in (7.83) may vary across the subject's doxastic alternatives.

(7.83) Every epistemologist who got a painted mule thinks it ruined epistemology.

§7.4.2 captured intensional gap readings by positing an optional F position under n. If choice-functional uses of indefinites such as 'a' may also occupy the lower position, one may expect intensional readings of donkey pronouns to be possible as well. An analysis for the nonspecific reading of (7.83) is in (7.84).

(7.84)

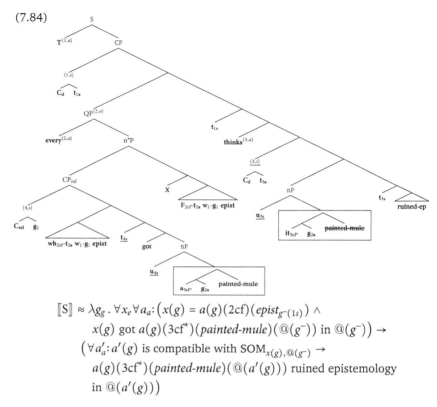

$$[\![S]\!] \approx \lambda g_g \,.\, \forall x_e \forall a_a \colon \big(x(g) = a(g)(2\mathrm{cf})(epist_{g^-(1s)}) \,\wedge$$
$$x(g) \text{ got } a(g)(3\mathrm{cf}^*)(painted\text{-}mule)(@(g^-)) \text{ in } @(g^-)\big) \rightarrow$$
$$\big(\forall a'_a \colon a'(g) \text{ is compatible with SOM}_{x(g),@(g^-)} \rightarrow$$
$$a(g)(3\mathrm{cf}^*)(painted\text{-}mule)(@(a'(g)))\big) \text{ ruined epistemology}$$
$$\text{in } @(a'(g))\big)$$

This says, roughly, that (7.83) is true on the relevant reading iff for all $o \in E$ selectable from the epistemologists and individual concepts of a painted mule $F^*(painted\text{-}mule)$ such that o got the manifestation of $F^*(painted\text{-}mule)$ in $@(g_c)$, in each of o's belief-worlds $@(h')$ the manifestation of $F^*(painted\text{-}mule)$ in $@(h')$ ruined epistemology.

As previously, the donkey pronoun is represented as a copy of its antecedent FP at LF — here, the intensional choice-function pronoun $[\mathbf{a}_{3\mathrm{cf}^*}\ \mathbf{g}_2]$, which selects an individual concept of a painted mule. The world-variable in the indefinite is anchored to the discourse. The quantifier phrase quantifies over individuals $o, o' \in E$ such that o is selectable among the epistemologists, o' is the manifestation in the actual world of an individual concept $F^*(painted\text{-}mule)$ of a painted mule, and o got o'. The world-variable in the donkey pronoun, in contrast, is anchored to the local attitude state by FC. For every belief-world $@(h')$ of the quantificational subject o, the individual $F^*(painted\text{-}mule)(@(h'))$ which ruined epistemology is a relevant counterpart of the individual $F^*(painted\text{-}mule)(@(g_c))$

which o received (§7.4.2). The relevant counterpart of $F^*(painted\text{-}mule)(@(g_c))$ might be the same across the subject's belief-worlds; but as far as the formal semantics is concerned, it need not be. The intuitively nonspecific reading of the donkey pronoun follows from the treatment of donkey pronouns as copies of their linguistic antecedent and the syntax/semantics for nPs.

King's (2004) "Context-Dependent Quantifier" (CDQ) account also treats donkey pronouns as representing material from the linguistic context. Donkey pronouns are analyzed as quantifiers which inherit their force and restriction from their linguistic antecedent and other features of the sentence. There are concerns for King's account. First, King diagnoses specific vs. nonspecific readings of donkey pronouns in examples such as (7.82) in terms of differences in scope: insofar as the pronoun is quantificational, it may take varying scopes with respect to attitude verbs. This diagnosis is problematic. Donkey pronouns can receive alternative specific/nonspecific readings when embedded in scope islands such as 'if'-clauses, as in (7.85).

(7.85) Every star who has a secret admirer$_i$ thinks that if he$_i$ is a stalker, he$_i$ should be arrested.

The account in this section diagnoses the distinction between specific vs. nonspecific readings of donkey pronouns under attitude verbs in terms of the structure of the noun phrase.

Second, King characterizes the nonspecific reading of (7.82) as follows:

> These sentences certainly appear to have readings on which they attribute *de dicto* beliefs to the [stars] in question. That is, they have readings on which they attribute to the [stars] in question *general* beliefs to the effect **that they are being stalked by secret admirers**. This is why these sentences can be true even though the [stars] in question don't know who their secret admirers are, and so have no beliefs about *particular* persons stalking them. (King 2004: 105; bold added)

We have seen that the de re/de dicto distinction cannot be assimilated to the specific/general distinction. The fact that the subject's beliefs aren't about a particular individual doesn't imply that the beliefs are de dicto, in the sense of representing the stalkers in question as secret admirers. The donkey pronouns in (7.86)–(7.87) are nonspecific yet non-de dicto. The stars in (7.86) don't represent their actual-world secret admirers as admirers but as pranksters; yet they still don't know who the individuals are "and so have no beliefs about particular persons." The quantified attitude ascription in (7.87) can be true even if the boys don't think that their coins are nickels.

(7.86) Every star who has a secret admirer thinks he is a prankster.

(7.87) [Context: The boys know that the meter says it "only takes quarters." Yet the boys confuse their coins and think that the nickels they have are quarters.]
Every boy who has a nickel thinks it will fit in the meter.

The analysis in (7.83) allows for such nonspecific non-de dicto readings of "intensional donkey pronouns." For (7.86), the pronoun $[\mathbf{F}_{cf*}\ \mathbf{g}]$ in the representations of 'a' and 'he' selects an individual concept of a secret admirer, $F^*(admirer)$. The "world-line" of $F^*(admirer)$ may be such that in some of the subject's belief-worlds u, the relevant counterpart of the given admirer $F^*(admirer)(@(g_c))$, $F^*(admirer)(u)$, is a prankster. The treatment of nonspecific non-de dicto readings of donkey pronouns is the mirror image of the treatment of intensional gap readings such as (7.78)–(7.79). In (7.78)–(7.79) with 'which monster', the relevant individual concept is manifested by a monster throughout the subject's belief-worlds and by a (non-monster) shadow in the actual world; in (7.86), the relevant individual concept is manifested by a secret admirer in the actual world and by (non-admirer) pranksters throughout the subject's belief-worlds.

7.4.4 Relativization and Operator Movement

Our examples thus far have focused on relativized quantifier phrases, where the choice-function pronoun is bound by the matrix quantifier. Relative clauses can also occur in nonpresuppositional noun phrases and free relatives, e.g.:

(7.88) The prize went to a woman (/several women) who got a perfect score.

(7.89) Bert likes what Alice likes.

It is common to analyze free relatives such as 'what Alice likes' in (7.89) with respect to an implicit definite-like operator (see n. 32). In some languages the definite element can be pronounced, as in (7.90).

(7.90) **le**   [$_{CP_{rel}}$ **ba'ax** k-in   tsikbal-t-ik   te'ex]-a'
         DET   what HAB-ERG.1S chat-TRANS-IND-ABS.3S 2.PL-CL
         'what (this thing which) I'm telling you'
                              (cf. Gutiérrez-Bravo 2012: ex. 10; Yucatec Maya)

One might wonder whether in some languages restrictive relative clauses can also introduce an implicit operator. Rather than yielding a definite interpretation, the implicit element in restrictive relative clauses would serve as a sort of existential closure operator. Such an operator would bind the choice-function pronoun in examples such as (7.88), as reflected in (7.91)–(7.92).[92]

(7.91) $\llbracket \exists_r \rrbracket = \lambda A_{at}.\lambda g_g . \exists a_a : A(a)(g)$

(7.92) a. $[_{n^*P} \exists_r^{\langle 2,a \rangle} [_{n^*P_1} [_{CP_{rel}} [C_{rel} \, g_1]^{\langle 2,s \rangle} [[wh_{2cf}\text{-}t_{2a} \, w_1\text{-}g_1\text{-woman}]$
   $[_{vP} \, t_{2s} \, \text{got-perfect}]]] \, [X \, [F_{2cf}\text{-}t_{2a} \, w_1\text{-}g_1\text{-woman}]]]]$

   b. $\llbracket n^*P \rrbracket = \llbracket \exists_r^{\langle 2,a \rangle} \rrbracket \circ \llbracket n^*P_1 \rrbracket = \lambda x_e.\llbracket \exists_r^{\langle 2,a \rangle} \rrbracket (\llbracket n^*P_1 \rrbracket(x))$
   $\approx \lambda x_e.\lambda g_g . \exists a_a : x(g) = a(g)(2cf)(woman_{g(1a)(1s)}) \wedge$
   $a(g)(2cf)(woman_{g(1a)(1s)}) \text{ got-a-perfect-score in } @(g(1a))$

$\exists_r^{\langle 2,a \rangle}$ of type $\langle t, t \rangle$ and the lower n^*P_1 segment of type $\langle e, t \rangle$ combine by function composition to yield the type $\langle e, t \rangle$ denotation for the noun phrase. The n^*P picks out the set of individuals o such that for some choice function F, F selects o from the women $(= woman_{g.(1s)})$ and $F(woman_{g.(1s)}) = o$ got a perfect score. In argument-position uses such as (7.88), the predicative denotation for the noun phrase can be shifted as described in §7.2.1.

Positing an implicit operator leads one to expect that there might be crosslinguistic variation in its presence or specific content. Suppose a language lacked an element such as $\exists_r$ for a given relative construction. The relative clauses would be incompatible with nonpresuppositional readings, invariably headed by a (possibly implicit) presuppositional quantifier. This is precisely what is observed with "maximalizing" relatives (Grosu and Landman 1998, Grosu 2002, 2012). Unlike its English counterpart, the maximalizing relative in (7.93) is incompatible with continuations implying a non-maximal interpretation.

(7.93) [Ken-ga mittu-no mangoo-o kattekitekure-ta no]-wa tabe-ta (#ga
   Ken-NOM 3-GEN   mango-ACC buy.come-PAST C-TOP eat-PAST but
   hoka-no mittu-wa tabe-nakat-ta)
   other   3-TOP   eat-NEG-PAST
   'I ate three mangoes that Ken bought for me (#but I didn't eat three
   others).'   (Hiraiwa et al. 2017: 19; Japanese)

---

[92] I assume that $\exists_r$ raises above the relative clause in the n^*P area. For simplicity I continue to represent the choice-function element in the high F position; a revised analysis is given in §7.5 in the context of a more general treatment of predicate nominals.

Given the (hypothesized) absence of $\exists_r$, the merely existential interpretation of the noun phrase is unavailable. A sample LF is in (7.95). The definite quantifier (cf. §6.2), overt in some languages (Hiraiwa 2005, Hiraiwa et al. 2017), binds the choice-function pronouns; a revised denotation incorporating plurality is in (7.94). (For readability I again use the metalanguage ι operator, understood as previously. I use '3-*mangoes*$_u$' for the set of individuals o such that $\#o'[o'$ is a mango in $u \;\wedge\; o' \sqsubseteq o] \geq 3$, i.e. individuals with three mangoes as atomic parts.)

(7.94) $\llbracket \iota_o \rrbracket = \lambda P^+_{\langle a,et \rangle} . \lambda Q^+_{\langle a,et \rangle} . \lambda g_g . \exists x_e \exists a_a : P^+(a)(x)(g) \wedge Q^+(a)(x)(g) \wedge$
$\left(\forall y_e : P^+(a)(y)(g) \rightarrow y(g) \sqsubseteq x(g) \right)$
$= \lambda P^+_{\langle a,et \rangle} . \lambda Q^+_{\langle a,et \rangle} . \lambda g_g . \exists x_e \exists a_a : \left(x(g) = \text{the maximal } o \text{ such that} \right.$
$\left({}^{\downarrow}P^+ \right)(a(g))(o) \right) \wedge Q^+(a)(x)(g)$
$= \lambda P^+_{\langle a,et \rangle} . \lambda Q^+_{\langle a,et \rangle} . \lambda g_g . \left[\iota x(g) \exists a_a : P^+(a)(x)(g) \right] Q^+(a)(x)(g)$

(7.95)   "Maximalizing" headed relative

a.   'three mangoes which Ken bought' (cf. (7.93))

b. $[_{QP^{\langle 2,a \rangle}} \; \iota_o^{\langle 2,a \rangle} \; [_{n^*P} \; [_{CP_{rel}} \; [C_{rel} \; g_1]^{\langle 2,s \rangle}$
[Ken $[_{vP} \; t_{2s}$ bought [wh$_{2cf}$-t$_{2a}$ w$_1$-g$_1$ three$_{\#}$-mangoes]]]]
[X [F$_{2cf}$-t$_{2a}$ w$_1$-g$_1$ three$_{\#}$-mangoes]]]]

c. $\llbracket (7.95b) \rrbracket \approx \lambda P_{et} . \lambda g_g . \left[\iota x(g) \exists a_a : x(g) = a(g)(2cf)(3\text{-}mangoes_{g(1a)(1s)}) \wedge \right.$
Ken bought $a(g)(2cf)(3\text{-}mangoes_{g(1a)(1s)})$ in $@(g(1a)) \big]$
$P(x)(g[a(g)/2a])$

Roughly put, the noun phrase denotes the maximal o such that o is selectable from the set of pluralities with three mangoes as atomic parts, and Ken bought o. Hence a continuation such as '... but I didn't eat three others' in (7.93) is infelicitous; every collection of three mangoes that Ken bought is a part of o.

   There are well-attested syntactic and semantic differences between headed relatives and free relatives crosslinguistically; however, the matching analysis in this section might be applied to free relatives in certain languages. It is common in various languages to express free relative interpretations via maximalizing relatives with a general class noun — e.g., free relative 'what' as 'the thing(s) that', free relative 'who' as 'the person(s) that', etc., as in (7.96) (cf. Citko 2004, Cinque 2017). In some cases the definite element is also pronounced (cf. (7.90)). The double-headed circumnominal relative in (7.96b) wears the matching structure on its sleeve.

(7.96)   a.   márô   [gìn   àmê   cámô]
             3SG.like.HAB thing REL+PRT 3SG.eat.HAB
             'He likes what/the thing he eats.'
                                    (Noonan 1992: 220; Lango (Nilo-Saharan))

b. [skə̀n nàm   dzá skə̀n syì] há diyà gáy kà
   thing 1DUAL find thing COM 2SG put spoil POV.SUBJ
   'What/the thing we found, you are ruining it.'
(Frajzyngier and Johnston 2005: 433; Mina (Chadic))

(7.97) "Light-headed" free relative

   a. 'what Alice found' (cf. (7.96b))

   b. $\iota_o^{(2,a)}$ $[_{n^*P}$ $[_{CP_{rel}}$ $[C_{rel}$ $g_1]^{(2,s)}$ [Alice $[_{vP}$ t_{2s} found [wh$_{2cf}$-t_{2a} w$_1$-g$_1$-thing]]]]
     [X [F$_{2cf}$-t_{2a} w$_1$-g$_1$-thing]]]

The free relative in (7.97) refers to the maximal o such that for some choice function F, F selects o from the set of things and Alice found $F(thing_{g_c(1s)}) = o$, i.e. the maximal thing that Alice found.

It is controversial how to capture the linguistic differences among free relatives and maximalizing and non-maximalizing headed relatives, and whether the different relative constructions have a common underlying structure.[93] Suffice it to say that the proposed matching analysis is compatible with overtly and non-overtly headed relative constructions, and maximalizing and non-maximalizing interpretations. It is worth investigating more carefully how the alternative head-raising and matching analyses developed here and in §5 might be applied to different types of (headed, light-headed, headless) relative constructions in different languages.

7.5   Appendix: Verb Phrases, Events, and the Structure of Predication

In §7.1 we noted the prominent move in syntax of distinguishing elements n/v determining nominal/verbal environments from lexical roots. It is rare to find the move represented in compositional semantics of nominal and verbal predicates, as for (7.98) (though see Levinson 2007, Copley and Harley 2015, Wood and Marantz 2017).

(7.98) a. $[_{nP}$ $[_n$ /ɑ/] √*muorr*] ⤳ *muorra* ('wood' (n.))
     b. $[_{vP}$ $[_v$ /e/] √*muorr*] ⤳ *murret* ('chop wood' (v.))
(cf. Julien 2015: 5–6; North Sámi (Uralic))

This section briefly considers how the layered N, n, n* analysis for noun phrases developed in this chapter might be extended to the verbal domain and incorporate events. Comparisons between predication structures in noun phrases and verb phrases are explored, yielding revised compositional semantics for

---

[93] See Dayal 1996, Grosu and Landman 1998, Grosu 2002, 2012, de Vries 2002, Caponigro 2003, Citko 2004, 2009, Hastings 2004, Gračanin-Yuksek 2008, Cinque 2013, 2017, Law 2014, Hiraiwa 2017, Hiraiwa et al. 2017, Sportiche 2017.

agentive sentences, possessives, and existentials. I leave further developments and extensions to other categories (aspect, tense) for future research.

Not all root phrases need be compatible with both nominalizing and verbalizing heads. In (7.99b), although the vP *viekhat* 'run' can be nominalized ('running'), the root √*viekh* cannot combine directly with n.

(7.99) a. [$_{nP}$ [$_n$ /ɑ/] √*viellj*] ⤳ *viellja* ('brother' (n.))   (/*vielljet/*vielljat* (v.))

      b. [$_{vP}$ [$_v$ /ɑ/] √*viekh*] ⤳ *viekhat* ('run' (v.))   (/*viekha/*viekhu* (n.))

       [$_{nP}$ [$_n$ /m/] [$_{vP}$ [$_v$ /ɑ/] √*viekh*]] ⤳ *viekhan* ('running')

                            (cf. Julien 2015: 5; North Sámi (Uralic))

The meanings of some roots may themselves be sortally restricted, whether in the lexicon or as a matter of world knowledge (cf. Harley 2005, Levinson 2007). Some roots may express properties satisfied only by particular sorts of things in *E*. The idea I wish to explore is to treat a semantic function of certain nominalizing/verbalizing heads as providing an explicit source of such sortal constraints.

Root phrases can again be given type-$\langle s, et \rangle$ denotations, as functions from worlds to sets of individuals ((7.100)).[94] The metalanguage predicate 'WOOD' in (7.100b) picks out a spectrum of wood-ish things — "wood objects," such as (say) twigs, branches, as well as a range of "wood doings" (which such range depending on the lexical semantics of North Sámi).

(7.100) a. $[\![\sqrt{barg}]\!] = \lambda w_s.\lambda x_e.\lambda g_g . \text{WORK}(w(g))(x(g))$

      b. $[\![\sqrt{muorr}]\!] = \lambda w_s.\lambda x_e.\lambda g_g . \text{WOOD}(w(g))(x(g))$

Following the Davidsonian tradition (Davidson 1967, Parsons 1990) it is standard to treat verbs as predicates of eventualities (events, states) — e.g., treating

---

[94] In §7.1 we saw how number features in nominal environments may modify these denotations by restricting them to properties of atomic or countable individuals. Parallels between the mass/count distinction and the atelicity/telicity distinction have led many theorists to treat an aspectual category as the verbal counterpart of number (cf. Rijkhoff 2002, Borer 2005a,b, Alexiadou et al. 2007, Megerdoomian 2008). In ǂHoan (i) the same marker *kí* indicates plurality for nouns and "pluractionality" for verbs. The modified plural noun in (i-a) denotes a set of (countable) house pluralities; likewise the modified plural verb in (i-b) "gives the sense of repeated action" (Collins 2001: 465) by denoting a set of (countable) shooting-pluralities.

(i)   a. ǂ'amkoe **kí**-!oa-qa
         person KÍ[PL]-house-PL
         'the person's houses'
    b. Jefo **kí**-tchi-tcu   -'a ⊙'u ki ‖a"a-qa.
         Jeff KÍ[PL]-shoot-REP PERF duiker PREP arrow-PL
         'Jeff shot at the duiker (repeatedly) with arrows.' (Collins 2001: 459, 464; ǂHoan (Kxʼa))

Following Hiraiwa 2005, number and aspect might be treated as different manifestations of a "supercategory" #, realized as Num under n and Asp under v. I will continue to ignore aspect.

'rain' as denoting a set of raining events.[95] Suppose that eventualities are conceived as being included among the entities in E (cf. Chierchia 1994, Kracht 2002, Moulton 2015). Along with unsorted type e variables x, y, we can use sorted variables x^κ for (functions from assignments to) things in E of particular sorts — e.g., atomic objects, plural objects, or, let's suppose, eventualities x^ε (events x^ν, states x^s). The v head phonologically realized with /e/ in (7.98) — call it '$\mathbf{v}_{\mathrm{do}}$' — can be treated as restricting the property denoted by its complement to a property of events, as in (7.101). The world variable in v^0 is now an internal argument of the verbalizing head, which receives a substantive lexical entry.

(7.101) a. $[_{vP}\ [_{v^0}\ v\ t_{1s}]\ \textit{muorr}]$

 b. $[\![\mathbf{v}_{\mathrm{do}}]\!] = \lambda w_s.\lambda P_{\langle s,et\rangle}.\lambda x_e^\nu.\lambda g_g\,.\,P(w)(x^\nu)(g)$
  $[\![vP]\!] = \lambda x_e^\nu.\lambda g_g\,.\,\mathrm{WOOD}(g(1s))(x^\nu(g))$

The vP picks out the set of wood-ish things in the given world ($=\mathrm{WOOD}(g(1s))$) that are events — for speakers of North Sámi, events of wood-chopping. Composition rules specific to the verbal domain for combining the root and verbalizer, such as Event Identification (Kratzer 1996), aren't required.

Despite gesturing at times at certain syntactic roles for v^*, thus far we have ignored v^* in the compositional semantics. The treatment of genitives in §6.2 drew on the comparison between the role of n^* in introducing possessors in free R readings, and the role of v^* in introducing external arguments in agentive sentences (cf. Chomsky 1995, Kratzer 1996, Folli and Harley 2007, Pylkkänen 2008, D'Alessandro et al. 2017, Wood and Marantz 2017). Just as the external possessor in a free R genitive is introduced in Spec,n^* with a relevant possession relation pronoun, the external subject in an active sentence can be introduced in Spec,v^* with a relevant agentive relation pronoun. As noted in §6.2, in some languages the connection between the semantic roles of thematic subjects and possessors is reflected in the morphology. In (7.102) the agentive subject is introduced with the same marker used in free R readings of possessive noun phrases (see n. 53).

(7.102) a. ngā kurī [a   Hata]
      ART dog POSS_fr Hata
      'Hata's dogs'

 b. ka whakamau [a   Hata] i   te   taura.
      T/A fasten   POSS_fr Hata ACC ART rope
      'Hata is fastening the rope.'
         (cf. Harlow 2007: 166, Chung 1973: 652, Maori (Austronesian))

---

[95] I will use 'event' for eventualities generally and for events proper; context should disambiguate.

In both cases the external argument+relation functions semantically as a restrictive modifier, as reflected in (7.104). The lexical entry for the v^* head **Y** in (7.103) is in effect an event-restricted version of the entries for n^* heads **X**, **'s** from §6. (I again ignore intensionality with thematic relation pronouns, and use 'R'/'**R**' in indices/pronouns for type $\langle e, et \rangle$.)

(7.103) $[\![\mathbf{Y}]\!] = \lambda P_{et}.\lambda P'_{et}.\lambda x^{\varepsilon}_{e}.\lambda g_g \,.\, P(x^{\varepsilon})(g) \wedge P'(x^{\varepsilon})(g)$

(7.104) Fluffy meowed

    a. $[_{v^*P} [R_2\text{-}g_1 \text{ Fluffy}] [_{\overline{v^*}} Y [_{vP} [v_{do} \, t_{1s}] \text{ meow}]]]$

    b. $[\![v^*P]\!] \approx \lambda x^{v}_{e}.\lambda g_g \,.\, \textsc{meow}(g(1s))(x^{v}(g)) \wedge g(1a)(2R)(\text{Fluffy})(x^{v}(g))$

Roughly put, the v^*P denotes the set of things o^v which are meowing events and which bear the relevant agent-relation (represented by $[R_2 \, g_1]$) to Fluffy. The set of event-entities o^v denoted by the verb phrase can be quantified over, as usual, by existential closure or a higher aspectual quantifier (Bonomi 1997, Kratzer 1998a, Hacquard 2006, 2009). A first approximation with a simple existential closure operation (represented syntactically with '∃') is in (7.105).[96]

---

[96] The proposed analysis would ultimately need to incorporate contributions of particular aspectual heads and their interactions with tense. For instance, a prominent move is to treat aspects such as perfective and imperfective as (existential) quantifiers which locate the "running time" of an event (written: $\tau(e)$) with respect to a "reference time," as may be supplied by a time pronoun in Tense (Klein 1994, Kratzer 1998a). A sample revised analysis of (7.105) is in (i) (l_i a variable for times, type l; ignore any presuppositional constraint associated with the past tense).

(i) $[_S T^{\langle 1,a \rangle} [_{CP} [C_d \, t_{1a}]^{\langle 1,s \rangle} [_{TP} \, l_1 \, g_1 [_{AspP} \text{ PRFV } [_{v^*P} [R_2\text{-}g_1 \text{ Fluffy}] [Y [_{vP} \, v_{do}\text{-}t_{1s} \text{ meow}]]]]]]]$

    $[\![\textsc{prfv}]\!] = \lambda P_{et}.\lambda t_l.\lambda g_g \,.\, \exists x^{\varepsilon}_{e}:P(x^{\varepsilon})(g) \wedge \tau(x^{\varepsilon}(g)) \subseteq t(g)$

    $[\![S]\!] \approx \lambda g_g \,.\, \exists x^{v}_{e}:\textsc{meow}(@(g^{-}))(x^{v}(g)) \wedge g^{-}(2R)(\text{Fluffy})(@(g^{-}))(x^{v}(g)) \wedge \tau(x^{v}(g)) \subseteq g^{-}(1l)$

Hacquard (2006, 2010) has argued that higher aspectual quantifiers raise for type reasons from inside the verb phrase (see also Moulton 2015). Comparisons with the present syntax/semantics of nominal quantifiers Q as raising from inside the noun phrase and introducing assignment-quantification would be worth exploring.

(7.105)

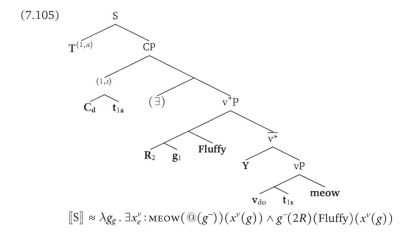

$$[\![S]\!] \approx \lambda g_g \,.\, \exists x_e^v : \text{MEOW}(@(g^-))(x^v(g)) \wedge g^-(2R)(\text{Fluffy})(x^v(g))$$

The sentence is true iff there is an event in the actual world of the sort described by the v*P in (7.104) — a meowing event of which Fluffy is the agent.

In §6.2 we saw how n* heads may differ with respect to semantic properties such as thematic role assignment. In free *R* readings of genitives, the genitive morpheme semantically constrains the relation in its specifier to broadly posses-sional relations; in inherent *R* readings, in contrast, the structural "possessor" originates in the NP as an argument of the head noun. Similar points hold in the verbal domain. In active transitives and unergatives such as (7.105), the external subject receives its thematic role in Spec,v*, and the relevant relation is constrained to broadly agentive relations (Agent, Experiencer). The analogue of inherent *R* readings would be, say, unaccusatives or passives, where the structural subject originates as an internal argument of the verb.[97] The v* head in (7.106) can be given the same (polymorphic) lexical entry for purposes of compositional semantics as the agentive v* head in (7.105) (cf. (6.35)).

(7.106) Fluffy was hugged

    a. $[_{v^*P} \ [P_{2et} \ g_1] \ [Y \ [_{vP} \ v_{do} \ t_{1s} \ [\text{hug Fluffy}]]]]$

    b. $[\![v^*P]\!] \approx \lambda x_e^v.\lambda g_g \,.\, \text{HUG}(\text{Fluffy})(g(1s))(x^v(g)) \wedge g(1a)(2et)(x^v(g))$

The passive verb phrase denotes the set of relevant things that are events of hugging Fluffy.

---

[97] Crosslinguistic work provides evidence that passives retain a layered V-v-v* structure (Collins 2005, Alexiadou et al. 2006, Harley 2013, 2017, Merchant 2013, Legate 2014, Julien 2015, Sundaresan and McFadden 2017, Wurmbrand and Shimamura 2017). What distinguishes passives from unergatives and active transitives needn't be the category of the verb phrase (vP vs. v*P), but whether the v* head takes a thematic argument in its specifier.

The proposed analysis of possessors in possessive noun phrases can thus be generalized to other types of thematic arguments. The discussion in §6.2 left open the nature of the category of the constituent in Spec,n*. One approach would be to analyze it as a Case phrase KP (Lamontagne and Travis 1987, Bittner and Hale 1996), identifying the relevant relational elements as K^0. The general semantic function of non-vacuous K heads would be to introduce thematic roles/relations — e.g., "possessor" in free R readings of genitives, "agent" or "experiencer" in active verb phrases (cf. n. 53). Predication structures in complete noun phrases n*P and verb phrases v*P can thus be given a common structure. The external argument is introduced in a relational KP in Spec,n*/v*, which functions semantically as a restrictive modifier. The nature of the relation expressed may be constrained by agreement with n*/v* or the specific lexical semantics of the K head. I leave more detailed analysis of K-case for future research.[98]

The examples thus far have involved eventive predicates. Let's turn to stative predicates, and consider how the approach to existential sentences from §7.2.3 might be revised in light of the present event-based syntax/semantics.

---

[98] We have seen semantically contentful/noncontentful K heads in noun phrases and verb phrases with/without external arguments. One additional prominent example in the verbal domain is applicative and double object constructions. In applicatives such as (i) — "true," or "high" applicatives (Pylkkänen 2000, 2008) — the direct object (e.g. 'the door') is merged as an internal argument of the verb, whereas the non-selected applied object (e.g. 'Jose') is introduced as a thematic participant (beneficiary, instrument, etc.) of the event described by the verb+direct object (see also Marantz 1993, Pesetsky 1995, Bosse et al. 2012, Larson 2014, Harley and Jung 2015). Like with the external subject, the KP introducing the applied object functions semantically as a restrictive modifier, as reflected in the alternative analyses in (ii)–(iii). The verb phrase denotes a certain set of closing-the-door events — those of which Jose is the beneficiary and Bert is the agent. ((ii) represents the applicative arguments as modifiers in the v*P layer, with a type-flexible entry for v* heads analogous to the type-flexible entry for X in n. 51. For morphosyntactic reasons, a likely more accurate analysis is to introduce the arguments via a verbal applicative head v_{appl}, e.g. as in (iii). Alternative argument structures are possible. For clarity I use 'R_{agt}', 'R_{ben}' etc. for the relevant relations.)

(i)   a.   Inepo Hose-ta   pueta-ta   eta-ria-k.
             I   Jose-ACC door-ACC close-APPL-PRF
             'I closed the door for Jose.'   (Harley 2013: ex. 8; Hiaki (Uto-Aztecan))
        b.   kit laa-lii-ȼuq-yaa-na   hun karta [hun pluma]$_{inst}$ [hun Mario]$_{com}$
             I   APPL$_{com}$-APPL$_{inst}$-write-IMPFV-APPL$_{com}$ DET letter DET   pen   DET Mario
             'I with Mario write a letter with a pen.'
                                              (MacKay 1999: 283; Misantla Totonac (Totonacan))

(ii)   a. $[_{v*P} [_{KP} R_{agt}$ Bert$] [_{\overline{v*}} [_{KP} R_{ben}$ Jose$]$ [Y $[_{vP} v_{do}$ t$_{1s}$ [close the-door]]]]]
        b. $[\![\textbf{close}]\!] = \lambda y_e.\lambda w_s.\lambda x_e.\lambda g_g \cdot \text{CLOSE}(y(g))(w(g))(x(g))$
             $[\![\textbf{Y}]\!] = \lambda P^1_{et} \dots \lambda P^n_{et}.\lambda x^\varepsilon_e.\lambda g_g \cdot P^1(x^\varepsilon)(g) \wedge \cdots \wedge P^n(x^\varepsilon)(g)$
        c. $[\![\textbf{v*P}]\!] \approx \lambda x^\varepsilon_e.\lambda g_g \cdot \text{CLOSE}(\text{the-door})(g(1s))(x^v(g)) \wedge R_{ben}(\text{Jose})(g(1s))(x^v(g)) \wedge$
             $R_{agt}(\text{Bert})(g(1s))(x^v(g))$

(iii)   a. $[_{v*P} [_{KP} R_{agt}$ Bert$]$ [Y $[_{vP} [_{KP} R_{ben}$ Jose$]$ [$_{vappl}$ $[_{vP} v_{do}$ t$_{1s}$ [close the-door]]]]]]
        b. $[\![\textbf{v}_{appl}]\!] = \lambda P_{et}.\lambda P'_{et}.\lambda x^\varepsilon_e.\lambda g_g \cdot P(x^\varepsilon)(g) \wedge P'(x^\varepsilon)(g)$
        c. $[\![\textbf{v*P}]\!] = [\![\text{(ii-c)}]\!]$

It is worth exploring how the above sorts of analyses might be extended to other double object constructions.

A preliminary analysis of a "bare" existential 'there' sentence without a coda phrase is in (7.107)–(7.108) (cf. (7.39)–(7.40)). (In 'There be YP (ZP)', the nominal YP is often called the "pivot" and the ZP, if present, the "coda." Following the approach to predicate nominals suggested in n. 85, I treat the complementizer as base-generated in n^0 in the main predicate. To fix ideas I assume that predicative 'be' realizes a stative verbalizer $\mathbf{v_{be}}$ (cf. Harley 1995, Kratzer 1996, Folli and Harley 2007). x_e^s is again a sorted variable over elements of D_e such that $x_e^s(g)$, for any g_g, is a state.)

(7.107) $[\![\mathbf{v_{be}}]\!] = \lambda P_{et}.\lambda x_e^s.\lambda g_g . P(x^s)(g)$

(7.108) There are three pillows.

 a. $[_S \, T^{\langle 1,a \rangle} \, [[C_d \, t_{1a}]^{\langle 1,s \rangle} \, [(\exists) \, [_{vP} \, v_{be} \, [_{nP} \, t_{1s} \, \text{three}_{\#} \, \text{pillows}]]]]]$

 b. $[\![S]\!] \approx \lambda g_g . \exists y_e^s \colon \#x(g)\big[\text{PILLOW}(@(g^-))(x(g)) \wedge x(g) \sqsubseteq y^s(g)\big] \geq 3$

 (to be revised)

The nominal predicate 'three pillows' denotes the property of being a plural entity with at least three pillows as atomic parts. The light verb $\mathbf{v_{be}}$ converts this predicate to a verbal predicate expressing a property of states. Suppose that we give '$\sqsubseteq$' in our metalanguage a generalized "part-of" interpretation, applicable to algebraic structures with plurals (e.g., where Fluffy is part of $[\![\mathbf{cats}]\!]$) as well as to locations, situations, states, events. The vP denotes the set of states $o^s \in E$ such that the number of pillows in $@(g_c)$ that are a part of o^s is at least three. The sentence is true iff there is such a state.

The analysis in (7.108) loses two key features of the account from §7.2.3. First, the account in (7.39)–(7.41) assumed a (possibly implicit) domain pronoun above the nominal predicate. The existential quantification over eventualities in (7.108) obviates the need for such an element, at least for type reasons. Yet the basis for capturing the apparent context-sensitivity of existential 'there' sentences is lost. Second, the analysis now fails to generalize to examples with quantifier words expressing downward entailing or non-monotone quantificational concepts. The truth condition in (7.109) is too weak.

(7.109) There are no unicorns.

 a. $[_S \, T^{\langle 1,a \rangle} \, [[C_d \, t_{1a}]^{\langle 1,s \rangle} \, [(\exists) \, [_{vP} \, v_{be} \, [_{nP} \, t_{1s} \, \text{no}_{\#} \, \text{unicorns}]]]]]$

 b. $[\![S]\!] \approx \lambda g_g . \exists y_e^s \colon \#x(g)\big[\text{UNICORN}(@(g^-))(x(g)) \wedge x(g) \sqsubseteq y^s(g)\big] = 0$

The truth of 'There are no unicorns' isn't guaranteed by there being some unicornless state.

Both problems can be addressed with a common solution. There is substantial crosslinguistic and syntactic evidence that the nominal predicates in existential sentences are n*Ps. It is crosslinguistically common to form existential sentences via a possessive construction where the pivot nominal functions as the "possessee" (see Creissels 2014, McNally 2016). The pattern of genitive morphology in Serbian (7.110a) parallels the pattern of genitive morphology on the quantifier complement in (7.110b); in both cases n* can be treated as assigning genitive Case to its complement (§6.2). Existential constructions such as (7.111) in Tagalog are identical to the possessive construction without an overt "possessor" subject (cf. Lynch 1978: 99–100, Fortescue 1984: 81, 171, 173, Onishi 2000: 133, Creissels 2014: 33–34). Existential and possessive sentences in languages such as Tolai are both expressed with a bare possessive n*P predicate ((7.112)). Indeed a prominent idea, following Szabolcsi (1983, 1994) and Kayne (1993, 1994), is that possessive 'have' sentences are (in at least some languages) derived from 'be' plus a possessive noun phrase — on the present architecture, v+n*P.[99] In languages such as Irish the v+n*P and relational phrase in Spec,n* are overt. In (7.113), using the PP *ag YP* 'at YP' yields a possessive interpretation; using the PP *ann* 'in it' yields an existential interpretation (see also Freeze 1992, 2001, Boneh and Sichel 2010). McCloskey (2014) reports that the PPs in such examples are obligatory. If the relevant n* head in Irish has an EPP-property or assigns a broadly possessional/locational θ-role, (7.113a) without *ann* is excluded insofar as the EPP-property/θ-role of n* isn't satisfied/discharged. Revealingly, whereas *ann* can co-occur with modifiers adjoined inside or outside the noun phrase ((7.114a)), it is in complementary distribution with *ag YP* ((7.114b)). On the present analysis, *ann* and *ag YP* cannot co-occur insofar as they compete for the same position in Spec,n*.[100]

---

[99] Cf. Kayne's suggestive remark: "Szabolcsi's claim that Hungarian possessive sentences [e.g., ≈ *John has a sister*] contain … a copula plus a single argument can become intuitively clear to an English speaker if the Hungarian sentences are thought of as parallel to the almost acceptable English *There is (exists) a sister of John's*" (1993: 108). For discussion see also Freeze 1992, den Dikken 1995, 1997, Harley 1995, 2002, Zeshan and Perniss 2008, Boneh and Sichel 2010, Creissels 2013, Myler 2016.

[100] McCloskey shows that *ann* in existential sentences isn't a verbal modifier or an expletive present for syntactic reasons. For instance, unlike with the noun-phrase-external modifier 'on the couch' in (i-a), the fronting of *ann* in (i-b) is ungrammatical. Unlike 'there', *ann* can be structurally focused in existential sentences (McCloskey 2014: 353–354).

(i)   a.   On the couch, there is a cat.
       b.   *Ann, níl   tae ar bith.
             in-it is-not tea any
             (Intended: 'There's no tea.')   (McCloskey 2014: 352; Irish)

McCloskey 2014 gives *ann* in Irish existential sentences the semantics of an existential generalized quantifier (type ⟨*et, t*⟩). For other languages McCloskey suggests that the existential meaning attributed to *ann* may be distributed among the copula or other verbal head. The meanings of *ann* and verbal element in existential sentences are thus distinguished from their meanings in other environments. If the approach to *ann* suggested in the main text is on the right track, *ann* in Irish existentials may be given its usual syntax and (bleached) semantics as a "preposition [which] projects a maximal phrase [PP] and selects a null pronominal as its complement" (McCloskey 2014: 377n.25; more on

(7.110) a. Bilo je   nekih   knjiga.
        be.SG AUX.SG some.GEN books.GEN
        'There were some books.'

   b. Mnogo [nekih   ljudi]   želi pravdu.
      many some.GEN people.GEN want justice
      'Many different people want justice.'
                (cf. Hartmann and Milićević 2009: exs. 2, 23; Serbian)

(7.111) Mayroong   maysakit na   aso (/si Maria).
        exist.there.LNKR sick   LNKR dog SBJ Maria
        'There is a sick dog.' (/'Maria has a sick dog.')
                (cf. Sabbagh 2009: 683, 700; Tagalog (Austronesian))

(7.112) a. A   lolovina lima-i-diat.
        ART long   hand-POSS.MRK-3PL
        'They had long arms.' (lit. '(there were) long arms of theirs')

   b. Pa ka-gu   ta   vabirau.
      NEG POSS$_{fr}$-1SG some light
      'I have not got a light.' (lit. '(there is) no light of mine')
                (cf. Mosel 1984: 157, 164; Tolai (Austronesian))

(7.113) a. Níl   arán ar bith ann.
        is-not bread any   in-it
        'There's no bread.'

   b. Tá leabhar ag mo dheirfiúr.
      is book   at my sister
      'My sister has a book.'

(7.114) a. Tá daoine ann [nach mbeadh sásta   glacadh   leis] / [ar
        is people in-it NEGC be.COND satisfied take.NONFIN with-it   on
        an bhaile]
        the town
        'There are people [who would not be willing to accept it] / [on
        the town]'

   b. *Tá leabhar ann ag mo dheirfiúr.
      is book   in-it at my sister
                (cf. McCloskey 2014: 347, 351; Irish)

---

this shortly). It would be interesting to compare the behavior of *ann* with the behavior of obligatory
locative elements in other languages lacking dedicated existential constructions (see Creissels 2014:
25–26; cf. n. 77 on certain Romance locative clitics and German *da*).

A revised v+n*P analysis for (7.109) is in (7.115). As in §7.4.4, the existential assignment-binder $\exists_r$ raises from inside F^0 in the predicative n*P. The broadly possessional/locational element in Spec,n* supplies the relevant contextual domain. (As previously I use '0-*unicorns*' to abbreviate the property of having zero unicorns as a part.)[101]

(7.115) There are no unicorns.

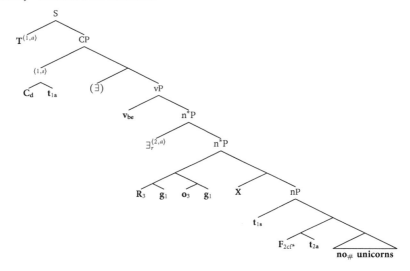

---

[101] I continue to ignore complications from distinguishing a sort/type for locations; and I leave open the relation between the interpreted pronoun supplying the relevant domain (the "subject" of the n*P) and overt grammatical subjects such as 'there' in particular languages (see n. 77). The proposed 'be'+n*P syntax and predicative semantics may help capture insights from alternative "small-clause analyses" (Moro 1997, Hazout 2004, McCloskey 2014) and "NP analyses" (Williams 1984, Chung 1987, McNally 1997, Sabbagh 2009): the n*P complement of the light verb is both a predicative noun phrase and a type of small clause (cf. Bittner and Hale 1996, Harley and Jung 2015, Wood and Marantz 2017). Given economy principles constraining implicit functional structure (Cardinaletti and Starke 1999, Katzir 2011), I assume that predicative uses may be realized with the implicit choice-function element inside the nP, as in (7.115). Additional support may come from languages in which the pivot nominal can appear with an overt determiner. For instance, Law (2011) reports that although Malagasy *ny* is otherwise generally interpreted as specific, it lacks a specific interpretation in the pivot of existential sentences, as reflected in (i)–(ii).

(i)   lasa ny mpianatra.
        gone DET student
        'The student(s) left.'

(ii)   a. tsy misy ny zaza intsony.
            not exist DET child any longer
            'There are no children any longer.'
        b. tsy misy ny fahamarinana.
            not exist DET justice
            'There is no justice.'   (Law 2011: exs. 113, 35, 116; Malagasy (Austronesian))

$$\llbracket S \rrbracket \approx \lambda g_g . \exists x_e^s \exists a_a : x^s(g) = a(g)(2cf^*)(0\text{-}unicorns)(@(g^-)) \wedge$$
$$g^-(3R)(g^-(3e))(x^s(g))$$

This says that (7.115) is true iff there is a state $o^s \in E$ that manifests some individual concept of an entity having no unicorn as a part, and that bears the relevant possessional/locational relation $g_c(3R)$ to the relevant domain $g_c(3e)$ — roughly put, a state of having no unicorn as a part, located at the contextually relevant location. The locational domain functions as a sort of metaphorical "possessor" of the witness state o^s.[102] The denotation of the vP is restricted to the set of "being-nP" states that are "possessed" by, in the sense of being located at, $g_c(3e)$. If the relevant domain corresponds to the entire world, the truth condition requires that the actual world-state be unicornless. Yet, as in §7.2.3, there is no implication of N-instantiation/existence associated with the "existential" construction itself. Continuations such as in (7.40) are still predicted coherent:

(7.116) There are no pillows (... so we should go buy some)
  a. $[_S \, T^{\langle 1,a \rangle} \, [[C_d \, t_{1a}]^{\langle 1,s \rangle} \, [(\exists) \, [_{vP} \, v_{be} \, [\exists_r^{\langle 2,a \rangle}$
      $[_{n^*P} \, [R_3\text{-}g_1 \, o_{4e}\text{-}g_1] \, [X \, [_{nP} \, t_{1s} \, F_{2cf^*}\text{-}t_{2a} \, no_{\#} \, pillows]]]]]]]]$
  b. $\llbracket S \rrbracket \approx \lambda g_g . \exists x_e^s \exists a_a : x^s(g) = a(g)(2cf^*)(0\text{-}pillows)(@(g^-)) \wedge$
      $g^-(3R)(g^-(4e))(x^s(g))$

The fact that no part of the witness state o^s at the relevant location $g_c(4e)$ is a pillow needn't imply that there are there are no pillows in the world.

The previous v+n*P analysis extends to existential sentences 'There be YP ZP' with a ZP "coda" adjoined inside or outside the noun phrase. In (7.118) the locative coda 'on the couch' modifies the verb phrase, restricting the denotation of the predicate to states of being on the couch. A generalized polymorphic entry for v_{be} is in (7.117) (cf. nn. 51, 98). (For simplicity I leave 'the couch' unanalyzed, and I ignore the additional domain pronoun. The world argument for the prepositional phrase can be determined by FC in the CP phase (§7.2.4).)

(7.117) $\llbracket v_{be} \rrbracket = \lambda P_{et}^1 \dots \lambda P_{et}^n . \lambda x_e^s . \lambda g_g . P^1(x^s)(g) \wedge \cdots \wedge P^n(x^s)(g)$

(7.118) There are three pillows on the couch.
  a. $[_S \, T^{\langle 1,a \rangle} \, [[C_d \, t_{1a}]^{\langle 1,s \rangle} \, [(\exists) \, [_{vP}$
      $[_{vP} \, v_{be} \, [_{n^*P} \, \exists_r^{\langle 2,a \rangle} \dots [X \, [_{nP} \, t_{1s} \, F_{2cf^*}\text{-}t_{2a} \, three_{\#} \, pillows]]]]$
      $[_{pP} \, u_{1s} \, on \, the\text{-}couch]]]]]$

---

[102] For relevant discussion see Lyons 1968: §8.4, Freeze 1992, Barker 1995, Langacker 1995, Heine 1997, Marantz 1997, Borschev and Partee 2002, Heine and Kuteva 2002, Uriagereka 2002b, Larson and Cho 2003, Francez 2007, Zeshan and Perniss 2008, Payne 2009, Creissels 2013.

b. $[\![S]\!] \approx \lambda g_g \,.\, \exists x_e^s \exists a_a \colon x^s(g) = a(g)(2\mathrm{cf}^*)(3\text{-}pillows)(@(g^-)) \wedge \cdots \wedge$
   $\mathrm{ON}(\text{the-couch})(@(g^-))(x^s(g))$

Roughly put, this says that (7.118) is true iff there is an on-the-couch state o^s with three pillows as parts.

The revised compositional semantics in this section helps systematize a range of syntactic and semantic features of existential 'there' sentences. As in §7.2.3, the account provides an independent basis for the context-sensitivity of existential sentences; it unifies the syntax/semantics of quantifier words in the pivot with their syntax/semantics in predicative uses generally; it avoids syntactic and compositional semantic problems with imposing a generalized quantifier structure (as in Barwise and Cooper 1981, Keenan 1987, Francez 2007, 2010; see McNally 2011); and it maintains that overt codas such as in (7.118) are optional modifiers (Williams 1984, McNally 1997, Hazout 2004, Sabbagh 2009, McCloskey 2014; contrast Barwise and Cooper 1981, Keenan 1987). The proposed analyses also provide structural grounds for commonalities between existential 'there' sentences and locative, copular, and possessive sentences, while distinguishing them in their syntax and semantics. (7.118) is intuitively true in our context iff (7.119) is. Yet in (7.120a) 'three floors' provides the main predicate; in (7.120b) it is an nP subject of a predication structure, generated in a potential θ-position (whether in a small clause complement of 'be' (cf. Wood and Marantz 2017), as in (7.119), or in an embedding v^*P; I assume the lexical rule option from (7.22)).[103]

(7.119) Three pillows are on the couch.

   $[_S \; T^{\langle 1,a\rangle} \; [[C_d \; t_{1a}]^{\langle 1,s\rangle} \; [(\exists) \; [_{vP} \; v_{be}$
      $[[_{nP^{\langle 1,e\rangle}} \; u_{1s} \; \text{three pillows}] \; [[R_3\text{-}g_1 \; t_{1e}] \; [Y \; [t_{1s} \; \text{on the-couch}]]]]]]]]$

(7.120) a. There are three floors in the building.
         b.??Three floors are in the building.

The 'be'+n^*P analysis for existentials also extends naturally to possessive sentences of the form in (7.111)–(7.113). Our treatment of the distinction between free R vs. inherent R readings in possessive noun phrases carries over directly, as

---

[103] The analyses of predicate nominals may shed light on the correlation, observed by Milsark (1974, 1977), between predicates excluded from codas and from copular sentences with nonpresuppositional noun phrase subjects. Though the predicted LFs for (i)–(ii) with the "individual level" predicate (Carlson 1980) 'jackass' are distinct, the derived semantic values both involve characterizing an indefinite number of individuals as jackasses (cf. (7.118)–(7.120)). Whatever exactly explains the oddity of doing so in (i) presumably carries over to (ii). Resources specific to existential constructions needn't be required (contrast McNally 1997, Francez 2007).

(i)   #sm people are jackasses (/^{ok}available).

(ii) #There are sm people jackasses (/^{ok}available).

reflected in (7.121)–(7.122).[104] In (7.121) ($\approx$ (7.113b)) the relevant relation is contextually supplied; in (7.122) it is supplied by the relational noun. Roughly put, the Irish free R possessive in (7.121) (literally 'a book is at Riley') is true iff there is some being-a-book state of which Riley is the possessor; the inherent R possessive in (7.122) is true iff there is a being-a-brother-of-Riley state.

(7.121) *Tá leabhar ag Riley* ('Riley has a book'; Irish)

    a. $[_S \ T^{\langle 1,a \rangle} \ [[C_d \ t_{1a}]^{\langle 1,s \rangle} \ [(\exists) \ [_{vP} \ v_{be} \ [\exists_r^{\langle 2,a \rangle}$

        $[_{n^*P} \ [_{pP} \ u_{1s} \ R_3\text{-}g_1 \ Riley] \ [X \ [_{nP} \ t_{1s} \ F_{2cf^*}\text{-}t_{2a} \ book]]]]]]]]$

    b. $[\![S]\!] \approx \lambda g_g \, . \, \exists x_e^s \exists a_a \colon x^s(g) = a(g)(2cf^*)(book)(@(g^-)) \ \wedge$

        $g^-(3R)(Riley)(@(g^-))(x^s(g))$

(7.122) *Tá deartháir ag Riley* ('Riley has a brother'; Irish)

    a. $[_S \ T^{\langle 1,a \rangle} \ [[C_d \ t_{1a}]^{\langle 1,s \rangle} \ [(\exists) \ [_{vP} \ v_{be} \ [\exists_r^{\langle 2,a \rangle}$

        $[_{n^*P} \ ... \ X \ [_{nP} \ t_{1s} \ F_{2cf^*}\text{-}t_{2a} \ [brother \ Riley]]]]]]]]]$

    b. $[\![S]\!] \approx \lambda g_g \, . \, \exists x_e^s \exists a_a \colon x^s(g) = a(g)(2cf^*)(bro\text{-}of\text{-}Riley)(@(g^-)) \ \wedge \ \cdots$

Yet it is controversial whether 'have' is analyzable in this way across languages (see nn. 99, 104).

One needn't assume that all types of existential constructions have a uniform underlying syntax (contrast Freeze 1992, 2001). As we have seen, there is variation within and across languages regarding the external syntax of codas, the morphosyntactic properties of n* and light verb, and the nature and presence of

---

[104] Morphological markers of the distinction (see §6.2) can be reflected in verbal possessives as well, as in (i)–(ii) with the added morphemes *-thá-* and *tháwa* in free R possessive pronouns and predicative possessives, respectively (see also Mosel 1984: §§4.3, 4.6, Tellier 1991, den Dikken 1995, Harley 1995, 2002, Español-Echevarría 1997, Heine 1997, Nedjalkov 1997: §1.10, Boneh and Sichel 2010, Dixon 2010: 301–305, Aikhenvald 2013, Myler 2016).

(i)   a. mi-thuŋkašila

          1SG-grandfather

          'my grandfather'

    b. mi-**thá**-wámakȟaškaŋpi kiŋ

          1SG-POSS-animals   DEF

          'my animals'

(ii)   a. Thuŋkášila-wa-ya.

          grandfather-1SG-have.kin

          'I have (him) as grandfather.'

    b. Ni-mi-**tȟawa**.

          2SG-1SG-belong

          'You are mine.'/'I have you.'

          (cf. Helmbrecht 2016: 448–451, Williamson 1979: 359; Lakota (Siouan))

a grammatical subject. Comparisons with related predicate nominal, possession, and double object constructions may provide additional directions for future research.

In the remaining chapters I will put aside the complications from this section regarding events, the semantics of verbalizing heads, the argument structure of verbs, and the introduction of external subjects via v^*. Unless otherwise noted I will assume familiar NP, VP, DP category labels — NP for nP, VP for vP, DP for the spread of argument-suitable functional projections above nP.

Part III

8

Conditionals

§§8–9 explore how the assignment-variable-based treatments of modals, relativization, and pronominal anaphora in the previous chapters may be extended to capture shifting phenomena in other types of clausal structures, such as conditionals and questions. §8.2 develops a syntax/semantics for 'if'-clauses as free relatives of assignments, interpreted as plural definite descriptions of possibilities. The account affords a uniform analysis of 'if'-clauses adjoined in noun phrases, verb phrases, and clauses (§§8.3–8.5), and in conditionals with or without a modal (§8.6) or proform such as 'then' (§8.7.2). Comparisons between conditional correlatives and correlatives of individuals are briefly considered (§8.7).

8.1 Local and Global Readings

Conditionals provide diverse sources of shifted and unshifted readings. There can be global readings in the 'if'-clause and main clause, as in (8.1); local readings in the 'if'-clause, as in (8.2); and local readings in the main clause, as in (8.3).

(8.1)   If it$_j$ breaks, he$_k$ will cry.

   ≈ "If $g_c(j)$ breaks, $g_c(k)$ will cry"

(8.2)   [Context: We know how much everyone's income is. We haven't settled on what level of income should count as rich.]
   If$_i$ Rita is rich$_i$, she shouldn't get a tax break.

   ≈ "If the relevant standard for richness is i and Rita is at least i-rich, ..."

(8.3)   [If John wasn't invited,]$_i$ everyone$_i$ will come.

   ≈ "[If John wasn't invited]$_i$ everyone who is relevant given i will come"

Semantic work on conditionals has focused nearly exclusively on examples where the 'if'-clause combines with a clause. Yet there are also conditionals where the 'if'-clause is sentence final and modifies the verb, and "adnominal" conditionals where the 'if'-clause modifies a noun.[105] Syntactic tests confirm that the 'if'-clause may combine at the level of the verb/noun phrase rather than scoping over the rest of the sentence, as reflected with the VP-ellipsis and Condition C data in (8.4) and coordination data in (8.5).

(8.4)   *Sentence-final 'if'-clause. VP-modification*
         a. I will leave if you do and John will {~~$_{VP}$ leave if you do}~~ too.
         b. *She$_i$ yells at Bill if Mary$_i$ is hungry.
                                      (Bhatt and Pancheva 2006: exs. 19a, 21a)

(8.5)   *Adnominal 'if'-clause. NP-modification*
         [[The [$_{NP}$ location if it rains]] and [the [$_{NP}$ location if it doesn't rain]]] are within five miles of each other.   (Lasersohn 1996: ex. 10)

Shifted readings can be observed in each of these positions, as in (8.6)–(8.7).

(8.6)   Everyone$_i$ will [$_{VP}$ come [if John wasn't invited]$_i$] (...or no one$_j$ will {~~$_{VP}$ come [if John wasn't invited]$_j$~~)

(8.7)   The [$_{NP}$ right$_i$ thing [if utilitarianism is true]$_i$] and the [$_{NP}$ right$_j$ thing [if deontology is true]$_j$] are the same in this case.

Santorio (2012) argues that in examples such as (8.8) the interpretation of 'I' in the consequent clause is shifted by the supposition, referring to an epistemic counterpart of the speaker in the hypothetical possibility. Such "shifted indexical" readings are possible with adnominal and adverbial conditionals as well ((8.9)).

(8.8)   [Context: Lingens and Lauben know they are kidnapped amnesiacs. They are informed that they will be anesthetized, and a coin will be flipped: if it lands tails, Lingens will be released in the Stanford library and Lauben will be killed; if it lands heads, Lauben will be released in the Harvard library and Lingens will be killed. After the experiment, one of them wakes up and says:]
         [If the coin landed heads,]$_i$ I$_i$ am in Widener Library, Harvard.
                                                  (cf. Santorio 2012: ex. 6)

(8.9)   a. I$_i$ [am in Widener Library [if the coin landed heads]$_i$].
         b. [My$_i$ location [if the coin landed heads]$_i$] and [my$_j$ location [if the coin landed tails]$_j$] are on opposite coasts.

---

[105] Dixon (1972) reports that in Dyirbal the adnominal NP+relative structure is the primary means for expressing hypothetical 'if' conditionals, as in (i).

(i)   bayi   yara rudu   balga-ŋu guyibi-ñ
         CL1.M man hollow hit-REL   die-FUT
         'If a man is hit in the hollow in the back of his neck, he will die.' (lit. 'A man if hit ... will die')
                                     (Dixon 1972: 362; Dyirbal (Pama–Nyungan))

Classic semantics for conditionals are inapplicable as they stand to examples where the 'if'-clause combines with a noun phrase or verb phrase. We must ensure that whatever type of semantics we go in for generalizes across environments in which 'if'-clauses (and other markers of conditionality) appear. The account must derive local readings in the 'if'-clause and main clause, i.e. shifting in a supposition and in the scope of a supposition, as in (8.2)–(8.3); and it must do so in a way that allows for global readings in both clauses, as in (8.1). The semantic type of the 'if'-clause must be suitable to combine directly with a nominal/verbal predicate and shift the interpretation of material inside or outside the modified NP/VP, as in (8.6)–(8.7), (8.9). The following sections show how we can satisfy these desiderata, drawing on independent syntactic work on 'if'-clauses as free relatives. The compositional semantics affords a uniform analysis of 'if'-clauses in diverse types of conditionals — conditionals with sentence-initial/-internal/-final 'if'-clauses, and in conditionals with or without an overt modal or a proform such as 'then'. A unified treatment of individual and conditional anaphoric proforms in correlative constructions is provided.

8.2 'If'-Clauses as Plural Definite Descriptions of Possibilities

A standard story following Lewis (1975) and Kratzer (1981, 1991) is that 'if'-clauses restrict the domain of a modal or other operator. Yet as von Fintel notes, "it is very probable … that tripartite structures are merely a convenient meta-level notation" (1994: 77), and movement operations don't literally generate operator-restrictor-scope LFs like (8.10) analogous to structures with nominal quantifiers (cf. Partee 1995).

(8.10) $[_S [\text{MOD}^i [\text{IF-CLAUSE}]^j] [_{CP} t_j [\dots t_i \dots]]]$

So I assume that our best syntactic story for conditionals will involve some other way of capturing the idea that 'if'-clauses function to modify a domain. The previous chapters drew on independent syntactic work and crosslinguistic data to motivate treatments of quantification in various nominal, verbal, and clausal structures. In what follows I suggest that syntactic analyses of 'if'-clauses as free relatives (Iatridou 1991, von Fintel 1994, Bittner 2001, Schlenker 2004, Bhatt and Pancheva 2006) provide analogous motivations for world- and assignment-quantification in conditionals. Like other free relatives (Jacobson 1995, Dayal 1996, Caponigro 2012), 'if'-clauses are interpreted as definite descriptions. In some languages conditionals are overtly realized as such. The Somali conditional clause in (8.11) is a remoteness-marked ("modal past") definite description. The Warlpiri construction in (8.12) is ambiguous between a conditional interpretation and an interpretation as an individual definite description (see also Furbee 1973: 15, Welmers 1973: 433–434).

(8.11) a. Nin **hád-díi**   uu seexdó oo sóo toosó,   waa
            man time-DEF.REM 3   sleeps and DIR wakes-up DECL
            isá-gíi   ún.
            him-EMPH.PAST only
            'If a man goes to sleep and then wakes up, he is only himself (i.e. the
            same as he was before).'
        b. **Hád-díi**   aad rabtó na ráac!
            time-DEF.REM you want us follow.IMP
            'Come along with us, if you want!'   (Lecarme 2008: ex. 19; Somali)

(8.12) [Maliki-rli **katji**-ŋki   yarlki-rni   nyuntu] ŋula-ju
        dog-ERG   SAME.TOP-3SG.2SG bite-NONPAST you   DEM-TOP
        kapi-rna   luwa-rni   ŋatjulu-rlu.
        FUT-1SG.3SG shoot-NONPAST me-ERG
        a. 'As for the dog that bites you, I'll shoot it.'
        b. 'If a dog bites you, then I'll shoot it.'
            (Hale 1976: 80, Bittner 2001: ex. 7; Warlpiri (Pama–Nyungan))

Rather than treating the variable relativized over in conditionals as a variable over worlds or events (as in Schein 2003, Schlenker 2004, Bhatt and Pancheva 2006, Haegeman 2010), we can treat it as a variable over assignments: 'if'-clauses are analyzed as definite descriptions of possibilities, represented via assignments.

Given the diverse linguistic means of expressing conditionality, it is common to treat conditional interpretations as arising independent of particular complementizers such as 'if' (Bhatt and Pancheva 2006, Rawlins 2008). A prominent approach is to treat the conditional element as raising above the complementizer from inside the 'if'-clause (Bhatt and Pancheva 2006, Arsenijević 2009, Haegeman 2010). Movement analyses of conditional clauses provide independently motivated resources for implementing the analysis of 'if'-clauses in the present framework — notably, a complementizer such as 'if', and clause-internal movement of an operator responsible for conditional interpretations. A schematic analysis is in (8.13), where ι_h is the raised definite-like operator (implicit in English), parallel to ι_o in free relatives of individuals (§§5.1.3, 7.4.4).[106]

---

[106] Though Bhatt and Pancheva (2006) don't specify the generation site of the conditional operator, Haegeman (2010) argues against treating it as moving from inside VP. Haegeman treats the operator as semantically modal and as sharing properties specifically with syntactically high (broadly epistemic) modals. Such a view may provide independent support for the present implementation of ι_h as raising from inside C^0, analogously to modal elements (§3).

(8.13)

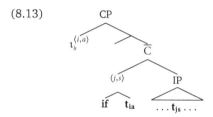

Like the declarative complementizer, 'if' is base-generated in the world-argument position of the clause's main predicate and moves for type reasons as a quantifier over worlds; the world argument of the main predicate receives an obligatory local reading under the supposition (cf. §§3–4). Like other modal elements, ι_h is base-generated in the complementizer's internal assignment-argument position and moves for type reasons (here clause-internally), introducing an assignment binder.

A preliminary semantics and derivation are as follows.[107] The lexical entry for 'if' in (8.14) is effectively an intensional analogue of the entry for the relative complementizer $\mathbf{C_{rel}}$ from §5. The type-$\langle at, \langle at, t \rangle \rangle$ entry for ι_h in (8.15) is a definite version of the semantics for modal verbs such as 'may' (§3.4).[108]

(8.14) $[\![\text{if}]\!] = \lambda a_a.\lambda p_{st}.\lambda w_s.\lambda g_g \,.\, @(a(g)) \sqsubseteq w(g) \wedge$
$\qquad\qquad \forall w_s' = [\lambda g_g'. @(a(g'))] \colon p(w')(g)$ *(to be revised)*

(8.15) $[\![\iota_h]\!] = \lambda A_{at}.\lambda A_{at}'.\lambda g_g \,.\, \exists a_a \colon \big(A(a)(g) \wedge \forall a_a'' \colon A(a'')(g) \to a''(g) \sqsubseteq a(g) \big)$
$\qquad\qquad \wedge A'(a)(g)$
$\qquad = \lambda A_{at}.\lambda A_{at}'.\lambda g_g \,.\, \exists a_a \colon \big(a(g) = \text{the maximal } h \in G \text{ such that } (^\downarrow A)(h) \big)$
$\qquad\qquad \wedge A'(a)(g)$
$\qquad = \lambda A_{at}.\lambda A_{at}'.\lambda g_g \,.\, \big[\iota a(g) \colon A(a)(g) \big] \, A'(a)(g)$

---

[107] In the definition of the binder-index (§3.5): with **if**, $\tau = s$, $\sigma = \langle s, t \rangle$; with ι_h, $\tau = a$, $\sigma = \langle at, t \rangle$.

[108] In languages such as Toqabaqita the same element *mada* used in introducing conditional clauses (as in (i-a) with the irrealis marker) introduces an epistemic possibility when used alone in main clauses ((i-b)) (cf. Dixon 1972: 113, 362, 2009, Stebbins 2009).

(i)   a.   **Mada sa** dani qe   qaru ...
            MADA IRR rain 3SG.NONFUT fall
            'If it rains, ...'
    b.   **Mada** qe   mataqi.
            MADA 3SG.NONFUT be.sick
            'He might be sick.'   (Lichtenberk 2008: 8, 38, 776; Toqabaqita (Austronesian))

(8.16)

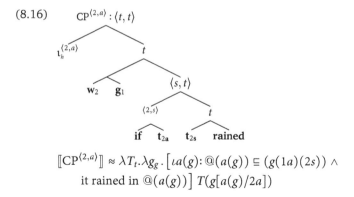

$$[\![CP^{\langle 2,a\rangle}]\!] \approx \lambda T_t.\lambda g_g.\left[\iota a(g)\colon @(a(g)) \sqsubseteq (g(1a)(2s)) \wedge \right.$$
$$\left.\text{it rained in } @(a(g))\right] T(g[a(g)/2a])$$

Following general treatments of free relatives as plural definite descriptions, the assignment described by the 'if'-clause may represent a plural possibility — a possibility that has multiple atomic possibilities as parts (cf. Jacobson 1995, Dayal 1996, Grosu and Landman 1998, Schein 2003, Bhatt and Pancheva 2006). The metalanguage ι operator is again used as in §§6–7 along the lines of Link's (1983) σ, which returns the maximal element of a set (formally, the m in the set S such that $\forall m' \in S\colon m' \sqsubseteq m$).[109] The external world argument of 'if' further restricts the quantification to possibilities in a relevant (salient/live/remote) domain. Intuitively put, the pronoun [$\mathbf{w}_2\ \mathbf{g}_1$] supplies a topical modal possibility which provides the backdrop for the supposition. The 'if'-clause in (8.16) is a definite description of the maximal relevant possibility in which it rained. (I won't distinguish singular vs. plural predicates; my saying that a property holds of an object leaves open whether the predication is of an atomic object, a plurality, or every atomic part of a plurality. For instance, saying that it rained in $@(h)$ can be understood as saying that it rained in the world of every possibility that is a part of h.)

The approach to free relatives of individuals mentioned in §5.1.3 (n. 32) treated the external argument of $\mathbf{C}_{\text{rel}}$ as a selected individual in a contextually relevant domain supplied by the relative phrase — schematically:

(8.17) $\iota_o^{\langle i,a\rangle}$ [wh-g$_i$ P$_{\text{et}}$-g [[C$_{\text{rel}}$ t$_{ia}$]$^{\langle j,e\rangle}$ [... t$_{je}$ ...]]]

One way of unifying the analyses of free relatives of individuals and possibilities is to treat the external argument of 'if' as being supplied by an implicit 'wh(ether)'-like element analogous to the relative phrase. Just as free relative

---

[109] Note that the uniqueness implication applies to items in the model. There may be multiple functions $a\colon D_g \to G$ mapping an assignment to the unique possibility $h \in G$ described by the 'if'-clause.

'what' is analyzed intuitively as "which relevant thing(s)," the external argument of 'if' in (8.19) is analyzed as "which relevant world(s)." The 'wh' component functions semantically as a choice function of worlds — a function which selects a world $u \in W$ from a given set of worlds (cf. (4.17)). A suitably revised lexical entry for 'if' is in (8.18). (For clarity I distinguish 'sf' in choice-function indices/pronouns of type $\langle st, s \rangle$; I continue to use 'cf' for choice functions of type $\langle et, e \rangle$.)

(8.18) $\quad [\![\mathbf{if}]\!] = \lambda a_a.\lambda p_{st}.\lambda w_s.\lambda g_g . @(a(g)) = w(g) \wedge \forall w'_s = [\lambda g'_g.@(a(g'))] : p(w')(g)$

(8.19)

$$CP^{\langle 2,a \rangle} : \langle t, t \rangle$$

$$[\![CP^{\langle 2,a \rangle}]\!] \approx \lambda T_t.\lambda g_g . \left[\iota a(g) : @(a(g)) = a(g)(2\mathrm{sf})(g(1a)(1\mathrm{st})) \wedge \right.$$
$$\left. \text{it rained in } @(a(g)) \right] T(g[a(g)/2a])$$

The proposition-pronoun $[\mathbf{p}_{1\mathrm{st}}\ \mathbf{g}_1]$ functions analogously to class restrictions (thing, person) in free relatives of individuals. Free relative 'what' selects an individual from a subdomain of things, and free relative 'who' selects an individual from a subdomain of persons; likewise the constituent $[\mathbf{wh}_{2\mathrm{sf}}\text{-}\mathbf{g}_2\ \mathbf{p}_{1\mathrm{st}}\text{-}\mathbf{g}_1]$ in the free relative 'if'-clause selects a world from a subdomain of relevant worlds.[110] The raised maximality operator $\iota_h^{\langle 2,a \rangle}$ binds the choice-function pronoun and quantifies over possibilities in the restricted set that satisfy the property denoted by 'if + IP'. The 'if-clause in (8.19) picks out the maximal possibility h such that the world of h, $@(h)$, is selected by $h(2\mathrm{sf})$ from the set of relevant worlds $g_c(1\mathrm{st})$ and it rained in $@(h)$ — roughly put, the sum of relevant possibilities in which it rained.

The semantic type of the 'if-clause CP is derived to be type $\langle t, t \rangle$ — the same type as the adjoined quantifier phrases in our examples with inverse linking and genitive binding from §6.4 (cf. §7.4.4). We will see that function composition can also be exploited in capturing shifted readings with 'if-clauses in various types of adjunction structures.

---

[110] Strict conditional and material conditional interpretations would be cases where the proposition pronoun is ultimately identified with W and $\{@(g_c)\}$, respectively.

8.3   Adnominal Conditionals

Adnominal conditionals such as (8.5) are rarely considered in semantics for conditionals (see Lasersohn 1996). A derivation in which the 'if'-clause combines with a noun phrase is in (8.20). (For present purposes I assume a simple $\langle et, \langle et, t \rangle \rangle$ entry for 'the'. Unless indicated otherwise I will treat free individual pronouns as simple type e pronouns. I again occasionally use asterisks for distinguishing different ZP segments.)

(8.20)   *Adnominal conditional* (NP-adjunction)
The fine if you drive is expensive.

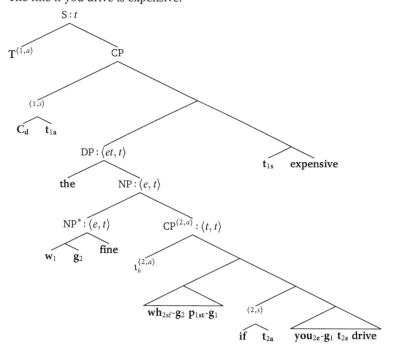

$$\llbracket CP^{\langle 2,a\rangle} \rrbracket \approx \lambda T_t.\lambda g.\left[\iota a(g):g(1a)(2e)\text{ drives in }@(a(g)) \wedge \right.$$
$$\left.@(a(g)) = a(g)(2\text{sf})(g(1a)(1\text{st}))\right] T(g[a(g)/2a])$$

$$\llbracket NP \rrbracket = \llbracket CP^{\langle 2,a\rangle} \rrbracket \circ \llbracket NP^* \rrbracket$$
$$= \lambda x_e.\llbracket CP^{\langle 2,a\rangle} \rrbracket (\llbracket NP^* \rrbracket (x))$$
$$\approx \lambda x_e.\lambda g_g.\left[\iota a(g):g(1a)(2e)\text{ drives in }@(a(g)) \wedge \right.$$
$$\left.@(a(g)) = a(g)(2\text{sf})(g(1a)(1\text{st}))\right] x(g[a(g)/2a])\text{ is a fine in }a(g)(1s)$$

$$\llbracket S \rrbracket \approx \lambda g_g . \big[\iota x(g) : [\iota a(g) : g^-(2e) \text{ drives in } @(a(g)) \wedge$$
$$@(a(g)) = a(g)(2\text{sf})(g^-(1st))] \, x(g) \text{ is a fine in } a(g)(1s) \big]$$
$$x(g) \text{ is expensive in } @(g^-)$$

The 'if'-clause of type $\langle t, t \rangle$ and nominal predicate 'fine' of type $\langle e, t \rangle$ combine via function composition to yield the complex NP of type $\langle e, t \rangle$. The assignment binder-index projecting in the conditional $CP^{\langle 2,a \rangle}$ shifts the coindexed world-pronoun $[w_1 \, g_2]$ in NP* to the world of the hypothetical possibility described by the 'if'-clause. The subject DP thus picks out the unique $o \in E$ such that o is a fine in the world $h(1s)$ $(= @(h))$ of the maximal relevant possibility h where you $g_c(2e)$ drive — i.e., the maximal possibility h such that $@(h)$ is selectable from the contextually relevant domain $g_c(1st)$ and you drive in $@(h)$. The sentence is true iff o is expensive in the actual world $@(g_c)$.

The analysis in (8.20) compositionally derives the local reading of the world argument of 'fine' in the subject noun phrase. Nothing said thus far excludes an LF where the world-pronoun in NP* is bound by the topmost assignment-binder, representing an unattested reading implying that the fine in the actual world is expensive. One response would be to derive the obligatory shifted reading via movement. In (8.21) the 'if'-clause is treated as moving for type reasons from the NP's world argument, leaving a coindexed trace.[111]

(8.21) *Adnominal conditional* (alternative)

    ... the $[_{NP} \, [_{NP^*} \, w_1 \, t_{2a} \, \text{fine}] \, CP^{\langle 2,a \rangle}]$

An alternative is to maintain that the 'if'-clause is base-generated in an adjoined position and exclude LFs representing global readings for conversational reasons. Treating the world argument of 'fine' in (8.20) as $[w_1 \, g_1]$ renders the 'if'-clause trivial in the interpretation of the subject noun phrase. An interpretive principle against such semantically trivial modifications might be formulated as in (8.22). Intuitively put, this says that binder-indices necessary for interpretability in a given step in a derivation must do nontrivial semantic work in that step in the derivation.

(8.22) *Nontriviality principle*

    Let i be a set of binder-index features $\{ \langle i_1, \tau_1 \rangle, \langle i_2, \tau_2 \rangle, \dots \}$, and γ be a branching node in the domain of $\llbracket \; \rrbracket$ whose daughters are α and β^i, where β^i occupies an $\overline{A}$-position. For any binder-index feature $k \in i$ that

---

[111] In terms of the architecture from §7, the 'if'-clause would QR out of n^0 and adjoin to nP. The pronounced word order could be derived by rightward QR (cf. Fox 2002), or by leftward QR followed by remnant movement of NP. For simplicity I assume the former.

is semantically necessary in γ, there are assignments $g \approx_k g'$ such that
$[\![\alpha]\!](\cdots)(g) \neq [\![\alpha]\!](\cdots)(g')$.

a. $g \approx_k g'$ iff g and g' are otherwise identical except that $g(k) \neq g'(k)$
b. k is *semantically necessary* in γ iff, for γ^* a branching node whose daughters are α and $\beta^{i\backslash\{k\}}$, γ^* is not in the domain of $[\![\ ]\!]$.

(8.22) is directly satisfied in cases of QR, where the moved expression binds its trace. In (8.20) with a base-generated adjunct, the 'if'-clause's assignment-binder is "semantically necessary" insofar as, without it, CP and NP* would be types $\langle at, t\rangle$ and $\langle e, t\rangle$, respectively, and the NP node would be uninterpretable. So, lest the nontriviality principle be violated, the nominal predicate's world-pronoun must be coindexed with the 'if'-clause, representing the shifted reading.

I won't attempt to adjudicate between these options here. Yet note that accepting (8.21) is compatible with treating certain 'if'-clauses as base-generated adjuncts; and accepting (8.20) is compatible with treating (8.22) as a violable extra-grammatical principle. Consider the analysis of the relevance conditional in (8.23) (leave 'made soup' as an unanalyzed predicate).

(8.23) *Biscuit conditional* (CP-adjunction)
    If you're hungry, Justin made soup.
    a. $[_S T^{\langle 1,a\rangle} [[_{CP\langle 2,a\rangle} \iota_h^{\langle 2,a\rangle} [wh_{2sf}\text{-}g_2 \; p_{1st}\text{-}g_1 [[if \; t_{2a}]^{\langle 2,s\rangle} \; you_{2e}\text{-}g_1 \; t_{2s} \; hungry]]]$
        $[_{CP} [_{C_d} t_{1a}]^{\langle 1,s\rangle} \; Justin \; t_{1s} \; made\text{-}soup]]]$
    b. $[\![S]\!] \approx \lambda g_g . \big[\iota a(g) : g^-(2e) \text{ is hungry in } @(a(g)) \wedge$
        $@(a(g)) = a(g)(2sf)(1st)\big] \text{ Justin made soup in } @(g^-)$

The 'if'-clause is base-generated in its interpreted position adjoined to the main clause. Like in simple sentences, the topmost assignment-binder raises from the assignment-argument position of the main clause complementizer, and the modal domain for the main clause is linked to the world of the discourse via the definition of truth-in-a-context. Roughly put, (8.23) is true iff the maximal relevant possibility where you $(=g_c(2e))$ are hungry is such that Justin made soup in the actual world $@(g_c)$.

The analysis in (8.23) derives features often associated with relevance conditionals such as the independence of the antecedent and consequent and the apparent assertion of the consequent. The 'if'-clause introduces a modal topic — the possibility that you're hungry — but then fails to comment on it in the main clause; the sentence implies that Justin actually made soup. The 'if'-clause in the relevance conditional is treated on a par with a "frame-setting" topic (Reinhart 1981), as in (8.24).

(8.24) As for cats, I like Fluffy.

Not all syntactic modifiers need do nontrivial semantic work in the sense of (8.22).

8.4 Sentence-Final 'If'-Clauses

Let's turn to conditionals with sentence-final 'if'-clauses that adjoin to verbal predicates. First, observe that treating the main predicate's world argument as a trace coindexed with the matrix complementizer would fail to capture the role of the 'if'-clause in shifting the modal domain. The LF in (8.25a) incorrectly derives a global reading for 'slept'.

(8.25) Fluffy slept if it rained.

    a. $[_\text{S} \, \mathbf{T}^{\langle 1,a \rangle} \, [_\text{CP} \, [_\text{C}_\text{d} \, t_{1a}]^{\langle 1,s \rangle} \, [\text{Fluffy} \, [_\text{VP} \, [_{\text{VP}^*} \, t_{1s} \, \text{slept}] \, \text{CP}^{\langle 2,a \rangle}]]]]$

    b. $[\![\text{VP}^*]\!] = \lambda x_e . \lambda g_g . x(g) \text{ slept in } g(1s)$

        $[\![\text{VP}]\!] = \lambda x_e . \lambda g_g . \left[\iota a(g) : \dots \right] x(g[a(g)/2a]) \text{ slept in } g[a(g)/2a](1s)$

        $[\![\text{CP}]\!] \approx \lambda g_g . \left[\iota a(g) : \dots \right] \text{Fluffy slept in } @(g(1a))$

        $[\![\text{S}]\!] \approx \lambda g_g . \left[\iota a(g) : \dots \right] \text{Fluffy slept in } @(g^-)$

We needn't assume that all occurrences of complementizers raise for type reasons from their base-generated position. The relevant modal domain for interpreting the main predicate in (8.25) with a VP-modifier is the domain as shifted by the modifier. Suppose that the main predicate's world argument in such examples may be supplied by a world-pronoun. A derivation for the "shifted indexical" example in (8.9a) (adapted from Santorio 2012) is as follows. The matrix complementizer $\mathbf{C}_\varnothing$ denotes the identity function. (Treat 'landed heads' and 'be in Widener Library' as unanalyzed predicates.)[112]

---

[112] As previously, I leave open whether the coindexing between the world-pronoun in VP* and the 'if'-clause may be derived via A̅-movement.

(8.26) *Sentence-final 'if'-clause. Shifted indexical* (VP-adjunction)
[Context: same as (8.8)]
I am in Widener Library if it landed heads.

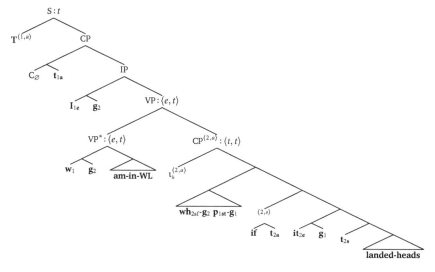

$$[\![IP]\!] = ([\![CP^{\langle 2,a\rangle}]\!] \circ [\![VP^*]\!])(\lambda g_g.g(2a)(1e))$$
$$\approx [\lambda x_e.[\lambda T_t.[\lambda g_g.[\iota a(g){:}g(1a)(2e) \text{ landed heads in } @(a(g)) \wedge$$
$$@(a(g)) = a(g)(2\mathrm{sf})(g(1a)(1st))] \, T(g[a(g)/2a])]]$$
$$(\lambda g_g.x(g) \text{ is in WL in } g(2a)(1s))] \, (\lambda g_g.g(2a)(1e))$$
$$\approx \lambda g_g.[\iota a(g){:}g(1a)(2e) \text{ landed heads in } @(a(g)) \wedge$$
$$@(a(g)) = a(g)(2\mathrm{sf})(g(1a)(1st))] \, a(g)(1e) \text{ is in WL in } a(g)(1s)$$
$$[\![C_\varnothing]\!] = \lambda a_a.\lambda T_t.\lambda g_g \, . \, T$$
$$[\![S]\!] \approx \lambda g_g \, . \, [\iota a(g){:}g(2e) \text{ landed heads in } @(a(g)) \wedge$$
$$@(a(g)) = a(g)(2\mathrm{sf})(g^-(1st))] \, a(g)(1e) \text{ is in WL in } a(g)(1s)$$

Roughly put, the 'if'-clause is a definite description of the maximal relevant possibility h such that the contextually relevant object $g_c(2e)$ landed heads in $@(h)$ ($=h(2\mathrm{sf})(g_c(1st))$). The conditional is true iff $h(1e)$ is in Widener Library in the world of that possibility.

Whereas the pronoun 'it' in the 'if'-clause is interpreted with respect to the discourse assignment, the clause's main predicate 'landed-heads' receives an obligatory local reading due to movement of the complementizer 'if'. As in (8.20), the 'if'-clause combines with the (here verbal) predicate via function composition, yielding the complex VP of type $\langle e, t\rangle$. The 'if'-clause shifts the interpretation of the coindexed world-pronoun [$\mathbf{w}_1$ $\mathbf{g}_2$], and the sentence's main predicate receives a local reading; the state of being in Widener Library occurs in the world of the hypothetical possibility. Although the 'if'-clause doesn't combine at the level of the main clause, the subject pronoun 'I' can still receive a local reading under the supposition. Following Santorio 2012 the denoted individual $h(1e)$ can be understood as an epistemic counterpart of the speaker $g_c(1e)$ (§§3.4, 4). The interpretation of 'I' in the main clause is determined relative to the possibility introduced by the 'if'-clause. The shifted reading of the subject is compositionally derived from the general analysis of 'if'-clauses and function composition.

8.5   Sentence-Initial 'If'-Clauses

Conditionals with sentence-initial 'if'-clauses may be treated as adjoined to IP or CP (cf. Iatridou 1991, von Fintel 1994, Izvorski 1996, Bhatt and Pancheva 2006). Consider the following alternative LFs for (8.27) on the reading where 'tall' receives a local reading targeted by the supposition (cf. (8.2)). (Assume a toy context-sensitive semantics for positive form relative gradable adjectives, where [$\mathbf{d}_i$ $\mathbf{g}_j$] is a pronoun for degrees $d \in D_d$, and 'o is s-tall' abbreviates that o's height is at least as great as the standard s for counting as tall (cf. Barker 2002, Kennedy 2007). Assume that the 'if'-clause $CP^{\langle 2,a \rangle}$ in (8.29) is as in (8.28).)

(8.27) [Context: We know everyone's height. We haven't settled on how tall one must be to count as tall.]
          If she is tall, she made the team.

(8.28) *Sentence-initial 'if'-clause* (CP-adjunction)

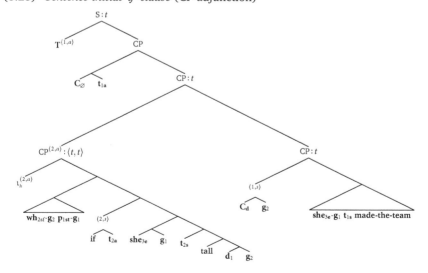

$$\llbracket \mathbf{tall} \rrbracket = \lambda d_d.\lambda w_s.\lambda x_e.\lambda g_g . x(g) \text{ is } d(g)\text{-tall in } w(g)$$

$$\llbracket S \rrbracket \approx \lambda g_g . \big[\iota a(g) : g^-(3e) \text{ is } a(g)(1d)\text{-tall in } @(a(g)) \wedge$$
$$@(a(g)) = a(g)(2sf)(g^-(1st)) \big] g^-(3e) \text{ made the team in } @(a(g))$$

(8.29)   *Sentence-initial 'if'-clause* (IP-adjunction)

    a. $[_S \, T^{\langle 1,a \rangle} \, [_{CP} \, C_\varnothing \, t_{1a} \, [_{IP} \, CP^{\langle 2,a \rangle} \, [_{IP} \, \text{she}_{3e} \, g_1 \, [w_1\text{-}g_2 \, \text{made-the-team}]]]]]$

    b. $\llbracket S \rrbracket \approx \lambda g_g . [\iota a(g) : \dots] \, g^-(3e) \text{ made the team in } a(g)(1s)$

In both (8.28) and (8.29) the world argument of the predicate 'is tall' in the 'if'-clause receives an obligatory local reading, captured via type-driven movement; and the degree-standard pronoun [d_1 g_2] associated with the adjective receives an optional local reading, captured via coindexing with the 'if'-clause. The relevant standard for tallness is the standard in the supposition. The possibility described by the 'if'-clause is a possibility h in which $g_c(3e)$'s height in $@(h)$ ($=h(2sf)(g_c(1st))$) meets the standard determined by h for counting as tall. The conditional is true iff $g_c(3e)$ made the team in the world of that possibility.

In (8.29) the world argument of the sentence's main predicate ('made-the-team') is supplied, as in (8.26),[113] by a world-pronoun [w_1 g_2]; and the derived modal domain is contextually identified with the world of the hypothetical possibility, i.e. $a(g)(1s) = @(a(g))$. By contrast, in (8.28) the modal domain for the main clause is explicitly identified with $@(a(g))$. The main predicate's world argument is supplied by a world-trace left from movement of the complementizer; and the complementizer's assignment argument is supplied by an assignment-variable g_2 coindexed with the 'if'-clause. In both cases the topmost assignment-binder raises from the internal assignment argument of $C_\varnothing$. However, in (8.28), where the 'if'-clause adjoins to a full CP, there is an independently motivated mechanism for generating the vacuous complementizer: CP-recursion (Iatridou and Kroch 1993, Nyvad et al. 2017). Conditionals with sentence-initial 'if'-clauses follow the complementizer in attitude ascriptions.

(8.30)   Alice thinks $[_{CP}$ that $[_{CP}$ [if it snows] $[_{CP}$ school will close]]]

Treating the complementizer embedding the conditional as vacuous satisfies the requirement for CP-recursion in Iatridou and Kroch 1993 that any content of

---

[113] The semantic value for (8.8) in (i) with IP-adjunction is equivalent to the semantic value in (8.26) where the 'if'-clause is sentence-final and adjoined to VP.

(i)   If it landed heads, I am in Widener Library.

    a. $[_S \, T^{\langle 1,a \rangle} \, [_{CP} \, C_\varnothing \, t_{1a}$

          $[_{IP} \, [_{CP^{\langle 2,a \rangle}} \, t_h^{\langle 2,a \rangle} \, [\text{wh}_{2sf}\text{-}g_2 \, p_{1st}\text{-}g_1 \, [[\text{if } t_{2a}]^{\langle 2,s \rangle} \, [\text{it}_{2e}\text{-}g_1 \, t_{2s} \, \text{landed-heads}]]]]$
          $[_{IP} \, I_{1e}\text{-}g_2 \, w_1\text{-}g_2 \, \text{am-in-WL}]]]]$

    b. $\llbracket S \rrbracket = \llbracket (8.26) \rrbracket$

the higher complementizer be recoverable from the content of the lower complementizer. In (8.30) the embedding complementizer is pronounced (=**that**$_\varnothing$), and what raises from the internal assignment argument is the attitude verb; in (8.28) the embedding complementizer is implicit (=**C**$_\varnothing$), and what raises is the topmost assignment-binder.

Hypothetical conditionals can be understood as a type of correlative construction, where the free relative clause binds a correlate in the main clause (Iatridou 1991, von Fintel 1994, Bittner 2001, Schlenker 2004, Bhatt and Pancheva 2006, Arsenijević 2009).

(8.31)   [[$_{CP}$ FREE RELATIVE]^i [... CORRELATE$_i$ ...]]

Crosslinguistic work on correlatives shows that fronted correlates must be structurally adjacent to the sentence-initial relative clause (Bhatt and Pancheva 2006, Lipták 2012). This requirement can help capture how in hypothetical 'if ...' conditionals the modal domain for the main clause is obligatorily shifted even if the 'if-clause is base-generated in its adjoined position. The 'if'-clause in (8.28) binds the assignment-variable g_2 in the adjacent main clause C^0, shifting the modal domain to that of the topical antecedent possibility.

It is common in analyses of 'if'-clauses as free relatives to treat conditional 'then' as the correlate in correlative constructions. Not all sentence-initial 'if...' conditionals are compatible with 'then':

(8.32)   a. If John is dead or alive, (#then) Bill will find him.
         b. Even if John is drunk, (#then) Bill will vote for him.
                                          (Iatridou 1994: exs. 6, 10)

(8.33)   What did John say that if his mother visits (*then) we should cook for
         her?   (cf. Iatridou and Kroch 1993: 13)

Such data lead Bhatt and Pancheva (2006) to deny that hypothetical 'if ...' conditionals without 'then' are correlatives. This strikes me as a cost. Unlike relevance conditionals, where the main clause intuitively describes a condition in the actual world, hypothetical conditionals shift the modal domain with or without 'then'. The main clause correlate needn't be overtly expressed — in conditionals such as (8.27) or in certain correlatives of individuals such as (8.35b) (see also Iatridou 2013). The relation between relevance conditionals and hypothetical conditionals with/without 'then' is analogous in this respect to the relation between "frame-setting" topics and individual correlatives ("aboutness" topics) with/without a proform (Reinhart 1981; cf. Lipták 2012).

(8.34) *Relevance conditionals vs. Hypothetical 'if ... (then)' conditionals*
    a. If you're cold, I have a jacket.
    b. If you're cold, (then) you should shut the window.

(8.35) *Frame-setting topics vs. Individual correlatives*
    a. As for music, I like jazz.
    b. [jo laRkii khaRii   hai] (vo) lambii hai
       REL girl   standing is   DEM tall   is
       'The girl who is standing is tall.'

(Srivastav 1991, Bhatt 2003; Hindi)

We will revisit 'then' and individual correlatives in §8.7. For now, note that treating hypothetical conditionals generally as correlatives is compatible with acknowledging differences between conditionals with and without 'then'. Overtly expressing the conditional proform requires raising it from its base position and topicalizing it (cf. Izvorski 1996, Arsenijević 2009, Lipták 2012), as schematized in (8.36).

(8.36) ... $[_{CP} [_{CP} \text{IF-CLAUSE}]^{\langle i,a \rangle} [_{CP} [... \text{then}_i ...]^k [_{\overline{C}} ... t_k ...]]]$

Topicalizing the proform can have syntactic and interpretive effects. It is often claimed that 'If p, then q' conditionals carry an implication that some/all $\neg p$-possibilities are $\neg q$-possibilities (Iatridou 1991, 1994, von Fintel 1994).

(8.37) If Fluffy barks, then Timmy will cry.
    ⤳ "In some/every possibility where Fluffy doesn't bark, Timmy won't cry"

Izvorski (1996) shows that this exhaustiveness implication associated with conditional 'then' arises with correlative proforms generally. It isn't implausible that focusing the proforms leads to the apparent exhaustivity effects—hence the exclusion of 'then' in (8.32) where the antecedent is already exhaustive. Topicalizing the proform can also have syntactic implications, as in (8.33). $\overline{\text{A}}$-raising the proform to Spec,C excludes further argument or adjunct extractions out of the main clause (Iatridou 1991, Iatridou and Kroch 1993, Dayal 1996, Izvorski 1996, Bhatt and Pancheva 2006, Lipták 2012).

    The assignment-variable-based syntax/semantics for hypothetical conditionals in this section unifies 'if... (then)' with correlatives in the sense that there is a left-adjoined free relative clause which binds a correlate in the main clause. In conditionals with 'then' the proform is topicalized. We can capture the idea that 'if'-clauses function notionally as topics (Haiman 1978, Bittner 2001) without analyzing all conditional constructions as involving topicalization-driven movement.

8.6 Modalized Conditionals: Restricting and Shifting

So far we have focused on "bare" conditionals without an overt operator in the main clause. Although there may be a covert operator in some bare conditionals (Lewis 1975, Kratzer 1991), the account in this chapter captures the function of 'if'-clauses in shifting a modal domain without needing to posit an additional operator. Let's turn now to hypothetical 'if …' conditionals with an overt modal.

8.6.1 Direct Restriction

The traditional Kratzerian (1981, 1991) line is that the 'if'-clause in a modalized conditional such as (8.38) restricts the domain of the modal. Adapting the approach to quantifier domain restriction in von Fintel 1994, one option is to treat modal verbs as taking a resource domain argument in addition to the modal background representing the intended reading (epistemic, deontic, etc.). The revised entry for 'may' in (8.39) treats the modal as quantifying over the accessible possibilities that are part of the relevant resource domain and satisfy the prejacent proposition (nn. 18, 47). (I again use 'r'/'$\mathbf{r}$' in indices/pronouns for type $\langle s, at \rangle$.)

(8.38) If it rains, he may cry.
$\approx$ "for some epistemic possibility i where it rains, he cries in i"

(8.39)

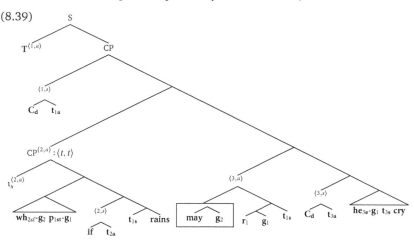

$$[\![\mathbf{may}]\!] = \lambda a_a.\lambda A_{at}.\lambda A'_{at}.\lambda g_g . \exists a'_a: a'(g) \sqsubseteq a(g) \wedge A(a')(g) \wedge A'(a')(g)$$

$$[\![S]\!] \approx \lambda g_g . \left[\iota a(g): \text{it rains in } @(a(g)) \wedge @(a(g)) = a(g)(2\mathrm{sf})(g^-(1st)) \right]$$
$$\exists a': a'(g) \sqsubseteq a(g) \wedge g^-(1r)(@(g^-))(a'(g)) \wedge g^-(3e) \text{ cries in } @(a'(g))$$

Roughly put, this says that the conditional is true iff the contextually relevant individual $g_c(3e)$ cries in some accessible possibility $h' \in g_c(1r)(@(g_c))$ that is part of the maximal relevant possibility where it rains.

The embedded modal in (8.39) is interpreted with respect to the same set of contextually relevant possibilities $(=g_c(1r)(@(g_c)))$ as an unembedded 'may' sentence. The reading of the modal is supplied by the discourse assignment, and the modal background is indexed to the actual world. The 'if'-clause functions to supply the modal's resource domain (via coindexing with $\mathbf{g_2}$) and thereby restrict the quantification to possibilities where it rained. As von Fintel (1994) notes, this relation between the 'if'-clause and the modal's restriction seems stronger than an optional binding relation. In nested conditionals the modal receives the restriction of the closest 'if'-clause.

(8.40)   If you get back in time for *Duck Tales*, then [if Timmy isn't tired]^i we should$_i$ let him watch.

The link between the topical possibility described by the 'if'-clause and the modal's resource domain may be understood as an instance of the locality requirement on correlative correlates (§8.5). Drawing on Dayal's (1996) account of individual correlatives, von Fintel suggests analyzing the relation between the 'if'-clause and restrictor argument as an $\overline{A}$-chain (1994: 88–89). On a movement-based implementation, obligatory coindexing between the 'if'-clause and the modal's resource domain would be derived from type-driven movement.

8.6.2   *Indirect Modification: "Double Modal" and "Information-Sensitive" Readings*

The §8.6.1-analysis captures the correlative binding requirement and the restricting role of the 'if'-clause via a posited resource domain argument of the modal. In (8.39) the resource domain variable is the correlate, and the matrix complementizer raises from the modal's world-argument position. One might wonder what would be predicted if the complementizer instead raised locally under the 'if'-clause:

(8.41)

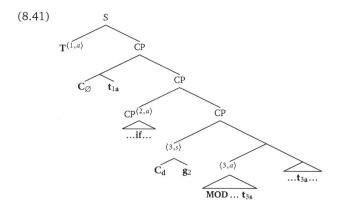

As with the bare conditional in (8.28), the complementizer adjacent to the 'if'-clause supplies the correlate, and the modal domain for the main clause is determined by the 'if'-clause. I suggest that LFs of this form can represent so-called "double modal" and "information-sensitive" readings of modalized conditionals.

Examples such as (8.42) have led some theorists to posit that overtly modalized conditionals may also have an implicit (epistemic) necessity modal (Frank 1996, Geurts 2004, von Fintel and Iatridou 2005). The 'if'-clause, on this line, restricts the domain of the posited covert modal, and the modalized main clause is evaluated at each world in the covert modal's restricted domain.

(8.42)   If marijuana is illegal, we have to report Alice.   (cf. Geurts 2004: ex. 1)

    ≈ "for every accessible world u where marijuana is illegal, every world v conforming to the laws in u is such that we report Alice in v"

The analysis in (8.43) captures such "double modal" readings without positing a covert modal. (Assume that in the intended interpretation r_2 represents a modal background for the relevant laws. I will ignore any resource domain arguments.)

(8.43)

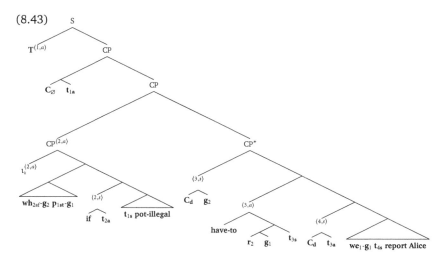

$$\llbracket S \rrbracket \approx \lambda g_g \,.\, \big[\iota a(g) \colon \text{marijuana is illegal in } @(a(g)) \,\wedge$$
$$@(a(g)) = a(g)(2\text{sf})(g^-(1st))\big]$$
$$\forall a'_a \colon g^-(2r)(@(a(g)))(a'(g)) \to g^-(1e) \text{ report Alice in } @(a'(g))$$

This says, roughly, that the maximal possibility h where marijuana is illegal is such that for every possibility h' compatible with the law in $@(h)$—i.e. every $h' \in g_c(2r)(@(h))$—we report Alice in $@(h')$.

As in (8.28), the 'if'-clause is coindexed with the assignment-variable $\mathbf{g}_2$ in the adjacent complementizer, which determines the modal domain for the main clause. The felt "double modal" interpretation follows from how the modal's modal-background pronoun $[\mathbf{r}_2\ \mathbf{g}_1]$ receives its interpretation from the discourse assignment g_c, as in (8.39), yet the world applied to the modal background is the world of the antecedent possibility $@(h)$. The discourse context supplies the relevant function $g_c(2r)$ from worlds to sets of possibilities, which represents the content of the law and the intended deontic reading of the modal. What the law provides may vary across worlds. The laws relevant for evaluating the modalized main clause are the laws in the possibility h in which marijuana is illegal. The 'if'-clause introduces a topical possibility, and the modal's deontic modal background is indexed to the world of that possibility.

Consider an example of an "information-sensitive" reading of a deontic conditional such as (8.44), adapted from Kolodny and MacFarlane 2010. The intuitive idea in the literature is that the priorities relevant for interpreting the deontic modal seem to be updated (in some sense to be explained) in light of the information in the antecedent, as reflected in the informal gloss (cf. also Dowell 2012, Charlow 2013, Dunaway and Silk 2014, Silk 2014, 2016b).

(8.44) [Context: Ten miners are trapped in shaft A or shaft B, but we don't know which, and floodwaters are threatening. All ten miners will be saved if we block the shaft they're in, but all ten will drown if we block the wrong shaft. One miner will drown if we block neither shaft.]

      If the miners are in shaft A, we have to block shaft A.

      ≈ "If the miners are in shaft A, then, given that information, the deontically preferred worlds are worlds where we block shaft A"

      (cf. Kolodny and MacFarlane 2010)

The "shifty" interpretation in (8.43) was derived by applying the worlds of the hypothetical possibility to the deontic modal background supplied by the discourse context. I suggest that LFs in which the modal background pronoun receives a shifted interpretation can represent information-sensitive readings, as in (8.45).

(8.45)

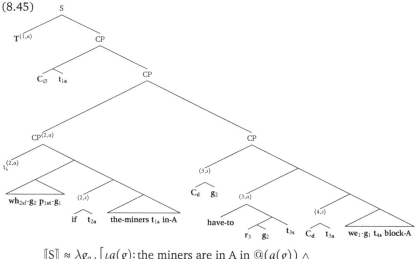

$$[\![S]\!] \approx \lambda g_g \, . \left[\iota a(g) \colon \text{the miners are in A in } @(a(g)) \, \wedge \right.$$
$$\left. @(a(g)) = a(g)(2\text{sf})(g^-(1\text{st})) \right]$$
$$\forall a_a' \colon a(g)(3r)(@(a(g)))(a'(g)) \to g^-(1e) \text{ blocks A in } @(a'(g))$$

This says, roughly, that the maximal possibility h where the miners are in shaft A is such that for every possibility h' compatible with the deontic ideal determined by h — i.e. every $h' \in h(3r)(@(h))$ — we block shaft A in $@(h')$.

As in (8.43), the modal domain for evaluating the modalized main clause is set by the assignment-variable g_2 coindexed with the adjacent 'if'-clause. However, the deontic modal background pronoun $[r_3\ g_2]$ also receives a local reading. The shifted value $a(g_c)(3r)$ represents the epistemic counterpart in the supposition of the priorities $g_c(3r)$ that would be determined in the discourse (§§3–4); the set of priorities relevant for evaluating the modal's prejacent is determined by the topical (plural) possibility $a(g_c)$, a possibility throughout which the miners are in shaft A. The discourse context may be such that $g_c(3r)$ implies that we block neither shaft; given our actual information, blocking neither shaft is the thing to do. Yet g_c's image under a, such that the miners are in shaft A in the world of every part of $a(g_c)$, may determine a deontic ideal $a(g_c)(3r)$ implying that we block shaft A.

Some theorists have appealed to information-sensitive readings to motivate revising traditional semantics for modals and conditionals — e.g., by relativizing modals' domains of quantification to an additional parameter such as an information state (cf. Kolodny and MacFarlane 2010, Cariani et al. 2013, Silk 2014). Plural domains may provide the structure to capture intuitions motivating certain revisionary approaches while relativizing modal backgrounds simply to worlds, as in the traditional semantics. An analysis of conditionals as plural definite descriptions may thus be of general interest independent of the assignment-variable implementation developed here.

8.7 Correlatives and Proforms: Individual and Conditional

This section briefly considers how the assignment-variable-based syntax/semantics for hypothetical conditionals might be extended to correlatives of individuals. Crosslinguistic work demonstrates robust links among conditionals, interrogatives, and individual correlatives (Dayal 1996, Bhatt and Pancheva 2006, Citko 2009, Dixon 2009, Lipták 2009b). For instance, there are systematic structural parallels between conditional and interrogative clauses, and many languages use the same complementizer in expressing conditionals and questions. Although English doesn't have correlatives of individuals, languages in which correlativization is more productive often use the same markers in conditionals and individual correlatives, such as in introducing the relative clause and for the main clause proforms. In some languages the same construction can be ambiguous between a conditional and individual correlative interpretation, as we saw in (8.12), reproduced in (8.46), and (8.47) (cf. Cable 2009 on Lhasa Tibetan).

(8.46) [Maliki-rli **katji**-ŋki   yarlki-rni   nyuntu] **ŋula-ju**
        dog-ERG   SAME.TOP-3SG.2SG bite-NONPAST you   DEM-TOP
        kapi-rna   luwa-rni   ŋatjulu-rlu.
        FUT-1SG.3SG shoot-NONPAST me-ERG
        a. '*If* a dog bites you, *then* I'll shoot it.'
        b. 'As for *the* dog that bites you, I'll shoot *it*.'
               (Hale 1976: 80, Bittner 2001: ex. 7; Warlpiri (Pama–Nyungan))

(8.47) [Ako je   ko   ve   ustao] onda neka taj i   izađe.
     if   AUX who already raised then let that and go.out
    a. '*If* anyone already stood up, *then* let him also go out.'
    b. '*Whoever* stood up, let *him* also go out.'

(Arsenijević 2009: ex. 10; Serbo-Croatian)

Suppose as a working hypothesis that correlative clauses are analyzed uniformly in conditionals and individual correlatives. (We will consider interrogatives in the next chapter.) I suggest that what distinguishes conditional and non-conditional interpretations of correlative clauses is the nature of the complementizer's world argument and its relation to the main clause correlate. In conditional correlatives the 'if'-clause introduces a topical modal possibility, and the correlate in the main clause is an element determining the local modal domain. In individual correlatives the topical possibility is still the possibility described by the correlative clause; however, rather than introducing a modal possibility, the correlative clause introduces an *actual* possibility about *topical individuals*. The correlative binding requirement is satisfied by binding an individual correlate in the main clause. Conditional and individual proforms are represented alike as copies of their antecedent relative/*wh* word (Part II).

8.7.1 Individual Correlatives and Proforms

An example with a multiple correlative of individuals is in (8.48). (To fix ideas I assume that the correlative clause adjoins to IP. I use C_{if} for the correlative clause complementizer, where $[\![C_{if}]\!] = [\![if]\!]$. The external world argument could also be represented via a complex $[wh_{sf}\text{-}g\ p_{st}\text{-}g]$, where the semantic value for the proposition-pronoun is ultimately identified with $\{g_c(1s)\} = \{@(g_c)\}$; however, for clarity I represent the external argument in individual correlative interpretations with a simple world-pronoun. For present purposes I represent the relative phrases and proforms with an F+nP structure (§7.4). I again use expressions such as '*baby_u*' for the characteristic function of the set of individuals $o \in E$ such that o is a baby in u. I use the English glosses and word order.)

(8.48) [jis laRkii-ne jis laRke-ke saath khelaa] us-ne us-ko haraayaa.
      REL girl   REL boy   with played DEM DEM liked
     'Which girl played with which boy, she defeated him.'

(Dayal 1996: 197; Hindi)

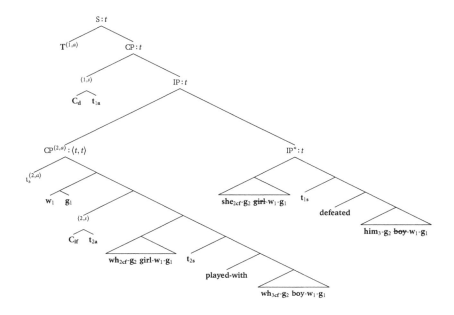

$[\![\text{IP}^*]\!] \approx \lambda g_g \cdot g(2a)(2\text{cf})(girl_{g(1a)(1s)})$ defeated $g(2a)(3\text{cf})(boy_{g(1a)(1s)})$
    in $g(1s)$

$[\![\text{CP}^{(2,a)}]\!] \approx \lambda T_t.\lambda g_g \cdot \big[\iota a(g): a(g)(2\text{cf})(girl_{g(1a)(1s)})$ played with
    $a(g)(3\text{cf})(boy_{g(1a)(1s)})$ in $@(a(g)) \wedge @(a(g)) = g(1a)(1s)\big]$
    $T(g[a(g)/2a])$

$[\![\text{S}]\!] \approx \lambda g_g \cdot \big[\iota a(g): a(g)(2\text{cf})(girl_{g^-(1s)})$ played with $a(g)(3\text{cf})(boy_{g^-(1s)})$
    in $@(a(g)) \wedge @(a(g)) = g^-(1s)\big]$
    $a(g)(2\text{cf})(girl_{g^-(1s)})$ defeated $a(g)(3\text{cf})(boy_{g^-(1s)})$ in $@(g^-)$

Intuitively put, this treats the correlative as saying that the assignment providing a true answer to the question "which girl$_i$ played with which boy$_j$?" verifies the matrix clause statement "that girl$_i$ defeated that boy$_j$". The correlative clause describes the maximal possibility h in the actual world ($@(h) = g_c(1s) = @(g_c)$) where the selected girl o ($=h(2\text{cf})(girl_{g_c(1s)})$) played with the selected boy o' ($=h(3\text{cf})(boy_{g_c(1s)})$). The sentence is true iff o defeated o' in $@(g_c)$.

The correlative clause in (8.48) is given the same structural representation as an 'if'-clause. The world $@(h)$ of the possibility introduced in the correlative clause is identified with $g_c(1s)$, which, given our metasemantic assumptions, is the world of the discourse $@(g_c)$. The topical possibility h is an actual possibility in which a certain girl played with a certain boy. The main clause comments on that possibility and says that that same girl defeated that same boy.

The correlative binding requirement is captured by the syntactic representation of the proforms as copies of their antecedent relative word and (here elided) NP,[114] and the assignment-quantification introduced by the correlative clause.

In a slogan: Individual correlatives are *material relevance conditionals with donkey pronouns*: (i) "material" insofar as the modal domain for the correlative clause is restricted to the actual world $g_c(1s)$; (ii) "relevance" insofar as the modal domain for the main clause is directly identified with $@(g_c)$ via type-driven movement of the matrix complementizer; and (iii) "donkey" insofar as the correlate proforms are anaphorically identified with their non-c-commanding antecedents.

Unifying the treatments of the anaphoric expressions in correlatives and donkey sentences doesn't require assimilating the constructions. For instance, although bare nominals in Hindi can in general serve as anaphoric expressions in donkey sentences ((8.49a)), using the bare nominal as the correlative correlate in (8.49b) is ungrammatical (§5.2).

(8.49) a. [har aadmii jis ke paas koi gadhaa hotaa hai] **gadheKO**
   every man REL with some donkey has   donkey
   maartaa hai.
   beats
   'Every man who has a donkey beats it.'
  b. *[jo aadmii aayaa] **aadmii** acchaa hai.
   REL man came man nice is
   'Which man came, man is nice.'   (Srivastav 1991: ex. 45; Hindi)

In correlatives with morphologically complex correlates the overt NP can potentially differ from the antecedent NP, typically denoting a contextual superset (Dayal 1996, Davison 2009, Beshears 2017) — hence the earlier qualification that correlative proforms are analyzed as copies of the antecedent relative word.

That said, there are crosslinguistic similarities between donkey sentences and correlatives. Though Cable (2009: 204–205, 219n.7) avoids giving "a 'simple' conditional analysis" of Tibetan correlatives, he notes that they can be glossed as conditional donkey sentences, as in (8.50). Indeed correlative proforms are typically formed from a demonstrative; the correlative binding requirement is often referred to as the "demonstrative requirement" (Dayal 1996, Bhatt 2003, Lipták 2009b).

(8.50) [Khyodra-s gyag gare nyos yod na] nga-s de bsad pa yin.
   you-ERG yak what buy AUX if I-ERG that kill PERF AUX

---

[114] Recall that the anaphoric expression need only be a copy with respect to material interpreted at LF (§5.2). Correlate proforms needn't be [+WH] or spelled out as relative/*wh* phrases.

(lit. 'If you bought what yak, I killed that')
'I killed whatever yak you bought.'   (Cable 2009: 204; Tibetan)

Individual correlates also pattern with donkey pronouns ((8.52)–(8.53)), in contrast to bound-variable pronouns ((8.51)), in being replaceable with an epithet.

(8.51)   Every donkey sued its/*the damn thing's owner.

(8.52)   Every farmer who had a donkey took it/the damn thing to court.

(8.53)   [jis aadmii-se tum bahut pyaar-se baat kar rahe the]
         REL man   you much love   talk do PROG be
         us   aadmii-ne/haraamii-ne mujh-pe muqadma Thonk   rakh-aa
         DEM man/bastard   me-on   court.case hammer.in keep
         hai.
         be
         'Which man you were talking with so nicely, that man/bastard is suing
         me.'   (Potts et al. 2009: exs. 27, 29; Hindi)

The account in this section provides a unified analysis of relative words and correlate proforms as choice-function pronouns. That there should be a demonstrative requirement with correlatives is in one sense unsurprising. A "demonstrative correlate" just is a copy of the interpreted material in a relative/*wh* phrase at LF; at some level of abstraction, REL/WH = [WH]-DEM. Put the other way, a relative/*wh* word in a correlative clause is a spelled-out [WH] demonstrative in agreement with [WH]-C_{if} (cf. Davison 2009). The "matching requirement" between correlates and antecedents is, in effect, a form of topic-comment congruence.[115]

In §§8.3–8.5 we saw how the proposed syntax and semantics for conditionals can be applied to 'if-clauses in various structural positions. This feature carries over to individual correlatives. Although correlative clauses characteristically appear sentence initially, modifying the main clause, in some languages they can be adjoined directly to the correlate DP, as in (8.54). A derivation is in (8.55).[116]

(8.54)   Ram-ne [$_{DP}$ [jo laRkaa tumhaare piichhe hai]$_i$ us   laRke-ko$_i$]
         Ram   REL boy your   behind is DEM boy

---

[115] For discussion of the matching requirement, topicalization, and locality effects in specific languages and crosslinguistically, see Bhatt 2003, Davison 2009, Leung 2009, Lipták 2012.

[116] Dayal (1996) argues that examples such as (8.55) actually involve IP adjunction, but for purposes of illustration I follow her in assuming an LF where the correlative clause forms a constituent with the correlate. Bhatt (2003) argues that Hindi single correlative clauses are in general base-generated adjoined to DP (see also Beshears 2017).

[$_{DP}$ [jo kitaab Shantiniketan-ne chhaapii thii]$_k$ vo   kitaab$_k$] dii
    REL book Shantiniketan   print   was DEM book   give
(lit. 'Ram gave [[which book Shantiniketan had published] that book] to [[which boy is behind you] that boy]')
'Ram gave the book that Shantiniketan had published to the boy behind you.'   (Bhatt 2003: ex. 32; Hindi)

(8.55) *Individual correlative* (DP-adjunction)

    [[jo laRkii khaRii   hai] vo] tez   hai.
    REL girl   standing be   DEM smart be
    'Which girl is standing, she is smart.'

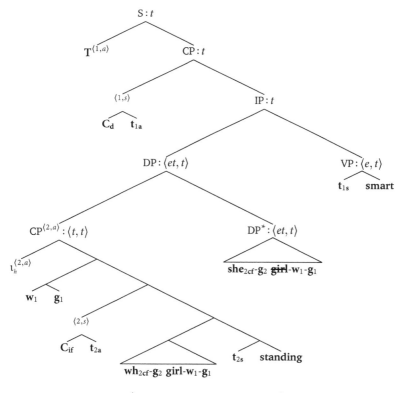

$$[\![\mathrm{DP^*}]\!] = \lambda P_{et}.\lambda g_g\,.\,P\big(\lambda g_g.g(2a)(2\mathrm{cf})(girl_{g(1a)(1s)})\big)(g)$$

$$[\![\mathrm{DP}]\!] = [\![\mathrm{CP}^{\langle 2,a\rangle}]\!] \circ [\![\mathrm{DP^*}]\!] = \lambda P_{et}.[\![\mathrm{CP}^{\langle 2,a\rangle}]\!]\big([\![\mathrm{DP^*}]\!](P)\big)$$

$$\approx \lambda P_{et}.\lambda g_g\,.\,\big[\iota a(g): a(g)(2\mathrm{cf})(girl_{g(1a)(1s)}) \text{ is standing in } @(a(g)) \wedge$$
$$@(a(g)) = g(1a)(1s)\big]\, P\big(\lambda g_g.g(2a)(2\mathrm{cf})(girl_{g(1a)(1s)})\big)(g[a(g)/2a])$$

$$[\![S]\!] \approx \lambda g_g . \big[\iota a(g) \colon a(g)(2\text{cf})(girl_{g^-(1s)}) \text{ is standing in } @(a(g)) \wedge$$
$$@(a(g)) = g^-(1s) \big] \, a(g)(2\text{cf})(girl_{g^-(1s)}) \text{ is smart in } @(g^-)$$

The correlative clause describes the unique possibility h in which the selected girl o $(=h(2\text{cf})(girl_{g_c(1s)}))$ is standing, where the world $@(h)$ of that possibility is the world of the discourse $(g_c(1s) = @(g_c))$. The sentence is true iff that girl o is smart in $@(g_c)$.

The type e individual proform is lifted to type $\langle et, t\rangle$ in the usual way. Analogous to our examples with NP-/VP-adjoined 'if'-clauses, the proform DP* of type $\langle et, t\rangle$ combines via function composition with the correlative CP$^{(2,a)}$ of type $\langle t, t\rangle$, yielding the complex subject DP of type $\langle et, t\rangle$. Roughly put, the subject DP denotes the set of properties characterizing the selected girl o $(=h(2\text{cf})(girl_{g_c(1s)})$ in the relevant actual possibility in which that girl o is standing. As in (8.48), the topical individual picked out by the relative phrase is identified with the individual picked out by the correlate via the representation of the anaphoric expression as a copy of its antecedent, here [$F_{2\text{cf}}$-g_2 **girl**-w_1-g_1], and the assignment-binder projecting to the correlative clause.

To my knowledge the only compositional semantics for correlatives that addresses DP-adjunction examples is Dayal's (1996). Dayal gives the correlative clause the semantics of a generalized quantifier of type $\langle et, t\rangle$. The correlate proform is represented as a bound variable. For DP-adjunction examples Dayal suggests a mechanism of cross-categorial quantification (1996: 207). Very roughly: The proform variable x is first lifted to type $\langle et, t\rangle$, yielding $\lambda P_{et}.P(x)$. This is converted to type $\langle e, t\rangle$ by adding a property variable Q and abstracting over the proform variable, yielding $\lambda x_e.[\lambda P_{et}.P(x)](Q) = \lambda x.Q(x)$. This combines with the type-$\langle et, t\rangle$ correlative clause to yield a type-t denotation for the subject DP, which is converted to type $\langle et, t\rangle$ by abstracting over the previously introduced variable Q, yielding $[\lambda Q_{et}.Q(\iota x_e \colon girl(x) \wedge standing(x))]$ for a DP such as in (8.55). Note that in combining the type-$\langle et, t\rangle$ nodes for the proform and the correlative clause, it must be stipulated which node is to be converted to predicative type (i.e., the node for the proform). This process is not compositional.

The account in this section avoids introducing additional semantic mechanisms for DP-adjoined correlatives. In correlatives with IP/CP-adjunction and DP-adjunction alike, the correlative clause is type $\langle t, t\rangle$, and the proform is represented as a copy of its linguistic antecedent. The semantics is fully compositional.

Many semantics for correlatives provide unified analyses of correlative clauses and ordinary DP-like free relatives (e.g. Srivastav 1991, Dayal 1996, Grosu and Landman 1998). Yet it is interesting that individual correlative clauses pattern with interrogative and conditional clauses, in contrast to DP-like free relatives, with respect to various syntactic and semantic properties. For instance, individual correlatives pattern with interrogatives regarding reconstruction effects, exhaustivity, and the availability of multiple *wh* words, as reflected in (8.48) and (8.56) (Dayal 1996, Cable 2009, Citko 2009).

(8.56) a. Which boy read which book?
  b. Everyone got what she/*who wants.

The account in this section analyzes individual correlative clauses and conditional clauses with respect to the same type of complementizer C_{if} and definite modal-like quantifier ι_h. The implicit quantifier ι_o in non-correlative free relatives, in contrast, may be given the same sort of assignment-quantificational semantics as nominal quantifiers, as in (7.94) reproduced in (8.57) (cf. n. 32).

(8.57) $[\![\iota_o]\!] = \lambda P^+_{\langle a,et\rangle}.\lambda Q^+_{\langle a,et\rangle}.\lambda g_g . \left[\iota x(g) \exists a_a : P^+(a)(x)(g) \right] Q^+(a)(x)(g)$

The definite-like element ι_o in DP-like free relatives picks out a unique maximal individual. The definite-like element ι_h in correlatives/conditionals picks out a unique maximal possibility.

8.7.2 Conditional Correlatives and 'Then'

Though there has been extensive syntactic and typological research on correlatives, little attention has been given to the compositional semantics of conditional proforms such as 'then'. Pioneering developments came with Iatridou (1991, 1994), who showed that conditional 'then' isn't semantically inert. A prominent approach is to analyze 'then' as a world pronoun (Schlenker 2004, Bhatt and Pancheva 2006, Arsenijević 2009). The analysis in (8.58) represents 'then' as a topicalized expression of the main predicate's world argument.

(8.58) $[_{CP} \text{ IF-CLAUSE}^{\langle k,a\rangle} \ [_{CP} [\text{then}_i \ g_k]^{\langle 1,s\rangle} \ [_{\bar{C}} \ ... \ t_{1s} \ ...]]]$

However, analyzing 'then' as a simple pronoun leaves various phenomena with conditional proforms unexplained.

Crosslinguistic work on correlatives shows that correlative proforms undergo movement to the left periphery of the main clause (Izvorski 1996, Lipták 2009b, 2012, also Bhatt 2003, Arsenijević 2009). Interestingly, whether this movement occurs overtly or covertly in a given language often patterns with certain $\bar{A}$-movements. For instance, in English, an overt *wh*-movement language (cf. (8.60)), 'then' raises overtly, as in (8.59). An individual correlative analogue of (8.59a) is in (8.61).

(8.59) a. If it rains then I think that we should stay at home.
        b. *If it rains I think that then we should stay at home.

(Izvorski 1996: ex. 29)

(8.60) Who$_i$ did you persuade (t_i) to come?

(8.61) [Akik korán jönnek]$_i$ **azokat**$_i$ Péter hallotta, hogy ingyen
        REL early come   those-ACC Peter heard   that free
        beengedik (t_i).
        admit
        lit. 'Who comes early, Peter heard that they will be admitted for free.'

(Lipták 2012: ex. 51; Hungarian)

For individual proforms, one might posit that the movement patterns with *wh*-movement given their association with the relative/*wh* phrases in the correlative clause. Analyzing conditional proforms like 'then' as simple variables leaves open why the movement's overt/covert status would correlate with that of *wh* words.

We noted earlier that many languages use the same type of marker for the proforms in conditionals and individual correlatives. In individual correlatives the correlate may be a bare proform or a complex with an explicit nominal, as reflected in (8.62).

(8.62) [jo laRkii khaRii   hai] vo   (laRkii) lambii hai
        REL girl standing is   DEM girl   tall   is
        (lit. 'Which girl is standing, that (girl) is tall')
        'The girl who is standing is tall.'   (cf. Srivastav 1991: ex. 13a; Hindi)

One might wonder whether conditional correlates may have analogous internal structure. The revised analysis of 'if'-clauses from §8.2 affords a basis for unifying the treatments of individual and conditional proforms: Correlative proforms are *topicalized copies* of their antecedent relative/*wh* word. In (8.62) the correlate is a copy of the choice-function pronoun of individuals and NP in the relative phrase. In conditional correlatives the correlate is a copy of the choice-function pronoun of worlds and proposition-pronoun in the 'whether'-like element in Spec,C of the 'if'-clause. Intuitively put, 'then' is to 'whether' as DEM is to REL.

A sample derivation for an 'if ... then' conditional is in (8.63). The 'then' phrase is a topicalization of the main predicate's world argument; the antecedent is the complex phrase [F_{2sf}-g_2 p_{1st}-g_1] supplying the world argument of 'if'.

(For purposes of illustration I represent 'then' in its fronted position, though I leave open whether it may be interpreted in its trace position (cf. Bhatt 2003, Sportiche 2006).)[117]

(8.63) If it rained, then Fluffy barked.

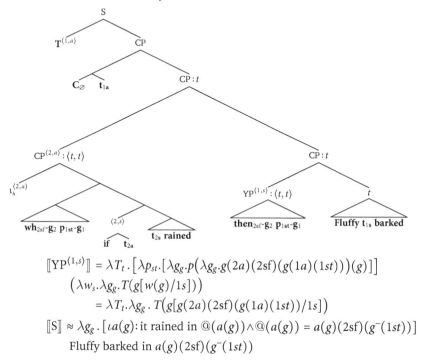

$$[\![\text{YP}^{\langle 1,s\rangle}]\!] = \lambda T_t \cdot \left[\lambda p_{st} \cdot \left[\lambda g_g \cdot p\big(\lambda g_g \cdot g(2a)(2\text{sf})(g(1a)(1st)) \big)(g) \right] \right]$$
$$\big(\lambda w_s \cdot \lambda g_g \cdot T(g[w(g)/1s]) \big)$$
$$= \lambda T_t \cdot \lambda g_g \cdot T\big(g[g(2a)(2\text{sf})(g(1a)(1st))/1s] \big)$$
$$[\![\text{S}]\!] \approx \lambda g_g \cdot \left[\iota a(g) \colon \text{it rained in } @(a(g)) \wedge @(a(g)) = a(g)(2\text{sf})(g^-(1st)) \right]$$
$$\text{Fluffy barked in } a(g)(2\text{sf})(g^-(1st))$$

The correlative 'if'-clause $\text{CP}^{\langle 2,a\rangle}$ binds the assignment-variable $\mathbf{g}_2$ in the representation of the proform 'then' and shifts the modal domain for the main clause. Roughly put, the 'if'-clause describes the maximal possibility h such that the world of h, $@(h)$, is identical to some part $h(2\text{sf})(g_c(1st))$ of the contextually relevant domain and it rained in $@(h)$. The consequent clause with 'then' says that Fluffy barked in that world $h(2\text{sf})(g_c(1st))$ $(=@(h))$.

Let's recap. This chapter has examined how our assignment-variable-based accounts of modals, relativization, and pronominal anaphora may be extended to conditionals and correlatives. 'If'-clauses are analyzed syntactically as free relatives and interpreted as plural definite descriptions of possibilities, represented

---

[117] The choice of representing the main clause complementizer position in (8.63) as empty is inessential. I return to this in §9.4 in discussion of conditional questions.

by assignments. The syntax/semantics in §8.2 yields a uniform analysis of 'if'-clauses in various positions and conditional structures — adjoined to NP in adnominal conditionals, adjoined to VP in sentence-final positions, and adjoined to IP/CP in sentence-initial positions; in conditionals with or without a main clause modal; and in conditionals with or without 'then'. The account compositionally derives how conditionals may shift the interpretation of expressions in the 'if'-clause and main clause, while allowing for global readings in both clauses. In correlative constructions the 'if'-clause binds a correlate in the main clause. In conditionals with 'then' the correlate is overtly expressed and topicalized with a proform. Correlatives of individuals and possibilities are given a unified general analysis. Correlate proforms are represented as topicalized copies of an antecedent relative/*wh* word, bound by the correlative clause. Alternative interpretations are derived from differences in individual/modal elements in the correlative clause and their relation to corresponding individual/modal elements in the main clause. §9 explores how the compositional semantics for conditionals and correlatives in this chapter may be extended to interrogatives.

9

Interrogatives

This chapter begins investigating how the assignment-variable framework may be applied to nondeclarative clauses. I focus on linguistic shifting phenomena in interrogative sentences. The proposed account yields a common structure for interrogative, conditional, and correlative clauses (§9.1); it provides a precise diagnosis of "interrogative flip" in terms of local readings under the question operator (§9.2); it extends the analyses of relative words and certain indefinites as choice-function pronouns to *wh* words (§9.3); and it affords a compositional semantics for interrogatives in conditional questions and correlatives (§9.4). (Following common practice I will generally use 'interrogative' for the clause type and 'question' for the semantic object.)

9.1   Syntax, Semantics, Metasemantics

A principal aim of the assignment-variable framework has been to capture various types of shifted (local) and unshifted (global) readings. Intuitively put, in interrogative sentences the interpretation of expressions receiving a local reading is targeted by the question. In (9.1), whereas the individual pronoun 'it' receives its interpretation from the discourse context, the world argument of the main predicate receives a local reading. The contextually relevant individual is constant across possible answers, yet the world in which the jumping did/didn't occur varies. Bert's question in (9.2a) targets the relevant standard associated with 'rich'—how rich one must be to count as rich. If Alice gives a *yes*-answer, Bert can infer that Alice assumes that the standard for richness is no greater than $X/yr. Bert's question in (9.2b), by contrast, is about Rita's income.

(9.1)   Did it jump?

(9.2)   Is Rita rich?

      a. [Context: Bert knows approximately how much money Rita earns (say, $X/yr), and he thinks Alice does too. Hoping to ascertain Alice's views on whether such a salary counts as rich, Bert utters (9.2).]
         ≈ "Is the relevant standard for richness, whatever it is, greater than around $X/yr?"   (*local reading*)

  b. [Context: We're millionaires and we agree that one must be a
     millionaire to count as rich. Hoping to ascertain Rita's income, Bert
     utters (9.2).]
     ≈ "Is Rita's income enough to make her a millionaire?"

                                                              (*global reading*)

In (9.2b) the value for the standards variable is supplied by the discourse
assignment; in (9.2b) the value is targeted by the question and varies across
possible answers.

It is common to distinguish at least two elements in interrogative sentences:
an interrogative complementizer (written: $C_?$), which may trigger interrogative
movement in languages such as English; and a question operator (written: Q),
which provides the source of the question semantics (Dayal 1996, Cable 2010,
Kotek 2014). Heim (2012) suggests a syntax in which Q is base-generated
as an internal argument of $C_?$ and raises as a quantifier over propositions.
Heim's account provides a precedent for an interrogative analogue of our
treatment of declaratives: the question operator Q raises for type reasons from
an assignment argument position of the interrogative complementizer $C_?$, as
schematized in (9.3). Whereas Heim treats the binder-index as occupying an
independent node and triggering a noncompositional Predicate Abstraction rule,
we can treat Q as combining via function application with the generalized
binder-index.

(9.3)

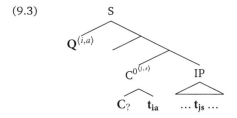

The semantic interactions among the question nucleus IP, interrogative complementizer, and question operator will be fully compositional.

In §8 we noted robust crosslinguistic links among conditionals, correlatives,
and interrogatives. An attractive idea is that interrogative clauses share a
common structure (at some relevant level of analysis) with conditional and
correlative clauses. Let's suppose as a working hypothesis that the interrogative
complementizer $C_?$ has a roughly parallel argument structure as 'if'/C_{if}. Lexical
entries for $C_?$ and Q are in (9.4)–(9.5)—where '$g \approx g'$' says that g and g' are
equivalent except possibly regarding which world is the world of the possibility
represented by the assignment.

(9.4) $[\![\mathbf{C}_?]\!] = \lambda a_a.\lambda p_{st}.\lambda w_s.\lambda g_g : @(a(g)) = w(g)\,.$
$\qquad \forall w'_s = [\lambda g'_g.@(a(g'))]\!:\!p(w')(g)$

(9.5) $[\![\mathbf{Q}]\!] = \lambda A_{at}.\lambda T_t.\lambda g_g\,.\,\forall a_a = [\lambda g_g.g^-]\!:\exists g''_g\!:$
$\qquad T = \big[\lambda g'_g\!:\!g' \approx g''.A(a)(g') = A(a)(g'')\big]$
$\qquad \bullet\; g \approx g' \text{ iff } \forall i\tau\!:\neg\big(g(i\tau) = g'(i\tau) = @(g) = @(g')\big) \to g(i\tau) = g'(i\tau)$

The interrogative complementizer $\mathbf{C}_?$ in effect forms an equivalence class with respect to the embedded proposition (cf. Groenendijk and Stokhof 1984). The question operator $\mathbf{Q}$ constructs a set of possible answers (type $\langle t,t\rangle$), where an answer is conceived as a set of possibilities, represented by a set of assignments (§2). The possibilities in a question's answers may fix facts including facts determining values for context-sensitive expressions. The values for items whose interpretation is targeted by the question — formally, items bound by $\mathbf{Q}^{\langle i,a\rangle}$ — may vary across possible answers; yet the constraint $g' \approx g''$ requires that the assignments in each answer agree on the particular value assigned.

Let's start with a simple *yes/no* question such as (9.1). (For readability I will represent the identity presupposition from the semantic value of the CP via subscripting, e.g. writing '$\lambda g_g.\ldots.u_{=v}\ldots$' for '$\lambda g_g\!:\!u = v.\ldots u\ldots$'; and I abbreviate '$\lambda g'_g\!:\!g' \approx g''$' in the question denotation with '$\lambda g' \approx g''$'.)[118]

(9.6) Did it jump?

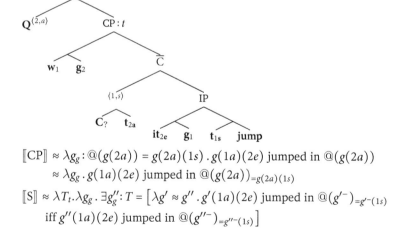

$[\![\text{CP}]\!] \approx \lambda g_g\!:\!@(g(2a)) = g(2a)(1s)\,.\,g(1a)(2e)$ jumped in $@(g(2a))$
$\qquad \approx \lambda g_g\,.\,g(1a)(2e)$ jumped in $@(g(2a))_{=g(2a)(1s)}$
$[\![\text{S}]\!] \approx \lambda T_t.\lambda g_g\,.\,\exists g''_g\!:\!T = \big[\lambda g' \approx g''\,.\,g'(1a)(2e)$ jumped in $@(g'^-)_{=g'^-(1s)}$
$\qquad \text{iff } g''(1a)(2e)$ jumped in $@(g''^-)_{=g''^-(1s)}\big]$

---

[118] I will continue to treat free individual pronouns as type e (§§5–6). Like with $\mathbf{T}$, I leave open whether $\mathbf{Q}$ raises to Spec,C or projects its own phrase such as ForceP. In the general definition of the binder-index (§3.5): with $\mathbf{C}_?$, $\tau = s$, $\sigma = \langle s,t\rangle$; with $\mathbf{Q}$, $\tau = a$, $\sigma = \langle t,t\rangle$.

Roughly put, the semantic value of the interrogative sentence is a set of propositions T, where each such proposition is a set of assignments g' that return the same truth value for the proposition that the individual $g'(1a)(2e)$ — the individual assigned to $2e$ by the assignment that g' happens to assign to $1a$ — jumped.

Note first the world-pronoun $[\mathbf{w}_1\ \mathbf{g}_2]$ that supplies the external argument of $\mathbf{C}_?$.[119] With free relatives and correlatives there was a natural story about what supplied the complementizer's external (individual, world) argument. In individual free relatives the relative clause describes a topical subdomain of individuals; in conditionals the 'if'-clause describes a topical subdomain of worlds that provides the backdrop for the supposition. For interrogatives a natural thought is that the external argument determines the possibility targeted by the question. In unembedded interrogatives such as (9.6) the world argument of $\mathbf{C}_?$ is a pronoun $[\mathbf{w}_1\ \mathbf{g}_2]$ bound by the question operator $\mathbf{Q}^{\langle 2,a\rangle}$; the question is about what is the case in the actual world. Here the argument is semantically trivial given our general metasemantic assumption that, for any assignment h, $h(1s)$ is the world of the possibility represented by h. We will see substantive roles for the world argument in more complex examples.

As in simple declarative sentences, the local reading of the world argument of the main predicate 'jump' is captured via type-driven movement of the complementizer $\mathbf{C}_?^{\langle 1,s\rangle}$ and embedding assignment quantifier $\mathbf{Q}^{\langle 2,a\rangle}$. However, in interrogatives the relevant world of evaluation is shifted across the possibilities in each possible answer. The possibilities g' in each answer T return the same truth value for the proposition that such-and-such individual $g'(1a)(2e)$ jumped in $@(g')$. Which world is the world of the possibility represented by the assignments may vary. The constraint $g' \approx g''$ ensures that the assignments in each answer are otherwise equivalent in the values assigned across indices. This constraint will help capture local readings of context-sensitive expressions (more on which shortly).

The semantic value in (9.6) clearly fails to represent the intended global reading of 'it'. The question is represented as targeting what assignment to associate with the index $\langle 1,a\rangle$, instead of targeting a property of the individual $g_c(2e) \in E$ determined by the discourse assignment g_c. The assignments in each answer T may not even agree on the identity of the individual that did/didn't jump.

One response would be to capture global readings by revising the semantics of $\mathbf{Q}$. An alternative is to maintain the present lexical entry and semantic value for interrogative clauses, and capture global readings in the metasemantics of answers. Our metasemantics for declaratives (§2) treats a declarative sentence

---

[119] As discussed in §8.7 with correlative clauses, the world argument could be represented with a complex $[\mathbf{wh}_{sf}\text{-}\mathbf{g}_2\ \mathbf{p}_{st}\text{-}\mathbf{g}]$; but to clarify the intended interpretation I use a simple world-pronoun.

S as true in a context c iff the semantic value $[\![S]\!]$ is true with respect to the assignment g_c representing the context. Correspondingly, I treat a proposition T_t in the semantic value $[\![S_?]\!]$ of an interrogative sentence as an *answer* to $S_?$ in c iff every assignment $g' \in T$ assigns g_c^- to all assignment-indices.

(9.7)   *Metasemantics*

    a. A declarative sentence S is **true** in c iff $[\![S]\!](g_c) = 1$

    b. T_t is an **answer** to an interrogative sentence $S_?$ in c iff (i) $T \in [\![S_?]\!]$, and (ii) for all $g' \in T$ and assignment-indices $\langle i, a \rangle$, $g'(ia) = g_c^-$.

Since $g'(1a) = g_c^-$, given (9.7b), answers to (9.6) will be sets of assignments g' such that $g_c^-(2e)$ $(=g'(1a)(2e))$ did/didn't jump in $@(g'^-)$. The assignments in each answer constitute an equivalence class with respect to the proposition that the individual $g_c^-(2e)$ jumped, as desired. (Hereafter I will continue to omit the superscripts in 'g'^-', 'g_c^-', etc., though they should be understood when relevant.)

Capturing global readings in the metasemantics maintains a uniform theoretical interpretation of assignment-indices. In effect, what **T** does in the semantics of declarative sentences, (9.7b) does in the metasemantics of interrogative sentences. Yet we shouldn't overstate the contrast. In both cases a bridge principle is required to link a sentence's compositional semantic value to an interpretation and discourse function (cf. Dummett 1973, Lewis 1980, Rabern 2012a, MacFarlane 2014). The semantics of **T** links a certain assignment-index $\langle i, a \rangle$ to the assignments in the sentence's semantic value $[\![S]\!]$; and the metasemantics of declaratives treats the sentence as true in c iff the assignment g_c representing the discourse is in that set of assignments $[\![S]\!]$. Analogously, the metasemantics of interrogatives treats a set of assignments T as constituting an answer in c only if every assignment in T assigns g_c to that same assignment-index $\langle i, a \rangle$. In this sense, for declarative sentences and interrogative sentences alike, global readings are ultimately captured in the metasemantics.

9.2   Interrogative Flip

In typological work on evidentials and certain epistemic expressions the phenomenon of local readings in questions often goes under the heading of "interrogative flip" (Speas and Tenny 2003). The assignment-variable-based account in this chapter affords a precise implementation. Consider (9.8), on the salient reading which questions what the relevant evidence is like and whether it (whatever it is) is compatible with the contextually relevant individual being the killer. (I leave 'be the killer' as an unanalyzed predicate. I again use '*r*'/'**r**' in indices/pronouns for type $\langle s, at \rangle$. When describing the answers to a question I will often omit the presuppositional constraint when trivial.)

(9.8)   Might he be the killer?

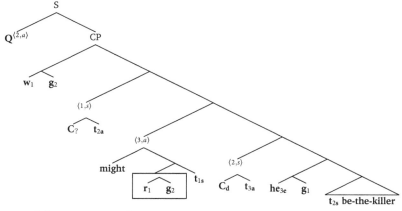

$\llbracket S \rrbracket \approx \lambda T_t . \lambda g_g . \exists g''_g$:

$$T = \left[\lambda g'_g \approx g'' . \exists a'_a : g'^-(1r)(@(g'^-)_{=g'-(1s)})(a'(g')) \wedge \right.$$
$$g'(1a)(3e) \text{ is the killer in } @(a'(g'))$$
$$\text{iff } \exists a''_a : g''^-(1r)(@(g''^-)_{=g''-(1s)})(a''(g'')) \wedge$$
$$\left. g''(1a)(3e) \text{ is the killer in } @(a''(g'')) \right]$$

A proposition $T_t \in \llbracket S \rrbracket$ is an *answer* to S in c iff $\exists g''_g$:

$$T = \left[\lambda g'_g \approx g'' . \exists a'_a : g'^-(1r)(@(g'^-))(a'(g')) \wedge \right.$$
$$g_c^-(3e) \text{ is the killer in } @(a'(g'))$$
$$\text{iff } \exists a''_a : g''^-(1r)(@(g''^-))(a''(g'')) \wedge$$
$$\left. g_c^-(3e) \text{ is the killer in } @(a''(g'')) \right]$$

Each possible answer T is a set of assignments g' that determine the same modal background R ($=g'(1r)$, via $g' \approx g''$), and return the same truth value for the proposition that the contextually relevant individual $g_c(3e)$ ($=g'(1a)(3e)$) is the killer in the world of some epistemic possibility, as determined by g'. Answers to the epistemic modal question are propositions that there is/isn't an epistemic possibility $h \in g'(1r)(@(g'))$ such that $g_c(3e)$ is the killer in $@(h)$.

The global reading of 'he' is captured again via the metasemantic condition on answerhood. A set of assignments T in the sentence's semantic value is an answer in the context c only if $g'(1a) = g_c$. Given the constraint that $g' \approx g''$, the assignments in each answer constitute an equivalence class with respect to a proposition about the contextually relevant individual $g'(1a)(3e) = g''(1a)(3e) = g_c(3e) \in E$.

The modal's world argument $\mathbf{t_{1s}}$ receives an obligatory local reading due to type-driven movement of the interrogative elements $C^{0^{\langle 1,s \rangle}}$ and $\mathbf{Q}^{\langle 2,a \rangle}$. The question nucleus places a constraint on the worlds of the possibilities g' in each possible answer, i.e. that $g_c(3e)$ is the killer in some world accessible from $@(g')$. Likewise the obligatory local reading of the world argument $\mathbf{t_{2s}}$ of the embedded predicate 'be-the-killer' is captured via movement of the embedding (declarative) complementizer $C^{0^{\langle 2,s \rangle}}$ and modal $\text{Mod}^{0^{\langle 3,a \rangle}}$.

The local reading of the epistemic modal is represented via coindexing between the modal-background pronoun $[\mathbf{r_1}\ \mathbf{g_2}]$ and question operator $\mathbf{Q}^{\langle 2,a \rangle}$. Given the constraint that $g' \approx g''$, the assignments in each possible answer T assign the same value to the index $\langle 1, sat \rangle$; however, what epistemic modal background is assigned may differ across answers. The question targets the nature of the relevant evidence. Although the assignments g' in each answer agree about whether the evidence $g'(1r)(@(g'))$ is compatible with $g_c(3e)$ being the killer, they may differ regarding other worldly facts. The possible answers T needn't be singleton sets.

In §4.3 we considered possible grounds for positing conventionalized locality/globality principles for certain context-sensitive expressions — e.g., a globality principle for gendered pronouns, or a locality principle for certain types of epistemic uses of modals. We noted that a locality principle requiring certain modal-background pronouns to be coindexed with the closest c-commanding assignment-binder may help capture the linking of epistemic modals to the subject in attitude ascriptions. Such a principle would apply to uses of epistemic modals in questions as well. An epistemic modal question such as (9.8) would typically be interpreted as being about what the evidence is — formally, what modal background is assigned to $1r$ — rather than about what the logical implications are of a contextually agreed-upon body of evidence $g_c(1r)$. For present purposes I leave open whether such an interpretation is conventionalized.

9.3 *Wh* Questions

There is a divide in approaches to *wh* interrogatives about whether *wh* words are to be analyzed like relative pronouns, often construed as λ-binders (Groenendijk and Stokhof 1984), or like indefinites (Karttunen 1977). On the one hand, in many languages the same forms can be used for interrogative pronouns and indefinites (Haspelmath 1997, Gair et al. 1999, Kratzer and Shimoyama 2002, Bhat 2004, Thurgood and LaPolla 2017). On the other hand, it is crosslinguistically common for interrogative words to be morphologically related to relative words. In languages such as Polish (Citko 2009), correlative clauses are introduced with interrogative *wh* words; on the flip side, in languages such as Sanskrit (Davison 2009) and Somali (Lecarme 1999a), complement questions are expressed by substituting the interrogative with a relative construction.[120]

§§5–8 developed analyses of relative words and certain indefinites and anaphoric pronouns as choice-function pronouns. A natural move is to extend the account to interrogative *wh* words. Indeed relative forms that are morphologically related to (anaphoric) demonstratives are also common (Heine and Kuteva 2002, de Vries 2002, Bhat 2004). Languages such as Lyele (Niger-Congo) use the same pro-forms for each of these functions (Showalter 1986; see also Bhat 2004: §8.3).

An example with a simple *wh* question is in (9.9). (For purposes of illustration I represent *wh* phrases with an F+nP structure (§7.4), and I show how the variation in values for the *wh* phrase can be derived while keeping the *wh* word in situ below $C_?$; more on this shortly. Ignore any contextual restriction associated with 'what', letting **E** represent a pronoun contextually identified with the set of individuals.)

(9.9)   What hit you?

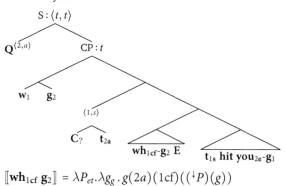

$$[\![\textbf{wh}_{1cf}\ \textbf{g}_2]\!] = \lambda P_{et}.\lambda g_g\,.\,g(2a)(1cf)((^{\downarrow}P)(g))$$

A proposition $T_t \in [\![S]\!]$ is an *answer* to S in c iff $\exists g''_g$:

$$T = \Big[\lambda g'_g \approx g''\,.\,g'^-(1cf)(E)\ \text{hit}\ g_c^-(2e)\ \text{in}\ @(g'^-)$$
$$\text{iff}\ g''^-(1cf)(E)\ \text{hit}\ g_c^-(2e)\ \text{in}\ @(g''^-)\Big]$$

The possible answers to the *wh* question are propositions T, where each such proposition is a set of assignments g' that return the same truth value for the proposition that a selected individual $g'(1cf)(E)$ hit $g_c(2e)$ in $@(g')$.

---

[120] See also Caponigro 2003, Gračanin-Yuksek 2008 on respects in which free relatives pattern with *wh* interrogatives in contrast to headed relatives crosslinguistically.

The variation in values for the *wh* phrase is captured via general mechanisms for capturing local readings of context-sensitive expressions. The choice-function pronoun $[\mathbf{wh}_{1\text{cf}}\, \mathbf{g}_2]$ in the representation of 'what' is bound by the question operator $\mathbf{Q}^{\langle 2,a\rangle}$.[121] Given that $g' \approx g''$, the assignments g' in each answer T assign the same value to the choice-function index and select the same individual; yet the particular value assigned and individual selected may vary across answers. For instance, if $E = \{o_1, o_2\}$, answers include that o_1 hit $g_c(2e)$, that o_2 hit $g_c(2e)$, etc. The interpretation of the *wh* phrase is targeted by the question, and the possible answers are about different individuals.

It is common in diverse approaches to the semantics of questions to require that *wh* phrases be interpreted in a specifier position of the interrogative complementizer (Karttunen 1977, Pesetsky 2000, Cable 2010, George 2011). A critical issue in such accounts is what in general requires the movement and how the order of *wh* phrases at LF is derived, given the crosslinguistic differences in pronunciation rules (e.g., requiring that all *wh* words be fronted (Bulgarian), requiring that all *wh* words be in situ (Japanese), or allowing variation (English)). Even for languages such as English with overt *wh*-movement, Rullmann and Beck (1998) argue that D-linked *wh* phrases ('which N') are obligatorily interpreted in situ (see also Boeckx and Grohmann 2004). The account in this section is compatible with alternative views on *wh*-movement and reconstruction in different languages. The semantics derives the local reading of *wh* words and the contribution of *wh* words to the semantics of the question without requiring or forbidding *wh*-movement to Spec,C at LF.

The analysis in (9.9) extends to interrogatives with multiple *wh* phrases; innovations such as a type-flexible question operator or tuple types which track the number of *wh* words and their relative positions (as in e.g. Groenendijk and Stokhof 1984, George 2011) aren't required.[122] A derivation for a multiple *wh* question is in (9.10). (I again use (e.g.) '*baby$_u$*' for the characteristic function of the set of individuals $o \in E$ such that o is a baby in u.)

(9.10)   Which baby liked which toy?

   $\approx$ "Timmy liked the doll, Clio liked the blocks, ..."

---

[121] Like with relative words, I assume that *wh* words must have the same assignment-variable as the local interrogative complementizer, e.g. due to agreement (cf. §§5.1.3, 8.2; Chung 1998, Kratzer and Shimoyama 2002, Kratzer 2009, Cable 2010, Johnson 2012).

[122] Multiple *wh* questions raise notorious challenges for syntax and semantics (see Rullmann 1995, Dayal 2006, 2016). As discussed earlier, the account is compatible with different views on *wh*-movement and reconstruction in the syntax and morphophonological component. I will put aside issues regarding single-list and pair-list readings, and exhaustivity and uniqueness implications.

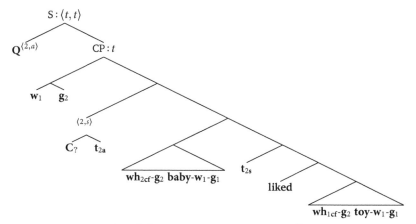

A proposition $T_t \in [\![S]\!]$ is an *answer* to S in c iff $\exists g''_g$:

$$T = \left[\lambda g'_g \approx g''. g'^-(2\mathrm{cf})(baby_{g_c^-(1s)}) \text{ liked } g'^-(1\mathrm{cf})(toy_{g_c^-(1s)}) \text{ in } @(g'^-) \right]$$
$$\text{iff } g''^-(2\mathrm{cf})(baby_{g_c^-(1s)}) \text{ liked } g''^-(1\mathrm{cf})(toy_{g_c^-(1s)}) \text{ in } @(g''^-)$$

Suppose $b_1, b_2 \in baby_{g_c(1s)}$ are the babies in the actual world and $t_1, t_2 \in toy_{g_c(1s)}$ are the toys; roughly put, the set of possible answers is the set of propositions that b_i liked/didn't like t_j. Given the metasemantic condition on answerhood, the world-pronouns in the noun phrases 'baby' and 'toy' receive global readings anchored to $g_c(1s)$, contextually identified with the world $@(g_c)$ of the discourse. Yet, as in (9.9), the *wh* words and the world argument of the clause's main predicate receive local readings, targeted by the question. For each possible answer T, the assignments $g' \in T$ constitute an equivalence class with respect to what actual baby $b_i = g'(2\mathrm{cf})(baby_{g_c(1s)})$ and what actual toy $t_j = g'(1\mathrm{cf})(toy_{g_c(1s)})$ are selected, and whether the selected baby b_i liked the selected toy t_j in $@(g')$. The account derives how each answer in the multiple *wh* question is about a particular pair of individuals.

The proposed analysis of *wh* interrogatives may yield an improved account of examples with donkey-style pronouns such as (9.11). The interpretations of the subject-internal pronoun 'his' and the object pronoun 'him' covary with the *wh* phrase, though the *wh* phrase doesn't c-command 'him' at LF (cf. §6.4).

(9.11)   *Which baby's picture of his dog scared him?*

Consider how we might capture such a reading in a traditional compositional semantic framework and Karttunen-style (1977) semantics for *wh* interrogatives. *wh* words, on Karttunen's account, are given the same quantificational lexical entry as indefinites; what distinguishes their contribution to the meanings of questions is a syntactic requirement that (all and only) [wʜ] elements be in Spec,C at LF, as in (9.12). (Recall that the binder index is treated as occupying its node and triggering an independent Predicate Abstraction rule. I put aside how the question meaning is compositionally derived from the interrogative complementizer and question operator; see Heim 2012.)

(9.12)   Which baby laughed?

    a. [$_{CP}$ ... [which baby [1 [C$_?$ [$_{IP}$ t$_1$ laughed]]]]]

    b. $\llbracket \textbf{which} \rrbracket^w = \llbracket \textbf{some} \rrbracket^w = \lambda P_{et}.\lambda Q_{et}.\exists x: P(x) \wedge Q(x)$

    c. $\llbracket CP \rrbracket^w = \lambda p_{st} . \exists x: x$ is a baby in $w \wedge p = [\lambda w' . x$ laughed in $w']$

The *wh* existential quantifier scopes over the interrogative complementizer that identifies the form of the answers, and the set of answers includes one proposition per baby quantified over.

For a complex DP such as 'which baby's NP' in (9.11), the [wʜ] feature of the *wh* phrase projects/percolates, triggering *wh*-movement of the entire phrase.

(9.13)   [$_{CP}$ ... [[$_{DP[wʜ]}$ [which baby] 's NP] [1 [C$_?$ [$_{IP}$ t$_1$ ...]]]]]

The challenge is to derive the intuitively anaphoric readings of both pronouns from operations on this (possibly intermediate) syntactic structure. One idea would be to posit that—unlike in the cases of DP-internal movement from §6.4—the *wh* phrase 'which baby' raises out of the genitive DP, as in (9.14). (Assume a simplified analysis of 'his dog' as 'the-dog-of-him', and an ad hoc type-$\langle et, \langle e, \langle et, t \rangle \rangle \rangle$ definiteness semantics for the genitive morpheme in D, with R the relevant possessional relation.)

(9.14)   a. [$_{CP}$ ... [which baby [2 [[$_{DP}$ t$_2$ [$_{\overline{D}}$'s pic-of-the-dog-of-him$_2$]] [1 [C$_?$ [$_{IP}$ t$_1$ scared him$_2$]]]]]]]

       b. $\llbracket CP \rrbracket^w = \lambda p_{st} . \exists x: x$ is a baby in $w \wedge$ the y such that y is a picture-of-the-dog-of-x in $w \wedge R(y)(x)$ is such that $p = [\lambda w' . y$ scared x in $w']$

Such an analysis derives how the *wh* phrase binds both pronouns, but at the cost of requiring an unlikely movement operation (cf. May 1985, Heim and Kratzer 1998) and denying that 'which baby's picture of his dog' forms a constituent.

Alternatively, one might treat the *wh* phrase as raising internal to the DP, and posit a mechanism of partial syntactic reconstruction whereby the non-*wh* portion of the DP is interpreted inside IP. The *wh* quantifier in Spec,C scopes over the interrogative complementizer, which identifies the form of the answers, and binds the pronouns, roughly as in (9.15).

(9.15) a. covert movement of 'which baby':
            [$_{CP}$ ... [[$_{DP}$ which baby [2 [t$_2$ ['s pic-of-the-dog-of-him$_2$]]]] [1 [$_{\overline{C}}$ C?
            [$_{IP}$ t$_1$ scared him$_2$]]]]]
        b. post-reconstruction LF:
            [$_{CP}$ ... [which baby [2 [$_{\overline{C}}$ C?
            [$_{IP}$ [$_{DP}$ t$_2$ ['s pic-of-the-dog-of-him$_2$]] scared him$_2$]]]]]
        c. $[\![CP]\!]^w = \lambda p_{st} \, . \, \exists x : x$ is a baby in $w \wedge p = [\lambda w' \, .$ the y such that y is a
            picture-of-the-dog-of-x in $w' \wedge R(y)(x)$ scared x in $w']$

Details of the requisite reconstruction operations are controversial (cf. Chomsky
1995, Sternefeld 1998, Fox 2000, Sportiche 2006). Note that 'which baby's
picture of his dog' still doesn't receive a semantic value.

The compositional semantics for *wh* interrogatives in this section derives the
anaphoric readings of the pronouns in examples such as (9.11) without requiring
specific commitments regarding pied-piping or syntactic reconstruction. The *wh*
phrase and complex DP may be interpreted in situ at LF, as in (9.16). As in the
previous chapters, the anaphoric pronouns are represented as copies for purposes
of interpretation of their linguistic antecedent (n. 114; cf. §§5.2, 6.3, 6.4, 8.7).
(I assume the D+XP analysis of free *R* genitives from §6.2. For present purposes
I continue to assume the simplified "the-N-of-him" analysis of the possessive
pronoun.)

(9.16)   S

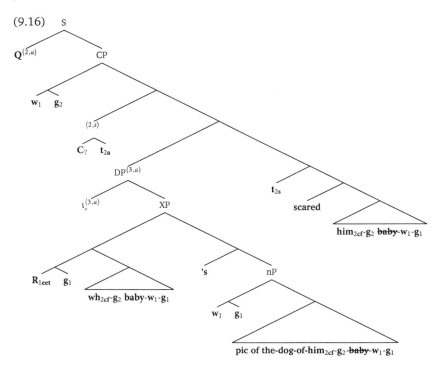

A proposition $T_t \in [\![S]\!]$ is an *answer* to S in c iff $\exists g''_g$:

$$T = [\lambda g'_g \approx g''.$$
$$[\iota x(g')\exists a'_a\colon g_c^-(1eet)(g'^-(2cf)(baby_{g_c^-(1s)}))(x(g')) \wedge$$
$$x(g') = a'(g')(3cf)(\textit{pic-of-the-dog-of-}g'^-(2cf)(baby_{g_c^-(1s)})\textit{-in-}g_c^-(1s))]$$
$$x(g') \text{ scared } g'^-(2cf)(baby_{g_c^-(1s)}) \text{ in } @(g'^-)$$

iff

$$[\iota x(g'')\exists a''_a\colon g_c^-(1eet)(g''^-(2cf)(baby_{g_c^-(1s)}))(x(g'')) \wedge$$
$$x(g'') = a''(g'')(3cf)(\textit{pic-of-the-dog-of-}g''^-(2cf)(baby_{g_c^-(1s)})\textit{-in-}g_c^-(1s))]$$
$$x(g'') \text{ scared } g''^-(2cf)(baby_{g_c^-(1s)}) \text{ in } @(g''^-)]$$

Each possible answer T is a set of assignments g' that return the same truth value for the proposition that [the o' that bears the contextually relevant relation $g_c(1eet)$ to a selected baby o $(=g'(2cf)(baby_{g_c(1s)}))$ and is a picture of the dog of o $(=g'(2cf)(baby_{g_c(1s)}))]$ scared o $(=g'(2cf)(baby_{g_c(1s)}))$ in $@(g')$. For each answer T, the assignments $g' \in T$ constitute an equivalence class with respect to what actual baby $o_i = g'(2cf)(baby_{g_c(1s)})$ is selected, and whether o_i's picture of o_i's dog scared o_i in $@(g')$.

The anaphoric connections between 'which baby' and the individual pronouns 'his'/'him' are derived via the local reading of the *wh* word $[\mathbf{wh}_{2cf}\,\mathbf{g}_2]$ under the question operator $\mathbf{Q}^{\langle 2,a\rangle}$, and the analyses of the pronouns as copies of their antecedent $[\mathbf{F}_{2cf}\text{-}\mathbf{g}_2\,\mathbf{baby}\text{-}\mathbf{w}_1\text{-}\mathbf{g}_1]$ at LF. The variation in values for the *wh* phrase across answers and the anaphoric readings of the pronouns can be captured while leaving the *wh* phrase in situ and giving the complex subject DP a semantic value.

The previous examples have ignored differences between interrogative 'which' phrases and simplex interrogative pronouns such as 'who'. Notable in light of our discussions of "specificity" with noun phrases (§§6.1, 7.2) are differences in D-linking and presuppositionality. Following Pesetsky (1987, 2000), 'which N' phrases are "D(iscourse)-linked" in the sense that uses generally imply that the individuals in the possible answers are from a contextually relevant domain (cf. Rullmann 1995, Rullmann and Beck 1998). Using 'which' in (9.17) is anomalous unless a set of musicians is salient in the discourse (e.g., if Pat is a writer for a music publication, and A and B have been talking about her recent efforts to scope out a new story).

(9.17)   A: Pat met someone famous.
           B: Who did she meet?
           B':#Which musician did she meet?

The syntax/semantics from §§6–7 captured contextual domain restriction in terms of structural properties of n*P noun phrases. One approach would be to analyze D-linked *wh* phrases as having a structure roughly analogous to the structure proposed for prenominal genitives — as n*Ps with an implicit definite-like element.[123] In a D-linked *wh* phrase, n* is implicit and the choice-function pronoun in F is realized by the *wh* word, bound by the question operator, as reflected in (9.18)–(9.19). The D-linked *wh* phrase might be represented in, say, a Top(ic) Phrase (cf. Rizzi 2001). (Let ι be an ordinary type-$\langle et, e \rangle$ definite.)

(9.18) $Q^{\langle i,a \rangle}$ ... $[_{\text{TopP}}$ ι $[_{\text{n*p}} P_{et}$ g $[X$ [wh$_{\text{cf}}$ g$_i$ nP]]]

(9.19)   Which baby laughed?

    a. $[_S Q^{\langle 2,a \rangle} [_{CP} w_1 g_2 [[C_? t_{2a}]^{\langle 1,s \rangle}$
        $[[_{\text{TopP}}$ ι $[_{\text{n*p}} P_{1et} g_1 [X$ [wh$_{1\text{cf}}$-g$_2$ w$_1$-g$_1$-baby]]]]
        $[t_{1s}$ laughed]]]]]

    b. $[\![\text{TopP}]\!] \approx \lambda g_g$. the o such that $g(1a)(1et)(o) \wedge$
        $o = g(2a)(1\text{cf})(baby_{g(1a)(1s)})$

    c.   A proposition $T_t \in [\![S]\!]$ is an *answer* to S in c iff $\exists g_g''$:
        $T = \left[\lambda g_g' \approx g'' \right.$.
        the o s.t. $g_c^-(1et)(o) \wedge o = g'(1\text{cf})(baby_{g_c^-(1s)})$ laughed in $@(g'^-)$
        iff
        the o s.t. $g_c^-(1et)(o)) \wedge o = g''(1\text{cf})(baby_{g_c^-(1s)})$ laughed in $@(g''^-) \left.\right]$

"Discourse linking" to a set of contextually relevant individuals is captured like with presuppositional uses of quantifier phrases. The domain pronoun $[P_{1et} \; g_1]$ restricts the denotation of the D-linked 'which NP' phrase and thereby restricts the possible answers to answers about individuals in the contextually relevant domain $g_c(1et)$. The possible answers in (9.19) are propositions T, where each such proposition is a set of assignments g' that return the same value for the proposition that a selected baby $g'(1\text{cf})(baby_{g_c(1s)})$ in the contextually relevant domain laughed.

9.3.1   Recap: Choice-Function Pronouns across Categories and Domains

Along the way we have appealed to variables for choice functions in the representations of various types of expressions, including names (§4.4), certain

---

[123] Indeed as Pesetsky remarks, "The semantics of D-linked *wh* phrases closely tracks the semantics of the definite article *the*. Context sets previously mentioned in the discourse qualify a phrase as D-linked, but so do sets that are merely salient" (2000: 16). It would be worth exploring how the phase-based analysis of presuppositional noun phrases from §7 might be applied to further syntactic and semantic independence properties of D-linked *wh* phrases, such as regarding island (in)sensitivity and Superiority effects (Dayal 2006).

indefinites (§§5, 7.4) and anaphoric proforms (§§5.2, 6.3, 6.4, 7.4, 8.7), relative words (§§5, 7.4), presuppositional noun phrases (§§6.1, 6.2, 7.2, 7.3), and *wh* words (§§8.2, 9.3). These analyses have been central in developing assignment-variable-based compositional semantics for noun phrases, relativization, donkey sentences, conditionals, and interrogatives. It is worth briefly recapping certain independent motivations for the common structure, and relevant dimensions of difference among the expressions.

Researchers in various subdisciplines have demonstrated crosslinguistically robust morphosyntactic parallels among the expressions. For instance, relative words generally have the same format as interrogative *wh*-words or *d*-words, and *wh*-words are often morphologically related to indefinites; it isn't uncommon for the same format to be used for certain pronouns and demonstratives as well, such as in various Chinese dialects with third-person pronouns and distal demonstratives (Jespersen 1924, Postal 1969, Haspelmath 1997, Gair et al. 1999, Heine and Kuteva 2002, de Vries 2002, Bhat 2004, Luján 2004, Thurgood and LaPolla 2017). In many languages strong quantifiers are composed from or are diachronically related to a relative/*wh* or definite/demonstrative form (Haspelmath 1995). The anaphoric proforms in correlatives are also generally formed from a demonstrative element (Dayal 1996, Bhatt 2003, Lipták 2009b). The $\overline{\text{A}}$-movement of the demonstrative correlate in a language often patterns with *wh*-movement (Izvorski 1996). Uniqueness and exhaustivity implications associated with *wh* interrogatives are also observed with correlatives (Dayal 1996, Izvorski 1996). Some languages even use the same pronouns for each of these functions — as relatives, indefinites, anaphoric proforms, and interrogatives (Bhat 2004).

The proposed unified choice-function-based analyses reflect such intralinguistic and crosslinguistic relations among the expressions. This isn't to say that there are no differences among them — e.g., morphosyntactically, semantically, distributionally. For instance, differences among pronominal elements in internal structure, pronunciation rules, and features such as φ-features or definiteness are to be expected (Déchaine and Wiltschko 2002, 2017, Lecarme 2008, 2012, Cowper and Hall 2009, Kratzer 2009, Grosz and Patel-Grosz 2016, Patel-Grosz and Grosz 2017). Simplex pronouns are in effect a conventionalized system of demonstratives prioritizing the expression of φ-features — over, say, spatial features or an overt nominal complement — for retrieving the relevant selectional subdomain. Even if both types of pronominal elements were represented via choice functions, the choice-function-qua-individual-pronoun plays a distinctive role in the expressive potential of the pronominal system (cf. n. 36). Other differences may be due to differences in [WH] features, e.g. distinguishing relative and *wh* words from indefinites and anaphoric pronouns. In languages such as Chinese the relation between *wh* words and indefinites is transparent; *wh* words just are, in some cases, indefinites with a phonetically unrealized [wh] feature. In other languages the [wh] feature may be realized via an interrogative morpheme, or indefinites and *wh* words may be derived from a more basic form, as in languages with systems of "indeterminate" pronouns such as Japanese.

Leaving matters here would of course be incomplete. Issues regarding syntactic/semantic relations between indefinites and interrogatives, the internal and external syntax of different classes of pronouns, and interactions between the syntax and morphophonological components in the realization of pronominal and anaphoric expressions are notoriously complex. The aim in these chapters has been to provide an account which captures a common semantic core among the expressions in question. For present purposes what relevantly unifies certain indefinites, relative words, interrogative *wh* words, and certain anaphoric proforms is that they are analyzed in terms of choice-function pronouns. I hope the proposed semantics may provide a fruitful basis for delineating further dimensions of difference.

9.3.2   Aside: Weak Crossover Revisited

The discussion of weak crossover in §6.4 remained neutral regarding phenomena with *wh* interrogatives ((9.20)–(9.21)) in light of independent contrasts between QR-chains and *wh*-chains. Not all languages with weak crossover effects exhibit those effects in *wh* interrogatives. In (9.22), although the bound reading of the pronoun is unavailable with the QR'd DP, the *wh* interrogative corresponding to (9.20b) is grammatical. In English, *wh* weak crossover examples improve in certain focus constructions, as in (9.23) with 'only'.

(9.20)   a.   Who$_i$ (t_i) likes her$_i$ child?
         b.   *Who$_i$ does her$_i$ child like (t_i)?

(9.21)   a.   [*Which boy$_i$*'s friend]$_k$ (t_k) accidentally introduced his$_i$ girlfriend to his$_i$ mother?
         b.   *[*Which boy$_i$*'s mother]$_k$ did his$_i$ friend accidentally introduce his$_i$ girlfriend to (t_k)?

(9.22)   a.   *Ìyá   rè$_i$ féràn enìkòòkan$_i$.
              mother his like   everyone
              (intended: 'everyone$_i$ is liked by his$_i$ mother')
         b.   Ta$_i$ ni ìyá   rè$_i$ féràn (t_i)?
              who be mother his like
              'Who$_i$ does his$_i$ mother like?'

                          (Adésolá 2005: 55, 11; Yorùbá (Niger-Congo))

(9.23)??[Which baby]$_i$ did only its$_i$ mother say (t_i) was cute?

Given such intralinguistic and crosslinguistic variation, it isn't implausible that *wh* weak crossover effects should follow from properties of *wh* chains within the language rather than general binding principles (cf. (6.59)). The semantics for *wh* interrogatives in this section is compatible with different views on *wh*-movement in the syntax and interfaces; yet it may be worth briefly speculating on binding configurations with pronouns.

To a rough (inadequate) first approximation, consider the constraint in (9.24) on relations among copies of *wh* phrases. Intuitively put, this says that any copy of a *wh* expression α must be c-commanded (perhaps trivially) by an element whose *wh* status "results from" α. (The superscripts are used simply to delineate the copies; they have no theoretical import. For simplicity one may assume a reflexive definition of percolation, i.e. so an expression's features can percolate (trivially) from itself.)[124]

(9.24) Let α_i be an expression with feature [WH] such that there is no coindexed γ_i higher than α_i; and let $C = (a_i^1, \ldots, a_i^n)$ be the sequence of copies coindexed with α_i. Then for every $a_i^j \in C$, there is some $a_i^k \in C$ and [WH]-β such that (β, a_i^j) is a chain and β's [WH] feature percolates from a_i^k.

Unlike copies of movement, non-movement copies need only be equivalent in elements relevant to satisfying requirements for coindexing; that is, they must have the same φ-features (e.g. Kratzer 2009; cf Nunes 2004, van Koppen 2007). The principle in (9.24) thus permits examples such as (9.20a). The copies of who$_i$ = [$_{[WH]}$ wh-g PERS-w-g]$_i$ (ignoring irrelevant internal indices) are the trace t_i and b_i = [her-g PERS-w-g]$_i$ in the representation of the possessive pronoun; t_i = [$_{[WH]}$ wh-g PERS-w-g]$_i$ has feature [WH]; and (t_i) and (t_i, b_i) are chains. Examples such as (9.20b), however, are excluded. There is no [WH]-β, whose [WH] feature arises from some $a_i^k \in C$, such that (β, b_i) is a chain. The pronoun b_i lacks a [WH] feature, and the [WH]-t_i trace doesn't c-command b_i. The treatment of "secondary weak crossover" effects ((9.21)) proceeds likewise. Unlike (9.21a), (9.21b) is excluded since the only potential [WH]-β is the trace t_k for 'which

---

[124] I continue to use 'copy' both for traces and for copies not derived via movement. The chains needn't be movement chains; the principle is compatible with treating chain relations as represented in the narrow syntax or the interfaces. The principle is formulated to apply at a level at which *wh*-movement has taken place, though it could be reformulated in other terms.

boy$_i$'s mother', and t_k doesn't c-command either copy [him-g boy-w-g]$_i$ in the representations of the possessive pronouns.

The binding principle in (6.59) (§6.4) functions to constrain movement repairing a type mismatch from introducing new kinds of binding relations. Whereas QR is a semantically driven mechanism that applies for reasons of interpretability, *wh*-movement and reconstruction depend on principles at various grammatical levels. Hence it might not be surprising to find greater crosslinguistic variation in weak crossover effects with *wh* interrogatives, as in fact we do. Crosslinguistic differences in *wh* weak crossover might be diagnosed in terms of differences in the status and formalization of a principle such as (9.24) — e.g., at what level the principle is checked, and what the relevant command relations are — along with independent differences regarding *wh*-movement, reconstruction, pied-piping. I leave further developments and investigation of different types of weak crossover configurations for future research.[125]

9.4 Conditional and Correlative Questions

Informally put, whereas the possible answers to a simple *yes/no* question partition the relevant space of possibilities, the possible answers to a conditional question such as (9.25) partition the subdomain of possibilities that verify the antecedent.

---

[125] In §§5.3, 7.4 we considered several arguments against the head-raising analysis of restrictive relative clauses from §5.1 and developed an alternative matching analysis. Possible additional support for the matching analysis may come from weak crossover effects in relative clauses, as in (i). (Absent further constraints, weak crossover effects wouldn't be predicted for languages with relatives that lack [WH]/[OP]-features.)

(i)   a. Every cat$_i$ which likes its$_i$ owner...
      b. *Every cat$_i$ which its$_i$ owner likes...

The matching analysis from §7.4 treats the relative phrase as originating in the gap position in the relative IP. The explanation of *wh* weak crossover in the main text carries over directly. However, on the head-raising analysis, the principle in (9.24) threatens to exclude ordinary cases of bound-variable pronouns such as (ii-a) (at least given the analysis from §6.3). The pronoun [it-g cat] in the representation of 'its' is a copy of its antecedent FP, which, on the head-raising analysis, is the relative phrase. Yet there is no suitable [WH]-β c-commanding the pronoun, as reflected in (ii-b) (ignoring worlds and irrelevant indices).

(ii) a. Every cat which meowed liked its toy.
      b. [every [[wh-g cat]$_k$ C^0_i t_i meowed]] liked ... [it-g cat]$_k$ ...

No such overgeneration problem arises with the matching analysis. The bound pronoun is represented as a copy of the external FP, as reflected in (iii). The principle in (9.24) doesn't apply since the external FP doesn't have a [WH] feature.

(iii) [every [[$_{CP_{rel}}$ ... wh-g cat meowed] X [F$_{cf}$-g cat]$_i$]] liked ... [it-g cat]$_i$ ...

(9.25)   If it snows, will school be canceled?

Capturing this idea has proven a persistent challenge for traditional approaches to questions and quantificational analyses of conditionals (see Isaacs and Rawlins 2008, Groenendijk and Roelofsen 2009, Starr 2010; cf. Charlow 2011 on conditional imperatives). A further challenge is to capture the range of shifted and unshifted readings in the 'if'-clause and interrogative main clause. Consider the following conditional-question analogues of the shifted indexical example from Santorio (2012) discussed in §§8.1, 8.4.

(9.26)   [Context: Lingens and Lauben know they are kidnapped amnesiacs. They are informed that they will be anesthetized, and a coin will be flipped: if it lands tails, Lingens will be released in the Stanford library and Lauben will be killed; if it lands heads, Lauben will be released in the Harvard library and Lingens will be killed. After the experiment, one of the amnesiacs wakes up. Feeling fuzzy about the experimental protocol, he asks himself:]
If the coin landed heads, might I be in Widener?

(cf. Santorio 2012)

(9.27)   [Context: as in (9.26). The awoken amnesiac also can't remember whether funds were going to be left in one of the libraries, or what the standards for richness are, wherever he is.]
(Q^k) [If it$_i$ landed heads]^j am I$_j$ in Widener and rich$_k$?

In (9.27), for instance, we need to capture the global reading of 'it' in the 'if'-clause; the shifted reading of 'I' in the consequent clause, interpreted with respect to the assignment representing the supposition; and the shifted reading of the world argument and standard of richness associated with '(be) rich' in the consequent, targeted by the question operator and varying across possible answers. The conditional question in (9.27) is in part a question about how rich one must be to count as rich, on the supposition that the coin landed heads.

In light of crosslinguistic links among conditionals, correlatives, and interrogatives, I treated the interrogative complementizer $\mathbf{C}_?$ as having an analogous argument structure and semantics as 'if'/$\mathbf{C_{if}}$ in relativization of possibilities. In developing the approach I suggested understanding the world argument of $\mathbf{C}_?$ as determining a relevant possibility targeted by the question. We will see that this argument, though semantically trivial in the examples thus far, can play a nontrivial role in other complex sentences.

9.4.1 Relevance Conditional Questions

Before considering hypothetical conditional questions, let's start with a "non-shifty" relevance conditional question such as (9.29). In an ordinary relevance conditional, the 'if'-clause introduces a modal topic and the declarative main clause is used to assert something about the actual world: in (9.28), that there are biscuits. Similarly, in (9.29), the 'if'-clause introduces a modal topic and the main clause interrogative is used to ask about what is actually the case: whether there are biscuits.

(9.28)   If Timmy is hungry, there are biscuits in the kitchen.

(9.29)   If Timmy is hungry, are there biscuits in the kitchen?

Relevance conditional questions such as (9.29) raise no new complications. The sentence-initial 'if'-clause in (9.30) is analyzed as in §8.5, and the interrogative main clause is analyzed like in our examples with unembedded interrogatives. (For present purposes I leave the existential 'there' construction unanalyzed, and I ignore the prepositional phrase. I resume representing the identity presupposition associated with the interrogative CP via the subscript (§9.1).)

(9.30)

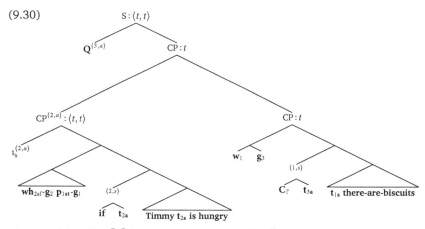

A proposition $T_t \in [\![S]\!]$ is an *answer* to S in c iff $\exists g''_g$:

$$T = \left[\lambda g'_g \approx g''\,. \right.$$
$$\left[\iota a(g') : \text{Timmy is hungry in } @(a(g')) \wedge @(a(g')) = a(g')(2\mathrm{sf})(g_c^-(1st))\right]$$
$$\quad \text{there are biscuits in } @(g'^-)_{=g'-(1s)}$$
$$\text{iff}$$
$$\left[\iota a(g'') : \text{Timmy is hungry in } @(a(g'')) \wedge @(a(g'')) = a(g'')(2\mathrm{sf})(g_c^-(1st))\right]$$
$$\left. \quad \text{there are biscuits in } @(g''^-)_{=g''-(1s)}\right]$$

Roughly put, each possible answer T is a set of assignments g' that return the same truth value for the proposition that the maximal relevant possibility where Timmy is hungry is such that there are biscuits in $@(g')$.

The global reading of the pronoun $[\mathbf{p}_{1st}\ \mathbf{g}_1]$, which supplies the contextually relevant background domain for the supposition, is captured in the metasemantic answerhood condition. For each answer T, every $g' \in T$ is such that $g'(1a)(1st) = g_c(1st)$. Just as external argument of 'if' determines the possibility targeted by the supposition, the external argument of $\mathbf{C}_?$ determines the possibility targeted by the question. In relevance conditional questions this possibility is the actual world. The external argument of $\mathbf{C}_?$ is again supplied by a world-pronoun bound by the question operator, and the interrogative introduces a question about whether there are actually any biscuits in the kitchen. The assignments g' in each answer T constitute an equivalence class with respect to whether there are biscuits in the world $@(g')$ of the possibility represented by g'.

A remark on interpreting the metalanguage quantification over assignments is in order. The argument of a in the denotation of the 'if'-clause varies across the assignments g', g'' in the possible answers; however, the items in terms of which the uniqueness condition is stated are images of the assignments under a, i.e. items $h \in G$ in the model (cf. §§2.2, 8.2). Varying the argument of a has no effect on which h constitutes the unique maximal possibility with the given property in the model.

9.4.2 Correlative Questions

Correlatives with interrogative main clauses are rarely if ever considered in semantics for questions or correlatives. It is instructive to compare the treatment of relevance conditional questions in (9.30) with the predicted analysis of an individual correlative question such as (9.31) (cf. §8.7.1). (Assume a context in which we haven't settled on how tall one must be to count as tall, and the standard for tallness associated with 'tall' receives a local reading targeted by the question. As in §8.5, assume a simplified context-sensitive semantics for positive form relative gradable adjectives, where 'o is *s*-tall' abbreviates that o's height is at least s, the degree standard for counting as tall.)

(9.31) jo laRkii khaRii hai vo lambii hai?
  REL girl standing is DEM tall is
  'Which girl is standing, is she tall?' (cf. Srivastav 1991: ex. 3a; Hindi)

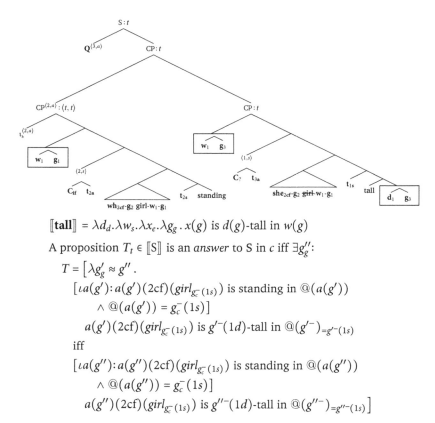

$\llbracket \mathbf{tall} \rrbracket = \lambda d_d.\lambda w_s.\lambda x_e.\lambda g_g \,.\, x(g)$ is $d(g)$-tall in $w(g)$

A proposition $T_t \in \llbracket S \rrbracket$ is an *answer* to S in c iff $\exists g_g''$:

$$T = \Big[\lambda g_g' \approx g'' \,.$$
$$[\iota a(g') \colon a(g')(2\mathrm{cf})(girl_{g_c^-(1s)}) \text{ is standing in } @(a(g'))$$
$$\wedge\ @(a(g')) = g_c^-(1s)]$$
$$a(g')(2\mathrm{cf})(girl_{g_c^-(1s)}) \text{ is } g'^-(1d)\text{-tall in } @(g'^-)_{=g'^-(1s)}$$

iff

$$[\iota a(g'') \colon a(g'')(2\mathrm{cf})(girl_{g_c^-(1s)}) \text{ is standing in } @(a(g''))$$
$$\wedge\ @(a(g'')) = g_c^-(1s)]$$
$$a(g'')(2\mathrm{cf})(girl_{g_c^-(1s)}) \text{ is } g''^-(1d)\text{-tall in } @(g''^-)_{=g''^-(1s)}\Big]$$

Like with the relevance conditional question in (9.30), the modal domain for the interrogative main clause is targeted by the question operator. The possibilities g' in each answer are equivalent with respect to whether the given individual counts as tall in $@(g')$ $(=g'(1s))$. But whereas the 'if-clause in (9.30) introduces a topical modal possibility, the correlative clause introduces an actual possibility about a topical individual (§8.7). The correlative clause describes a possibility h in the actual world $(=g_c(1s))$ in which a certain girl o $(=h(2\mathrm{cf})(girl_{g_c(1s)}))$ is standing. The interrogative main clause comments on that same girl, asking whether she $(=h(2\mathrm{cf})(girl_{g_c(1s)}))$ is tall. Each possible answer T is a set of assignments g' which determine the same standard s $(=g'(1d))$ for counting as tall, and return the same truth value for the proposition that the selected girl o who is standing in the actual world $g_c(1s)$ is at least s-tall in $@(g')$.

The global readings of the world-pronouns [$\mathbf{w}_1$ $\mathbf{g}_1$] determining the modal interpretation for 'girl' and the modal domain for the correlative clause are captured via the metasemantic condition on answerhood. The local reading of the correlate again follows from the representation as a copy of its antecedent, here [$\mathbf{F}_{2cf}$-$\mathbf{g}_2$ **girl**-$\mathbf{w}_1$-$\mathbf{g}_1$], and the assignment-quantification introduced by the correlative clause $CP^{\langle 2,a\rangle}$. The interpretation of the proform in the interrogative clause is shifted by the correlative clause without being targeted by the question. Conversely, the world argument and standard for tallness associated with '(be) tall' receive local readings under the question operator without being shifted by the correlative clause. (9.31) is in part a question about how tall one must be to count as tall. The assignments g' in each answer determine the same standard for tallness $g'(1d)$ (via $g' \approx g''$), though which standard is determined varies across possible answers. The correlative question is derived as being about whether a certain girl who is actually standing counts as tall.

9.4.3 Hypothetical Conditional Questions

Finally, let's return to hypothetical conditional questions such as (9.25)–(9.27). The syntax/semantics for interrogatives in this chapter can be layered directly into the account of conditionals from §8. The predicted LF and interpretation for (9.27) are as follows — again assuming the local reading targeted by the question of the standard for richness, and the local reading of 'I' shifted under the supposition.

(9.32)   If it landed heads, am I rich?

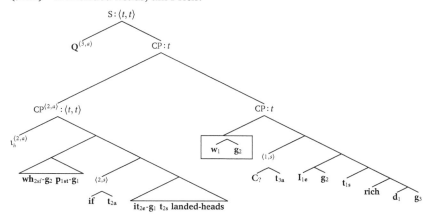

A proposition $T_t \in [\![S]\!]$ is an *answer* to S in c iff $\exists g''_g$:

$$T = \left[\lambda g'_g \approx g'' \, . \right.$$
$$\left[\iota a(g') : g_c^-(2e) \text{ landed heads in } @(a(g')) \right.$$
$$\left. \wedge \, @(a(g')) = a(g')(2\text{sf})(g_c^-(1st)) \right]$$
$$a(g')(1e) \text{ is } g'^-(1d)\text{-rich in } @(g'^-)_{=a(g')(1s)}$$

iff

$$\left[\iota a(g'') : g_c^-(2e) \text{ landed heads in } @(a(g'')) \right.$$
$$\left. \wedge \, @(a(g'')) = a(g'')(2\text{sf})(g_c^-(1st)) \right]$$
$$\left. a(g'')(1e) \text{ is } g''^-(1d)\text{-rich in } @(g''^-)_{=a(g'')(1s)} \right]$$

Each possible answer T is a set of possibilities g' which determine the same standard s ($=g'(1d)$) for counting as rich, and return the same truth value for the proposition that the relevant possibility h where the coin $g_c(2e)$ landed heads is such that $h(1e)$ is s-rich in that possibility ($@(g') = h(1s) = @(h)$).

The global readings of 'it' and the proposition-pronoun representing the relevant domain for the supposition are captured via the metasemantic condition on answerhood, which anchors their interpretation to the discourse context. The degree standard for 'rich' receives a local reading under the question operator. (9.32) is in part a question about what standard of richness to accept. The assignments in each answer agree in what standard of richness $g'(1d)$ they determine (via $g' \approx g''$), though which standard is determined varies across possible answers. By contrast, the interpretations of 'it' and 'I' are constant across answers. For each possible answer, the topical modal possibility h is about the same contextually relevant object $g_c(2e)$ and the individual $h(1e)$ representing (say) the epistemic counterpart of the speaker in that possibility (§§3.4, 4). The interpretation of 'I' in the interrogative consequent is shifted under the conditional supposition without being targeted by the question. I am not aware of other accounts of conditionals or questions that derive the observed range of local and global readings.

The present account captures the idea that the possible answers to a hypothetical conditional question are about the possibility described by the antecedent. There are two main moving parts. First, unlike in the lexical entries for 'if'/C_{if}, the condition on the external world argument in (9.4) with $C_?$ is treated as a presupposition. Intuitively, a *no*-answer to a conditional question such as (9.25) shouldn't include possibilities that are outside the contextually relevant *snow*-possibilities and where school is canceled (and perhaps even where it snows). The possibilities in each answer should count as relevantly equivalent due to being equivalent with respect to whether school is canceled. Implementing the identity condition as a presupposition captures this. The assignments in each possible answer T in (9.32) are restricted to assignments representing the topical modal possibility h described by the 'if'-clause — assignments g' such that $@(g'^-) = h(1s) = @(h)$.

By contrast, there isn't an analogous *no*-answer relevant in the semantics of relative clauses or 'if'-clauses. In deriving the embedding operator's restrictor argument, what matters is simply the items that satisfy both the identity condition and the embedded claim — e.g., for 'if it snows', the *snow*-possibilities which are part of the relevant background domain. That said, it may be interesting to consider presuppositional variants of the lexical entries for 'if/$\mathbf{C_{rel}}$' parallel to (9.4) (cf. n. 46). Developing the account in this way may provide a general presuppositional approach to quantifier domain restriction.

Second, the questions in our previous examples were about what is the case in the actual world. The external world argument of the interrogative complementizer — the argument determining the relevant possibility targeted by the question — received a local reading under the question operator, and the presupposition was trivial (given our general metasemantic assumptions). In contrast, in hypothetical conditional questions the possibility targeted by the question is the possibility introduced in the antecedent; the question is about what is the case in the topical hypothetical possibility. In (9.32) the external argument of $\mathbf{C_?}$ receives a local reading under the supposition, and the world-pronoun $[\mathbf{w}_1 \ \mathbf{g}_2]$ is coindexed with the 'if'-clause. The derived presupposition is the nontrivial constraint $@(g') = @(h)$ that the assignments g' in each possible answer represent the world of the topical possibility h. The possible answers T are propositions about the relevant possibility where the coin landed heads.

There is an important structural difference between correlative conditionals with interrogative vs. declarative main clauses. In §§8.5–8.7 the correlate of the 'if'-clause was directly linked to the main predicate's world argument. The assignment-binder $\mathbf{T}$ — or an embedding modal, as in (9.33) — raises from a vacuous complementizer generated by CP-recursion above the conditional.

(9.33)   Alice thinks [$_\text{CP}$ that [$_\text{CP}$ [if it snows] [$_\text{CP}$ (then) school will close]]]

In contrast, in correlative conditional questions, the non-vacuous embedded interrogative complementizer must be generated to trigger *wh*-movement, satisfy selection requirements of the question-embedding operator, and derive the question meaning. The correlate is instead the adjacent world argument in Spec,C — an adjacent world-pronoun, as in (9.32), or a topicalized proform such as 'then', as in (9.34). (For purposes of illustration I again leave 'then' in its fronted position.)

(9.34)   If it landed heads, then am I rich?

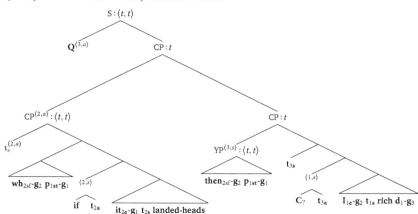

A proposition $T_t \in [\![S]\!]$ is an *answer* to S in c iff $\exists g''_g$:

$$T = \left[\lambda g'_g \approx g''\right].$$
$$[\iota a(g'):g_c^- (2e) \text{ landed heads in } @(a(g'))$$
$$\wedge\ @(a(g')) = a(g')(2\text{sf})(g_c^-(1st))]$$
$$a(g')(1e) \text{ is } g'^-(1d)\text{-rich in } @(g'^-)_{=a(g')(2\text{sf})(g_c^-(1st))}$$
iff
$$[\iota a(g''):g_c^- (2e) \text{ landed heads in } @(a(g''))$$
$$\wedge\ @(a(g'')) = a(g'')(2\text{sf})(g_c^-(1st))]$$
$$a(g'')(1e) \text{ is } g''^-(1d)\text{-rich in } @(g''^-)_{=a(g')(2\text{sf})(g_c^-(1st))}\big]$$

Like in our examples with unembedded interrogatives, the question operator raises from the assignment argument position of the main clause interrogative complementizer. No mechanism of CP-recursion is predicted. This is a significant feature since CP-recursion has been argued to be degraded or impossible under interrogative complementizers (e.g. Iatridou and Kroch 1993). Unlike (9.33), the examples in (9.35)–(9.36) are ungrammatical with 'then' (cf. Iatridou and Kroch 1993: 12).

(9.35)   Every boy asked if his mother visits (*then) what he should cook for her.

(9.36)   Every student asked whether if they fail (*then) they can retake the class.

The $\overline{A}$-movement from topicalizing the proform degrades the further *wh*-movement. The contrast between embedded 'then' conditionals with main clause declaratives vs. interrogatives falls out of our general analyses of correlatives and interrogative clauses.[126]

9.5 Recap: Standardizing Quantification

The syntax and compositional semantics for interrogatives in this chapter extends the treatments of type-driven movement with other quantifiers, complementizers, and modal elements developed throughout the book:

- Interrogative, conditional, and (non-vacuous) declarative complementizers raise from the main predicate's world argument position as quantifiers over worlds.

- Modal elements raise from inside their complement clause as quantifiers over assignments, determining the local modal domain. Analogously, nominal quantifiers raise from inside their complement, determining the relevant domain of individuals.

- Relative and *wh* words are choice-function pronouns — type $\langle et, e \rangle$ (alternatively $\langle \langle s, et \rangle, se \rangle$) in relativization of individuals, type $\langle st, s \rangle$ in relativization of possibilities. Correlative proforms are represented as copies at LF of their antecedent relative/*wh* word.

- Complementizers in free relatives and interrogatives relate a pair of individuals/worlds with respect to the property of individuals/worlds expressed by the complement. In interrogatives the interrogative clause characterizes an issue about the possibility targeted by the question; in individual relatives the relative clause characterizes a topical subset of individuals supplied by the relative phrase; in conditionals the 'if'-clause characterizes a topical subdomain of a relevant modal possibility; in individual correlatives the correlative clause characterizes a possibility about topical individuals in the actual world.

The proposed assignment-variable-based account affords a unified approach to conditionality, relativization, and questions, and a generalized treatment of quantification in various types of sentences and clausal structures.

---

[126] It is interesting that conditional 'then' questions like (9.34) (where 'then' is fronted) are ungrammatical in V2 languages. Unlike in declarative 'then' conditionals like (8.63), there is no empty complementizer position for the verb to move to.

10

Taking Stock

This book has investigated the prospects for a linguistic theory which posits explicit representations of context — formally, assignment variables — in the syntax and semantics of natural language. Contextually determined assignment functions are essential in contemporary linguistic theorizing, such as in the semantics of free pronouns, relativization, and quantification. I have argued that representing these assignments in the syntax can help capture a wide range of linguistic phenomena. A principal feature of the account is that it systematizes a spectrum of linguistic shifting data in which the context relevant for interpretation seems to depend on features of the linguistic environment. Central case studies include local and nonlocal contextual dependencies in nominal, verbal, and clausal domains, such as with intensionality, attitude ascriptions, presuppositional and nonpresuppositional noun phrases, donkey anaphora, questions, and relativization. The semantics affords a unified analysis of the context-sensitivity of pronouns, epistemic modals, etc., in the spirit of contextualist theories, while compositionally deriving certain recalcitrant shifting data. Resources for capturing these phenomena have grown increasingly complex in current theories. Binding across syntactic categories and semantic domains is derived uniformly from type-driven movement and a generalized binder-index feature. The account avoids added parameters of interpretation, interpretive principles, or quantification-specific composition rules. The semantics is fully compositional.

Certain developments may be of more general theoretical interest, such as the formalization of assignment modification; the approaches to the syntax–semantics interface with nominal, verbal, clausal quantifiers; fully compositional semantics for quantifier raising, *wh* interrogatives, and relativization across categories; a unified choice-function analysis of relative words, *wh* words, and certain indefinites and anaphoric proforms; a distinction between trace- and pronoun-binding, with applications to weak crossover; general treatments of donkey-style anaphora with quantifiers, genitives, and correlatives; unified compositional semantics for 'if'-clauses in nominal, verbal, and clausal environments, and for individual and conditional correlatives; and parallel phase-based layered n/v analyses of noun/verb phrases, with applications to "specificity," predication structures, and double object constructions.

Many issues call for more thorough investigation. Although I emphasized certain formal similarities among context-sensitive expressions, there are of course differences among them. The speculative discussions of varieties of pronoun binding, thematic arguments and relations, events, agreement-based constraints on readings, and comparisons among conditionals, individual correlatives, and interrogatives raise difficult questions about binding principles, (non-)linguistic anaphora, Case, locality and relativized minimality, tense/aspect, and *wh*-movement. Applications to other types of conventional meanings, such as conventional implicature and presupposition; categories, such as tense, aspect, voice, mood, and force; and expressions and constructions, such as expressives, imperatives, counterfactuals, modal adjectives/adverbs, nominal tense, and ellipsis, may provide further avenues to explore. I hope the preliminary developments here may illustrate the fruitfulness of an assignment-variable-based approach to investigating these and additional linguistic phenomena.

Bibliography

Abbott, Barbara. 2002. Donkey Demonstratives. *Natural Language Semantics*, **10**, 285–298. [See page 72.]

Abney, Steven Paul. 1987. *The English Noun Phrase in Its Sentential Aspect*. Ph.D. thesis, MIT. [See page 63.]

Aboh, Enoch Oladé. 2004. *The Morphosyntax of Complement-Head Sequences: Clause Structure and Word Order Patterns in Kwa*. Oxford: Oxford University Press. [See pages 81, 84, 113, 121.]

Adamou, Evangelia. 2011. Temporal Uses of Definite Articles and Demonstratives in Pomak (Slavic, Greece). *Lingua*, **121**(5), 871–889. [See page 90.]

Adésolá, Olúsèye. 2005. *Pronouns and Null Operators: A-Bar Dependencies and Relations in Yorùbá*. Ph.D. thesis, Rutgers University. [See page 218.]

Adger, David. 2003. *Core Syntax: A Minimalist Approach*. New York: Oxford University Press. [See pages 81, 132.]

Adger, David, de Cat, Cécile, and Tsoulas, George (eds). 2004. *Peripheries: Syntactic Edges and Their Effects*. Dordrecht: Kluwer. [See pages 235, 260.]

Åfarli, Tor A. 1994. A Promotion Analysis of Restrictive Relative Clauses. *The Linguistic Review*, **11**, 81–100. [See pages 58, 78.]

Aikhenvald, Alexandra Y. 2000. *Classifiers: A Typology of Noun Categorization Devices*. Oxford: Oxford University Press. [See page 89.]

Aikhenvald, Alexandra Y. 2008. Versatile Cases. *Journal of Linguistics*, **44**, 565–603. [See page 63.]

Aikhenvald, Alexandra Y. 2013. Possession and Ownership: A Cross Linguistic Perspective. Pages 1–64 of: Aikhenvald and Dixon (2013). [See pages 89, 92, 97, 98, 167.]

Aikhenvald, Alexandra Y., and Dixon, R. M. W. (eds). 2013. *Possession and Ownership: A Cross-Linguistic Typology*. Oxford: Oxford University Press. [See pages 233, 241.]

Alexiadou, Artemis. 2003. Some Notes on the Structure of Alienable and Inalienable Possessors. Pages 167–188 of: Coene and D'hulst (2003). [See pages 88, 91, 93, 97.]

Alexiadou, Artemis, and Wilder, Chris (eds). 1998. *Possessors, Predicates and Movement in the Determiner Phrase*. Amsterdam: John Benjamins. [See pages 63, 93.]

Alexiadou, Artemis, Anagnostopoulou, Elena, and Schäfer, Florian. 2006. The Properties of Anticausatives Crosslinguistically. Pages 187–221 of: Frascarelli (2006). [See page 159.]

Alexiadou, Artemis, Haegeman, Liliane, and Stravou, Melita. 2007. *Noun Phrase in the Generative Perspective*. Berlin: Mouton de Gruyter. [See pages 63, 69, 81, 84, 88, 156.]

Arsenijević, Boban. 2009. Correlatives as Types of Conditional. Pages 131–156 of: Lipták (2009a). [See pages 174, 185, 186, 193, 199.]

Bach, Emmon, Jelinek, Eloise, Kratzer, Angelika, and Partee, Barbara H. (eds). 1995. *Quantification in Natural Languages*. Dordrecht: Kluwer. [See pages 245, 246, 247, 255.]

Badulescu, Adriana, and Moldovan, Dan. 2008. A Semantic Scattering Model for the Automatic Interpretation of English Genitives. *Natural Language Engineering*, **15**(2), 215–239. [See pages 88, 98.]

Bagchi, Tista. 1994. Bangla Correlative Pronouns, Relative Clause Order, and D-Linking. Pages 13–30 of: Butt, Miriam, King, Tracy Holloway, and Ramchand, Gillian (eds), *Theoretical Perspectives on Word Order in South Asian Languages*. Stanford: CSLI. [See page 2.]

Baltin, Mark. 2012. *The Structural Signature of Pronouns*. MS, New York University. [See page 69.]

Baltin, Mark, and Collins, Chris (eds). 2001. *The Handbook of Contemporary Syntactic Theory*. Oxford: Blackwell. [See pages 234, 257.]

Barker, Chris. 1995. *Possessive Descriptions*. Stanford: CSLI Publications. [See pages 88, 93, 98, 165.]

Barker, Chris. 2002. The Dynamics of Vagueness. *Linguistics and Philosophy*, **25**, 1–36. [See page 183.]

Barwise, Jon, and Cooper, Robin. 1981. Generalized Quantifiers and Natural Language. *Linguistics and Philosophy*, **4**, 159–219. [See page 166.]

Bernstein, Judy. 2001. The DP Hypothesis: Identifying Clausal Properties in the Nominal Domain. Pages 536–561 of: Baltin and Collins (2001). [See pages 63, 112, 114.]

Bernstein, Judy, and Tortora, Christina. 2005. Two Types of Possessive Forms in English. *Lingua*, **115**(9), 1221–1242. [See page 93.]

Beshears, Anne. 2017. *The Demonstrative Nature of the Hindi/Marwari Correlative*. Ph.D. thesis, Queen Mary University of London. [See pages 195, 196.]

Bhat, D. N. S. 2004. *Pronouns*. New York: Oxford University Press. [See pages 3, 63, 69, 73, 102, 143, 209, 210, 217.]

Bhatt, Rajesh. 2002. The Raising Analysis of Relative Clauses: Evidence from Adjectival Modification. *Natural Language Semantics*, **10**, 43–90. [See pages 58, 59, 60, 62, 78, 140.]

Bhatt, Rajesh. 2003. Locality in Correlatives. *Natural Language and Linguistic Theory*, **21**, 485–541. [See pages 72, 186, 195, 196, 197, 199, 201, 217.]

Bhatt, Rajesh. 2006. *Covert Modality in Non-Finite Contexts*. Berlin: de Gruyter. [See pages 38, 81.]

Bhatt, Rajesh, and Pancheva, Roumyana. 2006. Conditionals. Pages 638–687 of: Everaert and van Riemsdijk (2006). [See pages 60, 172, 173, 174, 176, 183, 185, 186, 192, 199.]

Bhattacharya, Tanmoy. 1999a. Specificity in the Bangla DP. Pages 71–99 of: Singh, Rajendra (ed), *Yearbook of South Asian Language and Linguistics*, vol. 2. London: SAGE Publications. [See pages 63, 84, 86, 96.]

Bhattacharya, Tanmoy. 1999b. *The Structure of the Bangla DP*. Ph.D. thesis, University College London. [See pages 63, 81, 84, 86, 93, 96.]

Bianchi, Valentina. 1999. *Consequences of Antisymmetry: Headed Relative Clauses*. Berlin: Mouton de Gruyter. [See pages 58, 59.]

Bianchi, Valentina. 2011. Some Notes on the "Specificity Effects" of Optional Resumptive Pronouns. Pages 319–342 of: Rouveret (2011). [See page 148.]

Bittner, Maria. 2001. Topical Reference for Individuals and Possibilities. Pages 36–55 of: Hastings, Rachel, Jackson, Brendan, and Zvolenszky, Zsofia (eds), *Proceedings from SALT XI*. Ithaca: CLC Publications. [See pages 173, 174, 185, 186, 192.]

Bittner, Maria, and Hale, Ken. 1996. The Structural Determination of Case and Agreement. *Linguistic Inquiry*, **27**(1), 1–68. [See pages 63, 160, 164.]

Blutner, Reinhard. 2004. Pragmatics and the Lexicon. Pages 488–514 of: Horn, Laurence R., and Ward, Gregory (eds), *The Handbook of Pragmatics*. Malden: Blackwell. [See page 136.]

Boeckx, Cedric. 2003. *Islands and Chains: Resumption as Stranding*. Amsterdam: John Benjamins. [See pages 102, 148.]

Boeckx, Cedric, and Grohmann, Kleanthes K. 2004. SubMove: Towards a Unified Account of Scrambling and D-Linking. Pages 241–257 of: Adger et al. (2004). [See pages 86, 211.]

Boeckx, Cedric, Hornstein, Norbert, and Nunes, Jairo. 2007. Overt Copies in Reflexive and Control Structures: A Movement Analysis. Pages 1–45 of: Conroy, Anastasia, Jing, Chunyuang, Nakao, Chizuru, and Takahashi, Eri (eds), *University of Maryland Working Papers in Linguistics 15*. College Park: University of Maryland. [See pages 51, 100, 101.]

Boneh, Nora, and Sichel, Ivy. 2010. Deconstructing Possession. *Natural Language and Linguistic Theory*, **28**, 1–40. [See pages 93, 162, 167.]

Bonomi, Andrea. 1997. Aspect, Quantification and *When*-Clauses in Italian. *Linguistics and Philosophy*, **20**, 469–514. [See page 158.]

Borer, Hagit. 2005a. *Structuring Sense, Volume I: In Name Only*. Oxford: Oxford University Press. [See pages 43, 112, 113, 114, 156.]

Borer, Hagit. 2005b. *Structuring Sense, Volume II: The Normal Course of Events*. Oxford: Oxford University Press. [See page 156.]

Borschev, Vladimir, Paducheva, Elena V., Partee, Barbara H., Testelets, Yakov G., and Yanovich, Igor. 2008. Russian Genitives, Non-Referentiality, and the Property-Type Hypothesis. Pages 48–67 of: Antonenko, Andrei, Bailyn, John F., and Bethin, Christina Y. (eds), *Formal Approaches to Slavic Linguistics (FASL) 16*. Ann Arbor: Michigan Slavic Publications. [See page 96.]

Borschev, Vladimir, and Partee, Barbara H. 2002. The Russian Genitive of Negation in Existential Sentences: The Role of Theme–Rheme Structure Reconsidered. Pages 185–250 of: Hajičová, Eva, Sgall, Petr, Hana, Jiří, and Hoskovec, Tomáš (eds), *Prague Linguistic Circle Papers*, vol. 4. Amsterdam: John Benjamins. [See pages 126, 165.]

Bošković, Željko. 2006. Case and Agreement with Genitive of Quantification in Russian. Pages 99–121 of: Boeckx, Cedric (ed), *Agreement Systems*. Amsterdam: John Benjamins. [See pages 82, 96.]

Bošković, Željko. 2014. Phases beyond Clauses. Pages 75–127 of: Schürcks, Lilia, Giannakidou, Anastasia, and Etxeberria, Urtzi (eds), *The Nominal Structure in Slavic and Beyond*. Berlin: de Gruyter. [See page 96.]

Bošković, Željko, and Nunes, Jairo. 2007. The Copy Theory of Movement: A View from PF. Pages 13–74 of: Corver and Nunes (2007). [See page 101.]

Bosse, Solveig, Bruening, Benjamin, and Yamada, Masahiro. 2012. Affected Experiencers. *Natural Language and Linguistic Theory*, **30**(4), 1185–1230. [See page 160.]

Brasoveanu, Adrian. 2007. *Structured Nominal and Modal Reference*. Ph.D. thesis, Rutgers University. [See page 76.]

Bruening, Benjamin. 2009. Selectional Asymmetries between CP and DP Suggest that the DP Hypothesis Is Wrong. Pages 26–35 of: MacKenzie, Laurel (ed), *University of Pennsylvania Working Papers in Linguistics*, vol. 15.1. University of Pennsylvania. [See page 87.]

Bruening, Benjamin. 2010. Ditransitive Asymmetries and a Theory of Idiom Formation. *Linguistic Inquiry*, **41**(4), 519–562. [See page 27.]

Burge, Tyler. 1973. Reference and Proper Names. *Journal of Philosophy*, **70**(14), 425–439. [See page 43.]

Büring, Daniel. 2004. Crossover Situations. *Natural Language Semantics*, **12**, 23–62. [See pages 53, 69, 70, 79, 86, 103, 105, 109.]

Büring, Daniel. 2005. *Binding Theory*. Cambridge: Cambridge University Press. [See pages 53, 102.]

Büring, Daniel. 2011. Pronouns. Pages 971–996 of: von Heusinger et al. (2011). [See page 70.]

Cable, Seth. 2009. The Syntax of the Tibetan Correlative. Pages 195–222 of: Lipták (2009a). [See pages 192, 195, 196, 199.]

Cable, Seth. 2010. *The Grammar of Q: Q-Particles, Wh-Movement, and Pied-Piping*. Oxford: Oxford University Press. [See pages 204, 211.]

Campbell, Richard. 1996. Specificity Operators in SpecDP. *Studia Linguistica*, **50**, 161–188. [See pages 27, 63, 80, 87.]

Caponigro, Ivano. 2002. Free Relatives as DPs with a Silent D and a CP Complement. Pages 140–150 of: Samiian, Vida (ed), *Proceedings of the Western Conference on Linguistics 2000 (WECOL 2000)*. Fresno: California State University. [See page 80.]

Caponigro, Ivano. 2003. *Free Not to Ask: On the Semantics of Free Relatives and Wh-Words Cross-Linguistically*. Ph.D. thesis, UCLA. [See pages 64, 155, 210.]

Caponigro, Ivano. 2012. Acquiring the Meaning of Free Relative Clauses and Plural Definite Descriptions. *Journal of Semantics*, **29**, 261–293. [See pages 64, 173.]

Cardinaletti, Anna, and Giusti, Giuliana. 2017. Quantified Expressions and Quantitative Clitics. Pages 1–61 of: Everaert and van Riemsdijk (2017). [See page 82.]

Cardinaletti, Anna, and Starke, Michal. 1999. The Typology of Structural Deficiency: A Case Study of the Three Classes of Pronouns. Pages 145–233 of: van Riemsdijk, Henk (ed), *Clitics in the Languages of Europe*. Berlin: Mouton de Gruyter. [See pages 84, 114, 164.]

Cariani, Fabrizio, Kaufmann, Stefan, and Kaufmann, Magdalena. 2013. Deliberative Modality under Epistemic Uncertainty. *Linguistics and Philosophy*, **36**(3), 225–259. [See page 192.]

Carlson, Greg N. 1977. Amount Relatives. *Language*, **58**, 520–542. [See pages 78, 140.]

Carlson, Gregory N. 1980. *Reference to Kinds in English*. New York: Garland. [See page 166.]

Cecchetto, Carlo. 2004. Explaining the Locality Conditions of QR: Consequences for the Theory of Phases. *Natural Language Semantics*, **12**, 345–397. [See pages 31, 110, 132, 133.]

Chang, Henry Y. 2012. Nominal Tense in Tsou: *Nia* and Its Syntax/Semantics. Pages 43–58 of: Graf, Thomas, Paperno, Denis, Szabolcsi, Anna, and Tellings, Jos (eds), *Theories of Everything: In Honor of Ed Keenan*. UCLA Working Papers in Linguistics. [See page 80.]

Chappell, Hilary, and McGregor, William. 1989. Alienability, Inalienability and Nominal Classification. Pages 24–36 of: Hall, Kira, Meacham, Michael, and Shapiro, Richard (eds), *Proceedings of the Berkeley Linguistic Society 15*. Berkeley, Calif.: Berkeley Linguistics Society. [See pages 89, 97, 98.]

Chappell, Hilary, and McGregor, William. 1996. Prolegomena to a Theory of Inalienability. Pages 3–30 of: Chappell, Hilary, and McGregor, William (eds), *The Grammar of*

Inalienability: A Typological Perspective on Body Part Terms and the Part–Whole Relation. Berlin: Mouton de Gruyter. [See pages 89, 98.]

Charlow, Nate. 2011. *Practical Language: Its Meaning and Use*. Ph.D. thesis, University of Michigan. [See page 221.]

Charlow, Nate. 2013. What We Know and What to Do. *Synthese*, **190**, 2291–2323. [See page 190.]

Charlow, Simon, and Sharvit, Yael. 2014. Bound "De Re" Pronouns and the LFs of Attitude Reports. *Semantics and Pragmatics*, **7**(3), 1–43. [See pages 5, 43.]

Cheng, Lisa L.-S., and Huang, C.-T. James. 1996. Two Types of Donkey Sentences. *Natural Language Semantics*, **4**, 121–163. [See page 71.]

Chierchia, Gennaro. 1994. Intensionality and Context Change: Towards a Dynamic Theory of Propositions and Properties. *Journal of Logic, Language and Information*, **3**, 141–168. [See pages 17, 157.]

Chierchia, Gennaro. 1995. *Dynamics of Meaning*. Chicago: University of Chicago Press. [See page 75.]

Chierchia, Gennaro. 1998. Reference to Kinds across Languages. *Natural Language Semantics*, **6**, 339–405. [See pages 118, 146.]

Chomsky, Noam. 1977. On Wh-Movement. Pages 71–132 of: Culicover, Peter, Wasow, Tom, and Akmajian, Adrian (eds), *Formal Syntax*. New York: Academic Press. [See page 142.]

Chomsky, Noam. 1981. *Lectures on Government and Binding: The Pisa Lectures*. Dordrecht: Foris. [See pages 20, 25, 31.]

Chomsky, Noam. 1993. A Minimalist Program for Linguistic Theory. Pages 1–52 of: Hale, Kenneth, and Keyser, Samuel Jay (eds), *The View from Building 20: Essays in Linguistics in Honor of Sylvain Bromberger*. Cambridge: MIT Press. [See pages 25, 31, 101.]

Chomsky, Noam. 1995. *The Minimalist Program*. Cambridge: MIT Press. [See pages 20, 25, 31, 33, 61, 157, 214.]

Chomsky, Noam. 2000. Minimalist Inquiries: The Framework. Pages 89–155 of: Martin, Roger, Michaels, David, and Uriagereka, Juan (eds), *Step by Step: Essays on Minimalist Syntax in Honor of Howard Lasnik*. Cambridge: MIT Press. [See pages 99, 131.]

Chomsky, Noam. 2001. Derivation by Phase. Pages 1–52 of: Kenstowicz (2001). [See pages 99, 131, 132, 136.]

Chomsky, Noam. 2004. Beyond Explanatory Adequacy. Pages 104–131 of: Belletti, Adriana (ed), *Structures and Beyond: The Cartography of Syntactic Structures,* vol. 3. Oxford: Oxford University Press. [See page 132.]

Chomsky, Noam. 2007. Approaching UG from Below. Pages 1–29 of: Sauerland, Uli, and Gärtner, Hans-Martin (eds), *Interfaces + Recursion = Language? Chomsky's Minimalism and the View from Syntax-Semantics*. Berlin: Mouton de Gruyter. [See pages 83, 87, 132.]

Chomsky, Noam. 2008. On Phases. Pages 133–166 of: Freidin et al. (2008). [See page 131.]

Chung, Sandra. 1973. The Syntax of Nominalizations in Polynesian. *Oceanic Linguistics*, **12**, 641–686. [See pages 89, 97, 157.]

Chung, Sandra. 1987. The Syntax of Chamorro Existential Sentences. Pages 191–225 of: Reuland and ter Meulen (1987). [See pages 125, 164.]

Chung, Sandra. 1998. *The Design of Agreement: Evidence from Chamorro*. Chicago: University of Chicago Press. [See pages 66, 211.]

Chung, Sandra, and Ladusaw, William. 2004. *Restriction and Saturation*. Cambridge: MIT Press. [See page 127.]

Cinque, Guglielmo. 1995. On the Evidence for Partial N-Movement in the Romance DP. Pages 287–309 of: *Italian Syntax and Universal Grammar*. Cambridge: Cambridge University Press. [See pages 88, 117.]

Cinque, Guglielmo. 2003. *The Prenominal Origin of Relative Clauses*. MS, NYU Workshop on Antisymmetry and Remnant Movement. [See page 141.]

Cinque, Guglielmo. 2013. *Typological Studies: Word Order and Relative Clauses*. New York: Routledge. [See pages 78, 88, 140, 141, 155.]

Cinque, Guglielmo. 2015. Three Phenomena Discriminating between "Raising" and "Matching" Relative Clauses. *Semantics-Syntax Interface*, **2**(1), 1–27. [See pages 78, 140.]

Cinque, Guglielmo. 2017. *On the Double-Headed Analysis of "Headless" Relative Clauses*. MS, University of Venice. [See pages 140, 154, 155.]

Citko, Barbara. 2004. On Headed, Headless, and Light-Headed Relatives. *Natural Language and Linguistic Theory*, **22**(1), 95–126. [See pages 154, 155.]

Citko, Barbara. 2009. What Don't Wh-Questions, Free Relatives, and Correlatives Have in Common?. Pages 49–79 of: Lipták (2009a). [See pages 155, 192, 199, 210.]

Coene, Martine, and D'hulst, Yves (eds). 2003. *From NP to DP, Vol. II: The Expression of Possession in Noun Phrases*. Amsterdam: John Benjamins. [See pages 233, 250.]

Collins, Chris. 1993. *Topics in Ewe Syntax*. Ph.D. thesis, MIT. [See page 72.]

Collins, Chris. 2001. Aspects of Plurality in ǂHoan. *Language*, **77**(3), 456–476. [See page 156.]

Collins, Chris. 2005. A Smuggling Approach to the Passive in English. *Syntax*, **8**(2), 81–120. [See pages 114, 159.]

Collins, Chris, and Stabler, Edward. 2016. A Formalization of Minimalist Syntax. *Syntax*, **19**, 43–78. [See pages 25, 31.]

Copley, Bridget, and Harley, Heidi. 2015. A Force-Theoretic Framework for Event Structure. *Linguistics and Philosophy*, **38**(2), 103–158. [See page 155.]

Corver, Norbert, and Nunes, Jairo (eds). 2007. *The Copy Theory of Movement*. Philadelphia: John Benjamins. [See pages 235, 246, 248.]

Cowper, Elizabeth, and Hall, Daniel Currie. 2009. Argumenthood, Pronouns, and Nominal Feature Geometry. Pages 97–120 of: Ghomeshi et al. (2009b). [See pages 44, 69, 84, 112, 114, 117, 217.]

Creissels, Denis. 2013. Control and the Evolution of Possessive and Existential Constructions. Pages 461–476 of: van Gelderen, Elly, Cennamo, Michela, and Barðdal, Jóhanna (eds), *Argument Structure in flux*. Amsterdam: John Benjamins. [See pages 162, 165.]

Creissels, Denis. 2014. *Existential Predication in Typological Perspective*. MS, University of Lyon. [See pages 125, 162, 163.]

Cresswell, M.J. 1990. *Entities and Indices*. Dordrecht: Kluwer. [See page 4.]

Cumming, Samuel. 2008. Variabilism. *Philosophical Review*, **117**(4), 525–554. [See pages 5, 11, 30, 43, 49, 50.]

Czinglar, Christine. 2000. Pure Existentials as Individual-Level Predicates: Evidence from Germanic. *Wiener Linguistische Gazette*, **64–65**, 55–82. [See page 126.]

Czinglar, Christine. 2002. Decomposing Existence: Evidence from Germanic. Pages 85–126 of: Abraham, Werner, and Zwart, C. Jan-Wouter (eds), *Issues in Formal German(ic) Typology*. Amsterdam: John Benjamins. [See page 126.]

D'Alessandro, Roberta, Franco, Irene, and Gallego, Ángel J. (eds). 2017. *The Verbal Domain*. Oxford: Oxford University Press. [See pages 87, 113, 114, 157, 244, 256, 260, 262.]

Danon, Gabi. 1996. *The Syntax of Hebrew Determiners*. MA thesis, Tel-Aviv University. [See page 82.]

Danon, Gabi. 2001. Syntactic Definiteness in the Grammar of Modern Hebrew. *Linguistics*, **39**, 1071–1116. [See pages 84, 86.]

Davidson, Donald. 1967. The Logical Form of Action Sentences. Pages 105–121 of: *Essays on Actions and Events*, 2nd ed. New York: Clarendon Press. [See page 156.]

Davison, Alice. 2009. Adjunction, Features and Locality in Sanskrit and Hindi/Urdu Correlatives. Pages 223–262 of: Lipták (2009a). [See pages 195, 196, 210.]

Dayal, Veneeta. 1996. *Locality in WH Quantification*. Dordrecht: Kluwer Academic Publishers. [See pages 44, 64, 65, 155, 173, 176, 186, 188, 192, 193, 195, 196, 198, 199, 204, 217.]

Dayal, Veneeta. 2006. Multiple-*Wh*-Questions. Pages 275–326 of: Everaert and van Riemsdijk (2006). [See pages 211, 216.]

Dayal, Veneeta. 2016. *Questions*. Oxford: Oxford University Press. [See page 211.]

de Vries, Lourens. 1993. *Forms and Functions in Kombai, an Awyu Language of Irian Jaya*. Canberra: Australian National University. [See page 140.]

Déchaine, Rose-Marie, and Wiltschko, Martina. 2002. Decomposing Pronouns. *Linguistic Inquiry*, **33**, 409–442. [See pages 42, 69, 72, 73, 74, 83, 102, 217.]

Déchaine, Rose-Marie, and Wiltschko, Martina. 2015. When and Why Can 1st and 2nd Person Pronouns Be Bound Variables? Pages 1–50 of: Grosz, Patrick, Patel-Grosz, Pritty, and Yanovich, Igor (eds), *NELS 40: Semantics Workshop on Pronouns*. Amherst: GLSA. [See pages 69, 83, 102.]

Déchaine, Rose-Marie, and Wiltschko, Martina. 2017. A Formal Typology of Reflexives. *Studia Linguistica*, **71**, 60–106. [See pages 69, 83, 101, 102, 217.]

Diesing, Molly (ed). 1992. *Indefinites*. Cambridge: MIT Press. [See pages 117, 125, 132.]

den Dikken, Marcel. 1995. *Copulas*. MS, Vrije Universiteit Amsterdam/HIL. [See pages 91, 93, 115, 162, 167.]

den Dikken, Marcel. 1997. The Syntax of Possession and the Verb 'Have'. *Lingua*, **101**, 129–150. [See page 162.]

Dixon, R. M. W. 1969. Relative Clauses and Possessive Phrases in Two Australian Languages. *Language*, **45**, 35–44. [See page 92.]

Dixon, R. M. W. 1972. *The Dyirbal Language of North Queensland*. Cambridge: Cambridge University Press. [See pages 172, 175.]

Dixon, R. M. W. 1980. *The Languages of Australia*. Cambridge: Cambridge University Press. [See pages 89, 92.]

Dixon, R. M. W. 2002. Copula Clauses in Australian Languages: A Typological Perspective. *Anthropological Linguistics*, **44**, 1–36. [See page 115.]

Dixon, R. M. W. 2004. *The Jarawara Language of Southern Amazonia*. Oxford: Oxford University Press. [See page 130.]

Dixon, R. M. W. 2009. The Semantics of Clause Linking in Typological Perspective. Pages 1–55 of: Dixon and Aikhenvald (2009). [See pages 175, 192.]

Dixon, R. M. W. 2010. *Basic Linguistic Theory, Volume 2: Grammatical Topics*. Oxford: Oxford University Press. [See pages 3, 89, 93, 97, 98, 167.]

Dixon, R. M. W., and Aikhenvald, Alexandra Y. (eds). 2009. *The Semantics of Clause Linking: A Cross-Linguistic Typology*. Oxford: Oxford University Press. [See pages 239, 260.]

Donati, Caterina, and Cecchetto, Carlo. 2015. *(Re)labeling*. Cambridge: MIT Press. [See page 58.]

Doron, Edit. 1982. On the Syntax and Semantics of Resumptive Pronouns. Pages 289–318 of: Rouveret (2011). [See page 148.]

Dowell, J. L. 2011. A Flexible Contextualist Account of Epistemic Modals. *Philosophers' Imprint*, **11**(14), 1–25. [See page 2.]

Dowell, J. L. 2012. Contextualist Solutions to Three Puzzles about Practical Conditionals. Pages 271–303 of: Shafer-Landau, Russ (ed), *Oxford Studies in Metaethics*, vol. 7. Oxford: Oxford University Press. [See page 190.]

Drummond, Alex, Kush, Dave, and Hornstein, Norbert. 2011. Minimalist Construal: Two Approaches to A and B. Pages 396–426 of: Boeckx, Cedric (ed), *The Oxford Handbook of Linguistic Minimalism*. New York: Oxford University Press. [See pages 101, 102.]

Dryer, Matthew S. 2005. Order of Relative Clause and Noun. Pages 366–369 of: Haspelmath, Martin, Dryer, Matthew S., Gil, David, and Comrie, Bernard (eds), *The World Atlas of Language Structures*. Oxford: Oxford University Press. [See page 140.]

Dummett, Michael. 1973. *Frege: Philosophy of Language*, 2nd ed. London: Duckworth. [See page 207.]

Dunaway, Billy, and Silk, Alex. 2014. Whither Anankastics? *Philosophical Perspectives*, **28**, 75–94. [See page 190.]

Egli, Urs, and von Heusinger, Klaus. 1995. The Epsilon Operator and E-Type Pronouns. Pages 121–141 of: Egli, Urs, Pause, Peter E., Schwarze, Christoph, von Stechow, Arnim, and Wienold, Gotz (eds), *Lexical Knowledge in the Organization of Language*. Amsterdam: Benjamins. [See page 44.]

Elbourne, Paul D. 2005. *Situations and Individuals*. Cambridge: MIT Press. [See pages 4, 43, 59, 69, 71, 75, 86, 109.]

Elbourne, Paul D. 2013. *Definite Descriptions*. Oxford: Oxford University Press. [See pages 69, 86.]

Embick, David, and Noyer, Rolf. 2001. Movement Operations after Syntax. *Linguistic Inquiry*, **32**(4), 555–595. [See page 93.]

Enç, Mürvet. 1991. The Semantics of Specificity. *Linguistic Inquiry*, **22**(1), 1–25. [See pages 82, 83, 84, 85, 111, 122, 123, 124, 125.]

Epstein, Samuel David, and Seely, T. Daniel (eds). 2002. *Derivation and Explanation in the Minimalist Program*. Oxford: Blackwell. [See pages 248, 253.]

Español-Echevarría, Manuel. 1997. Inalienable Possession in Copulative Contexts and the DP-Structure. *Lingua*, **101**, 211–244. [See pages 93, 167.]

Evans, Gareth. 1977. Pronouns, Quantifiers, and Relative Clauses (I). *Canadian Journal of Philosophy*, **7**(3), 467–536. [See page 69.]

Everaert, Martin, and van Riemsdijk, Henk (eds). 2006. *The Blackwell Companion to Syntax*. Oxford: Blackwell. [See pages 234, 239, 259.]

Everaert, Martin, and van Riemsdijk, Henk (eds). 2017. *The Wiley Blackwell Companion to Syntax,* 2nd ed. Blackwell. [See pages 236, 246, 254, 256.]

Falco, Michelangelo, and Zamparelli, Roberto. 2016. The Only Real Pro-Nouns: Comparing English *One* and Italian *Ne* as Noun Phrase Pro-Forms. Pages 107–134 of: Grosz and Patel-Grosz (2016). [See page 73.]

Faller, Martina, and Hastings, Rachel. 2008. Cuzco Quechua Quantifiers. Pages 277–317 of: Matthewson (2008). [See pages 84, 124, 125.]

Fara, Delia Graff. 2015. Names Are Predicates. *Philosophical Review*, **124**, 59–117. [See page 43.]

Farkas, Donka. 1981. Quantifier Scope and Syntactic Islands. Pages 59–66 of: Hendrik, Roberta, Masek, Carrie, and Miller, Mary Frances (eds), *Proceedings of the Chicago Linguistic Society (CLS) 17*. Chicago: Chicago Linguistic Society. [See page 63.]

von Fintel, Kai. 1994. *Restrictions on Quantifier Domains*. Ph.D. thesis, University of Massachusetts, Amherst. [See pages 10, 71, 85, 86, 173, 183, 185, 186, 187, 188.]

von Fintel, Kai. 1998a. *Evidence for Presuppositional Indefinites*. MS, MIT. [See page 112.]

von Fintel, Kai. 1998b. *The Semantics and Pragmatics of Quantifier Domains*. Vilem Mathesius Lectures, Prague. [See page 83.]

von Fintel, Kai, and Heim, Irene. 2011. *Intensional Semantics*. MS, MIT. [See pages 13, 22, 29, 48.]

von Fintel, Kai, and Iatridou, Sabine. 2005. *What to Do If You Want to Go to Harlem: Anankastic Conditionals and Related Matters*. MS, MIT. [See page 189.]

Fodor, Janet Dean. 1970. *The Linguistic Description of Opaque Contexts*. Ph.D. thesis, MIT. [See page 37.]

Fodor, Janet Dean, and Sag, Ivan A. 1982. Referential and Quantificational Indefinites. *Linguistics and Philosophy*, **5**, 355–398. [See pages 63, 69.]

Folli, Raffaella, and Harley, Heidi. 2007. Causation, Obligation, and Argument Structure: On the Nature of Little v. *Linguistic Inquiry*, **38**(2), 197–238. [See pages 115, 157, 161.]

Fortescue, Michael. 1984. *West Greenlandic*. London: Croom Helm. [See page 162.]

Fox, Danny. 2000. *Economy and Semantic Interpretation*. Cambridge: MIT Press. [See pages 25, 31, 59, 62, 214.]

Fox, Danny. 2002. Antecedent-Contained Deletion and the Copy Theory of Movement. *Linguistic Inquiry*, **33**(1), 63–96. [See pages 25, 30, 32, 59, 62, 179.]

Fox, Danny. 2003. On Logical Form. Pages 82–123 of: Hendrick, Randall (ed), *Minimalist Syntax*. Oxford: Blackwell. [See pages 32, 62.]

Frajzyngier, Zygmunt. 2013. Possession in Wandala. Pages 243–260 of: Aikhenvald and Dixon (2013). [See pages 89, 92.]

Frajzyngier, Zygmunt, and Johnston, Eric. 2005. *A Grammar of Mina*. Berlin: Mouton de Gruyter. [See page 155.]

Francez, Itamar. 2007. *Existential Propositions*. Ph.D. thesis, Stanford University. [See pages 111, 125, 126, 165, 166.]

Francez, Itamar. 2009. Existentials, Predication, and Modification. *Linguistics and Philosophy*, **21**(1), 1–50. [See page 126.]

Francez, Itamar. 2010. Context Dependence and Implicit Arguments in Existentials. *Linguistics and Philosophy*, **33**, 11–30. [See pages 126, 166.]

Francez, Itamar, and Goldring, Katja. 2012. Quantifiers in Modern Hebrew. Pages 347–397 of: Keenan and Paperno (2012). [See page 82.]

Franco, Ludovico. 2013. A Typological *Rarum* in Sogdian: Overt Complmentizers in Indicative Root Clauses. *Lingua Posnaniensis*, **55**(1), 55–67. [See page 33.]

Frank, Anette. 1996. *Context Dependence in Modal Constructions*. Ph.D. thesis, University of Stuttgart. [See page 189.]

Franks, Steven. 1994. Parametric Properties of Numeral Phrases in Slavic. *Natural Language and Linguistic Theory*, **12**, 570–649. [See pages 82, 113.]

Frascarelli, Mara (ed). 2006. *Phases of Interpretation*. Berlin: Mouton de Gruyter. [See pages 233, 251.]

Freeze, Ray. 1992. Existentials and Other Locatives. *Language*, **68**, 553–595. [See pages 162, 165, 167.]

Freeze, Ray. 2001. Existential Constructions. Pages 941–953 of: Haspelmath et al. (2001). [See pages 162, 167.]

Freidin, Robert, Otero, Carlos P., and Zubizarreta, Maria Luisa (eds). 2008. *Foundational Issues in Linguistic Theory: Essays in Honor of Jean-Roger Vergnaud*. Cambridge: MIT Press. [See pages 237, 253.]

Fukui, Naoki, and Speas, Margaret. 1986. Specifiers and Projection. Pages 128–172 of: Fukui, Naoki, Rapoport, Tova R., and Sagey, Elizabeth (eds), *MIT Working Papers in Linguistics 8: Papers in Theoretical Linguistics*. Cambridge: MITWPL. [See page 63.]

Furbee, N. Louanna. 1973. Subordinate Clauses in Tojolabal-Maya. Pages 9–22 of: Corum, Claudia, Smith-Stark, Thomas Cedric, and Weiser, Ann (eds), *Proceedings of the Chicago Linguistic Society 9*. Chicago: CLS. [See page 173.]

Gair, James W. 1998. *Studies in South Asian Linguistics: Sinhala and Other South Asian Languages*. Oxford: Oxford University Press. [See page 3.]

Gair, James W., Lust, Barbara, Subbarao, K.V., and Wali, Kashi (eds). 1999. *Lexical Anaphors and Pronouns in Selected South Asian Languages: A Principled Typology*. Berlin: de Gruyter. [See pages 3, 73, 209, 217.]

Gallego, Ángel J. 2010. *Phase Theory*. Amsterdam: John Benjamins. [See page 132.]

George, Benjamin. 2011. *Question Embedding and the Semantics of Answers*. Ph.D. thesis, UCLA. [See page 211.]

Geurts, Bart. 1997. Good News about the Description Theory of Names. *Journal of Semantics*, **14**, 319–348. [See pages 43, 50.]

Geurts, Bart. 2004. *On an Ambiguity in Quantified Conditionals*. MS, University of Nijmegen. [See page 189.]

Ghomeshi, Jila, and Massam, Diane. 2009. The Proper D Connection. Pages 67–95 of: Ghomeshi et al. (2009b). [See page 43.]

Ghomeshi, Jila, Paul, Ileana, and Wiltschko, Martina. 2009a. Determiners: Universals and Variation. Pages 1–21 of: Ghomeshi et al. (2009b). [See page 44.]

Ghomeshi, Jila, Paul, Ileana, and Wiltschko, Martina (eds). 2009b. *Determiners: Universals and Variation*. Amsterdam: John Benjamins. [See pages 238, 242.]

Giannakidou, Anastasia. 2004. Domain Restriction and the Arguments of Quantificational Determiners. Pages 110–126 of: Young, Robert B. (ed), *Proceedings of SALT 14*. Ithaca: CLC Publications. [See page 97.]

Giannakidou, Anastasia, and Rathert, Monika (eds). 2009. *Quantification, Definiteness, and Nominalization*. Oxford: Oxford University Press. [See pages 244, 253.]

Gil, David. 2013. Genitives, Adjectives and Relative Clauses. In: Dryer, Matthew S., and Haspelmath, Martin (eds), *The World Atlas of Language Structures Online*. Leipzig: Max Planck Institute for Evolutionary Anthropology. wals.info/chapter/60. [See pages 88, 92, 93, 140.]

Gil, Kook-Hee, Harlow, Stephen, and Tsoulas, George (eds). 2013. *Strategies of Quantification*. Oxford: Oxford University Press. [See pages 114, 253.]

Gillon, Carrie. 2013. *The Semantics of Determiners: Domain Restriction in S̲k̲w̲x̲wú7mesh*. Newcastle upon Tyne: Cambridge Scholars Publishing. [See pages 82, 84, 85, 86.]

Giusti, Giuliana. 1991. The Categorial Status of Quantified Nominals. *Linguistiche Berichte*, **136**, 438–452. [See pages 81, 117.]

Giusti, Giuliana. 1992. Heads and Modifiers among Determiners: Evidence from Romanian and German. Pages 1–19 of: *University of Venice Working Papers in Linguistics*, vol. 1.3. University of Venice. [See pages 81, 86, 117.]

Giusti, Giuliana. 1997. The Categorial Status of Determiners. Pages 95–123 of: Haegeman, Liliane (ed), *The New Comparative Syntax*. London: Longman. [See pages 81, 84, 86, 117.]

Giusti, Giuliana. 2002. The Functional Structure of Noun Phrases: A Bare Phrase Structure Approach. Pages 54–90 of: Cinque, Guglielmo (ed), *Functional Structure in DP and IP: The Cartography of Syntactic Structures*, vol. 1. New York: Oxford University Press. [See pages 27, 63, 80, 84, 86, 114.]

Gorrie, Colin, Kellner, Alexandra, and Massam, Diane. 2010. Determiners in Niuean. *Australian Journal of Linguistics*, **30**(3), 349–365. [See page 84.]

Gračanin-Yuksek, Martina. 2008. Free Relatives in Croation: An Argument for the Comp Account. *Linguistic Inquiry*, **39**(2), 275–294. [See pages 64, 78, 155, 210.]

Groat, Erich, and O'Neil, John. 1996. Spell-Out at the LF Interface. Pages 113–139 of: Abraham, Werner, Epstein, Samuel David, Thráinsson, Höskuldur, and Zwart, Jan-Wouter (eds), *Minimal Ideas: Syntactic Studies in the Minimalist Framework*. Philadelphia: John Benjamins. [See page 31.]

Groenendijk, Jeroen, and Roelofsen, Floris. 2009. *Inquisitive Semantics and Pragmatics*. MS, ILLC. [See page 221.]

Groenendijk, Jeroen, and Stokhof, Martin. 1984. *Studies on the Semantics of Questions and the Pragmatics of Answers*. Ph.D. thesis, University of Amsterdam. [See pages 205, 209, 211.]

Groenendijk, Jeroen, and Stokhof, Martin. 1991. Dynamic Predicate Logic. *Linguistics and Philosophy*, **14**, 39–100. [See pages 17, 75.]

Grosu, Alexander. 2002. Strange Relatives at the Interface of Two Millennia. *Glot International*, **6**(6), 145–167. [See pages 78, 142, 153, 155.]

Grosu, Alexander. 2012. Towards a More Articulated Typology of Internally Headed Relative Constructions: The Semantics Connection. *Language and Linguistics Compass*, **6**(7), 447–476. [See pages 153, 155.]

Grosu, Alexander, and Landman, Fred. 1998. Strange Relatives of the Third Kind. *Natural Language Semantics*, **6**, 125–170. [See pages 64, 153, 155, 176, 198.]

Grosz, Patrick, and Patel-Grosz, Pritty (eds). 2016. *The Impact of Pronominal Form on Interpretation*. Berlin: de Gruyter. [See pages 69, 217, 241, 262.]

Guéron, Jacqueline, and Hoekstra, Teun. 1995. The Temporal Interpretation of Predication. Pages 77–107 of: Cardinaletti, Anna, and Guasti, Maria-Teresa (eds), *Small Clauses*. San Diego: Academic Press. [See pages 27, 63.]

Guéron, Jacqueline, and Lecarme, Jacqueline (eds). 2004. *The Syntax of Time*. Cambridge: MIT Press. [See pages 249, 250.]

Gutiérrez-Bravo, Rodrigo. 2012. Relative Clauses in Yucatec Maya: Light Heads vs. Null Domain. Pages 253–268 of: Comrie, Bernard, and Estrada-Fernández, Zarina (eds), *Relative Clauses in Languages of the Americas: A Typological Overview*. Amsterdam: John Benjamins. [See page 152.]

Hacquard, Valentine. 2006. *Aspects of Modality*. Ph.D. thesis, MIT. [See pages 4, 27, 158.]

Hacquard, Valentine. 2009. On the Interaction of Aspect and Modal Auxiliaries. *Linguistics and Philosophy*, **32**(3), 279–315. [See page 158.]

Hacquard, Valentine. 2010. On the Event Relativity of Modal Auxiliaries. *Natural Language Semantics*, **18**(1), 79–114. [See pages 4, 8, 27, 158.]

Haegeman, Liliane. 2010. The Movement Derivation of Conditional Clauses. *Linguistic Inquiry*, **41**(4), 595–621. [See page 174.]

Haïk, Isabelle. 1984. Indirect Binding. *Linguistic Inquiry*, **15**, 185–223. [See pages 103, 109.]

Haiman, John. 1978. Conditionals Are Topics. *Language*, **54**, 565–589. [See page 186.]

Haiman, John. 1985. *Natural Syntax: Iconicity and Erosion*. Cambridge: Cambridge University Press. [See pages 89, 97.]

Hale, Kenneth. 1976. The Adjoined Relative Clause in Australia. Pages 78–105 of: Dixon, R. M. W. (ed), *Grammatical Categories in Australian Languages*. Canberra: Australian Institute of Aboriginal Studies. [See pages 174, 192.]

Hallman, Peter. 2016. Universal Quantification as Degree Modification in Arabic. *Glossa*, **1**(1), 26, 1–31. [See pages 82, 86.]

Hankamer, Jorge, and Mikkelsen, Line. 2012. *CP Complements to D*. MS, UC Santa Cruz and UC Berkeley. [See page 80.]

Harley, Heidi. 1995. *Subjects, Events and Licensing*. Ph.D. thesis, MIT. [See pages 96, 115, 161, 162, 167.]

Harley, Heidi. 2002. Possession and the Double Object Construction. *Yearbook of Linguistic Variation*, **2**, 29–68. [See pages 162, 167.]

Harley, Heidi. 2005. How Do Verbs Get Their Names? Denominal Verbs, Manner Incorporation, and the Ontology of Verb Roots in English. Pages 42–64 of: Erteschik-Shir, Nomi, and Rapoport, Tova (eds), *The Syntax of Aspect: Deriving Thematic and Aspectual Interpretation*. Oxford: Oxford University Press. [See page 156.]

Harley, Heidi. 2009. The Morphology of Nominalizations and the Syntax of *v*P. Pages 320–342 of: Giannakidou and Rathert (2009). [See pages 113, 114, 143.]

Harley, Heidi. 2013. External Arguments and the Mirror Principle: On the Distinctness of Voice and v. *Lingua*, **125**, 34–57. [See pages 87, 113, 114, 143, 159, 160.]

Harley, Heidi. 2017. The "Bundling" Hypothesis and the Disparate Functions of Little v. Pages 3–28 of: D'Alessandro et al. (2017). [See pages 87, 113, 114, 143, 159.]

Harley, Heidi, and Jung, Hyun Kyoung. 2015. In Support of the P$_{\text{HAVE}}$ Analysis of the Double Object Construction. *Linguistic Inquiry*, **46**(4), 703–730. [See pages 160, 164.]

Harlow, Ray. 2007. *Māori: A Linguistic Introduction*. Cambridge: Cambridge University Press. [See pages 89, 98, 157.]

Hartmann, Jutta M. 2008. *Expletives in Existentials: English There and German Da*. Ph.D. thesis, Tilburg University. [See pages 83, 84, 126, 127.]

Hartmann, Jutta M., and Milićević, Nataša. 2009. Case Alternations in Serbian Existentials. Pages 131–142 of: Zybatow, Gerhild, Junghanns, Uwe, Lenertova, Denisa, and Biskup, Petr (eds), *Studies in Formal Slavic Phonology, Morphology, Syntax, Semantics and Information Structure*. Frankfurt: Peter Lang. [See pages 82, 96, 163.]

Haspelmath, Martin. 1995. Diachronic Sources of 'All' and 'Every'. Pages 363–382 of: Bach et al. (1995). [See pages 81, 217.]

Haspelmath, Martin. 1997. *Indefinite Pronouns*. Oxford: Clarendon Press. [See pages 81, 209, 217.]

Haspelmath, Martin. 2017. Explaining Alienability Contrasts in Adpossessive Constructions: Predictability vs. Iconicity. *Zeitschrift für Sprachwissenschaft*, **36**(2), 193–231. [See pages 89, 97.]

Haspelmath, Martin, König, Ekkehard, and Oesterreicher, Wulf (eds). 2001. *Language Typology and Language Universals: An International Handbook*. Berlin: de Gruyter. [See pages 242, 248.]

Hastings, Rachel. 2004. *The Syntax and Semantics of Relativization and Quantification: The Case of Quechua*. Ph.D. thesis, Cornell University. [See pages 78, 142, 155.]

Hawthorne, John, and Manley, David. 2012. *The Reference Book*. Oxford: Oxford University Press. [See page 43.]

Hazout, Ilan. 2004. The Syntax of Existential Constructions. *Linguistic Inquiry*, **35**(3), 393–430. [See pages 125, 134, 164, 166.]

Heath, Jeffrey. 2008. *A Grammar of Jamsay*. Berlin: Mouton de Gruyter. [See pages 92, 140.]

Heim, Irene. 1982. *The Semantics of Definite and Indefinite Noun Phrases*. Ph.D. thesis, University of Massachusetts Amherst. [See pages 69, 74, 75.]

Heim, Irene. 1990. E-Type Pronouns and Donkey Anaphora. *Linguistics and Philosophy*, **13**, 137–177. [See page 69.]

Heim, Irene. 2008. Features on Bound Pronouns. Pages 35–56 of: Harbour, Daniel, Adger, David, and Béjar, Susana (eds), *Phi Theory: Phi-Features across Modules and Interfaces*. Oxford: Oxford University Press. [See pages 11, 17, 69, 132.]

Heim, Irene. 2012. *Lecture Notes for 24.973: Advanced Semantics*. MIT. [See pages 27, 204, 213.]

Heim, Irene, and Kratzer, Angelika. 1998. *Semantics in Generative Grammar*. Oxford: Wiley-Blackwell. [See pages 8, 11, 17, 25, 30, 32, 58, 60, 69, 88, 99, 100, 102, 107, 213.]

Heine, Bernd. 1997. *Possession: Cognitive Sources, Forces, and Grammaticalization*. Cambridge: Cambridge University Press. [See pages 89, 91, 92, 97, 98, 165, 167.]

Heine, Bernd, and Kuteva, Tania. 2002. *World Lexicon of Grammaticalization*. Cambridge: Cambridge University Press. [See pages 73, 81, 89, 92, 113, 165, 210, 217.]

Heine, Bernd, Claudi, Ulrike, and Hünnemeyer, Friederike. 1991. *Grammaticalization: A Conceptual Framework*. Chicago: University of Chicago Press. [See page 89.]

Helmbrecht, Johannes. 2016. NP-Internal Possessive Constructions in Hoocąk and Other Siouan Languages. Pages 425–463 of: Rudin, Catherine, and Gordon, Bryan J. (eds), *Advances in the Study of Siouan Languages and Linguistics*. Berlin: Language Science Press. [See pages 89, 167.]

Hestvik, Arild. 1992. LF Movement of Pronouns and Antisubject Orientation. *Linguistic Inquiry*, **23**(4), 557–594. [See page 73.]

Hestvik, Arild, and Philip, William. 2000. Binding and Coreference in Norwegian Child Language. *Language Acquisition*, **8**(3), 171–235. [See page 74.]

von Heusinger, Klaus. 2002. Specificity and Definiteness in Sentence and Discourse Structure. *Journal of Semantics*, **19**, 245–274. [See pages 44, 84.]

von Heusinger, Klaus. 2011. Specificity. Pages 1025–1058 of: von Heusinger et al. (2011). [See pages 44, 63, 65, 69, 84.]

von Heusinger, Klaus, Maienborn, Claudia, and Portner, Paul (eds). 2011. *Semantics: An International Handbook of Natural Language Meaning*, vol. 2. Berlin: Mouton de Gruyter. [See pages 236, 245, 253, 260.]

Himmelmann, Nikolaus P. 2016. Notes on "Noun Phrase Structure" in Tagalog. Pages 319–341 of: Fleischhauer, Jens, Latrouite, Anja, and Osswald, Rainer (eds), *Explorations of the Syntax-Semantics Interface*. Düsseldorf: Düsseldorf University Press. [See pages 80, 96.]

Hiraiwa, Ken. 2005. *Dimensions of Symmetry in Syntax: Agreement and Clausal Architecture*. Ph.D. thesis, MIT. [See pages 58, 63, 65, 76, 80, 81, 87, 96, 114, 132, 142, 144, 154, 156.]

Hiraiwa, Ken. 2017. Internally Headed Relative Clauses. Pages 1–30 of: Everaert and van Riemsdijk (2017). [See pages 58, 76, 142, 155.]

Hiraiwa, Ken, Akanlig-Pare, George, Atintono, Samuel, Bodomo, Adams, Essizewa, Komlan, and Hudu, Fusheini. 2017. A Comparative Syntax of Internally-Headed Relative Clauses in Gur. *Glossa*, **2**(1), 1–30. [See pages 65, 76, 80, 139, 153, 154, 155.]

Hockett, Charles F., and Altmann, Stuart A. 1968. A Note on Design Features. Pages 61–72 of: Sebeok, Thomas A. (ed), *Animal Communication: Techniques of Study and Results of Research*. Bloomington: Indiana University Press. [See page 1.]

Holmberg, Anders. 1993. On the Structure of Predicate NP. *Studia Linguistica*, **47**(2), 126–138. [See page 86.]

de Hoop, Helen. 1995. On the Characterization of the Weak-Strong Distinction. Pages 421–450 of: Bach et al. (1995). [See page 84.]

Hornstein, Norbert. 2001. *Move! A Minimalist Theory of Construal*. Oxford: Blackwell. [See pages 25, 69, 101, 102.]

Hornstein, Norbert. 2007. Pronouns in a Minimalist Setting. Pages 351–385 of: Corver and Nunes (2007). [See pages 69, 101.]

Hyslop, Catriona. 2001. *The Lolovoli Dialect of the North-East Ambae Language, Vanuatu*. Canberra: Pacific Linguistics. [See page 90.]

Iatridou, Sabine. 1991. *Topics in Conditionals*. Ph.D. thesis, MIT. [See pages 60, 173, 183, 185, 186, 199.]

Iatridou, Sabine. 1994. On the Contribution of Conditional *Then*. *Natural Language Semantics*, **2**, 171–199. [See pages 185, 186, 199.]

Iatridou, Sabine. 2013. Looking for Free Relatives in Turkish (and the Unexpected Places This Leads to). Pages 129–152 of: Özge, Umut (ed), *Proceedings of the 8th Workshop on Altaic Formal Linguistics (WAFL8)*. Cambridge: MITWPL. [See page 185.]

Iatridou, Sabine, and Kroch, Anthony. 1993. The Licensing of CP-Recursion and Its Relevance to the Germanic Verb-Second Phenomenon. *Working Papers in Scandinavian Syntax*, **50**, 1–24. [See pages 184, 185, 186, 228.]

Iatridou, Sabine, Anagnostopoulou, Elena, and Izvorski, Roumyana. 2001. Observations about the Form and Meaning of the Perfect. Pages 153–205 of: Kenstowicz (2001). [See page 142.]

Ihsane, Tabea, and Puskás, Genoveva. 2001. Specific Is Not Definite. Pages 39–54 of: Shlonsky, Ur, and Ihsane, Tabea (eds), *Generative Grammar in Geneva 2*. University of Geneva. [See pages 27, 63, 80, 84.]

Ilkhanipour, Negin. 2016. Tense and Modality in the Nominal Domain. *Linguistica*, **56**, 143–160. [See pages 63, 80.]

Ionin, Tania, and Matushansky, Ora. 2006. The Composition of Complex Cardinals. *Journal of Semantics*, **23**(4), 315–360. [See pages 113, 117.]

Irwin, Patricia. 2018. Existential Unaccusativity and New Discourse Referents. *Glossa*, **3**(1), 24. [See pages 126, 127.]

Isaacs, James, and Rawlins, Kyle. 2008. Conditional Questions. *Journal of Semantics*, **25**, 269–319. [See page 221.]

Izvorski, Roumyana. 1996. The Syntax and Semantics of Correlative Proforms. Pages 133–147 of: Kusumoto, Kiyomi (ed), *Proceedings of NELS 26*. Amherst: GLSA Publications. [See pages 183, 186, 199, 200, 217.]

Jacobson, Pauline. 1995. On the Quantificational Force of English Free Relatives. Pages 451–486 of: Bach et al. (1995). [See pages 64, 173, 176.]

Jacobson, Pauline. 2000. Paycheck Pronouns, Bach-Peters Sentences, and Variable-Free Semantics. *Natural Language Semantics*, **8**, 77–155. [See page 69.]

Jaszczolt, K. M. 1997. The 'Default *De Re*' Principle for the Interpretation of Belief Utterances. *Journal of Pragmatics*, **28**, 315–336. [See page 45.]

Jensen, Per Anker, and Vikner, Carl. 1994. Lexical Knowledge and the Semantic Analysis of Danish Genitive Constructions. Pages 37–55 of: Hansen, Steffen L., and Wegener, Helle (eds), *Topics in Knowledge-Based NLP Systems*. Copenhagen: Samfundslitteratur. [See pages 90, 94.]

Jespersen, Otto. 1924. *The Philosophy of Grammar*. London: George Allen & Unwin. [See pages 91, 217.]

Jiménez-Fernández, Ángel L. 2012. A New Look at Subject Islands: The Phasehood of Definiteness. *Anglica Wratislaviensia*, **50**, 137–168. [See page 132.]

Johnson, Kyle. 2012. Toward Deriving Differences in How *Wh* Movement and QR Are Pronounced. *Lingua*, **122**, 529–553. [See pages 4, 30, 32, 211.]

Julien, Marit. 2005. *Noun Phrases from a Scandinavian Perspective*. Philadelphia: John Benjamins. [See page 81.]

Julien, Marit. 2015. Theme Vowels in North Sámi: Spanning and Maximal Expression. *Lingua*, **164**, 1–24. [See pages 113, 114, 155, 156, 159.]

Kadmon, Nirit. 1987. *On Unique and Non-Unique Reference and Asymmetric Quantification*. Ph.D. thesis, University of Massachusetts Amherst. [See page 74.]

Kamp, Hans. 1971. Formal Properties of 'Now'. *Theoria*, **37**, 227–274. [See page 4.]

Kamp, Hans. 1981. A Theory of Truth and Semantic Representation. Pages 277–322 of: Groenendijk, Jeroen, Janssen, T., and Stokhof, M. (eds), *Formal Methods in the Study of Language*. Amsterdam: Mathematical Centre. [See pages 69, 74, 75.]

Kaplan, David. 1989. Demonstratives. Pages 481–563 of: Almog, Joseph, Perry, John, and Wettstein, Howard (eds), *Themes from Kaplan*. Oxford: Oxford University Press. [See pages 2, 4, 13.]

Karttunen, Lauri. 1977. Syntax and Semantics of Questions. *Linguistics and Philosophy*, **1**, 3–44. [See pages 209, 211, 212.]

Katzir, Roni. 2011. Morphosemantic Mismatches, Structural Economy, and Licensing. *Linguistic Inquiry*, **42**, 45–82. [See page 164.]

Kayne, Richard S. 1993. Toward a Modular Theory of Auxiliary Selection. *Studia Linguistica*, **47**, 3–31. [See pages 93, 162.]

Kayne, Richard S. 1994. *The Antisymmetry of Syntax*. Cambridge: MIT Press. [See pages 38, 58, 80, 87, 91, 93, 162.]

Kayne, Richard S. 2002. Pronouns and Their Antecedents. Pages 133–166 of: Epstein and Seely (2002). [See pages 99, 102.]

Kazuhiro, Masutomi. 2010. On Nominal Phase and Its Interpretation: A Minimalist Approach. *Annals of the Institute for Research in Humanities and Social Sciences*, **19**, 1–19. [See page 132.]

Keenan, Edward L. 1987. A Semantic Definition of "Indefinite NP". Pages 286–317 of: Reuland and ter Meulen (1987). [See pages 122, 126, 166.]

Keenan, Edward L. 2002. Some Properties of Natural Language Quantifiers: Generalized Quantifier Theory. *Linguistics and Philosophy*, **25**, 627–654. [See page 122.]

Keenan, Edward L., and Paperno, Denis (eds). 2012. *Handbook of Quantifiers in Natural Language*. Dordrecht: Springer. [See pages 82, 241.]

Kennedy, Christopher. 2007. Vagueness and Grammar: The Semantics of Relative and Absolute Gradable Adjectives. *Linguistics and Philosophy*, **30**(1), 1–45. [See pages 9, 183.]

Kennedy, Christopher. 2014. Predicates *and* Formulas: Evidence from Ellipsis. Pages 253–277 of: Crnič, Luka, and Sauerland, Uli (eds), *The Art and Craft of Semantics: A Festschrift for Irene Heim*, vol. 1. Cambridge: MITWPL. [See pages 4, 25, 31.]

Kenstowicz, Michael (ed). 2001. *Ken Hale: A Life in Language*. Cambridge: MIT Press. [See pages 237, 246.]

Kim, Ji-yung, Lander, Yury A., and Partee, Barbara H. (eds). 2004. *Possessives and Beyond: Semantics and Syntax*. Amherst: GLSA. [See page 93.]

King, Jeffrey C. 2004. Context Dependent Quantifiers and Donkey Anaphora. *Canadian Journal of Philosophy*, **34 (supplement 1)**, 97–127. [See pages 149, 151.]

Klein, Wolfgang. 1994. *Time in Language*. London: Routledge. [See page 158.]

Kobele, Greg. 2010. Inverse Linking via Function Composition. *Natural Language Semantics*, **18**, 183–196. [See pages 4, 18, 22, 25, 31, 105.]

Kolodny, Niko, and MacFarlane, John. 2010. Ifs and Oughts. *Journal of Philosophy*, 115–143. [See pages 190, 191, 192.]

Koopman, Hilda. 1984. *The Syntax of Verbs: From Verb Movement Rules in the Kru Languages to Universal Grammar*. Dordrecht: Foris. [See page 28.]

Koopman, Hilda. 2003. Inside the "Noun" in Maasai. Pages 77–116 of: Mahajan, Anoop (ed), *Head Movement and Syntactic Theory*. UCLA Working Papers in Linguistics. [See pages 80, 88.]

Koopman, Hilda. 2005. On the Parallelism of DPs and Clauses: Evidence from Kisongo Maasai. Pages 281–302 of: Carnie, Andrew, Harley, Heidi, and Dooley, Sheila Ann (eds), *Verb First: On the Syntax of Verb-Initial Languages*. Amsterdam: John Benjamins. [See pages 63, 80, 88.]

van Koppen, Marjo. 2007. Agreement with (the Internal Structure of) Copies of Movement. Pages 327–350 of: Corver and Nunes (2007). [See pages 71, 219.]

Koptjevskaja-Tamm, Maria. 1996. Possessive Noun Phrases in Maltese: Alienability, Iconicity and Grammaticalization. *Rivista di Linguistica*, **8**(1), 245–274. [See pages 89, 90, 97, 98.]

Koptjevskaja-Tamm, Maria. 2001. Adnominal Possession. Pages 960–970 of: Haspelmath et al. (2001). [See page 89.]

Kotek, Hadas. 2014. *Composing Questions*. Ph.D. thesis, MIT. [See page 204.]

Kracht, Marcus. 2002. On the Semantics of Locatives. *Linguistics and Philosophy*, **25**, 157–232. [See pages 126, 157.]

Kratzer, Angelika. 1977. What 'Must' and 'Can' Must and Can Mean. *Linguistics and Philosophy*, **1**, 337–355. [See page 29.]

Kratzer, Angelika. 1981. The Notional Category of Modality. Pages 38–74 of: Eikmeyer, Hans-Jürgen, and Rieser, Hannes (eds), *Words, Worlds, and Contexts: New Approaches in Word Semantics*. Berlin: de Gruyter. [See pages 29, 173, 187.]

Kratzer, Angelika. 1991. Modality/Conditionals. Pages 639–656 of: von Stechow, Arnim, and Wunderlich, Dieter (eds), *Semantics: An International Handbook of Contemporary Research*. New York: de Gruyter. [See pages 173, 187.]

Kratzer, Angelika. 1995. Stage-Level and Individual-Level Predicates. Pages 125–175 of: Carlson, Gregory N., and Pelletier, Francis Jeffrey (eds), *The Generic Book*. Chicago: University of Chicago Press. [See page 71.]

Kratzer, Angelika. 1996. Severing the External Argument from Its Verb. Pages 109–137 of: Rooryck, Johan, and Zaring, Laurie (eds), *Phrase Structure and the Lexicon*. Dordrecht: Kluwer. [See pages 87, 114, 157, 161.]

Kratzer, Angelika. 1998a. More Structural Analogies between Pronouns and Tenses. Pages 92–110 of: Strolovitch, Devon, and Lawson, Aaron (eds), *Proceedings of Semantics and Linguistic Theory (SALT) 8*. Ithaca: CLC Publications. [See pages 13, 63, 158.]

Kratzer, Angelika. 1998b. Scope or Pseudoscope? Are There Wide-Scope Indefinites?. Pages 163–196 of: Rothstein, Susan (ed), *Events and Grammar*. Dordrecht: Kluwer. [See pages 44, 63, 69.]

Kratzer, Angelika. 2004. Telicity and the Meaning of Objective Case. Pages 389–424 of: Guéron and Lecarme (2004). [See page 25.]

Kratzer, Angelika. 2009. Making a Pronoun: Fake Indexicals as Windows into the Properties of Pronouns. *Linguistic Inquiry*, **40**, 187–237. [See pages 13, 66, 69, 101, 102, 132, 211, 217, 219.]

Kratzer, Angelika, and Shimoyama, Junko. 2002. Indeterminate Pronouns: The View from Japanese. Pages 1–25 of: Otsu, Yukio (ed), *Proceedings of the Third Tokyo Conference on Psycholinguistics*. Tokyo: Hituzi Syobo. [See pages 209, 211.]

Krifka, Manfred. 1989. Nominal Reference, Temporal Constitution, and Quantification in Event Semantics. Pages 75–115 of: Bartsch, Renate, van Bentham, Johan, and van Emde Boas, Peter (eds), *Semantics and Contextual Expressions*. Dordrecht: Foris. [See page 74.]

Kripke, Saul. 1979. A Puzzle about Belief. Pages 239–283 of: Margalit, Avishai (ed), *Meaning and Use*. Dordrecht: Reidel. [See pages 43, 48.]

Kripke, Saul. 1980. *Naming and Necessity*. Cambridge: Harvard University Press. [See page 43.]

Kupisch, Tanja, and Koops, Christian. 2007. The Definite Article in Non-Specific Object Noun Phrases: Comparing French and Italian. Pages 189–214 of: Stark, Elisabeth, Leiss, Elisabeth, and Abraham, Werner (eds), *Nominal Determination: Typology, Context Constraints, and Historical Emergence*. Amsterdam: John Benjamins. [See page 86.]

Ladusaw, William. 1982. Semantic Constraints on the English Partitive Construction. Pages 231–242 of: Flickinger, Daniel P., Macken, Marlys, and Wiegand, Nancy (eds), *WCCFL 1: Proceedings of the 1st West Coast Conference on Formal Linguistics*. Stanford: CSLI Publications. [See page 97.]

Laenzlinger, Christopher. 2005. French Adjective Ordering: Perspectives on DP Internal Movement Types. *Lingua*, **115**, 645–689. [See pages 63, 80.]

Lamontagne, Greg, and Travis, Lisa. 1987. The Syntax of Adjacency. Pages 173–186 of: Crowhurst, Megan (ed), *Proceedings of the West Coast Conference on Formal Linguistics 6*. Stanford: CSLI. [See page 160.]

Landman, Fred. 2003. Predicate-Argument Mismatches and the Adjectival Theory of Indefinites. Pages 211–238 of: Coene and D'hulst (2003). [See pages 117, 118.]

Langacker, Ronald W. 1995. Possession and Possessive Constructions. Pages 51–80 of: Taylor, John R., and MacLaury, Robert E. (eds), *Language and the Cognitive Construal of the World*. Berlin: Mouton de Gruyter. [See pages 98, 165.]

Larson, Brooke. 2016. The Representation of Syntactic Action at a Distance: Multidominance versus the Copy Theory. *Glossa*, **1**(1), 1–18. [See page 25.]

Larson, Richard, and Cho, Sungeun. 2003. Temporal Adjectives and the Structure of Possessive DPs. *Natural Language Semantics*, **11**, 217–247. [See pages 91, 165.]

Larson, Richard K. 2003. Event Descriptions in Fon and Hatian Creole. Pages 67–90 of: Adone, Dany (ed), *Recent Development in Creole Studies*. Tübingen: Niemeyer. [See page 80.]

Larson, Richard K. 2014. *On Shell Structure*. New York: Routledge. [See pages 63, 80, 160.]

Lasersohn, Peter. 1996. Adnominal Conditionals. Pages 154–166 of: Galloway, Teresa, and Spence, Justin (eds), *Proceedings of SALT 6*. Ithaca: CLC Publications. [See pages 172, 178.]

Lasersohn, Peter. 2009. Relative Truth, Speaker Commitment, and Control of Implicit Arguments. *Synthese*, **166**, 359–374. [See page 2.]

Lasnik, Howard. 1989. *Essays on Anaphora*. Boston: Kluwer. [See pages 51, 101.]

Law, Paul. 2011. Some Syntactic and Semantic Properties of the Existential Construction in Malagasy. *Lingua*, **121**, 1588–1630. [See pages 80, 127, 164.]

Law, Paul. 2014. A Unified Theory of Relative Clauses. Pages 203–221 of: Park, Jong-Un, and Lee, Il-Jae (eds), *SICOGG 16*. Seoul: The Korean Generative Grammar Circle. [See pages 141, 155.]

Lebeaux, David. 1983. A Distributional Difference between Reciprocals and Reflexives. *Linguistic Inquiry*, **14**, 723–730. [See page 101.]

Lecarme, Jacqueline. 1996. Tense in the Nominal System: The Somali DP. Pages 159–178 of: Lecarme, Jacqueline, Lowenstamm, Jean, and Shlonsky, Ur (eds), *Studies in Afroasiatic Grammar*. The Hague: Holland Academic Graphics. [See pages 63, 81, 83, 84, 86, 90, 97, 130.]

Lecarme, Jacqueline. 1999a. Focus in Somali. Pages 275–309 of: Rebuschi, Georges, and Tuller, Laurie (eds), *The Grammar of Focus*. Amsterdam: John Benjamins. [See pages 33, 83, 210.]

Lecarme, Jacqueline. 1999b. Nominal Tense and Tense Theory. Pages 333–354 of: Corblin, Francis, Dobrovie-Sorin, Carmen, and Marandin, Jean-Marie (eds), *Empirical Issues in Formal Syntax and Semantics 2*. The Hague: Thesus. [See pages 27, 63, 82, 84, 86, 90, 97, 130.]

Lecarme, Jacqueline. 2004. Tense in Nominals. Pages 441–475 of: Guéron and Lecarme (2004). [See pages 27, 81, 90, 93, 96, 97, 114, 130.]

Lecarme, Jacqueline. 2008. Tense and Modality in Nominals. Pages 195–226 of: Guéron, Jacqueline, and Lecarme, Jacqueline (eds), *Time and Modality*. Springer. [See pages 63, 80, 81, 83, 85, 88, 114, 130, 174, 217.]

Lecarme, Jacqueline. 2012. Nominal Tense. Pages 696–718 of: Binnick, Robert I. (ed), *The Oxford Handbook of Tense and Aspect*. Oxford: Oxford University Press. [See pages 80, 114, 217.]

Lechner, Winfried. 2006. An Interpretive Effect of Head Movement. Pages 45–71 of: Frascarelli (2006). [See page 27.]

Leckie, Gail. 2013. The Double Life of Names. *Philosophical Studies*, **165**, 1139–1160. [See page 136.]

Lee, Felicia. 2003. Anaphoric R-Expressions as Bound Variables. *Syntax*, **6**, 84–114. [See pages 4, 51, 100, 101.]

Lee-Schoenfeld, Vera. 2006. German Possessor Datives: Raised *and* Affected. *Journal of Comparative Germanic Linguistics*, **9**(2), 101–142. [See page 98.]

Lee-Schoenfeld, Vera. 2007. *Beyond Coherence: The Syntax of Opacity in German*. Amsterdam: Benjamins. [See page 132.]

Lees, Robert B. 1960. *The Grammar of English Nominalization*. The Hague: Mouton. [See pages 58, 78, 140.]

Legate, Julie Anne. 2014. *Voice and v: Lessons from Acehnese*. Cambridge: MIT Press. [See pages 87, 113, 114, 159.]

Leung, Tommi Tsz-Cheung. 2009. On the Matching Requirement in Correlatives. Pages 309–341 of: Lipták (2009a). [See page 196.]

Levinson, Lisa. 2007. *The Roots of Verbs*. Ph.D. thesis, New York University. [See pages 113, 114, 155, 156.]

Lewis, David. 1975. Adverbs of Quantification. Pages 3–15 of: Keenan, Edward L. (ed), *Formal Semantics of Natural Language*. Cambridge: Cambridge University Press. [See pages 74, 173, 187.]

Lewis, David. 1979. Attitudes De Dicto and De Se. *Philosophical Review*, **88**, 513–543. [See page 60.]

Lewis, David. 1980. Index, Context, and Content. Pages 79–100 of: Kanger, Stig, and Öhman, Helle (eds), *Philosophy and Grammar*. Dordrecht: D. Reidel. [See pages 4, 10, 207.]

Lichtenberk, Frantisek. 1985. Possessive Constructions in Oceanic Languages and in Proto-Oceanic. Pages 93–140 of: Pawley, Andrew, and Carrington, Lois (eds), *Austronesian Linguistics at the 15th Pacific Science Congress*. Canberra: Pacific Linguistics. [See pages 89, 97.]

Lichtenberk, Frantisek. 2002. The Possessive-Benefactive Connection. *Oceanic Linguistics*, **41**(2), 439–474. [See page 89.]

Lichtenberk, Frantisek. 2008. *A Grammar of Toqabaqita*. Berlin: Mouton de Gruyter. [See page 175.]

Lichtenberk, Frantisek. 2009a. Attributive Possessive Constructions in Oceanic. Pages 249–292 of: McGregor (2009). [See page 97.]

Lichtenberk, Frantisek. 2009b. Oceanic Possessive Classifiers. *Oceanic Linguistics*, **48**(2), 379–402. [See pages 89, 90, 92, 97.]

Lichtenberk, Frantisek, Vaid, Jyotsna, and Chen, Hsin-Chin. 2011. On the Interpretation of Alienable vs. Inalienable Possession: A Psycholinguistic Investigation. *Cognitive Linguistics*, **22**, 659–689. [See pages 88, 98.]

Link, Godehard. 1983. The Logical Analysis of Plurals and Mass Terms: A Lattice-Theoretical Approach. Pages 127–146 of: Portner, Paul, and Partee, Barbara H. (eds), *Formal Semantics: The Essential Readings*. Malden: Blackwell. [See pages 74, 113, 176.]

Lipták, Anikó (ed). 2009a. *Correlatives Cross-Linguistically*. Amsterdam: John Benjamins. [See pages 233, 236, 238, 239, 251, 252.]

Lipták, Anikó. 2009b. The Landscape of Correlatives: An Empirical and Analytical Survey. Pages 1–46 of: Lipták (2009a). [See pages 192, 195, 199, 217.]

Lipták, Anikó. 2012. Correlative Topicalization. *Acta Linguistica Hungarica*, **59**, 245–302. [See pages 72, 185, 186, 196, 199, 200.]

Löbel, Elisabeth. 1989. Q as a Functional Category. Pages 133–158 of: Bhatt, Christa, Löbel, Elisabeth, and Schmidt, Claudia Maria (eds), *Syntactic Phrase Structure Phenomena in Noun Phrases and Sentences*. Amsterdam: John Benjamins. [See page 81.]

Longobardi, Giuseppe. 1994. Reference and Proper names: A Theory of N-Movement in Syntax and Logical Form. *Linguistic Inquiry*, **25**(4), 609–665. [See pages 43, 63.]

Luján, Marta. 2004. Determiners as Pronouns. Pages 129–148 of: Castro, Ana, Ferreira, Marcelo, Hacquard, Valentine, and Salanova, Andres (eds), *Romance, Op. 47: Collected Papers on Romance Syntax*. Cambridge: MITWPL. [See pages 27, 63, 73, 80, 83, 88, 217.]

Lynch, John. 1973. Verbal Aspects of Possession in Melanesian Languages. *Oceanic Linguistics*, **12**, 69–102. [See pages 89, 90, 98.]

Lynch, John. 1978. *A Grammar of Lenakel*. Canberra: Pacific Linguistics. [See pages 98, 162.]

Lyons, Christopher. 1999. *Definiteness*. Cambridge: Cambridge University Press. [See pages 73, 83, 84, 86, 117.]

Lyons, John. 1968. *Introduction to Theoretical Linguistics*. Cambridge: Cambridge University Press. [See page 165.]

MacFarlane, John. 2014. *Assessment Sensitivity: Relative Truth and Its Applications*. Oxford: Clarendon Press. [See pages 3, 8, 207.]

MacKay, Carolyn J. 1999. *A Grammar of Misantla Totonac*. Salt Lake City: University of Utah Press. [See page 160.]

Marantz, Alec. 1991. Case and Licensing. Pages 234–253 of: Westphal, German, Ao, Benjamin, and Chae, Hee-Rahk (eds), *Proceedings of the 8th Eastern States Conference on Linguistics (ESCOL 8)*. Ithaca: CLC Publications. [See page 96.]

Marantz, Alec. 1993. Implications and Asymmetries in Double Object Constructions. Pages 113–150 of: Mchombo, Sam A. (ed), *Theoretical Aspects of Bantu Grammar 1*. Stanford: CSLI Publications. [See page 160.]

Marantz, Alec. 1997. No Escape from Syntax: Don't Try Morphological Analysis in the Privacy of Your Own Lexicon. Pages 201–225 of: Dimitriadis, Alexis, Siegel, Laura, Surek-Clark, Clarissa, and Williams, Alexander (eds), *University of Pennsylvania Working Papers in Linguistics*, vol. 4.2. University of Pennsylvania. [See pages 98, 113, 165.]

Martí, Luisa. 2002. *Contextual Variables*. Ph.D. thesis, University of Connecticut. [See page 85.]

Matisoff, James A. 1972. Lahu Nominalization, Relativization, and Genitivization. Pages 237–258 of: Kimball, John P. (ed), *Syntax and Semantics 1*. New York: Academic Press. [See page 92.]

Matthewson, Lisa. 1998. *Determiner Systems and Quantificational Strategies: Evidence from Salish*. The Hague: Holland Academic Graphics. [See pages 27, 44, 63, 80, 81, 82, 84, 86, 124, 128, 129.]

Matthewson, Lisa. 1999. On the Interpretation of Wide-Scope Indefinites. *Natural Language Semantics*, **7**, 79–134. [See pages 82, 86, 87.]

Matthewson, Lisa. 2001. Quantification and the Nature of Crosslinguistic Variation. *Natural Language Semantics*, **9**, 145–189. [See pages 81, 87, 114.]

Matthewson, Lisa (ed). 2008. *Quantification: A Cross-Linguistic Perspective*. Bingley: Emerald. [See pages 81, 241.]

Matthewson, Lisa. 2009. An Unfamiliar Proportional Quantifier. Pages 23–52 of: Giannakidou and Rathert (2009). [See page 124.]

Matthewson, Lisa. 2013. Strategies of Quantification in St'át'imcets and the Rest of the World. Pages 15–38 of: Gil et al. (2013). [See pages 81, 82, 84, 86, 87.]

Matushansky, Ora. 2006. Why Rose Is the Rose: On the Use of Definite Articles in Proper Names. Pages 285–308 of: Bonami, Olivier, and Cabredo Hofherr, Patricia (eds), *Empirical Issues in Syntax and Semantics 6*. CSSP. [See page 43.]

Mavrogiorgos, Marios. 2010. *Clitics in Greek: A Minimalist Account of Proclisis and Enclisis*. Amsterdam: John Benjamins. [See pages 38, 102.]

May, Robert. 1977. *The Grammar of Quantification*. Ph.D. thesis, MIT. [See page 109.]

May, Robert. 1985. *Logical Form*. Cambridge: MIT Press. [See pages 25, 31, 99, 105, 107, 213.]

McCloskey, James. 2002. Resumption, Successive Cyclicity, and the Locality of Operations. Pages 184–226 of: Epstein and Seely (2002). [See page 58.]

McCloskey, James. 2014. Irish Existentials in Context. *Syntax*, **17**(4), 343–384. [See pages 126, 127, 162, 163, 164, 166.]

McGregor, William B. (ed). 2009. *The Expression of Possession*. Berlin: Mouton de Gruyter. [See pages 251, 255.]

McNally, Louise. 1997. *An Interpretation for the English Existential Construction*. New York: Garland. [See pages 111, 127, 164, 166.]

McNally, Louise. 2011. Existential Sentences. Pages 1829–1848 of: von Heusinger et al. (2011). [See page 166.]

McNally, Louise. 2016. Existential Sentences Crosslinguistically: Variations in Form and Meaning. *Annual Review of Linguistics*, **2**, 211–231. [See pages 127, 162.]

McNeill, David. 1970. *The Acquisition of Language*. New York: Harper & Row. [See page 73.]

Megerdoomian, Karine. 2008. Parallel Nominal and Verbal Projections. Pages 73–104 of: Freidin et al. (2008). [See pages 63, 81, 96, 112, 114, 156.]

Megerdoomian, Karine. 2009. *Beyond Words and Phrases: A Unified Theory of Predicate Composition*. Berlin: VDM Verlag. [See page 96.]

Merchant, Jason. 2013. Voice and Ellipsis. *Linguistic Inquiry*, **44**, 77–108. [See pages 114, 159.]

Merlan, Francesca. 1982. *Mangarayi*. Amsterdam: North-Holland. [See page 89.]

Milsark, Gary. 1974. *Existential Sentences in English*. Ph.D. thesis, MIT. [See pages 111, 127, 166.]

Milsark, Gary. 1977. Toward an Explanation of Certain Peculiarities of the existential construction in English. *Linguistic Analysis*, **3**, 1–29. Reprinted in pages 40–65 of: Gutiérrez-Rexach, Javier (ed), *Semantics, Vol. III: Noun Phrase Classes*. London: Routledge. [See pages 115, 123, 166.]

Montgomery, Michael B., and Hall, Joseph S. 2004. *Dictionary of Smoky Mountain English*. Knoxville: University of Tennessee Press. [See page 126.]

Moro, Andrea. 1997. *The Raising of Predicates: Noun Phrases and the Theory of Clause Structure*. Cambridge: Cambridge University Press. [See page 164.]

Moro, Andrea. 2017. Copular Sentences. Pages 1–23 of: Everaert and van Riemsdijk (2017). [See page 115.]

Mortensen, David. 2003. *Two Kinds of Variable Elements in Hmong Anaphora*. MS, University of California–Berkeley. [See pages 51, 71, 100, 101.]

Mosel, Ulrike. 1984. *Tolai Syntax and Its Historical Development*. Canberra: Pacific Linguistics. [See pages 97, 98, 163, 167.]

Moulton, Keir. 2015. CPs: Copies and Compositionality. *Linguistic Inquiry*, **46**, 305–342. [See pages 27, 28, 59, 61, 157, 158.]

Musan, Renate. 1995. *On the Temporal Interpretation of Noun Phrases*. Ph.D. thesis, MIT. [See pages 129, 130.]

Myler, Neil. 2016. *Building and Interpreting Possession Sentences*. Cambridge: MIT Press. [See pages 162, 167.]

Nedjalkov, Igor. 1997. *Evenki*. London: Routledge. [See page 167.]

Nichols, Johanna. 1988. On Alienable and Inalienable Possession. Pages 557–609 of: Shipley, William (ed), *In Honor of Mary Haas*. Berlin: Mouton de Gruyter. [See pages 89, 97, 98.]

Nichols, Johanna. 1992. *Linguistic Diversity in Space and Time*. Chicago: University of Chicago Press. [See page 97.]

Nikolaeva, Irina, and Spencer, Andrew. 2013. Possession and Modification: A Perspective from Canonical Typology. Pages 207–239 of: Brown, Dunstan, Chumakina, Marina, and Corbett, Greville G. (eds), *Canonical Morphology and Syntax*. Oxford: Oxford University Press. [See page 92.]

Ninan, Dilip. 2012. Counterfactual Attitudes and Multi-Centered Worlds. *Semantics and Pragmatics*, **5**, 1–57. [See pages 5, 11, 30, 43.]

Nissenbaum, Jonathan W. 2000. *Investigations of Covert Phrase Movement*. Ph.D. thesis, MIT. [See pages 31, 133.]

Noguchi, Tohru. 1997. Two Types of Pronouns and Variable Binding. *Language*, **73**, 770–797. [See pages 69, 74.]

Noonan, Michael. 1992. *A Grammar of Lango*. Berlin: Mouton de Gruyter. [See page 154.]

Nunes, Jairo. 2004. *Linearization of Chains and Sideward Movement*. Cambridge: MIT Press. [See pages 25, 71, 93, 100, 142, 219.]

Nyvad, Anne Mette, Christensen, Ken Ramshøj, and Vikner, Sten. 2017. CP-Recursion in Danish: A cP/CP-Analysis. *The Linguistic Review*, **34**, 449–477. [See page 184.]

Ojeda, Almerindo. 1993. *Linguistic Individuals*. Stanford: CSLI Publications. [See page 144.]

Onishi, Masayuki. 2000. Transitivity and Valency-Changing Derivations in Motuna. Pages 115–144 of: Dixon, R. M. W., and Aikhenvald, Alexandra Y. (eds), *Changing Valency: Case Studies in Transitivity*. Cambridge: Cambridge University Press. [See page 162.]

Panagiotidis, Phoevos. 2002. *Pronouns, Clitics and Empty Nouns*. Amsterdam: John Benjamins. [See page 69.]

Parsons, Terence. 1990. *Events in the Semantics of English: A Study in Subatomic Semantics*. Cambridge: MIT Press. [See page 156.]

Partee, Barbara H. 1973. Some Structural Analogies between Tenses and Pronouns in English. Pages 50–58 of: Partee (2004). [See page 4.]

Partee, Barbara H. 1979. Semantics–Mathematics or Psychology? Pages 1–14 of: Bäuerle, Rainer, Egli, Urs, and von Stechow, Arnim (eds), *Semantics from Different Points of View*. Berlin: Springer. [See page 49.]

Partee, Barbara H. 1983. Genitives: A Case Study. Pages 182–189 of: Partee (2004). [See pages 88, 92, 94.]

Partee, Barbara H. 1984. Nominal and Temporal Anaphora. *Linguistics and Philosophy*, 7(3), 243–286. [See page 63.]

Partee, Barbara H. 1986a. Ambiguous Pseudoclefts with Unambiguous *Be*. Pages 190–202 of: Partee (2004). [See pages 115, 118.]

Partee, Barbara H. 1986b. Noun Phrase Interpretation and Type-Shifting Principles. Pages 203–230 of: Partee (2004). [See pages 117, 118, 128.]

Partee, Barbara H. 1989a. Binding Implicit Variables in Quantified Contexts. Pages 259–271 of: Partee (2004). [See page 69.]

Partee, Barbara H. 1989b. Many Quantifiers. Pages 241–258 of: Partee (2004). [See pages 117, 128.]

Partee, Barbara H. 1995. Quantificational Structures and Compositionality. Pages 541–602 of: Bach et al. (1995). [See pages 122, 173.]

Partee, Barbara H. 2004. *Compositionality in Formal Semantics: Selected Papers by Barbara H. Partee*. Malden: Blackwell. [See page 255.]

Partee, Barbara H., and Borschev, Vladimir. 2003. Genitives, Relational Nouns, and Argument-Modifier Ambiguity. Pages 67–112 of: Lang, Ewald, Maienborn, Claudia, and Fabricius-Hansen, Cathrine (eds), *Modifying Adjuncts*. Berlin: Mouton de Gruyter. [See pages 88, 90, 93, 94, 97, 98.]

Patel-Grosz, Pritty, and Grosz, Patrick. 2010. On the Typology of Donkeys: Two Types of Anaphora Resolution. Pages 339–355 of: Prinzhorn, Martin, Schmitt, Viola, and Zobel, Sarah (eds), *Proceedings of Sinn und Bedeutung 14*. Vienna: University of Vienna. [See page 71.]

Patel-Grosz, Pritty, and Grosz, Patrick G. 2017. Revisiting Pronominal Typology. *Linguistic Inquiry*, 48(2), 259–297. [See pages 69, 72, 74, 86, 217.]

Paul, Ileana, and Travis, Lisa. 2006. Ergativity in Austronesian Languages: What It Can Do, What It Can't, but Not Why. Pages 315–335 of: Johns, Alana, Massam, Diane, and Ndayiragije, Juvenal (eds), *Ergativity: Emerging Issues*. Dordrecht: Springer. [See page 82.]

Paul, Ileana, Cortes, Key, and Milambiling, Lareina. 2015. Definiteness without D: The Case of *Ang* and *Ng* in Tagalog. *Canadian Journal of Linguistics*, 60(3), 361–390. [See pages 83, 84, 114.]

Payne, Doris L. 2009. Is Possession Mere Location? Contrary Evidence from Maa. Pages 107–142 of: McGregor (2009). [See pages 98, 165.]

Percus, Orin. 2000. Constraints on Some Other Variables in Syntax. *Natural Language Semantics*, 8, 173–229. [See pages 4, 22, 24.]

Percus, Orin, and Sauerland, Uli. 2003. On the LFs of Attitude Reports. Pages 228–242 of: Weisgerber, Matthias (ed), *Proceedings of Sinn und Bedeutung 7*. Konstanz: Universität Konstanz. [See pages 4, 43.]

Pesetsky, David. 1987. *Wh*-In-Situ: Movement and Unselective Binding. Pages 98–129 of: Reuland and ter Meulen (1987). [See pages 85, 215.]

Pesetsky, David. 1995. *Zero Syntax: Experiencers and Cascades*. Cambridge: MIT Press. [See page 160.]

Pesetsky, David. 2000. *Phrasal Movement and Its Kin*. Cambridge: MIT Press. [See pages 211, 215, 216.]

Pesetsky, David. 2017. Complementizer-Trace Effects. Pages 1–34 of: Everaert and van Riemsdijk (2017). [See page 28.]

Peters, Stanley, and Westerståhl, Dag. 2013. The Semantics of Possessives. *Language*, **89**(4), 713–759. [See page 96.]

Peterson, Thomas H. 1974. On Definite Restrictive Relatives in Mooré. *Journal of West African Linguistics*, **9**(2), 71–78. [See page 65.]

Postal, Paul. 1969. On the So-Called "Pronouns" in English. Pages 201–224 of: Reibel, David A., and Schane, Sanford A. (eds), *Modern Studies in English: Readings in Transformational Grammar*. Englewood Cliffs: Prentice Hall. [See pages 69, 72, 73, 217.]

Potts, Christopher, Asudeh, Ash, Cable, Seth, Hara, Yurie, McCready, E., Alonso-Ovalle, Luis, Bhatt, Rajesh, Davis, Christopher, Kratzer, Angelika, Roeper, Tom, and Walkow, Martin. 2009. Expressives and Identity Conditions. *Linguistic Inquiry*, **40**(2), 356–366. [See page 196.]

von Prince, Kilu. 2016. Alienability as Control: The Case of Daakaka. *Lingua*, **182**, 69–87. [See pages 90, 97.]

Pylkkänen, Liina. 2000. What Applicative Heads Apply To. Pages 197–210 of: Kaiser, Elsi, Fox, Michelle Minnick, and Williams, Alexander (eds), *University of Pennsylvania Working Papers in Linguistics*, vol. 7.1. University of Pennsylvania. [See page 160.]

Pylkkänen, Liina. 2008. *Introducing Arguments*. Cambridge: MIT Press. [See pages 87, 113, 114, 157, 160.]

Rabern, Brian. 2012a. Against the Identification of Assertoric Content with Compositional Value. *Synthese*, **189**(1), 75–96. [See page 207.]

Rabern, Brian. 2012b. Monsters in Kaplan's Logic of Demonstratives. *Philosophical Studies*, 1–12. [See page 4.]

Rackowski, Andrea Stokes. 2002. *The Structure of Tagalog: Specificity, Voice, and the Distribution of Arguments*. Ph.D. thesis, MIT. [See pages 87, 113, 114.]

Radford, Andrew. 1997. *Syntactic Theory and the Structure of English: A Minimalist Approach*. Cambridge: Cambridge University Press. [See pages 69, 73.]

Ramchand, Gillian. 2017. The Event Domain. Pages 233–254 of: D'Alessandro et al. (2017). [See pages 114, 143.]

Rappaport, Gilbert C. 1986. On Anaphor Binding in Russian. *Natural Language and Linguistic Theory*, **4**, 97–120. [See page 42.]

Rawlins, Kyle. 2008. *(Un)conditionals: An Investigation in the Syntax and Semantics of Conditional Structures*. Ph.D. thesis, University of California, Santa Cruz. [See page 174.]

Reinhart, Tanya. 1981. Pragmatics and Linguistics: An Analysis of Sentence Topics. *Philosophica*, **27**, 53–94. [See pages 180, 185.]

Reinhart, Tanya. 1983. *Anaphora and Semantic Interpretation*. Chicago: University of Chicago Press. [See page 103.]

Reinhart, Tanya. 1987. Specifier and Operator Binding. Pages 130–167 of: Reuland and ter Meulen (1987). [See pages 103, 109.]

Reinhart, Tanya. 1997. Quantifier Scope: How Labor Is Divided between QR and Choice Functions. *Linguistics and Philosophy*, **20**, 335–397. [See page 69.]

Reuland, Eric J., and ter Meulen, Alice G. B. (eds). 1987. *The Representation of (In)definiteness*. Cambridge: MIT Press. [See pages 237, 248, 256, 257, 261.]

Richards, Marc D. 2007. On Feature Inheritance: An Argument from the Phase Impenetrability Condition. *Linguistic Inquiry*, **38**, 563–572. [See page 132.]

Rijkhoff, Jan. 2002. *The Noun Phrase*. Oxford: Oxford University Press. [See pages 63, 113, 156.]

Rijkhoff, Jan. 2008. Synchronic and Diachronic Evidence for Parallels between Noun Phrases and Sentences. Pages 13–42 of: Josephson, Folke, and Söhrman, Ingmar (eds), *Interdependence of Diachronic and Synchronic Analyses*. Amsterdam: John Benjamins. [See page 63.]

van Rijn, Marlou. 2017. *The Expression of Modifiers and Arguments in the Noun Phrase and Beyond: A Typological Study*. Ph.D. thesis, University of Amsterdam. [See pages 88, 89, 92, 93, 97.]

Ritter, Elizabeth. 1991. Two Functional Categories in Noun Phrases: Evidence from Modern Hebrew. Pages 37–62 of: Rothstein, Susan (ed), *Syntax and Semantics 25, Perspectives on Phrase Structure: Heads and Licensing*. San Diego: Academic Press. [See page 112.]

Ritter, Elizabeth, and Wiltschko, Martina. 2014. The Composition of INFL: An Exploration of *Tense*, *Tenseless* Languages, and *Tenseless* Constructions. *Natural Language and Linguistic Theory*, **32**, 1331–1386. [See page 26.]

Rizzi, Luigi. 1990. *Relativized Minimality*. Cambridge: MIT Press. [See page 131.]

Rizzi, Luigi. 1997. The Fine Structure of the Left Periphery. Pages 281–337 of: Haegeman, Liliane (ed), *Elements of Grammar: Handbook of Generative Syntax*. Dordrecht: Kluwer. [See page 33.]

Rizzi, Luigi. 2001. Extraction from Weak Islands, Reconstruction, and Agreement. Pages 155–176 of: Chierchia, Gennaro (ed), *Semantic Interfaces: Reference, Anaphora, Aspect*. Stanford: CSLI Publications. [See page 216.]

Roberts, Ian. 2001. Head Movement. Pages 113–147 of: Baltin and Collins (2001). [See page 26.]

Rouveret, Alain (ed). 2011. *Resumptive Pronouns at the Interfaces*. Philadelphia: John Benjamins. [See pages 102, 234, 240.]

Rullmann, Hotze. 1995. *Maximality in the Semantics of* Wh*-Constructions*. Ph.D. thesis, University of Massachusetts Amherst. [See pages 64, 211, 215.]

Rullmann, Hotze, and Beck, Sigrid. 1998. Presupposition Projection and the Interpretation of *Which*-Questions. Pages 215–232 of: Strolovitch, Devon, and Lawson, Aaron (eds), *Semantics and Linguistic Theory (SALT) 8*. Ithaca: CLC Publications. [See pages 86, 211, 215.]

Sabbagh, Joseph. 2009. Existential Sentences in Tagalog. *Natural Language and Linguistic Theory*, **27**, 675–719. [See pages 88, 125, 127, 163, 164, 166.]

Sabbagh, Joseph. 2016. Specificity and Objecthood in Tagalog. *Journal of Linguistics*, **52**, 639–688. [See pages 84, 89.]

Safir, Ken. 1985. *Syntactic Chains*. Cambridge: Cambridge University Press. [See page 126.]

Safir, Ken. 1999. Vehicle Change and Reconstruction in $\overline{\text{A}}$-Bar Chains. *Linguistic Inquiry*, **30**, 587–620. [See pages 62, 110.]

Safir, Ken. 2004. *The Syntax of (In)dependence*. Cambridge: MIT Press. [See pages 104, 109.]

Salmon, Nathan. 1986. *Frege's Puzzle*. Cambridge: MIT Press. [See page 43.]

Santelmann, Lynn. 1993. The Distribution of Double Determiners in Swedish: *Den* Support in D. *Studia Linguistica*, **47**, 154–176. [See pages 81, 86.]

Santorio, Paolo. 2010. Modals Are Monsters: On Indexical Shift in English. Pages 289–308 of: Li, Nan, and Lutz, David (eds), *Proceedings of SALT 20*. Ithaca: CLC Publications. [See pages 5, 11, 30, 43.]

Santorio, Paolo. 2012. Reference and Monstrosity. *Philosophical Review*, **121**(3), 359–406. [See pages 5, 10, 11, 30, 172, 181, 183, 221.]

Santorio, Paolo. 2013. Descriptions as Variables. *Philosophical Studies*, **164**, 41–59. [See page 48.]

Satık, Deniz. 2017. The Little nP Hypothesis. Pages 1–15 of: Monti, Andrew Alexander (ed), *Proceedings of the 2017 Annual Conference of the Canadian Linguistics Association*. CLA. [See page 87.]

Sato, Hiroko. 2009. Possessive Nominalization in Kove. *Oceanic Linguistics*, **48**(2), 346–363. [See pages 89, 90, 97.]

Sauerland, Uli. 1998. *The Meaning of Chains*. Ph.D. thesis, MIT. [See pages 25, 58, 78, 140.]

Sauerland, Uli. 2003. Unpronounced Heads in Relative Clauses. Pages 205–226 of: Schwabe, Kerstin, and Winkler, Susanne (eds), *The Interfaces: Deriving and Interpreting Omitted Structures*. Amsterdam: John Benjamins. [See pages 58, 78, 140.]

Sauerland, Uli. 2004. The Interpretation of Traces. *Natural Language Semantics*, **12**, 63–127. [See pages 140, 141.]

Saul, Jennifer M. 1998. The Pragmatics of Attitude Ascription. *Philosophical Studies*, **92**(3), 363–389. [See page 45.]

Schein, Barry. 2003. Adverbial, Descriptive Reciprocals. *Philosophical Perspectives*, **17**(1), 333–367. [See pages 174, 176.]

Schlenker, Philippe. 2003. A Plea for Monsters. *Linguistics and Philosophy*, **26**, 29–120. [See pages 4, 11, 17, 30.]

Schlenker, Philippe. 2004. Conditionals as Definite Descriptions (A Referential Analysis). *Research on Language and Computation*, **2**, 417–462. [See pages 173, 174, 185, 199.]

Schlenker, Philippe. 2005. Non-Redundancy: Towards a Semantic Reinterpretation of Binding Theory. *Natural Language Semantics*, **13**, 1–92. [See page 109.]

Schlenker, Philippe. 2006. Ontological Symmetry in Language: A Brief Manifesto. *Mind and Language*, **21**(4), 504–539. [See page 4.]

Schlenker, Philippe. 2010. Local Contexts and Local Meanings. *Philosophical Studies*, **151**, 115–142. [See page 5.]

Schwarz, Florian. 2009. *Two Types of Definites in Natural Language*. Ph.D. thesis, University of Massachusetts, Amherst. [See pages 72, 84, 86.]

Seiler, Hansjakob. 1983a. *Possession as an Operational Dimension of Language*. Tübingen: Gunter Narr Verlag. [See pages 89, 97, 98.]

Seiler, Hansjakob. 1983b. Possessivity, Subject and Object. *Studies in Language*, **7**(1), 89–117. [See page 97.]

Sells, Peter. 1987. Binding Resumptive Pronouns. *Linguistics and Philosophy*, **10**, 261–298. [See page 148.]

Sharvit, Yael. 1999. Resumptive Pronouns in Relative Clauses. *Natural Language and Linguistic Theory*, **17**, 587–612. [See page 148.]

Showalter, Catherine. 1986. Pronouns in Lyele. Pages 205–216 of: Wiesemann, Ursula (ed), *Pronominal Systems*. Tübingen: Günter Narr. [See page 210.]

Silk, Alex. 2013. Truth-Conditions and the Meanings of Ethical Terms. Pages 195–222 of: Shafer-Landau, Russ (ed), *Oxford Studies in Metaethics*, vol. 8. New York: Oxford University Press. [See page 2.]

Silk, Alex. 2014. Evidence Sensitivity in Weak Necessity Deontic Modals. *Journal of Philosophical Logic*, **43**(4), 691–723. [See pages 190, 192.]

Silk, Alex. 2016a. *Discourse Contextualism: A Framework for Contextualist Semantics and Pragmatics*. Oxford: Oxford University Press. [See pages 2, 8, 42, 136.]

Silk, Alex. 2016b. Update Semantics for Weak Necessity Modals. Pages 237–255 of: *Deontic Logic and Normative Systems (DEON 2016)*. Milton Keynes: College Publications. [See page 190.]

Silk, Alex. 2017. How to Embed an Epistemic Modal: Attitude Problems and Other Defects of Character. *Philosophical Studies*, **174**(7), 1773–1799. [See pages 2, 8, 42, 136.]

Silk, Alex. 2018. Commitment and States of Mind with Mood and Modality. *Natural Language Semantics*, **26**(2), 125–166. [See pages 11, 30.]

Siloni, Tal. 1997. *Noun Phrases and Nominalizations: The Syntax of DPs*. Dordrecht: Kluwer. [See pages 63, 93.]

Soames, Scott. 2002. *The Unfinished Semantic Agenda of* Naming and Necessity. Oxford: Oxford University Press. [See page 43.]

Song, Jae Jung. 1997. The History of Micronesian Possessive Classifiers and Benefactive Marking in Oceanic Languages. *Oceanic Linguistics*, **36**, 29–64. [See page 89.]

Speas, Margaret, and Tenny, Carol. 2003. Configurational Properties of Point of View Roles. Pages 315–344 of: Di Sciullo, Anna Maria (ed), *Asymmetry in Grammar*. Amsterdam: John Benjamins. [See page 207.]

Sportiche, Dominique. 2006. Reconstruction, Binding, and Scope. Pages 35–93 of: Everaert and van Riemsdijk (2006). [See pages 62, 201, 214.]

Sportiche, Dominique. 2017. *Relative Clauses: Promotion Only, in Steps*. MS, UCLA. [See pages 58, 78, 155.]

Srivastav, Veneeta. 1991. The Syntax and Semantics of Correlatives. *Natural Language and Linguistic Theory*, **9**, 637–686. [See pages 72, 186, 195, 198, 200, 223.]

Stalnaker, Robert. 1970. Pragmatics. Pages 31–46 of: Stalnaker (1999). [See page 4.]

Stalnaker, Robert. 1988. Belief Attribution and Context. Pages 150–166 of: Stalnaker (1999). [See pages 5, 35, 43, 49.]

Stalnaker, Robert. 1999. *Context and Content: Essays on Intentionality in Speech and Thought*. Oxford: Oxford University Press. [See page 259.]

Stalnaker, Robert. 2014. *Context*. New York: Oxford University Press. [See pages 5, 35.]

Stanley, Jason. 2002. Nominal Restriction. Pages 365–388 of: Preyer, Gerhard, and Peter, Georg (eds), *Logical Form and Language*. Oxford: Oxford University Press. [See pages 10, 85.]

Stanley, Jason, and Szabó, Zoltán Gendler. 2000. On Quantifier Domain Restriction. *Mind and Language*, **15**, 219–261. [See pages 10, 85.]

Starr, William. 2010. *Conditionals, Meaning, and Mood*. Ph.D. thesis, Rutgers University. [See page 221.]

Stebbins, Tonya N. 2009. The Semantics of Clause Linking in Mali. Pages 356–379 of: Dixon and Aikhenvald (2009). [See page 175.]

von Stechow, Arnim. 2003. Feature Deletion under Semantic Binding: Tense, Person, and Mood under Verbal Quantifiers. Pages 397–403 of: Kadowaki, Makoto, and Kawahara, Shigeto (eds), *Proceedings of the North East Linguistics Society 33*. Amherst: GLSA. [See page 69.]

von Stechow, Arnim. 2008. *Tense, Modals, and Attitudes as Verbal Quantifiers*. Paper presented at ESSLLI 2008. [See page 27.]

Stephenson, Tamina. 2007. *Towards a Theory of Subjective Meaning*. Ph.D. thesis, MIT. [See page 8.]

Sternefeld, Wolfgang. 1998. The Semantics of Reconstruction and Connectivity. Pages 1–58 of: *Arbeitspapier des SFB 340 97*. Universität Tübingen. [See pages 4, 18, 40, 214.]

Sternefeld, Wolfgang. 2001. Partial Movement Constructions, Pied Piping, and Higher Order Choice Functions. Pages 473–486 of: Féry, Caroline, and Sternefeld, Wolfgang (eds), *Audiatur Vox Sapientiae: A Festschrift for Arnim von Stechow*. Berlin: Akademie Verlag. [See page 64.]

Stockwell, Robert P., Schachter, Paul, and Partee, Barbara Hall. 1973. *The Major Syntactic Structures of English*. New York: Holt, Rinehart, and Winston. [See page 116.]

Stolz, Thomas, Kettler, Sonja, Stroh, Cornelia, and Urdze, Aina (eds). 2008. *Split Possession: An Areal-Linguistic Study of the Alienability Correlation and Related Phenomena in the Languages of Europe*. Amsterdam: John Benjamins. [See page 89.]

Stone, Matthew. 1997. *The Anaphoric Parallel between Modality and Tense*. IRCS TR 97-06, University of Pennsylvania. [See page 63.]

Storto, Gianluca. 2003. *Possessives in Context: Issues in the Semantics of Possessive Constructions*. Ph.D. thesis, UCLA. [See pages 93, 98.]

Sudo, Yasutada. 2012. *On the Semantics of Phi Features on Pronouns*. Ph.D. thesis, MIT. [See page 69.]

Sundaresan, Sandhya, and McFadden, Thomas. 2017. The Articulated v Layer: Evidence from Tamil. Pages 153–178 of: D'Alessandro et al. (2017). [See page 159.]

Svenonius, Peter. 2004. On the Edge. Pages 259–288 of: Adger et al. (2004). [See pages 63, 132.]

Swanson, Eric. 2011. Propositional Attitudes. Pages 1538–1560 of: von Heusinger et al. (2011). [See pages 5, 43.]

Szabolcsi, Anna. 1983. The Possessor that Ran Away from Home. *The Linguistic Review*, **3**, 89–102. [See pages 93, 162.]

Szabolcsi, Anna. 1994. The Noun Phrase. Pages 179–274 of: Kiefer, Ferenc, and Kiss, Katalin É. (eds), *Syntax and Semantics 27: The Syntactic Structure of Hungarian*. New York: Academic Press. [See pages 63, 84, 162.]

Szabolcsi, Anna. 2011. Certain Verbs Are Syntactically Explicit Quantifiers. Pages 1–26 of: Partee, Barbara H., Glanzberg, Michael, and Š ilters, Jurģis (eds), *The Baltic International Yearbook of Cognition, Logic and Communication*, vol. 6: *Formal*

Semantics and Pragmatics: Discourse, Context and Models. Manhattan: New Prairie Press. [See page 27.]

Takahashi, Shoichi. 2010. Traces or Copies, or Both. *Language and Linguistics Compass*, 4(11), 1091–1115. [See page 25.]

Tanaka, Misako. 2015. *Scoping Out of Adjuncts: Evidence for the Parallelism between QR and Wh-Movement.* Ph.D. thesis, University College London. [See pages 31, 133.]

Tănase-Dogaru, Mihaela. 2007. *The Category of Number: Its Relevance for the Syntax and the Semantic Typology of the Nominal Group.* Ph.D. thesis, University of Bucharest. [See page 113.]

Taylor, John R. 1989. Possessive Genitives in English. *Linguistics*, **27**, 663–686. [See pages 93, 98.]

Tellier, Christine. 1991. *Licensing Theory and French Parasitic Gaps.* Dordrecht: Kluwer. [See pages 63, 93, 167.]

Thurgood, Graham, and LaPolla, Randy J. (eds). 2017. *The Sino-Tibetan Languages*, 2 ed. London: Routledge. [See pages 73, 81, 92, 209, 217.]

Türker, Lola. 2019. *Noun Phrases in Article-less Languages: Uzbek and Beyond.* Amsterdam: John Benjamins. [See pages 84, 114, 124.]

Uriagereka, Juan. 1998. A Note on Rigidity. Pages 361–382 of: Uriagereka (2002a). [See pages 43, 80.]

Uriagereka, Juan. 2002a. *Derivations: Exploring the Dynamics of Syntax.* London: Routledge. [See page 261.]

Uriagereka, Juan. 2002b. From Being to Having: Questions about Ontology from a Kayne/Szabolcsi Syntax. Pages 192–211 of: Uriagereka (2002a). [See page 165.]

Vikner, Carl, and Jensen, Per Anker. 2002. A Semantic Analysis of the English Genitive: Interaction of Lexical and Formal Semantics. *Studia Linguistica*, **56**, 191–226. [See page 94.]

Villalba, Xavier. 2013. Eventive Existentials in Catalan and the Topic-Focus Articulation. *Italian Journal of Linguistics*, **25**, 147–173. [See page 125.]

de Vries, Mark. 2002. *The Syntax of Relativization.* Ph.D. thesis, University of Amsterdam. [See pages 58, 76, 80, 142, 143, 155, 210, 217.]

Weatherson, Brian. 2008. Attitudes and Relativism. *Philosophical Perspectives*, **22**, 527–544. [See page 2.]

Welmers, Wm. E. 1973. *African Language Structures.* Berkeley: University of California Press. [See page 173.]

Williams, Edwin. 1984. *There*-Insertion. *Linguistic Inquiry*, **15**, 131–153. [See pages 125, 164, 166.]

Williams, Edwin. 1997. Blocking and Anaphora. *Linguistic Inquiry*, **28**, 577–628. [See page 84.]

Williamson, Janis S. 1979. Patient Marking in Lakhota and the Unaccusative Hypothesis. Pages 353–365 of: Clyne, Paul R., Hanks, William F., and Hofbauer, Carol L. (eds), *Papers from the Fifteenth Regional Meeting of the Chicago Linguistic Society (CLS).* Chicago: CLS, University of Chicago. [See page 167.]

Williamson, Janis S. 1987. An Indefiniteness Restriction for Relative Clauses in Lakhota. Pages 168–190 of: Reuland and ter Meulen (1987). [See pages 65, 66, 76, 142.]

Wiltschko, Martina. 1998. On the Syntax and Semantics of (Relative) Pronouns and Determiners. *Journal of Comparative Germanic Linguistics*, **2**, 143–181. [See pages 69, 72, 73.]

Wiltschko, Martina. 2002. The Syntax of Pronouns: Evidence from Halkomelem Salish. *Natural Language and Linguistic Theory*, **20**(1), 157–195. [See page 73.]

Wiltschko, Martina. 2014. *The Universal Structure of Categories: Towards a Formal Typology*. Cambridge: Cambridge University Press. [See pages 26, 63.]

Wiltschko, Martina. 2016. Fake Form and What It Tells Us about the Relation between Form and Interpretation. Pages 13–52 of: Grosz and Patel-Grosz (2016). [See pages 3, 69.]

Winter, Yoad. 1997. Choice Functions and the Scopal Semantics of Indefinites. *Linguistics and Philosophy*, **20**, 399–467. [See page 44.]

Wood, Jim, and Marantz, Alec. 2017. The Interpretation of External Arguments. Pages 255–278 of: D'Alessandro et al. (2017). [See pages 87, 114, 155, 157, 164, 166.]

Wurmbrand, Susi, and Shimamura, Koji. 2017. The Features of the Voice Domain: Actives, Passives, and Restructuring. Pages 179–204 of: D'Alessandro et al. (2017). [See page 159.]

Yalcin, Seth. 2007. Epistemic Modals. *Mind*, **116**, 983–1026. [See pages 2, 8.]

Yalcin, Seth. 2011. Nonfactualism about Epistemic Modality. Pages 295–332 of: Egan, Andy, and Weatherson, Brian (eds), *Epistemic Modality*. Oxford: Oxford University Press. [See page 2.]

Zamparelli, Roberto. 2000. *Layers in the Determiner Phrase*. New York: Garland Publishing. [See pages 81, 86, 96, 111, 114, 117.]

Zeshan, Ulrike, and Perniss, Pamela (eds). 2008. *Possessive and Existential Constructions in Sign Languages*. Nijmegan: Ishara Press. [See pages 162, 165.]

Ziff, Paul. 1960. *Semantic Analysis*. Ithaca: Cornell University Press. [See page 79.]

Zribi-Hertz, Anne. 2008. From Intensive to Reflexive: The Prosodic Factor. Pages 591–632 of: König, Ekkehard, and Gast, Volker (eds), *Reciprocals and Reflexives: Theoretical and Typological Explorations*. Berlin: Mouton de Gruyter. [See pages 101, 102.]

Zucchi, Allesandro. 1995. The Ingredients of Definiteness and the Definiteness Effect. *Natural Language Semantics*, **3**, 33–78. [See page 125.]

Languages Index

Subject Index

Milton Keynes UK
Ingram Content Group UK Ltd.
UKHW021503060823
426405UK00029B/1121